PERIPLU

POCKET

INDONESIAN
DICTIONARY

Indonesian–English
English–Indonesian

REVISED AND EXPANDED

Compiled by Katherine Davidsen

PERIPLUS

Published by Periplus Editions (HK) Ltd.

www.periplus.com

Copyright © 2017 Periplus Editions (HK) Ltd.

All rights reserved. No part of this publication may be reproduced or utilized in any form or by any means, electronic or mechanical, including photocopying, recording, or by any information storage and retrieval system, without prior written permission from the publisher.

ISBN: 978-0-7946-0829-3

Distributed by:

Indonesia
PT Java Books Indonesia
Jl. Rawa Gelam IV No. 9
Kawasan Industri Pulogadung
Jakarta 13930, Indonesia
Tel: 62 (21) 4682 1088; Fax: 62 (21) 461 0206
crm@periplus.co.id; www.periplus.com

Asia Pacific
Berkeley Books Pte Ltd
3 Kallang Sector #04-01
Singapore 349278
Tel: (65) 6741-2178; Fax: (65) 6741-2179
inquiries@periplus.com.sg; www.tuttlepublishing.com

Japan
Tuttle Publishing
Yaekari Building, 3rd Floor,
5-4-12 Osaki, Shinagawa-ku,
Tokyo 141-0032, Japan
Tel: (81) 3 5437 0171; Fax: (81) 3 5437 0755
sales@tuttle.co.jp; www.tuttle.co.jp

North America, Latin America & Europe
Tuttle Publishing
364 Innovation Drive
North Clarendon, VT 05759-9436 U.S.A.
Tel: 1 (802) 773-8930; Fax: 1 (802) 773-6993
info@tuttlepublishing.com; www.tuttlepublishing.com

27 26 25 24 23   5 4 3 2 1   2301VP

Printed in Malaysia

Contents

Introduction

A brief introduction to Indonesian

Indonesian is the national language of the world's fourth-largest nation, spoken by at least 70% of the nation's 250 million people. It is a mother tongue to over 27%, connecting speakers of 750 regional languages. As a variety of Malay, it is also understood in Singapore and Malaysia, making it a major language of Southeast Asia. An Austronesian language, modern Indonesian developed from Riau Malay into the official language of post-war independent Indonesia. It has borrowed widely from other languages and absorbed myriad influences, making it dynamic and always in flux.

Indonesian is considered relatively easy to learn, having very regular grammar. Adjectives follow the noun, as in French, and there is a wide range of verbs. Word order generally follows a subject-verb-object pattern. Words may be left out if the context is clear. Pronunciation is similar to Spanish or Italian, although accents vary.

Vowels:	**a**	as in *father*
	e	mostly as in *loosen* (swallowed "shwa" sound); sometimes as in *egg*. In older texts this is written as **é**
	i	as in *marine*
	o	as in *open*
	u	as in *blue*

Diphthongs:	**ai**	as in *aisle*
	au	as in *sauerkraut*

Consonants: as in English, except for:

	c	like **ch** in *child*
	g	always hard, as in *gum*, never soft as in *gem*
	kh	throaty sound as in *loch*
	ng	as in *thing*
	ngg	as in *finger* (ng+g)
	r	rolled, as in Spanish
	sy	**sh** as in *show*

This pocket Indonesian dictionary aims to represent the modern, standard usage of Indonesian, through common entries, new terminology and authentic terms, as well as identify parts of speech. A helpful, unusual feature is that this volume does not presume knowledge of word structure, which is vital when using most quality Indonesian dictionaries. For example, the word **mengalahkan** is listed under **mengalahkan** as well as its base, **kalah** in this dictionary. In most dictionaries, only the latter would appear.

Selection of entries

By definition, a pocket dictionary is a selection of useful words and phrases, rather than a complete compendium. This dictionary attempts to reflect general, everyday usage throughout Indonesia and the English-speaking world, including words that are important to students, language learners and tourists. American spelling is used. Entries cover survival language for tourists, common everyday words, national culture and language heard on the street.

Guide to using this dictionary

The dictionary is divided into two sections, Indonesian–English and English–Indonesian.

menghadap	entry (in bold type)
halang: halangan	first word is not found (or commonly used) alone. Sub-entries follow after semi-colon, in bold black type
v	word type (ie part of speech). Not always given if more than one word type exists. eg. **cas** charge (could be N, v)
child N **children**	irregular plurals follow the noun symbol N
put v **put put**	irregular past tense forms (simple past and past perfect) follow the verb symbol v
[nait]	irregularly-spelt words are given in Indonesian phonetic pronunciation
malam	meaning (in plain type)
session, meeting; hearing	Similar meanings are divided by commas; other meanings are divided by a semi-colon
~ *tiri* stepmother; *bahasa* ~ mother tongue	Entries or sub-entries are indicated by ~ (in italics). On the left, ~ represents *ibu*.
ouch! ow! (expressions of pain) to (be able to) speak or use a language	Round brackets contain additional information; or perhaps an extra meaning.
baik ... maupun ... both ... and ...	... represents any word, in a set phrase
bersih, membersihkan, pembersih	Where possible, all entries and sub-entries are grouped alphabetically.
handwriting N [handraiting] tulisan tangan ← **hand**	A left-pointing arrow indicates the base word.
abis → habis **became → become**	A right-pointing arrow shows an entry for further information or reference; or the base of an irregular past tense verb form.

List of Abbreviations

ABBREV	abbreviation	ISL	Islamic
ADJ	adjective	M	masculine
ADV	adverb	N	noun
ARCH	archaic	PL	plural
CATH	Catholic	POL	polite
CHILD	child(ren)	PREF	prefix
CHR	Christian	PREP	preposition
COLL	colloquial	PRON	pronoun
CONJ	conjunction	S	singular
DEROG	derogatory	SL	slang
EJAC	ejaculation	SUF	suffix
F	feminine	V	verb
GR	greeting	V, AUX	auxiliary verb
HIND	Hindu	V, PF	past perfect form of verb

Indonesian–English

A

abad N century; age, era; ~ *keemasan* golden age

abadi eternal, everlasting; *cinta* ~ endless love

abang N, PRON elder brother; ~ *None* Mr and Miss Jakarta → **bang**

abis COLL → **habis**

abjad N alphabet

abon N shredded dry meat, eaten as a side-dish

ABRI ABBREV *Angkatan Bersenjata Republik Indonesia* Indonesian Armed Forces

abu N ash; ~ *rokok* cigarette ash

abu-abu ADJ gray

AC ABBREV air-conditioner, air-conditioning

acar N finely-cut pickles, eaten with fried rice, satay etc

acara agenda, program, event; **pengacara** N lawyer, solicitor

acung: acungan N ~ *jempol* thumbs-up

AD ABBREV *Angkatan Darat* Army

ada V to be (present); to have, exist; ~ *Firman?* Is Firman here?; ~ *apa?* What's up? What's wrong?; *tidak* ~ there isn't, there aren't; not here; **adalah** V is, are (followed by a noun); **adanya** N the existence of; *apa* ~ as it is, without any pretensions; **berada** V to be somewhere; ADJ well-to-do, well-off; **keadaan** N situation, condition; ~ *darurat* emergency situation; **mengadakan** V to create, organize, make available; **seadanya** ADJ what's there; *makan* ~ eat what's there

adalah V is, are (followed by a noun) → **ada**

adanya *apa* ~ as it is, without any pretensions → **ada**

adat N tradition, custom, customary law, esp. of an ethnic group; ~ *istiadat* customs and traditions;

~ *Sunda* Sundanese traditions

adegan N scene

adik N younger brother or sister; ~ *ipar* (younger) brother- or sister-in-law; ~ *laki-laki* (younger) brother; *kakak-ber* ~ siblings; ~ *kandung* (younger) blood brother or sister; ~ *sepupu* cousin (of lower status)

adil ADJ just, righteous; **keadilan** N justice; **pengadilan** N court of justice or law, trial

administrasi N administration, management

adon: adonan N batter, dough, mixture

adu: mengadu V to complain, report; ~ *domba* to play two parties against each other; **pengaduan** N complaint; *surat* ~ letter of complaint

aduh EJAC ouch! ow! (expression of pain); EXCL oh! (expression of sorrow); wow!

aduk *campur* ~ mixed up; **mengaduk** V to stir, mix

adzan → **azan**

Afrika N Africa; *orang* ~ African; ~ *Selatan (Afsel)* South Africa

agak ADV rather, somewhat; ~ *gemuk* rather fat

agama N religion; ~ *Budha* Buddhism; **beragama** V to have a religion; ADJ religious

agar CONJ in order that/to

agar, agar-agar N a kind of jelly made from seaweed

agén N agent, agency, distributor

agénda N agenda; appointment diary

agrowisata N agricultural tourism

agung ADJ high, supreme

Agustus *bulan* ~ August

ah EXCL oh (showing mild annoyance)

Ahad → **Minggu**

ahli N expert, specialist; member; ~ *bedah* surgeon; ~ *waris* heir

air N water; juice; ~ *jeruk* orange

A

juice; ~ *ledeng* reticulated water; ~ *mata* tears; ~ *minum*, ~ *putih* drinking water; ~ *pasang* incoming tide; ~ *terjun* waterfall; *buang* ~ to go to the toilet

ajaib ADJ miraculous, strange

ajak: mengajak v to invite, ask out; to urge; ~ *jalan-jalan* to ask out

ajar: ajaran N teaching; **belajar** v to learn, study; **mempelajari** v to study something in depth; **mengajar** v to teach; **pelajar** N pupil, student; **pelajaran** N lesson; **terpelajar** ADJ educated; **pengajar** N teacher

akad N contract, agreement; ~ *nikah* Muslim marriage contract

akal N mind, intellect; *mencari* ~ to find a way

akan v will, going to (marks future time); *minggu yang* ~ *datang* next week; PREP about, concerning, regarding; ~ *tetapi* however

akar N root

akhir N end; ~*nya* finally; **berakhir** v to end; **mengakhiri** v to end, finish something; **terakhir** ADJ last, final, latest

aki N vehicle battery

akibat N result, consequence; CONJ due to, consequently; ~*nya* as a result

akrab ADJ close, intimate, friendly

aksén N accent

aksi N action, demonstration; **beraksi** v to take action, do something

akta, akte N official document, certificate; ~ *lahir*, ~ *kelahiran* birth certificate; ~ *nikah*, ~ *pernikahan* marriage certificate

aktif ADJ activated, active, on, working; **aktivitas** N activity

aktual ADJ latest, up-to-date; *berita* ~ current affairs

aku PRON I, me; **mengaku** v to admit, confess, acknowledge; to claim; ~ *salah* to admit guilt

akuntan N accountant; **akuntansi** N accounting

AL ABBREV *Angkatan Laut* Navy

ala ADJ in the style of, à la

alam N nature, world; ~ *(ter-)buka* open-air

alam: mengalami v to experience; **pengalaman** N experience

alamat N address; sign, omen

alangkah ADV how ...! what a ...!

alas N foundation, basis, base; ~ *kaki* footwear; **alasan** N cause, reason, motive

alat N tool, instrument, means; ~ *kontrasepsi*, ~ *KB* form of contraception; ~ *tulis* stationery; **peralatan** N equipment

album N album; ~ *foto* photo album

alérgi allergy, allergic; ~ *terhadap mangga* allergic to mangoes

alhamdulillah EJAC, ISL thanks be to God; bless you! (when sneezing)

alih v to shift, change position

alir flow aliran N stream, current; ideology, school, sect; **mengalir** v to flow

alis N eyebrow; *mengangkat* ~ to raise your eyebrows

aljabar N algebra

Alkitab N the Bible

alkohol N alcohol; **beralkohol** v containing alcohol

Allah N God, Allah

almarhum ADJ, M, ISL the late; **almarhumah** ADJ, F, ISL the late

alpukat, apokat, avokat N avocado; *jus* ~ avocado drink

Alqur'an, Al-quran, Alquran N the Koran

AL(RI) ABBREV *Angkatan Laut (Republik Indonesia)* (Indonesian) Navy

alu N pestle; ~ *lumpang* mortar and pestle

alun-alun N town square

amal N charity

aman ADJ safe, in peace; **keamanan** N safety, security; **mengamankan** v to make safe, restore order; place in custody

amat ADV very, extremely

amat: mengamati v to watch closely, keep an eye on; **pengamat** N observer; **pengamatan** N observation, monitoring

ambeien N hemorrhoids, piles

ambil v to take; to subtract; to bring; ~ *saja* help yourself; **mengambil** v to take, get, fetch

INDONESIAN—ENGLISH

ambisi N ambition

ambruk V to collapse, break, crash

ambulans N ambulance

amén: (me)ngamén V to sing in the street for money, busk; **pengamén** N street singer, busker

Amérika N America; ~ *Serikat* United States of America

amin EJAC amen

amis ADJ putrid, smelling fishy

amplop N envelope; COLL bribe

ampuh ADJ powerful, potent

ampun N mercy, forgiveness, pardon; EJAC Mercy! (expression of astonishment or disapproval); *minta* ~ beg for mercy

amuk: mengamuk V to run amok, go berserk

anak N child; young (of an animal); member of a group; small part of a whole; ~ *angkat* adopted child; ~ *buah* assistants, staff; ~ *bungsu* youngest child; ~ *cucu* descendants; ~ *emas* favorite; ~ *haram* illegitimate child; ~ *jalanan* street kid; ~ *kunci* key; ~ *perempuan* daughter; ~ *sulung* eldest child; ~ *tiri* stepchild; ~ *tunggal* only child; ~ *yatim* orphan; **anak-anak** N, PL children; **beranak** V (of animals) to give birth to, have offspring; **peranakan** ADJ of mixed Chinese and Indonesian blood, Straits Chinese

analisa, analisis N analysis

ancam V to threaten; **ancaman** N threat; **mengancam** V to threaten, intimidate; **terancam** ADJ threatened

anda, Anda PRON you (neutral, without status)

andai, andaikan, andainya, seandainya CONJ if, supposing that

andal ADJ reliable; **mengandalkan** V to rely on, trust

andong N four-wheeled horse-drawn carriage in Jogja and Solo

anéh ADJ strange, peculiar; ~*nya* the strange thing is...

anéka ADJ all kinds of, various; ~ *jenis* all sorts; ~ *macam*, ~ *ragam* varied

anggap V to consider; **menganggap** V to consider, regard

anggaran N budget, estimate

anggota N member; ~ *badan* limb; ~ *DPR* Member of Parliament; ~ *keluarga* family member; **keanggotaan** N membership; *kartu* ~ membership card

anggrék N orchid

angguk, mengangguk V to nod

anggun ADJ elegant, stylish, graceful

anggur N wine, grapes; ~ *putih* white wine; *buah* ~ grapes

anggur: pengangguran N unemployment, unemployed person

angin N wind, breeze

angka N figure, numeral, digit; score, mark; ~ *Romawi* Roman numeral

angkasa N space, sky

angkat V to lift; ~ *besi* weight-lifting; ~ *tangan* give up; raise your hand; ~ *telepon* to pick up, answer the phone; **angkatan** N generation, year level (at school or university); force; ~ *darat (AD)* army; **berangkat** V to depart, leave; **keberangkatan** N departure; *pintu* ~ departure gate; **mengangkat** V to lift or pick up, raise; appoint; to remove, amputate

angkét N survey (form)

angklung N bamboo instrument, played in an orchestra

angkot N, COLL public minibus → **angkutan kota**

angkut V to carry, lift, transport; **angkutan** N transport, transportation; ~ *kota (angkot)* city transportation; ~ *umum* public transport

angpao, angpau N a red envelope containing money, given at Chinese New Year

angsa N goose

anjing N dog (also insult)

anjlok V to derail; *kereta api* ~ derailed train

anjung: anjungan N gallery, upper level, ship's bridge

anjur: menganjurkan V to suggest, propose

anoa N dwarf buffalo of Sulawesi

antar take, escort; ~ *jemput* pick up and take home, door-to-door; **mengantar** V to take, escort, accompany; **mengantarkan** V to take someone or something

INDONESIAN–ENGLISH

A

antara CONJ between; among them; **perantara** N broker, intermediary, go-between

antarpropinsi ADJ interprovincial

antem: berantem V, COLL to fight, scuffle → **hantam**

anti- PREF, ADJ against, resistant to; ~ *perang* anti-war

anting N earring

antré, antri queue; **antréan** N queue; **mengantri** V to queue

anut, menganut V to follow; **penganut** N follower, believer

anyam, menganyam V to weave, plait, braid; **anyaman** N plait, braid

apa INTERROG, N what; ~ *lagi* what else; ~ *saja* anything; ~ *kabar?* how are you?; **apa-apa** N something; *tidak* ~ it doesn't matter; **apabila** CONJ if, when; **berapa** INTERROG how many? what number?; ~ *harganya?* how much is it?; *umur* ~ how old; **beberapa** ADJ several, a number of; *jauh* ~ as far as; **mengapa** INTERROG why; *tak* ~ it doesn't matter; **ngapain** SL why, do what; **siapa** INTERROG, N who; ~ *saja* whoever; **siapa-siapa** N anybody

apakah, apa (question marker) → **apa**

apalagi ADV, CONJ especially, moreover

apartemén N apartment, flat

apel N apple

api N fire, flame; **berapi** V to produce fire; **perapian** N fireplace, oven

apik ADJ neat, tidy

apoték N pharmacy, chemist (shop), dispensary; **apotéker** N pharmacist

April *bulan* ~ April

apung float; **mengapung** V to float, be suspended

Arab *bahasa* ~ Arabic; *orang* ~ an Arab

arah N direction; *satu* ~ one way; same direction

arak N alcoholic drink

arang N charcoal

arca N statue

arén N areca palm

argo, argométer N taxi meter

arit N sickle

arogan ADJ arrogant

arsip N archive, file

arti N meaning; ~ *nya* it means, that is to say; **berarti** V to mean; ADJ meaningful

artikel N article (in print media)

artis N celebrity; actor, actress or singer

arung ~ *jeram* white water rafting

arus N stream, current, flow; ~ *listrik* electric current

AS ABBREV *Amerika Serikat* the United States

asal N origin; ~-*usul* origins; **berasal** V to come from

asal, asalkan CONJ as long as, providing that

asam, asem sour, tamarind; acid; ~ *manis* sweet and sour

asap N smoke, exhaust, pollution; vapor; **berasap** ADJ smoky

asar N, ISL the afternoon prayer

asas, azas: asasi, azasi ADJ basic

asbak N ashtray

ASI ABBREV *air susu ibu* breast milk

Asia N Asia; ~ *Tenggara* Southeast Asia

asin ADJ salty, salted; **asinan** N sour vegetable and fruit dish

asing ADJ strange, alien, foreign; *orang* ~ stranger; foreigner

asli ADJ original, indigenous; *orang* ~, *penduduk* ~ indigenous person, native

asma N asthma

asong: asongan N street vendor; goods sold on the street (cigarettes, magazines, drinking water etc.)

aspal N asphalt

asrama N boarding house, dormitory; MIL barracks

asri ADJ beautiful, scenic (of a view)

assalamualaikum, assalamu alaikum salam alaikum GR, ISL peace be upon you

asuh care; *orang tua* ~ foster parents; **pengasuh** N carer; ~ *anak* nursemaid, babysitter

asuransi N insurance

asyik ADJ fun; ADV absorbed, engrossed; eager

atap N roof; **beratap** V to have a roof

atas PREP up; N upper part; *di* ~ on (top of), upon, above, over;

INDONESIAN—ENGLISH

B

upstairs; **atasan** N superior, boss; **mengatasi** v to overcome

atau CONJ or

ati ampela N liver and gizzards

atlét, atlit N athlete

atur arrange; **aturan** N rule, regulation; **mengatur** v to arrange, organize, regulate; **peraturan** N rule, regulation; **teratur** ADJ organized, regular

aula N hall (at school), auditorium

AU(RI) ABBREV *Angkatan Udara (Republik Indonesia)* (Indonesian) Air Force

Australia N Australia; *orang ~* Australian

awak N person; *~ pesawat* cabin crew

awal beginning, early; **awalan** N prefix; **berawal** v to begin with

awan N cloud; **berawan** ADJ cloudy, overcast

awas EJAC be careful, beware; **mengawasi** v to supervise

awét ADJ durable, long-lasting

ayah, Ayah N, PRON father; *~ bunda* parents

ayam N chicken, hen; *~ kampung* free-range chicken; *~ negeri* battery hen

ayat N verse (of a religious text)

ayo come on, let's go

ayu ADJ beautiful

ayun: ayunan N swings

azan, adzan N call to prayer

B

bab N chapter

babi N pig, boar (also as an insult); *~ hutan* wild boar; *daging ~* pork

baca v to read; **bacaan** N reading material; **membaca** v to read; **pembaca** N reader

badai N hurricane, storm; *~ topan* typhoon

badak N rhino, rhinoceros

badan N body; board, committee

badut N clown

bagai CONJ like, as; **berbagai** ADJ various, several; **sebagai** CONJ like, as

bagaimana INTERROG, CONJ how, in what way

bagasi N baggage; boot (of vehicle); hold (of ship or aircraft)

bagi v divide; **bagian** N part, share, section; **berbagi** v to share; **membagi** v to divide, distribute; **sebagian** N some, a section of

bagi PREP for

bagus ADJ good, fine, excellent (external qualities of concrete objects)

bahagia ADJ happy, joyous; **berbahagia** v to be happy

bahan N materials, ingredients; cloth, fabric; *~ bakar* fuel

bahas v to discuss; **membahas** v to discuss, debate

bahasa N language; *~ Indonesia* Indonesian; **berbahasa** v to (be able to) speak or use a language

bahaya N danger; **berbahaya** v to be dangerous

bahkan CONJ moreover; on the contrary; indeed, even

bahu N shoulder

bahwa CONJ that

baik ADJ good, fine, well, OK (ie. internal qualities of abstract objects); **baik-baik** ADJ fine; respectable; *~ hati* kind; **membaik** v to improve; **memperbaiki** v to repair, fix; **perbaikan** N repair, improvement; **sebaiknya** ADV preferably, it's best if; **terbaik** ADJ the best

baja N steel

bajaj N three-wheeled motorized form of transport in Jakarta

bajak N plow; **membajak** v to plow

bajak, membajak v to hijack; to copy illegally; **bajakan** ADJ pirated; *CD ~* pirated CD

baju N, INF clothes; clothing for the upper body; *~ dalam* singlet; underwear

bak N tub; *~ mandi* large tank in the bathroom from which water is taken

bakal ADJ future, potential

bakar v to burn; **kebakaran** N fire; **membakar** v to burn; **terbakar** ADJ burnt

bakat N talent, gift; **berbakat** ADJ talented, gifted

bakau N mangrove

bakmi, bami N Chinese noodles

INDONESIAN–ENGLISH

B

bakpao N steamed white bread with filling of nuts or chicken

bakpia N sweet cake from Jogja with nutty filling

bakso, baso N meatball; meatball soup; ~ *tahu* meatballs and tofu (specialty of Bandung)

bakul N basket hung on a pole for selling goods

bakwan N dish of various sweetmeats, a specialty of Malang

balai ~ *kota* town hall

balap race; **balapan** N race; **membalap** v to race

balas reply; **balasan** reply, answer; **membalas** v to reply, respond

balét N ballet

Bali N *pulau* ~ Bali; *bahasa* ~, *orang* ~ Balinese

balik v to return, reverse, retreat; N back, flipside; return; **membalik** v to return, reverse, turn over; **membalikkan** v to turn something over; **sebaliknya** conj on the contrary; **terbalik** adj overturned, upside-down, opposite

balon N balloon

balut: pembalut N sanitary pad

bambu N bamboo

ban N tire; ~ *serep* spare tire

bandara N airport → **bandar udara**

bandel adj naughty, disobedient

banding: membandingkan v to compare something; **perbandingan** N comparison, ratio

bandrék N ginger drink

bang pron older brother (in Jakarta or Malay areas) → **abang**

banget adj, sl fast, quick

bangga adj proud

bangkai N corpse (usually of animals); *bunga* ~ the Rafflesia flower

bangkit v to rise, get up

bangkrut adj bankrupt

bangku N bench (for sitting); stool; desk

bangsa N people, nation, race

bangun v get up, wake up; **membangunkan** v to wake someone up

bangun: bangunan N building; **membangun** v to build or create; **pembangunan** N development

banjir N flood

bank N bank; ~ *negara* state-owned bank; **perbankan** adj banking; **bankir** N banker

bantal cushion; pillow

banteng N (Javan) ox

banting: membanting v to throw down (with a bang)

bantu v to help; **bantuan** N assistance, help, aid; **membantu** v to help (someone); **pembantu** N servant, maid; assistant

banyak adj many, much; **kebanyakan** N, adj too much; most

Bapa pron Father (title for own father or respected older man), also Bapak; chr God, Father, Lord

Bapak pron Father (title for own father or respected older man)

bapak N father

baptis adj baptist

barang N goods, things

barangkali conj perhaps, maybe

Barat N the West

barat adj west; ~ *daya* southwest; ~ *laut* northwest

Barelang *Batam, Rempang, Galang* group of islands in Riau Archipelago province

bareng conj, sl with; v to go together

baris N line, row, rank; **barisan** N line; forces; **berbaris** v to line up

barongsai N Chinese dragon for dance performances

baru adj new, recent; just; ~~ *ini* just the other day; **terbaru** adj latest, newest; **barusan** adv, sl just now

basa-basi N good manners, politeness; platitudes

basah adj wet, moist, soaked

basi adj off, rotten, inedible (of food)

batagor N fried tofu and meatballs, a specialty of Bandung → **bakso tahu goreng**

Batak adj ethnic group of North Sumatra

batal adj cancelled; broken (a fast); **membatalkan** v to cancel, repeal

batang N trunk, stem, stick (of a tree); shaft; handle; penis; counter for long cylindrical objects

batas N limit, border; **berbatasan** v to be adjacent to; **perbatasan** N border, frontier; **terbatas** adj limited

INDONESIAN—ENGLISH

B

baterai N battery

batik N application of wax onto fabric to create a pattern after dyeing; fabric or clothes with designs produced in this manner; ~ *cap* stamped batik; ~ *tulis* handmade batik; **membatik** V to apply wax onto fabric

batu N stone; **berbatu** ADJ rocky, stony

batuk V cough

bau N, V, ADJ smell, smelly; **berbau** V to smell, have connotations of

baut N bolt

bawa V to take, bring, carry; to conduct; **membawa** V to take, bring, carry; to conduct; **terbawa** ADJ (accidentally) taken away

bawah PREP below; *di* ~ below, under; *di* ~ *umur* underage

bawang N onion; ~ *putih* garlic

baya N age; *setengah* ~ middle-aged

bayam, bayem N spinach

bayang N shadow, image; **bayangan** N shadow; **terbayang** ADJ imagined, conceivable

bayar V to pay; **membayar** V to pay; **pembayaran** N payment

bayi N baby

béa N tax, duty, excise; ~ *cukai* customs

béasiswa N scholarship, bursary

beban N burden, load; responsibility

bébas ADJ free

bébék N duck

beberapa ADJ several, a number of → apa, berapa

becak N pedicab, rickshaw tricycle; *tukang* ~ bécak driver

bécék ADJ muddy, wet

béda ADJ different; *~nya* ... the difference is, ...; **berbéda** ADJ different; **membédakan** V to discriminate, differentiate between, consider different; **perbédaan** N difference

bedah N surgery

bedak N powder

begadang V to stay up all night; to sleep late

begini ADV like this, in this manner → ini

begitu ADV like that, in that manner → itu

béha N bra

bekal N provisions

bekas ADJ used, old, former (for objects)

bekerja V to work; ~ *sama* to cooperate, work together → kerja

beku ADJ frozen; **membeku** V to freeze

bél N bell

béla V defend; ~ *diri* self-defense; **membéla** V to defend

belah N crack, fissure, divide, splinter; **belahan** N half, side; **membelah** V to split in two; **sebelah** PREP next to; N half, side; (*din kanan*) on the right (side)

belajar V to learn, study → ajar

belakang PREP, N behind; back, rear; **belakangan** ADV recently; after others; ~ *ini* recently

belalang N grasshopper, locust

Belanda N the Netherlands, Holland; *bahasa* ~; *orang* ~ Dutch

belanja V to go shopping; **belanjaan** N shopping; **berbelanja** V to go shopping; **perbelanjaan** *pusat* ~ shopping center, mall

belas N number between 10–20; *lima* ~ fifteen; **belasan** N dozens; **sebelas** N, ADJ eleven

belérang N sulfur

Bélgia N Belgium

beli V to buy; **membeli** V to buy, purchase; **pembelian** N purchase

beliau PRON he, she; him, her (respectful form of **dia**)

belimbing N starfruit

bélok turn; **bélokan** N bend, turn in the road; **berbélok, membélok** V to bend, turn

belum ADV not yet; ~ *pernah* until now, never (but possibly in the future); **sebelum** ADJ before; **sebelumnya** ADV previously, before

belut N eel

benang N thread

benar, bener ADJ true, correct, right; **benar-benar** ADV truly, really; **kebenaran** N truth; **membenarkan** V to confirm, verify; to justify; **sebenarnya** ADV in fact, actually

bencana N disaster, catastrophe
benci v to hate; **membenci** v to hate
bendéra N flag
béndi N two-wheeled horse-carriage
bendung: bendungan N dam
bener → benar
bengkak ADJ swollen
béngkél N garage; workshop
béngkok ADJ bent, crooked
bening ADJ clear, transparent, clean (of glass, water etc)
bénjol, bénjolan N mole, lump, tumor
bénsin N petrol, gasoline
bénténg N fort, fortress
bentrok v to clash head-on; **bentrokan** N clash, conflict
bentuk N shape, form; **berbentuk** ADJ shaped, with the shape of; **membentuk** v to form, set up something (eg. committee); **terbentuk** ADJ formed, shaped, created
benua N continent
bepergian v to travel, be away → pergi
beracun ADJ poisonous, containing poison → racun
berada v to be somewhere; ADJ well-to-do, well-off → ada
beragam ADJ various → ragam
beragama ADJ religious; v to have a religion
bérak v to poo, defecate; N poo, feces
berakhir v to end → akhir
beralkohol v containing alcohol; *minuman* ~ alcoholic drink → alkohol
berambut ADJ hairy; v to have hair
beranak v (of animals) to give birth to, have offspring → anak
beranda N veranda, balcony; home (on webpage)
berang ADJ furious, enraged
berangkat v to depart, leave; **keberangkatan** N departure → angkat
berani ADJ brave, courageous; **keberanian** N bravery, courage
berantakan ADJ messy, in a mess → antak
berantas, memberantas v to wipe out, fight against
berantem v, COLL to fight, scuffle → antem, hantam

berapa INTERROG how many? what number?; ~ *harganya?* how much is it?; *umur* ~ how old; **beberapa** ADJ several, a number of → apa
berapi ADJ burning, fire-producing (of volcanoes) → api
berarti v to mean; ADJ meaningful → arti
beras N rice (husked and uncooked, as sold in shops)
berasal v to come from → asal
berasap ADJ smoky → asap
berat heavy, severe, difficult; weight; **keberatan** N objection; v to object
beratap v to have a roof → atap
berawal v to begin with → awal
berawan ADJ cloudy, overcast → awan
berbagai ADJ various, several → bagai
berbagi v to share → bagi
berbahagia v to be happy → bahagia
berbahasa v to (be able to) speak or use a language → bahasa
berbahaya v to be dangerous → bahaya
berbakat ADJ talented, gifted → bakat
berbaris v to line up → baris
berbatasan v to be adjacent to → batas
berbatu ADJ rocky, stony → batu
berbau v to smell, have connotations of → bau
berbéda ADJ different → béda
berbelanja v to go shopping → belanja
berbentuk ADJ shaped, with the shape of → bentuk
berbicara v to speak; ~ *dalam bahasa Sunda* to speak in Sundanese → bicara
berbincang, berbincang-bincang v to chat, discuss → bincang
berbintang v to have a star → bintang
berbisa ADJ poisonous; *ular* ~ poisonous snake → bisa
berbisnis v to do business → bisnis
berbohong v to lie → bohong
berbuah v to bear fruit, produce → buah

INDONESIAN–ENGLISH

berbuat v to do → buat
berbuka ~ *puasa* to break the fast → buka
berbukit ADJ hilly → bukit
berbunyi v to sound, make a noise → bunyi
bercampur ADJ mixed with → campur
bercanda v to joke → canda
bercelana v to wear trousers, trousered → celana
bercerita v to tell (a story) → cerita
bercinta v to make love; to be in love → cinta
berciuman v to kiss each other → cium
berdagang v to trade, do business → dagang
berdamai v to make peace → damai
berdampak v to have a (negative) effect → dampak
berdandan v to dress, put on make-up → dandan
berdansa v to dance (Western-style) → dansa
berdarah v to bleed → darah
berdebar v to beat quickly → debar
berdebat v to have a debate → debat
berdebu ADJ dusty → debu
berdekatan ADJ close (of two or more things) → dekat
berdémo v to hold a protest → démo
berdering v to ring, tinkle → dering
berdesakan v to push each other → desak
berdoa v to pray, say a prayer → doa
berdosa v to sin, commit a sin → dosa
berdua ADJ together, in pairs → dua
berduka ~ *(cita)* to grieve, be in mourning → duka
berduri ADJ thorny → duri
berebut v to fight for; **berebutan** v to fight each other for → rebut
berékor v to have a tail → ékor
berempat ADJ in a group of four → empat
berenang v to swim → renang
berencana v to plan → rencana
bérés finished, ready; **memberéskan** v to clear up, make ready

berfungsi v to work, go; to act as → fungsi
bergabung v to join together → gabung
bergambar ADJ illustrated → gambar
berganti v to change; ~-*ganti*, ~*an* in turns → ganti
bergaris ADJ lined → garis
bergaul v to mix or associate with → gaul
bergaya ADJ stylish, with style → gaya
bergegas-gegas v to hurry → gegas
bergelar v titled → gelar
bergelombang ADJ wavy → gelombang
bergembira v to be happy, joyous → gembira
bergéngsi ADJ prestigious → géngsi
bergerak v to move → gerak
bergilir, bergiliran ADJ in turns → gilir
bergizi ADJ nutritious → gizi
bergosip v to gossip → gosip
bergoyang v to shake, sway; to dance → goyang
bergulat v to wrestle, fight → gulat
berguna ADJ useful, worthwhile → guna
berhadapan v *(~ muka)* face to face → hadap
berhadiah ADJ with prizes → hadiah
berhak v to have a right to, be entitled to → hak
berhalangan v to be prevented from, unable → halang
berharap v to hope → harap
berharga ADJ precious, valuable → harga
berhari-hari ADV for days → hari
berhasil v to succeed → hasil
berhenti v to stop, cease → henti
berhubung CONJ in connection to, related with; **berhubungan** v, PL to have a link or connection → hubung
beri v to give; ~ *tahu* to inform, let know → **beritahu**; **memberi** v to give; **memberikan** v to give someone (as an act of kindness); to give something (for someone)

beribu, beribu-ribu ADJ thousands of → ribu

berikut ADJ following → ikut

berimbang ADJ balanced, proportional → imbang

beringin N banyan (tree)

berisi v to contain; ADJ full, filled out → isi

berisik ADJ noisy, loud; to rustle → risik

berisiko v to be risky → risiko

beristeri, beristri ADJ, M married → isteri, istri

beristirahat v to rest, take a break → istirahat

berita N news, information; **memberitakan** v to report

beritahu, beri tahu v to inform, let know; **memberitahu** v to advise, inform, tell; **pemberitahuan** N announcement, notice

berjabat, berjabatan ~ *tangan* to shake hands → jabat

berjalan v to walk, move → jalan

berjam-jam ADJ for hours and hours → jam

berjamur ADJ moldy → jamur

berjanji v to promise → janji

berjemur v to sunbathe, sun yourself → jemur

berjénggot ADJ bearded → jénggot

berjilbab v to wear the veil → jilbab

berjogét v to dance → jogét

berjuang v to fight, struggle → juang

berjudi v to gamble → judi

berjudul v to have a title; ADJ titled → judul

berjumlah v to number → jumlah

berjumpa v to meet → jumpa

berjuta v to have millions of → juta

berkali-kali ADV repeatedly, again and again → kali

berkapasitas v with a capacity of → kapasitas

berkarat ADJ rusty → karat

berkas N bundle; file, dossier, brief

berkata v to say, speak → kata

berkawan v to have or be friends with → kawan

berkedip v to blink (two eyes) or wink (one eye); **berkedip-kedip** ADJ blinking → kedip

berkelahi v to quarrel, fight, fall out → kelahi

berkelas ADJ classy → kelas

berkeliling v to go around → keliling

berkeluarga v to have a family, be married → keluarga

berkémah v to camp, go camping → kémah

berkembang v to develop, expand; *negara* ~ developing country → kembang

berkencan v to go on a date → kencan

berkeringat v to sweat → keringat

berkesan ADJ impressive → kesan

berkibar v to wave, flutter → kibar

berkilau ADJ glittering, sparkling → kilau

berkisah v to tell a story → kisah

berkisar v to revolve, rotate, turn → kisar

berkoméntar v to (make a) comment → koméntar

berkorban v to make sacrifices, do without → korban

berkualitas ADJ quality → kualitas

berkuasa ADJ powerful, mighty → kuasa

berkuda v to ride a horse, go (horse-)riding → kuda

berkuku ADJ having nails or claws; clawed → kuku

berkulit to have skin, skinned → kulit

berkumpul v to assemble, meet → kumpul

berkumur(-kumur) v to gargle → kumur

berkunjung v to visit, pay a visit to → kunjung

berkurang v to decrease, diminish, subside → kurang

berlaku ADJ effective, valid; v to behave → laku

berlambang v to have a symbol → lambang

berlangganan v to subscribe to → langgan

berlangsung v to take place → langsung

berlari v to run → lari

berlayar v to sail → layar

berlebihan ADJ excessive → lebih

INDONESIAN—ENGLISH

berlian N diamond
berlibur v to go or be on holiday → libur
berlindung v to (take) shelter → lindung
berlomba v to compete, race → lomba
berlumuran ADJ smeared, stained → lumur
berlutut v to kneel (down) → lutut
bermacam-macam ADJ various → macam
bermain v to play → main
bermaksud v to intend → maksud
bermalam v to spend or stay the night → malam
bermalas-malas(an) v to lie or laze around, be lazy → malas
bermanfaat ADJ useful, of benefit → manfaat
bermasalah ADJ problematic, troublesome → masalah
bermérek ADJ branded → mérek
bermimpi v to dream → mimpi
berminggu-minggu ADV for weeks → minggu
berminyak ADJ oily, greasy → minyak
bermotif v to have a design → motif
bermuka v to have a face; ~ dua two-faced → muka
bermula v to start, begin → mula
bermutu ADJ quality → mutu
bernafaskan, bernapaskan v with a breath of → nafas
bernafsu ADJ passionate, lusty → nafsu
bernama ADJ named → nama
berniat v to intend → niat
bernyanyi v to sing → nyanyi
berobat v to go to the doctor, seek medical advice → obat
beroda ADJ wheeled → roda
berolahraga v to do or play sport → olahraga
berombak ADJ wavy → ombak
berontak, memberontak v to rebel, revolt; **pemberontakan** N rebellion, revolt, mutiny
berotot ADJ muscular → otot
berpakaian ADJ dressed in → pakai
berpangkat v to have the rank of → pangkat

berpegang v to hold onto → pegang
berpendapat v to have an opinion, believe → dapat
berpendidikan ADJ educated; v to have an education
berpengaruh ADJ influential → pengaruh
berperan v to play the role or part → peran
berperang v to wage war, go to war → perang
berpésta v to (have a) party → pésta
berpidato v to make a speech, give an address → pidato
berpihak v to take sides → pihak
berpikir v to think → pikir
berpindah v to move → pindah
berpisah v to part, separate → pisah
berpose v to pose for a photograph → pose
berpréstasi ADJ prestigious; successful → préstasi
berpuasa v to fast → puasa
berpusar N to revolve, whirl → pusar
berpusat ~ pada to focus or center on → pusat
berputar v to rotate, turn → putar
bersabar v to be patient → sabar
bersahabat ADJ to be friends → sahabat
bersaing v to compete; harga ~ competitive price → saing
bersalah ADJ guilty → salah
bersalin v to give birth → salin
bersalju ADJ snowy, snow-covered → salju
bersama ADV together; jointly → sama
bersambung ADJ in parts; to be continued → sambung
bersampingan ADJ next to each other → samping
bersandar v to lean → sandar
bersangka v to suspect or think → sangka
bersangkutan ADJ concerned, involved → sangkut
bersatu v to unite → satu
bersaudara v to be related; to have brothers and sisters; ~ enam to be one of six (children) → saudara

INDONESIAN–ENGLISH

B

bersayap ADJ winged → sayap
bersedia v to be prepared or willing → sedia
bersedih v to be or feel sad → sedih
bersejarah ADJ historic, historical → sejarah
bersekolah v to go to school → sekolah
berselancar v to surf, go surfing → lancar
berselingkuh v to have an affair → selingkuh
bersemangat ADJ spirited, enthusiastic → semangat
bersembahyang v to pray, perform a prayer → sembahyang
bersembunyi v to hide (yourself) → sembunyi
bersenang-senang v to enjoy yourself, have fun → senang
bersenda ~ *gurau* to joke around → senda
bersendawa v to burp, belch → sendawa
bersenjata ADJ armed → senjata
bersepatu ADJ in shoes → sepatu
bersepéda v to ride a bicycle → sepéda
bersiap v to get ready; bersiap-siap v to make preparations → siap
bersifat v to have the quality of → sifat
bersih ADJ clean, neat; kebersihan N cleanliness, hygiene; membersihkan v to clean; wipe out (eg. disease); pembersih N cleaning agent
bersikap v to display an attitude → sikap
bersikeras v to maintain, stick to, be obstinate → keras
bersilaturahmi v to maintain good relations, visit or meet friends → silaturahmi
bersin v to sneeze
bersinar v to shine, gleam → sinar
bersiul v to whistle → siul
berskala v to be on a scale; ~ *besar* large-scale → skala
bersoda ADJ carbonated; *minuman* ~ carbonated drink → soda
bersolék v to put on make-up, dress up → solék
bersorak v to cheer, shout → sorak

bersuami ADJ, F married
bersuara v to sound, have a voice → suara
bersulang v to toast, drink to → sulang
bersumpah v to swear → sumpah
bersyarat ADJ conditional → syarat
bersyukur ADJ grateful → syukur
bertaburan ADJ scattered over → tabur
bertahap ADJ in stages → tahap
bertahun-tahun ADV for years and years → tahun
bertambah v to increase → tambah
bertanda ADJ marked → tanda
bertanding v to compete, play → tanding
bertanggung jawab ADJ responsible → tanggung jawab
bertanya v to ask; bertanya-tanya v to wonder, ask yourself → tanya
bertaruh v to bet → taruh
berteduh v to take shelter → teduh
berteman v to be friends → teman
bertempat v to take place or happen → tempat
bertemu v to meet; *sampai* ~ *lagi* see you later, so long → temu
bertengkar v to quarrel → tengkar
bertentangan ADJ contradictory, contrary, opposing → tentang
bertepuk tangan v to clap, applaud → tepuk tangan
berteriak v to scream or shout → teriak
berterima kasih v to be grateful or thankful → terima kasih
bertiga ADJ in threes → tiga
bertingkat ADJ having different levels → tingkat
bertinju v to box → tinju
bertumpuk v to be in piles → tumpuk
berturut-turut ADJ consecutive, successive → turut
beruang N bear; ~ *putih* polar bear
berubah v to change → ubah
berulang v to happen again, recur; berulang-ulang ADV again and again, repeatedly → ulang
berumur ADJ aged → umur
beruntung ADJ lucky, fortunate → untung

INDONESIAN – ENGLISH

berupa ADJ in the shape or form of → rupa

berurusan V to have dealings with, deal with → urus

berusaha V to try, make an effort → usaha

berusia V to be (aged) → usia

berutang V to owe; ~ *budi* to have a debt of gratitude → utang

berwarna ADJ colored → warna

berziarah V to make a pilgrimage, visit a holy place → ziarah

bésan N relationship between two couples whose children have married

besar ADJ big, large, great; ~ *kepala* big-headed, arrogant; **besar-besaran** ADJ large-scale; **kebesaran** ADJ too big; **membesarkan** V to bring up, raise (children); **memperbesar** V to enlarge something; **terbesar** ADJ largest, biggest

beserta CONJ along with, and → serta

besi N iron

bésok ADV tomorrow; COLL in the future → ésok

besuk V to visit someone in hospital

betah V to settle in, feel at home

betapa ADV how (very); ~ *cantiknya!* How pretty she is! → alangkah

Betawi N original inhabitants of Jakarta (since 1527)

betina ADJ female (of animals); *anjing* ~ bitch

betis N calf, lower part of leg

beton N concrete

betul ADJ true, correct, right; **betul-betul** ADV truly, completely; **kebetulan** ADV by chance, accidentally; N coincidence; **membetulkan** V to correct, repair; **sebetulnya** ADV in fact, actually

bi PRON aunt; term of address for older housemaid → bibi

biar let, no matter if; ~*lah!* Never mind!; **membiarkan** V to let, allow, permit

biasa ADJ normal, usual, common, ordinary; ~*nya* usually; **kebiasaan** N habit, custom; **terbiasa** ADJ used to, accustomed

biaya N cost, expense (for a service)

bibi N, PRON aunt, sister of parent; mother's female cousin → bi

bibir N lips

bibit N seedling

bicara V speak; **berbicara** V to speak; **membicarakan** V to discuss; **pembicaraan** N discussion

bidan N midwife

bidang ADJ spacious, wide; N area, field

bihun N vermicelli noodles

bijak ADJ wise; **kebijakan** N policy

biji N seed, grain; counter for very small objects; SL testicle

bikin V, COLL to make; ~ *marah* make angry; **bikinan** N product; **dibikin** V to be made → buat

biksu N Buddhist monk

bila CONJ if

bilang V, SL to say; **dibilang** V to be said

bilas, membilas V to rinse

biliar, bilyar N billiards

biliun, bilyun N billion (1 000 000 000)

bimbing V to lead, guide; **membimbing** V to lead, guide, coach

bina V to build up; **membina** V to build up, found

binatang N animal

binatu N (commercial) laundry

bincang: berbincang(-bincang) V to chat, discuss

bingkai N frame(s)

bingkis: bingkisan N wrapped or free gift

bingung ADJ confused; **membingungkan** ADJ confusing

bintang N star; **berbintang** V to have a star; **membintangi** V to star (in)

bintik N spot, stain, freckle

biodata N personal profile (name, address, date of birth, hobbies etc)

biola N violin, fiddle

bioskop N cinema, movie theater

bir N beer

biro N office, center; ~ *perjalanan* travel agent

biru ADJ blue; ~ *tua* dark blue

bis ~ *surat* letter box, mailbox (for posting)

bis, bus N bus

bisa V, AUX can, be able; **sebisanya, sebisa-bisanya** ADV as well as you can, to the best of your ability

INDONESIAN–ENGLISH

B

bisa N poison (of animals), venom; **berbisa** ADJ poisonous; *ular* ~ poisonous snake

bisbol N baseball

bisik whisper; v to whisper; **membisik** v to whisper something

bisnis N business, trade; **berbisnis** v to do business

bistik N steak

bisu ADJ mute, dumb; ~ *tuli* deaf-mute

bius N drug; *obat* ~ anesthetic; **membius** v to drug, anesthetize

blangko N form

blasteran ADJ mixed, hybrid; *Sari* ~ *Sunda-Jerman* Sari is half-Sundanese, half-German

bléwah N kind of melon

blits N flash (of camera)

blok N block (in addresses)

blokir, memblokir v to block

blong ADJ loose, not taut

blus N blouse

bobo, bobok v, SL to sleep (children's language)

bocor v to leak; **kebocoran** N leak; **membocorkan** v to leak something

bodoh ADJ stupid

bohlam N light bulb

bohong lie; **berbohong** to lie; **membohong** v to lie; **pembohong** N liar

boikot N boycott; **memboikot** v to boycott something

boks N playpen, bassinet

bola N ball; football, soccer; ~ *basket* basketball; *main* ~ play football

bolak-balik ADV back and forth, to and fro, there and back

boléh may, can; allowed, permitted; okay; ~~ *saja* sure you can; **memperboléhkan** v to allow, permit

boling N ten-pin bowling

bolong ADJ holey, perforated

bolos, membolos v to skip, be absent, to play truant, wag, skive

bolpoin N ballpoint pen, biro

bom N bomb; **mengebom** v to bomb something

bon N bill, check, receipt

bonéka N doll (like a person); soft toy (animal); puppet

bongkar, membongkar v to pull apart, dismantle; unpack; to unearth

bor N drill; *mata* ~ drill bit

bordir, bordiran N embroidery, lace edging; **membordir** v to embroider

borgol N handcuffs

boro-boro CONJ what's the point of ...? It's not even worth ...

borong, memborong v to buy up, buy in bulk; **borongan** N goods bought in bulk; *taksi* ~ un-metered taxi; **pemborong** N developer, contractor

boros ADJ wasteful

bos PRON, SL boss, sir; N boss

bosan ADJ bored, fed up with, tired of; **membosankan** ADJ boring, tiresome

botak ADJ bald

botok, bothok N Javanese side-dish of shredded coconut and fresh vegetables

botol N bottle; *teh* ~ bottled tea

brahmana, brahmin, brahma N highest Hindu caste in Bali

brankas, brangkas N safe

bréngsék EXCL blast! damn!; N bastard!; ADJ damn, bloody

brem N a soft white biscuit made from fermented rice

bréwok, beréwok N beard, whiskers, sideburns; **bréwokan** ADJ whiskered, bearded

brokoli N broccoli

bros N brooch

brosur N brochure

bu PRON Mother (to respected older women); Mum(my), Mom(my)

buah N fruit; piece, general counter for objects; ~ *nangka* jackfruit; **buah-buahan** N fruit(s); **sebuah** ADJ a, one (generic counter)

buang v to throw (away); ~ *air* to urinate; **membuang** v to throw out; waste; exile; **terbuang** ADJ thrown out, wasted

buas ADJ fierce, wild

buat PREP for; v to do, make; **buatan** N made in, product of; **berbuat** v to do; **membuat** v to make; **pembuat** N producer; **pembuatan** N production, manufacture; **perbuatan** N act, deed

buaya N crocodile, alligator

bubar v to disperse, break up,

INDONESIAN – ENGLISH

C

spread out; **membubarkan** v to break something up

bubuk n powder, dust

bubur n porridge; ~ *ayam* chicken porridge

budak n slave

budaya n culture; **kebudayaan** n culture, civilization

Budha *agama* ~ Buddhism; *orang* ~ Buddhist

bufét n buffet meal

bugar adj fit; **kebugaran** *pusat* ~ gym, fitness center

Bugis n ethnic group from South Sulawesi

bujang adj single, unmarried (man); **bujangan** n bachelor

bujuk, membujuk v to coax

bujur n longitude; vertical line down a sphere; ~ *timur* east longitude

buka open; ~ *baju* take off clothes; **berbuka** ~ *puasa* to break the fast; **membuka** v to open; **terbuka** adj open

bukan no, not (of things, nouns); *Ini* ~ ? This one, isn't it?

bukit n hill; **berbukit** adj hilly

bukti n proof, evidence; **membuktikan** v to prove; **terbukti** adj proven

buku n book; ~ *pelajaran* textbook; ~ *panduan* guide(book)

bulak-balik → bolak-balik

bulan n moon, month; ~ *Februari* February; ~ *madu* honeymoon; ~ *puasa* fasting month, Ramadan; ~ *purnama* full moon

bulat adj round; fat; **bulatan** n circle

bulé n, DEROG white person, whitey, paleface; albino

bulu n feather; fur; body hair; ~ *mata* eyelashes; ~ *tangkis* badminton

bumbu n spice

bumerang n boomerang

bumi n earth, ground

buncis n string bean

buncit adj pot-bellied, fat

bundar, bunder adj round; **bundaran** n roundabout

Bung pron brother; ~ *Karno* President Soekarno; *ayo* ~! Come on, mate!

bunga n flower, blossom; interest; ~ *mawar*, ~ *ros* rose

bungalo n bungalow, cottage, one-story house

bungkus n takeaway, pack; *nasi* ~ a takeaway rice meal; **membungkus** v to wrap; ~ *kado* to wrap a gift

bungsu n youngest child in a family; *anak* ~, *si* ~ youngest child

buntu adj one-way, useless; *jalan* ~ dead-end; cul-de-sac, court

buntut n tail; *sop* ~ oxtail soup

bunuh, membunuh v to kill; **pembunuh** n murderer, killer; **pembunuhan** n murder, killing; **terbunuh** adj killed

bunyi n sound, noise; **berbunyi** v to sound, make a noise; **membunyikan** v to sound, ring something

bupati n regent; **kabupatén** n regency

buram adj cloudy, frosted, dull

bursa n exchange; ~ *efek* stock exchange

buru, memburu v to hunt, chase; **buruan, buron** n the hunted; **keburu** SL in time; too early; **pemburu** n hunter; **terburu-buru** adj in a hurry

buruh n laborer

buruk adj bad (of a situation, weather); ugly

burung n bird; ~ *béo* parrot; ~ *dara* pigeon, dove; ~ *gereja* sparrow; ~ *hantu* owl

busa n foam, lather; **berbusa** adj foamy; with a layer of foam

busana n clothing, wear

busuk adj rotten

buta adj blind; ~ *huruf* illiterate

butik n boutique

butir n grain, counter for small oval objects; *tiga* ~ *telur* three eggs

butuh v to need; **kebutuhan** n need, necessity; **membutuhkan** v to need something

C

cabang n branch; ~ *pohon* tree branch

cabé, cabai n chilli; ~ *rawit* small, hot red chilli

cabut v to pull out, remove; SL to leave; **mencabut** v to pull out, remove

INDONESIAN–ENGLISH

C

cacar N pock, pox; ~ *air* chicken pox; **cacaran** v to have chicken pox

cacat N fault, defect, flaw; ADJ disabled, handicapped; *orang* ~ disabled or handicapped person

caci ~ *maki* insults

cacing N worm; **cacingan** ADJ to have (intestinal) worms

cadang *suku* ~ spare part; **cadangan** ADJ spare, reserve; stocks

cadel, cedal ADJ to have a speech impediment

cagar N preserve; ~ *alam* nature reserve

cahaya N light, shine, glow

cair flow; **cairan** N liquid; **mencair** v to melt, turn into liquid

cakap ADJ **cakep** SL handsome; SL pretty

cakap: percakapan N conversation

cakar N claw; **mencakar** v to scratch

cakram N disc; discus; *rem* ~ disc brakes

calo N ticket scalper, profiteer

calon N candidate; ~ *suami* husband-to-be; **mencalonkan** v to nominate someone

camar *burung* ~ seagull

camat N sub-district head; **kecamatan** N sub-district

cambuk N whip; **mencambuk** v to whip

campak N measles; *penyakit* ~ measles

campur mix; ~ *baur* mix with society; ~ *sari* a blend of traditional and modern Javanese music; ~ *tangan* get involved, interfere; **mencampuradukkan** v to mix up, confuse; **campuran** N mix, mixture; *anak* ~ child of mixed descent; **bercampur** ADJ mixed with

canda N joke; ~ *gurau* joking, jokes; **bercanda** v to joke

candi N temple, ancient Hindu or Buddhist temple or monument

canggih ADJ sophisticated

cangkir N cup, mug

cangkok graft, transplant; ~ *ginjal* liver transplant

cangkul N hoe

cantik ADJ beautiful, pretty; **kecantikan** N beauty

cantum: tercantum ADJ attached, included, inserted

cap N seal; brand, mark; **mengecap** v to brand

cap go méh N 15th day of the Chinese New Year

capai, mencapai v to reach, attain; **tercapai** ADJ achieved

capcay, cap cai N chop suey, Chinese vegetables in sauce

capék, capai ADJ tired; **kecapékan** ADJ tired out; N exhaustion

capung N dragonfly

cara N way, style, means; **secara** ADV in a way (used to form adverbs)

cari v to look for, search for, seek; **mencari** v to look or search for, seek; **mencari-cari** v to search repeatedly, everywhere

cas charge; **mengecas** v to charge (electrical equipment)

cat N **cét** COLL paint; **mengecat** v to paint, dye

catat, mencatat v to note; **catatan** N notes; **tercatat** ADJ noted, registered

catur N chess

cébok to wash your bottom after using the toilet

cebur v to fall into water

cedera, cidera injured, injury; ~ *lutut* knee injury

cegah, mencegah v to prevent, fight against

ceguk, cekuk: cegukan N hiccups; v to have the hiccups

cék N cheque, check; ~ *kosong* blank cheque

cék, mengecék v to check, confirm

cékér N, SL claw

cekik, mencekik v to strangle

ceking ADJ thin, gaunt, skin and bones

Céko N the Czech Republic

cekung ADJ concave, sunken

celah N gap, crack, crevice

celaka accident, bad luck, misfortune; **kecelakaan** N accident, disaster

celana N trousers; ~ *pendek* shorts

celémék N apron

céléng, céléngan N piggy bank, savings box

celurit, clurit N crescent-shaped knife, sickle

INDONESIAN—ENGLISH

cemar: mencemari v to dirty, pollute; **pencemaran** n pollution; **tercemar** ADJ polluted

cemara n casuarina (tree)

cemas ADJ worried, anxious

cemberut ADJ bad-tempered, in a bad mood

cemburu ADJ jealous; ~ *buta* blind jealousy

cemerlang ADJ glittering, sparkling, brilliant

cemilan n snack food

cempaka n a white kind of gardenia or magnolia

cempedak n fruit which is cut into slices and fried

cendana *kayu* ~ sandalwood

cendekiawan n intellectual

cenderung v to tend; **kecenderungan** n tendency, trend

céndol n sweet drink of green rice flour, molasses and coconut milk

cendramata, cinderamata n souvenir, keepsake

cengéng ADJ whiny, complaining

cengkéh n cloves

cengkeram v to grip; **cengkeraman** n grip, squeeze; **mencengkeram** v to grip, squeeze

centong ~ *nasi* spoon for serving rice

cepak ADJ shaven-headed

cepat ADJ cepet COLL fast, quick; **kecepatan** n speed; **mempercepat** v to speed up, accelerate; **secepat** CONJ as fast as; ~ *mungkin*, **secepat(-cepat)nya** ADV as fast as possible; **tercepat** ADJ fastest

ceplas-ceplos ADV forthright, blunt, straight from the heart (of speech or behavior)

ceplok *telur* ~ fried egg

cerah ADJ clear, sunny

cerai divorce; ~ *mati* widowed; **mencerai(kan)** v to divorce someone; **perceraian** n divorce

ceramah n lecture, talk

cerdas ADJ intelligent, bright; **kecerdasan** n intelligence

cerdik ADJ clever, smart; cunning

cerét, crét: mencrét v to have diarrhea

ceréwét ADJ fussy, finicky, hard to

please; talkative

céri *buah* ~ cherry

ceria ADJ happy, in a good mood

cerita, ceritera story, tale; ~ *pendek (cerpen)* short story; ~ *rakyat* folk tale; **bercerita** v to tell (a story); **menceritakan** v to describe, relate

cermai, cermé n small, sour plum

cermin mirror; **mencerminkan** v to reflect

cerna: mencerna v to digest; **pencernaan** n digestion

ceroboh ADJ careless

cerobong n chimney

cerutu n cigar

cét → cat

cétak print; **cétakan** n mold; impression, printing; **mencétak** v to print

céwék N, COLL girl, young woman; ADJ female

cicak, cecak n gecko, house lizard

cicil pay in instalments; **mencicil** v to pay by instalments

cicip taste; **mencicipi** v to try, taste something

cicit n great-grandchild

cidera → cedera

cidomo n horse-drawn cart in Lombok → **cikar dokar mobil**

ciduk, cédok n dipper

Cik PRON you, Sister (for Chinese women)

Cilé n Chile; *orang* ~ Chilean

cilik ADJ small, little

Cina n China; *bahasa* ~, *orang* ~ Chinese; **Pecinan** n Chinatown

cincang minced

cincau n jelly made from cinchona leaves, used in drinks

cincin n ring

cinderamata, cendramata n souvenir, keepsake

cinta love, like; **bercinta** v to make love; to be in love; **mencintai** v to love someone; **pencinta, pecinta** n lover; **tercinta** ADJ dear, beloved

cipta idea, creativity; **ciptaan** n creation; **mencipta, menciptakan** v to create, make; **tercipta** ADJ created

ciri n characteristic, identifying mark

cita-cita n ideal, dream, ambition

INDONESIAN–ENGLISH

C

citra N image
cium kiss; smell; **ciuman** N kiss; **berciuman** v to kiss each other; **mencium** v to smell; to kiss; **ter-cium** ADJ smelt; found out
coba v, AUX try; please; **cobaan** N trial, ordeal; **mencoba** v to try, attempt; **percobaan** N experiment, test
cobék, coék N pestle for grinding chillies
coblos, mencoblos v to vote, pierce
cocok fit, match, suitable; **mencocokkan** v to match
cokelat, coklat chocolate; *warna* ~ brown
colok v to put in a plug; **colokan** N powerpoint
conték, menconték, menyonték v to copy, cheat
contoh N example, model, sample; ~*nya* for example
copét N pickpocket; **kecopétan** ADJ to be pickpocketed, robbed; N pick-pocketing; **mencopét** v to pick someone's pocket
copot v to come off (accidentally)
corak N design, pattern, motif, style
corét scratch; **corét-corét** doodle, graffiti; **corétan** N scratch; **men-corét** v to scratch, cross out
corong N funnel, spout
coto N clear meat soup, specialty of Makassar
cuaca N weather
cubit pinch; **mencubit** v to pinch; **secubit** N pinch
cuci v to wash; **cucian** N laundry; **mencuci** v to wash, clean
cucu N grandchild
cuék ADJ uncaring, unfeeling, ignor-ing; independent
cuka N vinegar
cukup ADJ enough, sufficient; ADV quite; **secukupnya** ADV sufficient, adequate
cukur shave; **mencukur** v to shave
cula N horn
culik, menculik v to kidnap; **pen-culikan** N kidnapping
cuma, cuman COLL but, only; **cuma-cuma** free, at no cost

cumi, cumi-cumi N squid
curam ADJ steep, sloping, pre-cipitous
curang ADJ dishonest, cheating
curi steal; **curi-curi** surreptitious, secret; **mencuri** v to steal; **pencuri** N thief, burglar
curiga ADJ suspicious; **mencuriga-kan** ADJ suspicious, suspect
cuti leave; ~ *hamil* maternity leave

D

da, dag, dah GR bye; **da-da** GR (children) bye-bye
d/a *dengan alamat* care of, c/-
dada N breast, chest, bosom; *buah* ~ F breast
dadak: dadakan ADJ sudden; **men-dadak** ADJ sudden
dadar *telur* ~ omelet
daérah N region, territory, area; provinces, country(-side); *bahasa* ~ regional language
daftar list, register, roll; **mendaftar** v to register; **mendaftarkan** v to register something; **pendaftaran** N enrolment, registration; **terdaftar** ADJ registered, enrolled
dagang trade; **dagangan** v to sell goods informally; N merchandise; **berdagang** v to trade, do business; **pedagang** N merchant; **perda-gangan** N commerce, trade
daging N meat, flesh; ~ *babi* pork; ~ *sapi* beef
dagu N chin
dahak N phlegm, mucus
dahi N forehead
dahulu ADJ before, former(ly); first (more formal than **dulu**); *lebih* ~ first(ly); **mendahului** v to precede, overtake
daki: mendaki v to climb, ascend; ~ *gunung* (to go) mountaineering, bushwalking
dakwa, dakwaan N charge, accusa-tion; **terdakwa** N the accused
dalam PRON in, inside, into; ADJ deep, profound; *celana* ~ under-pants; *di* ~ in, inside; *ke* ~ into; **mendalam** ADJ deep; **pedalaman** N inland, hinterland

INDONESIAN—ENGLISH

D

dalang, dhalang N puppeteer (in shadow puppet plays); mastermind; **mendalangi** v to orchestrate (events)

daluwarsa, kedaluwarsa, kadaluwarsa ADJ expired, overdue

damai peace; **berdamai** v to make peace; **mendamaikan** v to reconcile, pacify; **perdamaian** N peace, reconciliation

dampak N ill-effect; **berdampak** v to have a (negative) effect

damping next to, close; **berdampingan** ADJ side by side; **mendampingi** v to accompany, flank; **pendamping** N companion

dan CONJ and

dana N funds, money, grant

danau N lake

dandan v to dress up, put on make-up; **dandanan** N dress, make-up; **berdandan** v to dress, put on make-up; **mendandani** v to decorate, dress, adorn

dangdut N popular Indian-inspired music

dangkal ADJ shallow, superficial

dansa N Western-style dance; **berdansa** v to dance

dapat find, get, obtain; be able to, can; **mendapat** v to obtain, receive; **mendapatkan** v to obtain; discover; **pendapat** N opinion, point of view; **berpendapat** v to have an opinion, believe; **pendapatan** N income, revenue; **sedapatnya** ADV what you can get

dapur N kitchen

darah N blood; **berdarah** v to bleed; **pendarahan** N bleeding

darat N land, shore; **daratan** N mainland; **mendarat** v to land

dari PREP from, of; CONJ from the time; **daripada** CONJ than

darurat ADJ emergency, pressing

dasar N base, basis, foundation; SL all because

dasi N necktie

daster N house-coat, nightgown, nighty

datang v to come, arrive; **kedatangan** N arrival; **mendatang** ADJ coming, next; **mendatangkan** v to bring, import; **pendatang** N immigrant, migrant; newcomer

datar ADJ level, flat; **dataran** N plain; **mendatarkan** v to make flat, level

daun N leaf; **dedaunan** N leaves, foliage

daur N cycle; *~ ulang* recycling; **mendaur-ulang** v to recycle

dawet N sweet Javanese drink of green rice flour, pink syrup and coconut milk

daya N power, energy

Dayak generic name for indigenous (non-Malay) inhabitants of Kalimantan and Borneo; *orang ~* Dayak

dayung N oar; **mendayung** v to stroke (an oar), row; to pedal

debar pulse, beat; **berdebar** v to beat quickly

debat N debate; **berdebat** v to have a debate; **perdebatan** N debate, discussion

débet, débit N debit; **mendébet** v to debit

debu N dust; **berdebu** ADJ dusty

dedaunan N leaves, foliage → **daun**

deg: **deg-degan** ADJ anxious, worried

déh OK then, well; *Ayo, ~ !* Come on, then! → **sudah**

dékan N (university) dean

dekat PREP close, near; **berdekatan** ADJ close (of two or more things); **mendekati** v to approach; **pendekatan** N approach; getting to know; **terdekat** ADJ closest, nearest

delapan ADJ eight; *~ belas* eighteen; *~ puluh* eighty

délman N two-wheeled horse-drawn carriage

demam N fever

demi CONJ for (the sake of); by

demikian ADV such, so, in this way, thus

démo, démonstrasi N demo, demonstration, protest; **mendémo** v to protest against

démokrasi N democracy; **démokrat** N democrat; **démokratis** ADJ democratic

démonstrasi N demo, demonstration, protest

dénah N plan, map, diagram

INDONESIAN–ENGLISH

denda fine; *kena* ~ be fined; **mendenda** v to fine
dendam revenge; grudge
déndéng n dried meat, jerky
dengan conj with
dengar v to hear; **kedengaran, terdengar** adj audible; **mendengar** v to hear; **mendengarkan** v to listen; **pendengar** n listener; **pendengaran** n hearing
dengkul n knee
dengkur, mendengkur v to snore; to purr (of a cat)
denyut pulse; throb
déodoran n deodorant
depak, mendepak v to kick something, kick out
depan prep front; *di* ~ front, in front of; *ke* ~ forward, to the front; *tahun* ~ next year
departemén n department, ministry
derajat n degree, rank
deras adj swift; heavy; *hujan* ~ heavy rain
dérék tow (a vehicle); *mobil* ~ tow truck; **mendérék** v to tow
dérét n row, line; **dérétan** n row
dering ring, chime; **berdering** v to ring, tinkle
derita n suffering; **menderita** v to suffer, endure
dermaga n pier, jetty
dermawan n donor, philanthropist; adj charitable
désa n village; hometown; **pedésaan** n country(side), rural areas
desak push; **mendesak** adj pressing, urgent; v to press, urge, push
Désémber *bulan* ~ December
déterjén n detergent
detik n second
déwa n, m god; **déwa-déwi, déwata** n, pl, m & f gods
déwan n council, board
déwasa adult; *orang* ~ adult, grown-up
déwata n, pl, m & f gods → déwa
déwi n, f goddess → déwa
di prep at; on; in; ~ *atas* above, on top of; ~ *dalam* inside; ~ *samping* beside
dia pron he, she, it; him, her (often replaced by –nya for possessive)

diabét, diabétés *(penyakit)* ~ diabetes
dialék n dialect
diam silent, not moving; **diam-diam** adv secretly
diaré n diarrhea
dibikin v, coll to be made → bikin
dibilang v to be said → bilang
didih: mendidih adj boiling
didik educate; **mendidik** v to educate, bring up, teach; **pendidikan** n education; **berpendidikan** adj educated; v to have an education
diét n diet; **berdiét** v to diet, go on a diet
difaks v to be faxed → faks
diinfus v to be put on a drip → infus
dikontrakkan adj for rent, lease → kontrak
dikté n dictation
dilarang v to be prohibited; ~ *masuk* no entry, no admittance; ~ *merokok* no smoking → larang
dimengerti v to be understood → erti, arti
dinas (to work at a) government office
dinding n (inner) wall
dingin n cold, cool, chilly; **kedinginan** n cold; feeling cold
dini adj very early, premature
diopname v to be admitted to hospital, be hospitalized → opname
dipél v to be mopped, cleaned → pél
dipermak v to be altered, shortened → permak
dipingpong v to be sent here and there, messed about → pingpong
diplomasi n diplomacy; **diplomat** n diplomat
diportal v to be blocked by a barrier, have a barrier lowered → portal
diri n self; ~ *saya* me, myself
diri: berdiri v to stand, get up; **mendirikan** v to build, establish, erect; **sendiri** adv alone; pron self; **sendirian** adv alone; single-handedly; **tersendiri** adj its own; apart, separate; **terdiri** ~ *atas*, ~ *dari* to consist of, be based or founded on
diserut v to be sharpened → serut
disérvis v to be serviced → sérvis
diskon n discount

INDONESIAN–ENGLISH

diskoték N disco, nightclub
diskriminasi N discrimination; **mendiskriminasi(kan)** V to discriminate against
distrik N district
disunat V to be circumcised → sunat
ditilang V to be fined → tilang
divonis V to be sentenced → vonis
DIY ABBREV *Daerah Istimewa Yogyakarta* Special Region of Yogyakarta
DKI ABBREV *Daerah Khusus Ibukota* Special Capital City Region
dll *dan lain-lain* et cetera
doa N prayer; **berdoa** V to pray, say a prayer; **mendoakan** V to pray for
dobel ADJ double, twice as much
dobrak, mendobrak V to break open, smash
dodol N soft, chewy sweet made from brown sugar or fruit
dok PRON Doc, Doctor (used when addressing a doctor) → dokter
dokar N (two-wheeled horse-drawn) buggy
dokter, dr N doctor, surgeon; ~ *gigi (drg)* dentist; **kedokteran** ADJ medical
dolar N dollar; ~ *Amerika* US dollar
domba N sheep
dompét N purse, wallet; ~ *saya hilang!* I've lost my wallet!
donat N donut, doughnut
dong, donk SL you should know that
dongéng N tale, story, fable
dongkrak N (car) jack, lever
dorong V to push; **mendorong** V to push, encourage; **terdorong** ADJ pushed, shoved
dosa N sin; **berdosa** V to sin, commit a sin
dosén N (university) lecturer
DPR ABBREV *Dewan Perwakilan Rakyat* People's Representative Council
Dr Doktor PRON holder of a Ph.D.
dr *dokter* doctor
drastis ADJ drastic
drg *dokter gigi* dentist
dsb *dan sebagainya* and so on
dua ADJ two; ~ *belas* twelve; ~ *kali* twice; ~ *puluh* twenty; **dua-duanya** ADJ both, the two of them; **berdua**

ADJ together, in pairs; **kedua** ADJ second; **kedua(-dua)nya** ADJ both
duda N widower; divorced man
duduk V to sit, be placed; **kedudukan** N position; **menduduki** V to sit on something; to occupy; **penduduk** N inhabitant, citizen, resident; **pendudukan** N occupation
duga, menduga V to suppose, suspect; **dugaan** N suspicion
duit N, SL money, cash, dirt, dosh; *cari* ~ earn a living
duka N sorrow; ~ *cita* grief, sorrow; **berduka** ~ *(cita)* to grieve, be in mourning
duku N small sweet fruit with light brown skin, clear flesh and large dark seed
dukun N traditional or spiritual healer, shaman
dukung support; **dukungan** N support; **mendukung** V to support; **pendukung** N supporter
dulu ADV first, former, before; **duluan** ADV, COLL first, before others → dahulu
dunia N world; ~ *maya* online, Internet
dupa N incense
duri N thorn; **berduri** ADJ thorny; **durian** N durian, spiky yellow-skinned fruit with a strong smell
dus, dos N cardboard box → kardus
duta ~ *besar (dubes)* N ambassador; **kedutaan** ~ *(besar)* embassy
duyung N seacow
dwi- PREF two; ~*bahasa* bilingual

E

é EJAC hey (showing recognition, disagreement)
ébi N (dried) shrimp
édisi N edition; **éditor** N editor
égois ADJ egoist, egotistical, selfish
éja: éjaan N spelling
éjék, mengéjék V to tease, mock, ridicule
ékonom N economist; **ékonomi** N economy
ékor N tail; counter for animals; **berékor** V to have a tail
éks- PREF ex-, former → mantan

INDONESIAN–ENGLISH

E

éksékutif executive

ékskul N extra-curricular activities, classes outside school → **ékstra kurikulér**

ékspatriat *orang* ~ expatriate (esp. Caucasian)

ékspor export; **mengékspor** v to export

éksprés ADJ express

éléktronik ADJ electronic; **éléktronika** N electronics

élit, élite [élit] N elite

élpiji N liquid petroleum gas, LPG

elus stroke, caress; **mengelus** v to caress, stroke or pat (an animal)

émail N (tooth) enamel

emak, mak N mother

emas, mas N gold

émbér N bucket, pail

embun N dew; **berembun** ADJ moist, dewy

emis: mengemis v to beg; **pengemis** N beggar

émisi N emission

émosi, émosional ADJ emotional

empat ADJ four; ~ *belas* fourteen; ~ *puluh* forty; **berempat** ADJ in a group of four; **keempat** ADJ fourth; **perempat** N quarter; **perempatan, prapatan** N crossroads, intersection; **seperempat** N one quarter

emping N chips made from the melinjo bean

empuk ADJ soft, tender

emut, kemut, mengemut v to suck on (sweets etc)

énak ADJ nice, tasty, delicious; pleasant; ~*nya* the good thing is, ...; ~ *saja*, ~ *aja* (sarcastically) that's nice! how dare they!; **énakan** ADJ, SL better, nicer, tastier; **seénaknya** ADV, NEG just how you like, at will

enam ADJ six; ~ *belas* sixteen; ~ *puluh* sixty; *segi* ~ hexagon; **keenam** ADJ sixth

éncér ADJ liquid, runny, watery

éncik, cik PRON form of address to Chinese woman

enggak COLL no, not → **tidak**

enggan ADJ reluctant, unwilling

enggang N hornbill

engkau, kau, dikau PRON you

entah who knows

entar soon → **sebentar**

énténg ADJ light; flippant

Éropa, Éropah N Europe; *orang* ~ European

érosi N erosion

érotis ADJ erotic

és N ice; ~ *krim*, ~ *puter* ice cream; ~ *teler* sweet dessert with ice; *lemari* ~ refrigerator

ésok ADV ~ *hari* tomorrow; **ke-ésokan** ~ *harinya* the next day → **bésok**

étika N ethics, good manners

étnik, étnis N ethnic group; ADJ ethnic, non-Western

évakuasi N evacuation → **ungsi**

F

fajar N dawn, daybreak

faks N fax, facsimile; **difaks** v to be faxed

fakultas N faculty

fals ADJ off-key, false (of music)

falsafah → **filsafat**

famili ADJ related, distant family

fanatik N fan; fanatic

fasih ADJ fluent, eloquent; ~ *berbahasa Indonesia* to speak Indonesian fluently

fatal ADJ very bad; fatal

fatwa N *fatwa*, religious ruling

favorit ADJ favorite; *sekolah* ~ top school

Fébruari *bulan* ~ February

fénoména N phenomenon

féodal, féodalis ADJ feudal, feudalistic; **féodalisme** N feudalism

féri N ferry

fésbuk N Facebook

fiksi N fiction

Filipina N the Philippines

film N film

filsafat, falsafah N philosophy

Finlandia N Finland

firasat N presentiment, foreboding, bad feeling

fisik ADJ physical

fisika N physics

fisiotérapi N physiotherapy

fitnah N slander, libel

flék N blemish, spot (on face)

flu N flu, influenza

INDONESIAN–ENGLISH

fokus N focus; **berfokus** ADJ focused; **memfokuskan** V to focus something

formulir N (blank) form

foto N photo, photograph; **berfoto** V to take, pose for a photo; **fotokopi** N photocopy; **difotokopi** to be photocopied

frustrasi ADJ frustrated

fungsi N function; **berfungsi** V to work, go; to act as

fuyung hai, puyung hai N sweet-and-sour omelet

G

G. *Gunung* Mt (Mount, name of mountain)

gabung connect, join; **gabungan** ADJ joint; **bergabung** V to join together; **menggabungkan** V to connect, combine, fuse

gadai: menggadaikan V to pawn something; **pegadaian** N pawnshop

gadang *rumah* ~ traditional Minangkabau house

gading tusk, ivory

gadis N girl, maiden, virgin, unmarried woman

gado-gado N cooked salad with peanut sauce; ADJ mixed; *bahasa* ~ mixture of Indonesian and another language

gagah ADJ strong; ~ *perkasa* heroic; handsome

gagak *burung* ~ crow, raven

gagal V to fail; **kegagalan** N failure

gagang N handle; ~ *telepon* handset, telephone cradle

gagap stammer, stutter; ~ *teknologi (gaptek)* technophobe

gagas: gagasan N idea, concept

gagu ADJ mute

gaib ADJ mysterious, invisible

gairah N passion, lust; enthusiasm

gajah N elephant

gaji N (monthly) salary, pay; ~ *bersih* net salary, take-home pay; **menggaji** V to pay, remunerate, employ

galak ADJ fierce, wild, vicious; *anjing* ~ vicious dog

galéri N gallery → **paméran**

gali V to dig; **galian** N excavations, diggings; **menggali** V to dig; **penggalian** N digging

gambar picture, drawing, illustration; **gambaran** N sketch, idea; **bergambar** ADJ illustrated; **menggambar** V to draw, depict; **menggambarkan** V to describe, illustrate

gamelan N traditional orchestra

gampang ADJ, COLL easy → **mudah**

ganas ADJ fierce, wild, ferocious; uncontrolled

ganda double; -fold

gandéng link, join; **bergandéngan** ~ *tangan* to link arms or hands

gandum N wheat; wholemeal

gang N alley, lane

ganggu, mengganggu V to bother, disturb; **gangguan** N disturbance, interference; problem; **terganggu** ADJ bothered, disrupted, disturbed

ganja N marijuana

ganjal V to wedge; to fill a gap

ganjil ADJ uneven, odd

ganteng ADJ, COLL handsome

ganti change, substitute; ~ *baju*, ~ *pakaian* change your clothes; **gantian** V, SL change over; **berganti** V to change; *~-ganti*, *~an* in turns; **mengganti** V to change, substitute, replace; **menggantikan** V to substitute or replace someone/something; **pengganti** N replacement, substitute, successor

gantung hang; **menggantung** V to hang, suspend; **tergantung** ADJ depending (on), it depends

gapték N technophobe → **gagap téknologi**

gapura N (ornamental) gateway, entrance

gara-gara ADV, SL all because of → **goro-goro**

garam N salt

garansi N guarantee (on a product); **bergaransi** ADJ guaranteed

garasi N carport, garage

garing ADJ dry, crisp

garis line, scratch; **bergaris** ADJ lined; **menggarisbawahi** to underline, emphasize; **penggaris** N ruler

garong N robber

garpu N fork

INDONESIAN—ENGLISH

G

garuda N eagle, national symbol of Indonesia

garuk, menggaruk V to scratch, scrape

gas N gas; ~ *bumi* natural gas

gasing N (spinning) top

gatal ADJ itchy; **gatal-gatal** V to have a rash

gaul V to mix, associate; ADJ, SL trendy; **bergaul** V to mix or associate; **pergaulan** N mixing, social intercourse; association

gaun N (evening) gown

gawang N goal (in field sports); hurdle; *penjaga* ~ goalkeeper

gawat ADJ serious, very bad

gaya energy, strength; style; **bergaya** ADJ stylish, with style

gayung N water dipper; stick

gedé ADJ, COLL big, large

gedung N building, public hall

gegar shake, quiver

gegas: bergegas-gegas V to hurry

gejala N symptom, sign

geladak N deck of a ship

gelang N bracelet; **pergelangan** ~ *kaki* ankle; ~ *tangan* wrist

gelanggang N arena, stadium

gelantung hang, suspend

gelap ADJ dark; **kegelapan** N darkness

gelar N title; **bergelar** V titled; **menggelar, menggelarkan** V to hold (an event)

gelatik *burung* ~ kind of bird, finch

gelembung N bubble

geléng: menggéléng to shake your head

geli ticklish; uncomfortable; **menggelikan** ADJ funny, comic; off-putting

gelincir: tergelincir ADJ skidded, slipped

gelisah ADJ nervous, restless

gelitik, menggelitik V to tickle

gelombang N wave; (radio) frequency; **bergelombang** ADJ wavy

gelora N storm, surge, passion; **gelanggang olah raga** sports complex

gema N echo, reverberation; **bergema** V to echo, reverberate

gemar like, enjoy; **kegemaran** N hobby; **penggemar** N fan, enthusiast

gemas, gemes COLL cute, sweet (often said to children); annoyed

gembira ADJ cheerful, happy, joyous; **bergembira** V to be happy, joyous; **kegembiraan** N joy, happiness; **menggembirakan** ADJ exciting, happy

gembok N padlock; **menggembok** V to padlock

gemetar shiver, tremble; **gemetaran** ADJ shivering, trembling

gemilang glitter, shine; brilliant

gempa N quake, shudder; ~ *bumi* earthquake

gempar clamor, noise, uproar

gemuk ADJ fat, plump, obese; N grease; *jalur* ~ busy route

gén N gene; **génétik** ADJ genetic

genang: genangan N puddle, flood; **tergenang** ADJ flooded

genap ADJ even, complete, exact; *angka* ~ even number

gencat: gencatan ~ *senjata* ceasefire, truce, armistice

gendang N (kettle) drum

géndong, menggéndong V to carry on the hip

gendut ADJ fat, pot-bellied

géng, génk N gang

genggam N fist; **menggenggam** V to grip, grasp

géngsi N prestige, face; **bergéngsi** ADJ prestigious

genit ADJ flirtatious

génsét N generator

genténg N roof tile

gépéng ADJ flat, concave, sunken

gerabah N earthenware pot

gerak move; **gerakan** N movement; **bergerak** V to move; **menggerakkan** V to move, shift something

gerbang N gate, gateway, door

gerbong N carriage

geréja N church

gergaji N saw

gerhana N eclipse

gerigi N, PL teeth, points; **bergerigi** ADJ serrated, jagged

gerilya N guerrilla

gerimis *(hujan)* ~ drizzle

gerobak N cart

gersang ADJ arid

gerutu: menggerutu V to grumble,

INDONESIAN—ENGLISH

G

complain, gripe

gesa: tergesa-gesa ADJ in a hurry or rush

gésék rub; **gésékan** N stroke, scrape; **menggésék** V to rub, scrape

gésér: menggésér V to move aside or over

gesit ADJ nimble, adept, adroit

getah N sap, latex, gum

getar shake, tremor; **getaran** N vibration, shake, tremor

giat: kegiatan N activity

gigi N tooth

gigil: menggigil V to shiver

gigit: menggigit V to bite

gila ADJ crazy, mad, insane

giling *daging ~* mincemeat

gilir: giliran N turn; **bergilir, bergiliran** ADJ in turns

gimana COLL how; *~ sih?* what about that? → **bagaimana**

gini ADV, COLL like this, in this way → **begini**

ginjal N kidney

giok *batu ~* jade

gips N plaster, plaster cast

girang ADJ pleased, glad, happy

gitar N guitar

gitu ADV, COLL like that, in that way → **begitu**

gizi N nutrient; *ahli ~* nutritionist; **bergizi** ADJ nutritious

gladi, geladi *~ resik, ~ bersih* dress-rehearsal

goa, gua N cave, tunnel

goda tempt; **godaan** N temptation; **menggoda** V to tempt; **tergoda** ADJ tempted

golf N golf

golok N machete, chopping knife

golong: golongan N group, category; rank; **tergolong** ADJ to include, be part of or considered

goncang, guncang rock, sway; **goncangan** N shock wave, quake; **menggoncangkan** V to rock or make something move

gondrong (excessively) long hair

gonggong: gonggong, menggonggong V to bark

gonta-ganti V to change constantly → **ganti**

GOR ABBREV *Gelanggang Olah*

Raga stadium, sports complex

gordén, hordén N curtain(s)

goréng fry; **goréngan** N fried snacks; **menggoréng** V to fry; **penggoréngan** N wok, frying pan; process of frying

gorés line, scratch; **gorésan** N scratch, stroke; **menggorés** V to scratch, make a stroke; **tergorés** ADJ scratched

gosip gossip

gosok rub; **menggosok** V to rub, polish

gosong ADJ burnt, singed, scorched; *bau ~* burnt smell

got N roadside drain or ditch

gotong carry; **menggotong** V to carry together

goyang shake, wobble, unsteady; **bergoyang** V to shake, sway; to dance; **menggoyangkan** V to shake or rock something

grup N group (esp business)

gua → **goa**

gubernur N governor

gubuk N hut

gudang N warehouse, shed, store

gugat sue; **gugatan** N lawsuit, accusation; **menggugat** V to sue, accuse

gugup ADJ nervous

gugur V to fall, be killed (in action) or eliminated; **keguguran** N miscarriage

gula N sugar

gulai, gulé N curry; *~ kambing* goat curry

gulat wrestling; **bergulat** V to wrestle, fight

guling *(bantal) ~* bolster, Dutch wife

gumpal N clot, lump; **gumpalan** N clot, lump

guna use, benefit; for; **berguna** ADJ useful, worthwhile; **menggunakan** V to use; **pengguna** N user

guna-guna N black magic

guncang, goncang rock, sway; **guncangan** N shock wave, quake; **mengguncangkan** V to rock or make something move

gundul ADJ bald

gunting scissors, cut; *~ kuku* nail clippers; **guntingan** N cutout;

INDONESIAN–ENGLISH

G

menggunting v to cut (out)
guntur N thunder
gunung N mountain, mount; remote area; ~ *(ber)api* volcano; **gunungan** N symbolic mountain used in shadow-puppet plays; **pegunungan** N mountain range
guramé, guraméh, gurami *ikan* ~ large freshwater fish
gurih ADJ tasty, delicious, mouth-watering
gurita *ikan* ~ octopus
guru N teacher; **perguruan** ~ *tinggi* university
gusi N gums
gusur: menggusur v to evict, sweep aside, forcibly remove

H

H. *Haji* title for man who has performed the major pilgrimage to Mecca
habis ADJ finished; empty; ADV entirely; COLL after; **kehabisan** v to run out of (water; food; stock); **menghabiskan** v to finish, use up, spend; **sehabis** CONJ after
hadap face; **berhadapan** (~ *muka*) v face to face; **menghadap** v to face, appear before; **menghadapi** v to face someone or something; **terhadap** CONJ regarding; against; with respect to
hadiah N present, gift; prize; **berhadiah** ADJ with prizes
hadir present; available; **kehadiran** N presence; attendance; **menghadiri** v to attend
hafal, hapal know by heart; **menghafalkan** v to learn by heart
hai SL hi
haid N menstruation
haji N, ISL person who has made the pilgrimage to Mecca; *Lebaran* ~ Idul Adha, Feast of the Sacrifice (performed during the annual pilgrimage)
hak N right; **berhak** v to have a right to, be entitled to
hak N heel
hakim N judge
hal N matter, case

halal ADJ, ISL permitted (to eat); killed according to Islamic practice
halaman N yard, open area, page; ~ *rumah* yard
halang: halangan N obstacle; hindrance; **berhalangan** v to be prevented; unable; **menghalangi** v to hinder, prevent; **terhalang** ADJ blocked; prevented
halte N stop; ~ *bis* bus stop
halus ADJ fine; soft; refined
HAM ABBREV *Hak Asasi Manusia* Human Rights
hama N pest; plague
hambat, menghambat v to obstruct, impede, hamper; **hambatan** N obstacle
hamil ADJ pregnant; **kehamilan** N pregnancy
hampir ADV nearly, almost
hancur smashed, crushed; **menghancurkan** v to smash, crush, destroy
handphone N [hénpon; hénfon] mobile phone, cell phone
handuk N towel
hangat ADJ warm, hot; **kehangatan** N warmth, friendliness
hangus ADJ burnt, scorched; expired
hansip N local security guard; para-military → **pertahanan sipil**
hantu N ghost
hanya ADV only
hapé, HP N mobile phone, cell phone → **handphone**
haram ADJ, ISL forbidden, not permitted
harap hope; please; **harapan** N hope, expectation; **berharap** v to hope; **mengharapkan** v to expect
harga N price; value; **berharga** ADJ precious; valuable; **menghargai** v to appreciate; **penghargaan** N appreciation; award
hari N day; ~ *ini* today; ~ *kerja* weekday, working day; ~ *libur* holiday, day off; ~ *ulang tahun (HUT)* birthday, anniversary; **harian** ADJ daily; **berhari-hari** ADV for days; **sehari-hari** ADV every day, daily; **seharian** ADV, COLL all day
harimau N tiger
harta N wealth, belongings

INDONESIAN—ENGLISH

H

haru emotion; touched; **mengharu-kan** ADJ moved, touched (emotionally); **terharu** ADJ moved, touched
harum ADJ fragrant; perfumed
harus v must, ought to, have to; **keharusan** N obligation, necessity, requirement; **mengharuskan** v to require; **seharusnya** should
hasil N product; result; **berhasil** v to succeed; **menghasilkan** v to produce
hati N liver; heart; ~ *kecil* conscience; **hati-hati** take care; **memperhatikan** v to notice, pay attention to; **perhatian** N attention
haus ADJ thirsty; **kehausan** ADJ to be thirsty; N thirst
havermut N oatmeal porridge
hawa N air, atmosphere, climate; **berhawa** ~ *sejuk* cool climate
hébat ADJ great; violent; terrific
héboh sensational
héktar N hectare
héla, menghéla v to draw; drag
helai N (counter) sheet; counter for thin flat objects; *se~ kertas* a piece of paper
héli, hélikopter N helicopter
hélm N helmet
hémat ADJ economical, thrifty; ~ *air* save water; **menghémat** v to save on or economize
hembus, embus blow, puff; **menghembus** v to blow
hendak v to will, wish, intend; *~nya* should; **kehendak** N will; **menghendaki** v to want
hening clear; quiet
henti stop; **berhenti** v to stop, cease; **menghentikan** v to stop something; **memberhentikan** v to stop (a vehicle); to dismiss
héran ADJ astonished, amazed; **menghérankan** ADJ astonishing, astounding
héwan N animal, beast
hias decorative; **hiasan** N decoration; **menghiasi** v to adorn; to decorate something; **perhiasan** N jewelry
hibur: hiburan N entertainment; **menghibur** v to entertain; to comfort, console
hidang: hidangan N dish, food served

hidung N nose
hidup live; alive; lively; **kehidupan** N life, existence; **menghidupkan** v to bring to life; to start or turn on (a device)
hijau, hijo, héjo ADJ green; ~ *tua* dark green
hijriah, H *tahun* ~ the Islamic calendar
hikmah N wisdom, insight, moral
hilang disappear; lost, missing; **kehilangan** N (feeling of) loss; v to lose something; **menghilang** v to disappear, vanish; **menghilangkan** v to remove
hilir, ilir downstream
hina low, insulting; humble; **hinaan** N insult; **menghinakan** v to humiliate, insult; **penghinaan** N insult, libel (written), slander (spoken)
hindar: menghindar v to steer clear of, avoid; **menghindari** v to avoid something
Hindu *agama* ~ Hinduism; *orang* ~ Hindu
hingga until; **sehingga** CONJ to the point that, as far as, until, so that
hirup inhale; suck; **menghirup** v to breathe in
hitam ADJ black
hitung count; **menghitung** v to count, calculate, reckon; **menghitungkan** v to count or calculate something; **perhitungan** N calculation; **terhitung** ADJ counted, included
Hj. *Hajjah* title for woman who has performed the major pilgrimage to Mecca
hobi N hobby
hoki N good luck or fortune
homo M, SL *(orang)* ~ homosexual, gay
honai N round hut in Papua (Irian Jaya)
Hongaria N Hungary
hong sui, féng sui N feng shui
hordén, gordén N curtain(s)
horé EJAC hooray!
horisontal ADJ horizontal; at one level
hormat respect, honor; **kehormatan** N respect; **menghormat, menghor-**

INDONESIAN–ENGLISH

H

mati v to honor or respect; **terhormat** ADJ respected

hotél N hotel; ~ *melati* cheap hotel; ~ *(ber)bintang lima* five-star hotel; **perhotélan** N hotel studies; hospitality

hubung: hubungan N link, connection, relationship; **berhubung** CONJ in connection with, relating to; **berhubungan** v, PL to have a link or connection; **menghubungi** v to contact someone; **menghubungkan** v to connect, join, link different parts; **perhubungan** N communications, connection; ~ *udara* air route

hujan rain; *musim* ~ rainy season, monsoon; **kehujanan** ADJ caught in the rain

hukum law; punish; **hukuman** N punishment; **menghukum** v to punish, sentence, condemn

hulu N source, beginning

huni: penghuni N occupant, resident

huruf N letter, character

HUT ABBREV *hari ulang tahun* birthday, anniversary

hutan N forest, jungle, wood; ~ *rimba* jungle; **kehutanan** N forestry

I

iba pity, compassion

ibadah N worship, religious devotion; **beribadah** v to worship, serve

ibarat CONJ like, as, example

ibu N, PRON, F mother; ~ *angkat* adopted mother; ~ *bapak* parents; ~ *jari* thumb; ~ *kota* capital (city); ~ *rumah tangga* housewife, homemaker; ~ *tiri* stepmother; *bahasa* ~ mother tongue; **ibu-ibu** N, PL ladies

idam: idaman ADJ dream, ideal; **mengidam** v ngidam COLL to crave (esp of pregnant woman)

idap: mengidap v to suffer from

idé, ide N idea

idéntik ADJ identical, same

idéntitas N (proof of) identity

idola N idol, star

Idul, Ied ul ISL ~ *Adha* Feast of the Sacrifice; ~ *Fitri* end of fasting celebrations

ijab ~ *kabul* ISL marriage contract

ijazah N certificate, qualification; **berijazah** ADJ certified, qualified

ijin, izin permission; **mengijinkan** v to permit, allow

ikal ADJ curly

ikan N fish; ~ *asin* salty fish; ~ *hiu* shark; **perikanan** N fisheries

ikat tie, knot; weaving, ikat; ~ *pinggang* belt; **ikatan** N alliance, union; **mengikat** v to tie, fasten; **terikat** ADJ bound

iklan N advertisement

iklim N climate

ikut v join in, go along with; ~ *serta* take part, participate; **berikut** ADJ following; **mengikut** v to follow, accompany; **mengikuti** v to follow, join, participate in

ilir → hilir

ilmu N science, study; ~ *filsafat* philosophy; ~ *fisika* physics; ~ *kimia* chemistry; ~ *pasti* the physical sciences, mathematics; ~ *sejarah* history; **keilmuan** ADJ scientific

imbal: imbalan N compensation, reward, repayment

imbang balanced; **berimbang** ADJ balanced, proportional; **seimbang** ADJ balanced, well-proportioned; **keseimbangan** N balance

imél N email

imigrasi N immigration

imitasi N fake

Imlék N *(Tahun Baru)* ~ Chinese New Year

impi: impian N dream

impor import; **mengimpor** v to import; **pengimpor** N importer

inai N henna

inap stay the night; **menginap** v to stay the night, stay over; **penginapan** N accommodation, hotel

inci N inch

indah ADJ beautiful; **keindahan** N beauty

indera, indra N sense; ~ *penglihatan* sense of sight

India N India; *orang* ~ Indian

Indian *orang* ~ Native American, (South) American Indian

Indo *orang* ~ person of mixed Western and Indonesian descent

INDONESIAN—ENGLISH

Indonésia Indonesia; *Bahasa ~, orang ~* Indonesian
induk mother (animal); *~ ayam* mother hen
indung mother, home
inféksi N infection; **terinféksi** ADJ infected
info, informasi N information, info
informatika N information technology (IT)
infus N (saline) drip; **diinfus** V to be put on a drip
ingat remember; **ingatan** N memory; **mengingat** V to remember, bear in mind; **mengingatkan** V to remind someone about something; **memperingati** V to commemorate; **peringatan** N warning; commemoration, remembrance
Inggris Britain; England, English; *~ Raya* Great Britain; *bahasa ~* English; *orang ~* English; British
ingin V to wish, desire; **keinginan** N desire, wish
ingkar V to break (a vow etc)
ingus N nasal mucus
ini PRON this, these; **begini** ADV like this; **segini** ADJ this much
injak V to tread, pedal; **menginjak** V to step, tread, or stamp on
injil N gospel, Bible
insinyur, Ir N engineer
insya Allah ISL God willing
intan N diamond
interlokal ADJ long-distance (dialing)
intérn ADJ internal
internasional ADJ international
intérnis N specialist (doctor)
interviu, interpiu N interview; **menginterviu** V to interview
inti N core, kernel, nucleus
intim ADJ intimate, close
intip, mengintip V to peep at, spy on
IPA ABBREV *ilmu pengetahuan alam* natural sciences
ipar in-law
IPS ABBREV *ilmu pengetahuan sosial* social sciences
Ir title for holder of a degree in engineering or architecture
Irak N Iraq; *orang ~* Iraqi
irama N rhythm
Iran N Iran; *orang ~* Iranian

iri envy; *~ (hati)* envious
Irian N (West) Papua, Irian; *~ Jaya* Indonesian province between 1963 & 2000; *orang ~* Papuan
irigasi N irrigation
iris slice thinly; **irisan** N slice
irit economical; save money
Irlandia N Ireland
Isa N Jesus → Yesus
isak sob; **terisak(-isak)** ADJ sobbing
isap V to suck on; **mengisap** V to suck
iseng for fun, not serious; waste or kill time
isi contents, volume, full; **berisi** V to contain; ADJ full, filled out; **mengisi** V to fill, load
Islam Islam; *agama ~* Islam; *orang ~* Muslim
Isra Miraj N, ISL holiday commemorating Muhammad's ascent to Heaven
istana N palace
isteri, istri N wife; **beristeri, beristri** ADJ, M married
istilah N term, word
istiméwa ADJ special
istirahat rest, recreation, break; **beristirahat** V to rest, take a break
istri, isteri N wife; **beristeri, beristri** ADJ, M married
isu N issue, controversy
isya night prayer (during the hours of darkness)
isyarat N signal, sign, gesture
Itali, Italia N Italy
itik N duck
itu PRON that, those; **begitu** ADV like that; **segitu** ADJ that much
iya COLL yes; *~ ya* it is, isn't it?
izin, ijin permission; **mengizinkan** V to permit, allow

J

jabat: jabatan N position, work; **berjabat(an)** *~ tangan* to shake hands; **pejabat** N (government) official
jadi V to become, happen; CONJ so; *tidak ~* it didn't happen, it fell through; **kejadian** N event, happening; creation; **menjadi** V to be or become; **terjadi** V to happen, become

J

jadwal N timetable, schedule
jaga guard, night watchman; **men-jaga** v to guard, keep watch
jago N champion; cock, rooster
jagung N corn, maize; ~ *bakar* roasted sweet corn
jahat ADJ bad, wicked, evil; **keja-hatan** N crime; **penjahat** N criminal
jahé N ginger
jahit v to sew; *tukang* ~ tailor; **jahitan** N stitches; sewing; **men-jahit** v to sew
jajah: jajahan N colony, territory; **menjajah** v to colonize, rule another country; **penjajah** N colo-nizer, ruler, colonial power
jajan buy cheap goods; *uang* ~ pocket money; **jajanan** N cheap snacks
jaksa N judge
jala N fishing net; *roti* ~ kind of Malay pancake
jalak N starling, mynah
jalan street, road, way; walk; oper-ate, go; ~ *besar* main road; ~ *keluar* exit, way out; ~ *masuk* entrance; ~ *raya* highway; **jalan-jalan** v to go for a walk; to go out (for fun); **jalanan** N streets, on the road; **ber-jalan** v to walk, move; **menjalan-kan** v to operate, run, set in motion; **perjalanan** N journey, trip
jalin: jalinan N net, network; **men-jalin** v to forge links, network
jalur N lane, track
jam N hour; clock; ~ *berapa?* what time is it?; ~ *besuk* visiting hours; ~ *buka* opening hours; ~ *karet* rub-ber time, lack of punctuality; ~ *lima* five o'clock; ~ *tangan* (wrist) watch; **berjam-jam** ADJ for hours and hours
jaman, zaman N age, era, time, period; ~ *dahulu*, ~ *dulu* in the old days, times past
jambu N *(buah)* ~ guava, rose-apple; kind of fruit; ~ *air* rose-apple; ~ *batu*, ~ *biji* guava
jamin, menjamin v to guarantee, promise; **jaminan** N guarantee; **terjamin** ADJ guaranteed
jamrud, zamrud N emerald
jamu N traditional herbal medicine

jamur N mushroom, mold, fungus; **berjamur** ADJ moldy
janda N widow
jangan NEG don't, do not
janggal ADJ odd, strange
janggut, jénggot N beard, goatee; **berjénggot** ADJ bearded
jangka N distance, term; ~ *pendek* short term
jangkar N anchor
jangkrik, jéngkerik N cicada, cricket
janin N fetus, embryo
janji promise; **janjian** v, SL to make a date, promise; **berjanji** v to prom-ise; **menjanjikan** v to promise something; **perjanjian** N agreement, contract
jantan male (animal), manly
jantung N heart, core
Januari *bulan* ~ January
jarak N distance, space
jarang ADJ, ADV seldom, rare, rarely, hardly ever
jari N finger; ~ *kaki* toe; ~ *kelingking* little or baby finger; ~ *manis* ring finger; ~ *telunjuk* forefinger, index finger; ~ *tengah* middle finger
jaring net, shoal; **jaringan** N net-work; **menjaring** v to fish with a net; to filter or sift
jarum N needle; hand
jas N coat; ~ *hujan* raincoat
jasa N service, merit
jatah N ration, serve
Jateng N Central Java → **Jawa Tengah**
jati ~ *diri* identity; **sejati** ADJ genu-ine, original, real
Jatim N East Java → **Jawa Timur**
jatuh fall; ~ *cinta* fall in love; ~ *sakit* fall ill; **menjatuhkan** v to fell, let drop; **terjatuh** ADJ (accidentally) fallen
jauh ADJ far; *jarak* ~ long-distance; **kejauhan** ADJ too far
Jawa Java; ~ *Barat (Jabar)* West Java; *bahasa* ~, *orang* ~ Javanese; *pulau* ~ Java
jawab answer, reply; **jawaban** N answer, reply, response; **menjawab** v to answer, reply; **terjawab** ADJ answered

INDONESIAN—ENGLISH

J

jebak: jebakan N trap; **menjebak** V to trap; **terjebak** ADJ trapped, caught

jejak N footprint, track; ~ *langkah* footprint

jejaka N bachelor, young single man

jelajah: menjelajahi V to travel through or explore a place

jelang: menjelang V to approach (usu time)

jelas ADJ clear, obvious; **menjelaskan** V to explain, clarify; **penjelasan** N explanation

jelék ADJ bad, ugly

jemaah, jemaat N congregation, followers of a religion

jembatan N bridge

jempol N thumb

jemput pick up; **jemputan** N vehicle which picks you up; **menjemput** V to pick up

jemur dry (in the sun); **jemuran** N clothes or food drying in the sun; **berjemur** V to sunbathe, sun yourself; **menjemur** V to air, dry in the sun

jenazah N dead body, corpse

jendéla N window

jénderal N general

jénggot, janggut N beard; **berjénggot** ADJ bearded

jéngkél ADJ annoyed

jéngkol N pungent vegetable

jenis N kind, sort, type; species; ~ *kelamin* sex, gender; *lawan* ~ opposite sex; **sejenis** ADJ same type or species

jenuh ADJ fed up, bored; saturated

Jepang N Japan; *bahasa* ~, *orang* ~ Japanese

jepit N tweezers; **jepitan** N clip; tweezers; **terjepit** ADJ pinched, caught in an uncomfortable situation

jeprét: jeprétan, penjeprét N stapler; **menjeprét** V to snap, staple

jerapah N giraffe

jerawat N pimple; **jerawatan** ADJ pimply

jerit scream, shriek; **menjerit** V to scream, shriek

Jerman N Germany; *bahasa* ~, *orang* ~ German

jernih ADJ clear, transparent, pure; *air* ~ clear water

jero: jeroan N innards

jeruk *buah* ~ orange, mandarin; ~ *nipis* lemon

jihad N, ISL crusade, holy war

jijik ADJ disgusting, revolting, filthy; **menjijikkan** ADJ disgusting, revolting, foul

jika, jikalau CONJ if, should

jilat lick; **menjilat** V to lick; SL to suck up, flatter

jilbab N, ISL (full) veil; **berjilbab** V to wear the veil

jilid N volume

jimat N lucky charm, talisman

jin N spirit

jinak ADJ tame, domesticated, friendly

jingga ADJ orange (color)

jinjing *tas* ~ carrybag

jip *mobil* ~ jeep

jiwa N life, soul

Jl(n) *Jalan* street, road

jodoh N life partner, match; M Mr Right; **menjodohkan** V to set up, match

jogét, jogéd (spontaneous) dance; **berjogét** V to dance

jok N seat (in vehicle)

jongkok V to squat

joran N fishing rod

jorok ADJ obscene, disgusting; sloppy; *cerita* ~ dirty story

jual V to sell; ~ *beli* business, buying and selling; **jualan** V to sell informally; **menjual** V to sell; **penjual** N seller, dealer; **penjualan** N sale, sales; **terjual** ADJ sold; *habis* ~ sold out

juang: berjuang V to fight, struggle; **perjuangan** N battle, fight, struggle

juara N champion; ~ *satu* first place; **kejuaraan** N championship

judi V to gamble; *main* ~ to gamble; **berjudi** V to gamble

judul N title; **berjudul** ADJ titled

juga too, also

jujur ADJ honest; **kejujuran** N honesty

Juli *bulan* ~ July

Jumat, Jum'at *hari* ~ Friday; *sholat* ~ Friday prayers

jumlah N amount, total, sum, number; **berjumlah** V to number

jumpa meet; **berjumpa** V to meet

Juni *bulan* ~ June

INDONESIAN–ENGLISH

J

junior, yunior N junior; student in a younger year level; co-worker of a lower rank

jurang N ravine, gorge

jurnal N journal; **jurnalis** N journalist, reporter → **wartawan**

juru expert, skilled; ~ *bicara* spokesperson; ~ *masak* cook

jurus: jurusan N direction; major (at university)

jus N juice

justru ADV precisely, exactly

juta N million; *sepuluh* ~ ten million; **jutaan** ADJ millions; **berjuta** V to have millions of; **jutawan** N millionaire

K

KA ABBREV *kereta api* train

kabar N news; ~ *baik* good news; I'm well

kabupatén N regency

kabur ADJ blurry, hazy

kabur V to disappear, vanish

kabut N fog, mist

kaca N glass; ~ *mata* glasses, spectacles; ~ *mata hitam* sunglasses, dark glasses

kacang N bean, legume; ~ *kedelai* soybean, soya bean; ~ *tanah* peanut

kacau ADJ disordered, confused, chaotic

kadal N lizard

kadaluwarsa, kedaluwarsa ADJ expired; *tanggal* ~ expiry date, use-by date (food) → **daluwarsa**

kadang, kadang-kadang, terkadang ADV sometimes, occasionally

kadar N level, degree; **sekadar** ADJ just; ~*nya* as necessary

kafé N café, bar, pub, nightspot

kagét N startled, surprised; **mengagétkan** V to surprise, startle

kagum ADJ admiring; **mengagumi** V to admire

-kah (suffix to make a question) *bisa*~? Can you?

kail N fishing rod

kailan N Chinese broccoli, kailan

kain N cloth; ~ *kebaya* national dress for women

kaisar N, PRON emperor

kait hook; **kaitan** N relationship, link; **mengaitkan** V to link, connect, join → **gaét, gait**

kaji: kajian N studies

kaji: mengaji, ngaji V to recite or read the Koran; **pengajian** N Koranic recitation

kak PRON term for older sibling or slightly older person; **kakak** N, PRON elder brother or sister; ~ *laki-laki* elder brother

kakas: perkakas N tool, implement

kakatua N *burung* ~ cockatoo

kakék N, PRON grandfather; old man

kaki N foot, leg

kaku ADJ stiff, frozen

kala N time; CONJ when

kalah lose, be defeated; **mengalahkan** V to conquer, defeat

kalajengking N scorpion

kalang: kalangan N circle, group

kalau CONJ if; **kalau-kalau** CONJ in case; **kalaupun** CONJ even if

Kalbar N West Kalimantan → **Kalimantan Barat**

kaldu N broth

kalem ADJ calm, steady

kaléndar, kalénder N calendar

kaléng N tin, can

kali time, times; *satu* ~, *se*~ once; *dua* ~ twice; **berkali-kali** ADV repeatedly, again and again; **sekali** ADV once; very; *besar* ~ very large; **sekali-sekali, sesekali** ADV every now and then, occasionally; **sekali-kali** *jangan* ~ never (do this); **sekalian** ADV all together, all at once; ADV, COLL at the same time; **sekaligus** ADV all at once; **sekalipun** CONJ even though

kali N creek, stream, river

kali COLL maybe, perhaps → **barangkali**

kalian PRON, PL you; *anda se*~ all of you

Kalimantan N Kalimantan, Borneo; ~ *Timur (Kaltim)* East Kalimantan

kalimat N sentence

kalkun N turkey

Kalsél N South Kalimantan → **Kalimantan Selatan**

INDONESIAN–ENGLISH

K

Kalteng N Central Kalimantan → Kalimantan Tengah
Kaltim N East Kalimantan → Kalimantan Timur
kalung N necklace
kamar N room; SL bedroom; ~ *kecil* toilet, lavatory; ~ *mandi* bathroom; ~ *pas* fitting room
kambing N goat, sheep
kamboja *bunga* ~ frangipani
Kamboja N Cambodia
kami PRON, EXCL we, us, our; (very polite) I
Kamis *hari* ~ Thursday
kampanye N campaign
kampung, kampong N village, hometown; ~ *pulang* to go home to the village; **kampungan** ADJ uneducated, backward, provincial
kampus N university, campus
kamu PRON S you (to children and familiars)
kamus N dictionary; ~ *saku* pocket dictionary
kan, 'kan you know; isn't it? → bukan
Kanada N Canada
kanan ADJ right; *ke* ~ to the right; *tangan* ~ right hand
kancil N mousedeer
kancing N button, stud
kandang N stable, pen
kandung N uterus; bladder; **kandungan** N fetus, unborn child; contents; **mengandung** v to contain, carry; to be pregnant
kangen ADJ long for, miss
kangguru, kanguru N kangaroo
kangkung N water spinach
kanker N cancer; ~ *payudara* breast cancer
kano N canoe
kantin N canteen
kantong, kantung N pocket, pouch
kantor N office; ~ *pos* post office; ~ *pusat* head office; *pergi ke* ~ go to work; **perkantoran** N office block
kantuk: mengantuk, ngantuk ADJ sleepy
kantung → kantong
kaos → kaus
kapak N ax
kapal N ship, vessel; ~ *terbang* aeroplane, airplane; *awak* ~ crew; **perkapalan** N shipping
kapan INTERROG when; ~ *saja* whenever, any time; **kapan-kapan** ADV one day, some time in the future
kapas N cotton, cotton wool
kapasitas N capacity; **berkapasitas** v with a capacity of
kapsul N capsule
kapuk, kapok N kapok
kapur N lime(stone), chalk
karamél N caramel pudding
karang N coral reef; *batu* ~ coral reef
karang: karangan N essay; **mengarang** v to write, compose; **pengarang** N author, writer, composer
karantina N quarantine
karapan ~ *sapi* Madurese bull races
karat N rust; **karatan, berkarat** ADJ rusty
karat N carat
karburétor, karburator N carburettor
karcis N ticket (of small value); ~ *bis* bus ticket; ~ *masuk* entrance ticket; *loket* ~ ticket office
kardus N cardboard (box)
karé → kari
karédok N Sundanese fresh salad with peanut sauce
karena CONJ because, since
karét N rubber; rubber band; ~ *gelang* rubber band; *kebun* ~ rubber plantation; *permen* ~ chewing gum
kari, karé N curry
karton N cardboard
kartu N card; ~ *nama* name card; ~ *pos* postcard; *main* ~ play cards
kartun N cartoon, anime; **kartunis** N cartoonist
karung N sack
karya N works; **karyawan** N (salaried) employee; **karyawati** N, F (salaried) employee
kasar ADJ rough, rude, vulgar; **kekasaran** N coarseness, roughness
kasét N cassette
kasih, kasi v, COLL give; ~ *lihat* show; ~ *pinjam* lend; ~ *tahu* inform, tell
kasih N affection, love; ~ *sayang* love; **kasihan** pity, feel sorry for; ~ *dia* poor thing!; **kekasih** N darling, sweetheart, beloved

INDONESIAN—ENGLISH

K

kasir, kassa N cashier
kasuari *burung* ~ cassowary
kasur N mattress
kasus N case
kata N word; *~nya, ~ orang* people say; *~ sandi* password; **berkata** V to say, speak; **mengatakan** V to say
katak N frog, toad
katédral N cathedral
Katolik Catholic
katrol N pulley
katulistiwa, khatulistiwa N the Equator
katun N cotton
katup N valve
kau PRON, S you (to equals or inferiors) → **engkau**
kaum N people, community
kaus, kaos N stocking, sock; garment; *~ kaki* sock; stocking; *~ tangan* glove, mitten
kawah N crater
kawal guard; **pengawal** N (body) guard, sentry
kawan N friend; **berkawan** V to have or be friends with
kawas: kawasan N area, region
kawat N wire; *~ berduri* barbed wire; *~ listrik* electrical wire
kawin V to marry, mate; **kawinan** N, COLL wedding ceremony or reception; **perkawinan** N marriage, wedding
kaya ADJ rich; *~ raya* very rich; **kekayaan** N wealth, riches
kayak, kaya CONJ, COLL like, as; **kayaknya** it seems, apparently
kayu N wood; *~ jati* teak; *~ manis* cinnamon
kayuh: mengayuh V to paddle or pedal something; *~ sepeda* to ride a bicycle
KB ABBREV *Keluarga Berencana* Family Planning
KBRI ABBREV *Kedutaan Besar Republik* Indonesia Embassy of the Republic of Indonesia
ke PREP to, towards; *~ atas* up, upwards; *~ dalam* into; *~ luar* out; *~ muka* to the front; *~ samping* to the side; *~ tengah* to the middle
keadaan N situation, condition → **ada**

keadilan N justice → **adil**
keamanan N safety, security → **aman**
keanggotaan N membership; *kartu ~* membership card → **anggota**
kebakaran N fire; *~ hutan* forest fire, bushfire; *ada ~!* fire! → **bakar**
kebaktian N (Protestant) service → **bakti**
kebangsaan ADJ national → **bangsa**
kebanyakan N, ADJ too much; most → **banyak**
kebaya N, F women's blouse worn as national costume
kebenaran N truth → **benar**
keberangkatan N departure; *pintu ~* departure gate → **angkat, berangkat**
keberanian N bravery, courage → **berani**
keberatan N objection; V to object → **berat**
kebersihan N cleanliness, hygiene → **bersih**
kebetulan ADV by chance, accidentally; N coincidence → **betul**
kebiasaan N habit, custom → **biasa**
kebijakan N policy → **bijak**
kebisingan N noise, buzz → **bising**
kebocoran N leak → **bocor**
kebudayaan N culture, civilization → **budaya**
kebugaran N health; *pusat ~* gym, fitness center → **bugar**
kebuli *nasi ~* lamb and rice dish of Middle Eastern origin
kebun, kebon N garden, plantation; *~ binatang* zoo; *~ raya* botanical garden; *tukang ~* gardener; **berkebun** V to garden, do gardening; **perkebunan** N plantation, estate; *~ teh* tea plantation
keburu ADJ, ADV, COLL in time; too early → **buru**
kebut: mengebut V to speed → **bugar**
kebutuhan N need, necessity → **butuh**
kecam; mengecam V to criticize; **kecaman** N criticism
kecamatan N sub-district → **camat**
kecantikan N beauty → **cantik**
kécap N soy sauce; *~ asin* soy sauce; *~ manis* sweet soy sauce

INDONESIAN–ENGLISH

kecapékan ADJ tired out; N exhaustion → capék

kecelakaan N accident, disaster → celaka

kecenderungan N tendency, trend → cenderung

kecepatan N speed → cepat

kecerdasan N intelligence → cerdas

kecéwa ADJ disappointed; kekecéwaan N disappointment; mengecéwakan V to disappoint; ADJ disappointing

kecil ADJ small, little; young; ~ hati disappointed, offended; orang ~ the little people, the poor; dari ~, sejak ~ since youth; kekecilan ADJ too small; mengecilkan V to make smaller, decrease

kecipratan ADJ be splashed, sprayed accidentally → ciprat

kecolongan ADJ to be robbed; to lose unjustly → colong

kecopétan ADJ to be pickpocketed, robbed; N pickpocketing → copét

kecuali CONJ except; terkecuali tidak ~, tanpa ~ without exception

kecubung batu ~ ruby

kecut ADJ sour, acidic

kecut ADJ shrivelled; pengecut N coward

kedai N stall, kiosk

kedaluwarsa, kadaluwarsa ADJ expired → daluwarsa

kedamaian N peace → damai

kedap ADJ free from; ~ air waterproof; ~ suara soundproof; ~ udara air-tight

kedatangan N arrival → datang

kedekatan N close relationship → dekat

kedelai, kedelé soy; susu kacang ~ soya milk, soymilk

kedengaran ADJ audible → dengar

kedinginan cold; feeling cold → dingin

kedip blink; wink; berkedip V to blink (two eyes) or wink (one eye); berkedip-kedip ADJ blinking; mengedipkan ~ mata to blink

kedondong buah ~ kind of fruit

kedua ADJ second; kedua(-dua)nya ADJ both → dua

kedudukan N position → duduk

kedutaan ~ (besar) embassy → duta

keempat ADJ fourth → empat

keénakan ADJ too enjoyable or good → énak

keenam ADJ sixth → enam

keésokan ~ harinya the next day → ésok, bésok

kegagalan N failure → gagal

kegelapan N darkness → gelap

kegemaran N hobby → gemar

kegembiraan N joy, happiness → gembira

kegiatan N activity → giat

keguguran miscarry, miscarriage → gugur

kehabisan V to run out of (water, food, stock) → habis

kehadiran N presence, attendance → hadir

kehamilan N pregnancy → hamil

kehangatan N warmth, friendliness → hangat

keharuman N fragrance

keharusan N obligation, necessity, requirement → harus

kehausan to be thirsty; thirst → haus

kehendak N will, wish; menghendaki V to wish, want → hendak

kehidupan N life, existence → hidup

kehilangan (feeling of) loss → hilang

kehormatan N respect → hormat

kehujanan ADJ caught in the rain → hujan

kehutanan N forestry → hutan

keindahan N beauty → indah

keinginan N desire, wish → ingin

kejadian N event, happening; creation → jadi

kejahatan N crime → jahat

kejam ADJ cruel, merciless

kejang N spasm, convulsion

kejap: sekejap N moment, flash, blink

kejar V to chase; kejar-kejaran V chase each other; mengejar V to chase

kejauhan ADJ too far → jauh

kejawén N Javanese traditional mysticism

kéju N cheese

kejuaraan N championship → juara

kejujuran N honesty → jujur

INDONESIAN–ENGLISH

K

kejut ADJ surprised, startled; **mengejutkan** ADJ surprising, startling; V to surprise or startle; **terkejut** ADJ surprised

kekacauan N chaos → kacau

kekasaran N coarseness, roughness → kasar

kekasih N sweetheart, beloved, darling → kasih

kekayaan N wealth, riches → kaya

kekebalan N immunity

kekecéwaan N disappointment → kecéwa

kekecilan ADJ too small → kecil

kekeliruan N mistake, error → keliru

kekerasan N violence

kekeringan N dryness, aridity → kering

kekosongan N emptiness → kosong

kekuasaan N power; authority → kuasa

kekuatan N strength, power → kuat

kekuatiran N worry, fear → kuatir

kekurangan N shortcoming (of a person), lack; flaw, mistake, defect → kurang

kelab, klab N club; ~ malam nightclub

kelabu ADJ gray, cloudy

kelahi: berkelahi V to quarrel, fight, fall out; **perkelahian** N fight, scuffle

kelahiran N birth; ADJ born → lahir

kelakuan N act, behavior → laku

kelalaian N forgetfulness, negligence → lalai

kelamaan ADJ too long (a time) → lama

kelambu N mosquito net

kelamin jenis ~ sex, gender

kelapa N coconut; ~ muda young coconut; ~ sawit oil-palm; air ~ coconut milk; coconut juice

kelaparan N hunger, famine, starvation → lapar

kelas N class; ~ kakap big-time

keledai N donkey

kelelawar, kelalawar N bat

kelemahan N weakness → lemah

kelembaban N humidity → lembab

keléngkéng buah ~ small lychee → léngkéng

kelenjar N gland

kelénténg, klénténg N Chinese temple, pagoda

keléréng N marble; main ~ to play marbles

kelihatan ADJ visible; ~nya apparently, it seems → lihat

keliling around; edge, perimeter; **berkeliling** V to go around; **mengelilingi** V to circle, go around

kelinci N rabbit; ~ percobaan guinea-pig

kelingking N little or baby finger

kelipatan N multiple → lipat

keliru ADJ wrong, mistaken; **kekeliruan** N mistake, error

kélok N bend, curve

kelola: mengelola V to manage, run; **pengelolaan** N management

kelom, klompen N clogs

kelompok N group

kelontong toko ~ shop selling cheap goods

kelopak ~ mata eyelid

keluar go out; be issued; PREP out, outside; **mengeluarkan** V to issue, send out, release, publish → ke luar

keluarga N family; **berkeluarga** V to have a family, be married

keluh sigh; **keluhan** N complaint; **mengeluh** V to complain

kelupaan N something forgotten → lupa

kelupas, mengelupas V to peel, come off (of a skin)

kelurahan N administrative unit, village → lurah

kemacetan N (traffic) jam → macet

kémah N tent; **berkémah** V to camp, go camping; **perkémahan** N camping, camp

kemajuan N progress, advance → maju

kemalaman ADV too late (at night); after dark → malam

kemaluan N genital, sex organ → malu

kemampuan N ability, capability → mampu

kemangi N Indonesian mint

kemarahan N anger → marah

kemarau musim ~ dry season

kemari here, in this direction

K

kemarin ADV yesterday; the other day; last; ~ *dulu* the day before yesterday

kemas: kemasan N packaging

kemasyarakatan ADJ social

kematian N death, passing → mati

kemauan N want, will, desire → mau

kembali back, return; again; *(terima kasih)* ~ you're welcome; **kembalian** N small change; **kembalinya** N the return; **mengembalikan** V to give or send back, return

kembang N flower; **berkembang** V to develop, expand; *negara* ~ developing country; **mengembangkan** V to develop something; **perkembangan** N development

kembar N twin

kembung, gembung ADJ filled with air, inflated; bloated

keméja N Western-style shirt (with collar)

kemenangan N victory → menang

kementerian N ministry, department, office → menteri

kemerdékaan N freedom, independence, liberty → merdéka

keméwahan N luxury → méwah

kemih *saluran* ~ urinary tract

kemis, emis: mengemis V to beg; **pengemis** N beggar

kemiskinan N poverty → miskin

kemocéng, kemucing N feather duster

kempés, kempis ADJ deflated, flat; hollow; *ban* ~ flat tire

kemudahan N ease, facility → mudah

kemudi N rudder, steering wheel; **mengemudikan** V to drive, steer; **pengemudi** N driver

kemudian CONJ then

kemuka: terkemuka ADJ prominent → ke muka

kemungkinan N possibility → mungkin

kemut, emut, mengemut V to suck on, chew

kena touch; **kenapa** COLL why, how come; what did you say?; **mengenai** CONJ about, concerning

kenaikan N rise, raise

kenal V to know, be acquainted with; **kenalan** N acquaintance; **mengenal** V to know, be acquainted with, to recognize; **memperkenalkan** V to introduce; **perkenalan** N introduction; **terkenal** ADJ well-known

kenang recall; **kenangan** N memories; **kenang-kenangan** N souvenir, keepsake; **mengenang** V to commemorate, remember

kenapa INTERROG, COLL why, how come; what did you say? → kena apa

kenari *burung* ~ canary

kencan N date; **berkencan** V to go on a date

kencang tight, taut; **mengencangkan** V to tighten

kencing urine; urinate; ~ *manis* diabetes

kencur *beras* ~ traditional Javanese drink

kendali N reins; **mengendalikan** V to control; **terkendali** ADJ controlled

kendang N small drum → gendang

kendara: kendaraan N vehicle

kendi N earthen water flask

kendor, kendur ADJ slack, loose

kenduri N feast, celebration

kenék, kernét N bus assistant acting as conductor

kening N forehead, brow

kental ADJ thick, sticky, congealed

kentang N potato; COLL french fries; ~ *goreng* hot potato chips, french fries

kentut fart, break wind

kenyamanan N comfort → nyaman

kenyang ADJ full, not hungry

kenyataan N fact → nyata

kéong N snail

kepada PREP to (someone)

kepal fist; **kepalan** N fist

kepala N head, chief

kepanjangan ADJ too long → panjang

kepariwisataan N tourism industry

kepastian N certainty → pasti

kepedasan ADJ too hot or spicy → pedas

kepéndékan N abbreviation → péndék

INDONESIAN–ENGLISH

K

kepéngén, kepingin v, coll really want to → **péngén**

kepentingan n importance, interest → **penting**

kepercayaan n belief, faith → **percaya**

kepergian n departure → **pergi**

keperluan n needs, requirements → **perlu**

keping n piece (counter for flat objects); splinter

kepiting n crab

kepompong n cocoon

keponakan, kemenakan n niece or nephew; cousin

Kepri (Kepulauan Riau) Riau Archipelago, a province in Sumatra

kepribadian n personality → **pribadi**

kepulauan n archipelago, chain

kepunyaan n possession, belonging → **punya**

keputihan n thrush, vaginal itching (white discharge) → **putih**

keputusan n decision, decree → **putus**

kera n ape

keracunan adj poisoned → **racun**

keraguan, keragu-raguan n doubt, uncertainty → **ragu**

kerah n collar

kerajaan n kingdom → **raja**

kerajinan n crafts → **rajin**

keram cramp

keramahan n friendliness → **ramah**

keramaian n noise, din; lively atmosphere → **ramai**

keramas to wash your hair

keramik ceramic, earthenware

keran n tap, faucet

kerang n shell; mollusc

kerangka n skeleton, framework

keranjang n basket

keras adj hard, strong, severe, strict, violent; loud; **bersikeras** v to maintain, stick to, be obstinate; **kekerasan** n violence; **mengeraskan** v to make something harder, louder; **pengeras** ~ *suara* loudspeaker

kerasan coll settled, comfortable, feel at home → **rasa**

keraton, kraton n Javanese palace

kerbau, kebo n buffalo

kerén adj, coll great, cool; trendy

keréta n train; carriage; ~ *api* train

kericuhan n chaos → **ricuh**

kerikil n gravel, pebble

kerinduan n longing, craving → **rindu**

kering adj dry; **kekeringan** n dryness, aridity; **mengeringkan** v to dry something

keringat n sweat, perspiration; **keringatan** adj sweaty, sweating; **berkeringat** v to sweat

keripik, kripik n small chip or crisp

keris, kris n traditional dagger, creese

keriting curl, curly

kerja work; job, occupation; ~ *sama* co-operation; **kerjaan** n work, job, things to do; **bekerja** v to work; ~ *sama* to co-operate, work together; **mengerjakan** v to do, carry out; **pekerja** n worker, laborer; **pekerjaan** n work, profession

kernét, kenék n assistant on a bus or truck

kerok traditional treatment for minor illnesses by rubbing the back with a coin; **kerokan** v to be massaged in this way

keroncong, kroncong n traditional songs and music of Portuguese origin

kerongkongan n throat

keropos adj eroded, eaten away; *tulang* ~ osteoporosis

keroyok, mengeroyok v to beat savagely in a mob

kertas n paper

kerucut, cerucut n cone

kerudung, kudungan n, isl veil

kerugian n loss; damage → **rugi**

keruk dredge; **mengeruk** v to dredge, scrape out

kerupuk, krupuk n large cracker, crisp, chip

kerusakan n damage → **rusak**

kerusuhan n riot, disturbance → **rusuh**

kesabaran n patience → **sabar**

kesadaran n consciousness, awareness → **sadar**

kesakitan adj in pain → **sakit**

kesaksian n evidence, testimony → **saksi**

INDONESIAN – ENGLISH

kesal ADJ **kesel** COLL annoyed, in a bad mood

kesalahan N mistake → salah

kesampaian ADJ achieved, reached, realized → sampai

kesan N impression; berkesan, mengesankan ADJ impressive; terkesan ADJ impressed; seemed

kesasar COLL to lose your way, (get) lost → sasar

kesayangan favorite, pet → sayang

kesedihan N sadness, sorrow → sedih

keséhatan N health → séhat

keseimbangan N balance → imbang

kesejahteraan N welfare → sejahtera

keselamatan N safety; salvation → selamat

keseléo sprain; sprained

keseluruhan *secara* ~ totally, completely → seluruh

kesempatan N opportunity → sempat

kesemutan V to have pins and needles → semut

kesenangan N amusement, hobby → senang

kesenian N art (form) → seni

kesepakatan N agreement → pakat

kesepian N loneliness, solitude → sepi

kesenangan N frequency; too often

kését N door mat

kesetrum V, COLL to receive an electric shock → setrum

kesiangan ADJ late, too late in the day → siang

kesibukan N activity, fuss, bustle, business → sibuk

kesimpulan N conclusion → simpul

kesopanan N manners, politeness → sopan

kesoréan ADV too late → soré

kesukaan N hobby; enjoyment → suka

kesukaran N difficulty → sukar

kesulitan N difficulty, trouble → sulit

kesusahan N trouble, difficulty → susah

ketagihan ADJ addicted to → tagih

ketahuan to be found out → tahu

ketakutan ADJ frightened, terrified, scared → takut

ketan N sticky rice; ~ *bakar* grilled slices of sticky rice

ketapél N catapult

ketat ADJ tight, strict

ketawa V, COLL to laugh → tawa

ketéla N yam

ketemu V, COLL to meet → temu

ketentuan N condition, stipulation → tentu

keterangan N explanation → terang

keterlaluan N excess, too much → lalu

keterlambatan N delay → lambat

keterlibatan N involvement, association → libat

kétiak, kéték N armpit

ketiduran V to fall asleep → tidur

ketiga ADJ the third → tiga

ketik V type; mengetik V to type

ketika CONJ when (in past)

ketimbang CONJ, COLL than; instead of → timbang

ketimun → mentimun

ketimuran ADJ Eastern, Oriental → timur

ketinggalan ADJ left behind → tinggal

ketinggian N altitude, height → tinggi

ketinting N water taxi used on the rivers of Kalimantan

ketok V to knock; panel-beat; ~ *magic* 'magic' panel-beating

ketombé N dandruff

ketoprak N Betawi dish of vegetables in peanut sauce; folk play

ketrampilan N skill → trampil

ketua N chief, chair, president, elder

ketuk, ketok knock; mengetuk V to knock

ketularan ADJ infected, caught something → tular

ketumbar N (ground) coriander

ketupat N coconut fronds woven into a diamond-shape for cooking rice

keturunan N descendant

keuangan N finance → uang

keunikan N unique thing, uniqueness → unik

keuntungan N advantage, profit → untung

INDONESIAN–ENGLISH

K

kewajiban N obligation, duty → wajib

kewarganegaraan N citizenship → warga negara

keyakinan N belief, conviction, faith → yakin

kg kilogram

khas ADJ special, specific

khatulistiwa, katulistiwa N the Equator

khawatir, kuatir V to worry, fear; *jangan* ~ don't worry; **kekuatiran** N worry, fear; **menguatirkan** V to worry about something

khayal: khayalan N dream, hallucination

khianat: mengkhianati V to betray someone; **pengkhianat** N traitor

khitan N circumcision; **khitanan** N feast held in honor of a circumcision; **mengkhitan(kan)** V to circumcise

khotbah N sermon

khusus ADJ special, particular; *~nya* in particular, especially

kian ADV such; increasingly, more and more; **sekian** ADV so much, this much

kibar: berkibar(-kibar) V to wave, flutter; **mengibarkan** V to wave, unfurl

kibor N keyboard

kidal ADJ left-handed

kijang N barking deer, kind of antelope

kikir ADJ stingy, tight, miserly

kikis ADJ scraped; **terkikis** ADJ eaten away, eroded

kilang N refinery, mill; **perkilangan** N refinery

kilap shine; **mengkilap** V to shine, gleam

kilas: sekilas N flash, glance

kilat N lightning

kilau: berkilau ADJ glittering, sparkling

kilir twist; **terkilir** ADJ twisted, sprained

kilo N kilo, kilogram; kilometer; **kiloan** ADV by the kilogram, in kilograms

kimia N chemistry

kimono N kimono; dressing gown

kincir N wheel; ~ *air* waterwheel; ~ *angin* windmill

kini ADV now, nowadays (often when comparing with past)

kios N stall, kiosk; **kiostél, kiospon** N small phone agency, phone kiosk → kios télépon

kipas N fan; ~ *angin*, ~ *listrik* (electric) fan

kiper N (goal)keeper

kira V to think, guess, estimate; **kira-kira** ADV approximately, around, about; **mengira** V to assume, think; **memperkirakan** V to estimate, calculate; **perkiraan** N estimate, guess; **terkira** *tak* ~ unsuspected, not thought of

kiri ADJ left; ~ *kanan* left and right; *belok* ~ turn left

kirim V to send; ~ *salam* to send your best wishes; **kiriman** N parcel; **mengirim** V to send; **pengirim** N sender; **pengiriman** N dispatch, forwarding; **terkirim** ADJ sent

kisah N tale, story; **berkisah** V to tell a story

kisar: berkisar V to revolve, rotate, turn

kismis N sultana, currant

kita PRON we, us, our (inclusive); ~ *punya* our

kitab N holy book

kitar: sekitar ADV around; near; PREP around; **sekitarnya** *di* ~ around (a place)

KITAS ABBREV *Kartu Izin Tinggal Sementara* temporary residence permit for foreigners

KKN ABBREV *korupsi, kolusi, nepotisme* corruption (collusion and nepotism)

klakson N horn

klasik ADJ classic, classical

klénténg, kelénténg N Chinese temple, pagoda

klép, kelép N valve, catch

klik V to click (a mouse)

klinik N clinic

klosét N cistern (of toilet)

klub N (sports) club

km *kamar* room (in a hotel); kilometer

knalpot N exhaust pipe, muffler

K

koalisi N coalition
koboi N cowboy
kocok *mie* ~ kind of noodles; **mengocok** v to shake, shuffle
kode N code; ~ *pos* postcode
kodok N frog
kok you know (emphasizing contrary argument); *tidak apa-apa* ~ really, it's OK; INTERROG how come, why
koki N cook
kokoh, kukuh ADJ strong, robust
kokpit N cockpit
kol N cabbage
kolaborasi N collaboration
kolak N sweet fruit stew
kolam N pond, pool
koléga N colleague
koléksi N collection
kolintang N large wooden xylophone from Minahasa
Kolombia N Colombia
kolonél N, PRON colonel
kolong N space under a large object; ~ *meja* under the table
kolor N drawstring shorts
kolot ADJ old-fashioned, out of date; conservative
koma N comma
komandan N commander
kombinasi N combination
koméntar N comment; **berkoméntar** v to (make a) comment
komik *(buku)* ~ comic (book); **komikus** N comic book author or artist
komisaris N commissioner
komisi N committee, commission
komité N committee → **panitia**
kompas N compass
komplék, kompléks, kompléx N housing complex, compound
komplét, komplit ADJ complete
kompor N stove, cooker
komprés N compress, pack
kompromi N compromise
komputer N computer
komunis ADJ, N communist; **komunisme** N communism
konci → **kunci**
kondéktur N conductor, guard (on a train or city bus)
kondisi N condition
kondom N condom

konéksi N connections, contacts (at an institution)
konferénsi, konperénsi N conference
konfrontasi N confrontation; Indonesian aggression towards Malaysia in the 1960s
Kong Hu Cu Confucius, Confucian, Confucianism
kongkol: persekongkolan N plot, intrigue
konglomerat N wealthy financier
kongrés N congress, convention
konséling N counselling; **konsélor** N counsellor
konsén, konséntrasi ADJ focused, concentrating
konsép N concept, draft
konsér N concert
konsul N consul; **konsulat** N consulate; ~ *jenderal (konjen)* consulate-general
konsumén N consumer
kontak contact
kontés N contest
kontra ADJ against, opposing, anti
kontrak N contract; **kontrakan** N rented (house); **dikontrakkan** ADJ for rent, lease
konyol ADJ silly, foolish
koper N suitcase, baggage
koperasi N co-operative, co-op
kopi N coffee; ~ *susu* white or milk coffee; ~ *tubruk* ground coffee
kopi N copy → **fotokopi**
kopyor *es* ~ sweet drink made from this coconut
koran N newspaper
korban N victim; **berkorban** v to make sacrifices, do without; **mengorbankan** v to sacrifice
Koréa N Korea; ~ *Selatan (Korsel)* South Korea; ~ *Utara* North Korea; *bahasa* ~, *orang* ~ Korean
korék ~ *api* matches; **mengorék** v to scrape, scratch
koréksi N correction; **mengoréksi** v to correct
korma, kurma N date
Korsél N South Korea → **Koréa Selatan**
kortsléting, korsléting N short-circuit

INDONESIAN–ENGLISH

K

korup ADJ corrupt; **korupsi** N corruption; ADJ corrupt; ~ *kolusi dan nepotisme (KKN)* corruption; **koruptor** N corrupt person

Korut N North Korea → **Koréa Utara**

kos board, lodging; **kos-kosan** N boarding-houses, rooms for board

kosa ~ *kata* vocabulary

kos-kosan N boarding-houses, rooms for board → **kos**

kosong ADJ empty, blank; hollow; zero; **kekosongan** N emptiness; **mengosongkan** V to empty

kota N town, city; **perkotaan** N metropolitan area; **kotamadya** N municipality

kotak N box; square; **kotak-kotak** ADJ checked pattern

kotamadya N municipality → **kota**

kotor ADJ dirty, filthy; gross; **kotoran** N excrement; dirt

kraton, keraton N Javanese palace

krédit N credit; *kartu* ~ credit card

kriminal ADJ criminal

kring sound of telephone ringing

kripik, keripik N small chip or crisp

krisis N crisis

kristal crystal

Kristen ADJ Christian, Protestant; *gereja* ~ Protestant church

Kristus *Yesus* ~ Jesus Christ

krupuk → **kerupuk**

ksatria, kesatria N knight, warrior; ADJ chivalrous

KTP ABBREV *Kartu Tanda Penduduk* national identity card

ku, -ku PRON I, my, mine; *rumah*~ my home

kuah N soup, sauce, gravy (accompanying a food)

kualitas, kwalitas N quality; **berkualitas** ADJ quality

kuas N brush (for art or cosmetics); paintbrush

kuasa N power; **berkuasa** ADJ powerful, mighty; **kekuasaan** N power; authority; **menguasai** V to control, have power over

kuat ADJ strong; **kekuatan** N strength, power; **menguatkan** V to strengthen

kuatir, khawatir V to worry, fear; *jangan* ~ don't worry; **kekuatiran** N worry, fear; **menguatirkan** V to worry about something

Kuba N Cuba

kubik ADJ cubic

kubis N cabbage

kubu N block, faction

kubur N grave, tomb; **kuburan** N cemetery, graveyard; **menguburkan** V to bury; **terkubur** ADJ buried in an accident

kucing N cat

kuda N horse; ~ *laut* seahorse; ~ *nil* hippo, hippopotamus; **berkuda** V to ride a horse, go (horse-)riding

kudéta N coup, coup d'etat

kudung, kerudung N loose veil

kudus ADJ, CHR holy

kué N cake, pastry

kuil N, CH, HIND temple

kuis N quiz

kuku N nail (of people), claw (of animals); *cat* ~ nail polish

kukuh, kokoh ADJ strong, robust

kukus steam; **mengukus** V to steam (food)

kuliah N lecture; V, COLL to study at university or college

kulit N skin, hide (of animals); leather; peel, rind (of fruit); **berkulit** to have skin, -skinned

kulkas N refrigerator, fridge

kuman N germ, bacteria

kumat, komat relapse

kumbang N beetle; bumblebee

kumis N mustache

kumpul V to get together, gather; **kumpulan** N collection; group; **berkumpul** V to assemble, meet; **mengumpulkan** V to collect, gather; **ngumpul** V, SL to get or come together; **perkumpulan** N association, club; assembly

kumuh ADJ dirty, slummy

kumur *obat* ~ mouthwash; **berkumur(-kumur)** V to gargle

kunang-kunang N firefly

kunci key; lock; fastener; **mengunci** V to lock (up)

kuncup N bud

kuning ADJ yellow; COLL light brown; ~ N saffron, turmeric; ~ *telur* yolk; **kuningan** N brass

kunjung: kunjungan N visit, excur-

INDONESIAN—ENGLISH

sion; **berkunjung** v to visit, pay a visit to; **mengunjungi** v to visit a place

kuno ADJ ancient, historic; old-fashioned, out-of-date, conservative

kunyit, kunir, kuning N saffron; turmeric

kupas peel; **mengupas** v to peel; to analyze

kuping N ear; **menguping** v to eavesdrop, listen in

kupu: kupu-kupu N butterfly

kura-kura N tortoise

kurang ADJ, ADV less, lacking; **berkurang** v to decrease, diminish, subside; **kekurangan** N shortcoming (of a person), lack; flaw, mistake, defect; **mengurangi** v to take from, subtract, minus; **sekurang(-kurang)nya** ADV at least

kurban, qurban N, ISL sacrifice, usu goats or cattle

kurir N courier

kurma, korma N date

kurs N exchange rate

kursi N chair, seat; ~ *roda* wheelchair

kursus course

kurung cage; **mengurung** v to cage, put in a cage, lock up

kurus ADJ thin, skinny

kusén, kosén N frame (of door or window)

kusut ADJ tangled, tousled, unkempt; complicated

kutak, utak: mengutak-ngatikkan v to work on or tinker with

kutik: mengutik v to tinker with; to touch on

kutil N wart

kutip, mengutip v to quote, cite an extract; **kutipan** N extract, quotation

kutu N louse, flea

kutub N pole; ~ *selatan* the South Pole; *beruang* ~ polar bear

kutuk curse; **kutukan** N curse; **mengutuk** v to curse; **terkutuk** ADJ cursed, accursed

kwalitas → kualitas

kwétiau, kwétiauw N large Chinese egg noodles

kwitansi, kuitansi N bill, receipt

laba: laba-laba N spider

laboratorium, lab N laboratory

labu N gourd, pumpkin, squash

labuh: pelabuhan port, harbor

lacak: melacak v to trace

laci N drawer; chest of drawers, dresser

lacur: pelacur N prostitute

lada N pepper

ladang N field; area of opportunity

lafal N pronunciation; **melafalkan** v to pronounce

laga N fight; *film* ~ action film

lagi SL in the act of; ~ *makan* eating → sedang

lagi ADV again; more; **lagipula** N furthermore, moreover

lagu N song, music; ~ *anak-anak* children's song; ~ *daerah* song or music from a certain region; ~ *kebangsaan* national anthem

-lah added after a word to soften the message; *baik*~ OK then; *mari*~ let us go

lahan N ground, land, terrain

lahar N lava

lahir born; external; **kelahiran** N birth; ADJ born; **melahirkan** v to give birth to; to create; **terlahir** ADJ born

lain ADJ other, different; ~ *lagi* different again; **melainkan** CONJ rather, instead; **selain** except, apart from

lajang ADJ single, unmarried

laju fast, rapid, quick; rate

lajur N lane (one of many); ~ *kiri* left lane → jalur

laki ADJ, SL male; N, SL husband; **lelaki** ADJ, N male; **laki-laki** ADJ, N male; *saudara* ~ brother; *anak* ~ son

lakon N play; act

laksa N Malay dish of vermicelli noodles with chicken in coconut sauce

laku ADJ popular, in vogue; salable; **berlaku** ADJ effective, valid; v to behave; **kelakuan** N act, behavior; **melakukan** v to do, perform, carry out

lalai ADJ careless, negligent; **kelalaian** N forgetfulness, negligence

INDONESIAN–ENGLISH

L

lalap, lalapan N raw vegetables, eaten as a side-dish

lalat, laler N fly

lalu CONJ then; ADJ last; ~ *lintas* traffic; **melalui** V to pass through; CONJ through, via; **selalu** ADV always; **terlalu** ADV too; **keterlaluan** ADJ too much, overly, unacceptable

lama ADJ long; old; former; lama-lama ADJ too long; **kelamaan** ADJ too long (a time); **selama** CONJ for, during, as long as; **selamanya** ADV always, forever

laman N webpage, website

lamar, melamar V to apply; **lamaran** N application; proposal

lambai: melambaikan V to wave something; ~ *tangan* to wave (goodbye)

lamban ADJ slow

lambang N symbol; **berlambang** V to have a symbol

lambat ADJ slow, late; **melambatkan** V to slow down; **selambat-lambatnya** ADV at the latest; **terlambat** ADJ (too) late, delayed; **keterlambatan** N delay

lambung N stomach

lambung: melambung V to bounce

laminasi N laminating

lampion N paper lantern

lampir: lampiran N attachment, appendix; **melampirkan** V to attach, enclose; **terlampir** ADJ attached, enclosed

lampu N light, lamp; ~ *lalu lintas*, ~ *merah* traffic light

lampung: pelampung N floater; flotation device

lamun: melamun V to day-dream, fantasize

lancang ADJ impudent, impolite, shameless

lancar ADJ smooth, fluent; **selancar** *papan* ~ surfboard; **berselancar** V to surf, go surfing

lancip ADJ pointed, pointy

landak N porcupine, echidna

landas N base, ground; *lepas* ~ take-off

langgan: langganan N subscription; regular customer; **berlangganan** V to subscribe to; **pelanggan** N subscriber, customer

langgar: melanggar V to disobey, offend

langgeng ADJ everlasting, eternal

langit N sky; langit-langit N palate, roof of your mouth; ceiling

langka ADJ rare

langkah N step; **melangkah** V to step

langsing ADJ slim, slender

langsung ADJ direct, straight; **berlangsung** V to take place

lanjur: terlanjur ADV too late, already

lanjut ADJ advanced, further; **melanjutkan** V to continue something; **selanjutnya** ADV then, after that

lansia ADJ elderly → *lanjut usia*

lantai N floor (of building), story (of house)

lantar: terlantar, telantar ADJ neglected, abandoned

lantik: pelantikan N inauguration

lap N rag, cloth; **mengelap** V to wipe, mop

lapang ADJ wide, spacious; **lapangan** N field; ~ *tenis* tennis court; ~ *terbang*, ~ *udara (lanud)* airfield, airport

lapar ADJ hungry; **kelaparan** N hunger, famine, starvation

lapis layer, fold, lining; **lapisan** N coat, layer

lapor, melapor V to report; **laporan** N report; **melaporkan** V to report, inform

lapuk rotten, decayed

larang: melarang V to ban, prohibit, forbid; **dilarang** V prohibited; ~ *masuk* no entry, no admittance; ~ *merokok* no smoking; **larangan** N ban, prohibition; **terlarang** ADJ forbidden, banned

larat: melarat ADJ miserable, poor; poverty-stricken

lari run; **berlari** V to run; **melarikan** V to run off with, abduct, kidnap; **pelari** N runner

laron N flying white ant

larut dissolve; **larutan** N solution

las weld; **mengelas** V to weld

laskar N army, troops

latar N base; ~ *belakang* background

INDONESIAN—ENGLISH

L

latih, melatih v to train; **latihan** n training, practice, exercise; **pelatih** n coach, trainer; **pelatihan** n training

lauk (~) pauk side-dish

laut n sea; **lautan** n ocean; ~ Hindia the Indian Ocean; **pelaut** n sailor, seaman

lawak: pelawak n comedian, comic, clown

lawan n opponent, adversary; opposite; **melawan** v to oppose, resist; **perlawanan** n opposition, resistance

layak, laik ADJ proper, suitable

layan: layanan n service; **melayani** v to serve; **pelayan** n attendant, M waiter, F waitress; **pelayanan** n service

layang: layang-layang kite

layar sail; **berlayar** v to sail; **pelayaran** n voyage

layat: melayat v to visit a house in mourning, pay your respects

lebah n bee

lébar ADJ wide, broad; **lébarnya** n width; **melébarkan** v to widen

Lebaran n Idul Fitri, first two days after the Ramadan fast

lébarnya n width → lébar

lebat ADJ thick, dense

lebih ADV more; ~ baik, ~ bagus better; **berlebihan** ADJ excessive; **kelebihan** n extra, excess; **melebihi** v to exceed, surpass

lécét sore, blister

léci n lychee

ledak: ledakan n explosion; **meledak** v to explode

lédék, melédék v to tease, provoke

léděng, léding tukang ~ plumber

lega ADJ relieved

légal ADJ legal; **melégalisasi, melégalisir** v to legalize

légénda n legend, myth; **légéndaris** ADJ legendary

légong tari ~ Balinese trance dance performed by young girls

léhér n neck

lekas ADJ fast, quick, speedy; (semoga) ~ sembuh get well soon

lekat: melekat v to stick; **pelekat** bahan ~ adhesive

lelah ADJ tired, weary; **melelahkan** ADJ tiring

lelaki, laki-laki ADJ male; n man, male

lélang n auction

lelap ADJ sound, fast, completely; tidur ~ sound asleep

lélé ikan ~ catfish

léléh melt, run; **meléléh** v to drip, run

leluhur n ancestor → luhur

lém n glue

lemah ADJ weak; **kelemahan** n weakness

lemak n fat; grease

lemari n cupboard, closet, shelf; ~ baju wardrobe

lemas, lemes ADJ weak, drained

lembab, lembap ADJ humid, damp, moist; **kelembaban** n humidity; **pelembab, pelembap** n moisturizer

lembaga n institute, foundation, board

lembah n valley

lembap → lembab

lembar n sheet (of paper), page

lembék ADJ soft, weak, flimsy

lembur v to work overtime, stay late

lembut ADJ soft, gentle

lémpar, melémpar v to throw; **lémparan** n throw; **terlémpar** ADJ thrown, flung

lemper n sweet cake of sticky rice with a meat filling

léncéng: meléncéng v to deviate, go out of your way

lendir n mucus

lengan n arm, sleeve

lengkap ADJ complete; **melengkapi** v to furnish, supply; **pelengkap** n an accessory; **perlengkapan** n outfit, equipment

léngkéng, keléngkéng n (buah) ~ small lychee

léngkét ADJ sticky, close

lénsa n lens; ~ kontak contact lenses

lentur ADJ elastic, pliable

lenyap ADJ disappeared, gone, vanished

lepas loose, free; escape; **melepaskan** v to release, let free

léréng n slope

lés (to attend) a private class or course

lésbi lesbian

INDONESIAN–ENGLISH

lését: melését v to slip, skid; to miss the target; **terpelését** ADJ slipped

lesu ADJ tired, weary

letak place, location; **letaknya** N the location, position; **meletakkan** v to put in place, set down; **terletak** ADJ situated, located

letih ADJ tired

létnan N lieutenant

letus: letusan N eruption; **meletus** v to erupt

léwat PREP past; via; *jam empat ~ lima* five past four; **meléwati** v to pass or go through

lezat ADJ delicious, tasty

lho you know (used to emphasize a statement, often denying something); EJAC well!

liang N hole, passage

liar ADJ wild, untamed; unregulated

Libanon N Lebanon

libat: melibatkan v to involve, include; **terlibat** ADJ involved, implicated; **keterlibatan** N involvement, association

libur be free, on holiday (from school or work); **liburan** N holiday; **berlibur** v to go or be on holiday

licik ADJ cunning, tricky

licin ADJ smooth; slippery

lidah N tongue

lidi N palm-leaf rib

liga N (football) league

lihat v to see; **kelihatan** ADJ visible; *~nya* apparently, it seems; **melihat** v to see, look; **melihat-lihat** v to look around, have a look

lilin N candle; wax

lilit turn, twist; **terlilit** ADJ caught up, twisted

lima ADJ five; *~ belas* fifteen; *~ puluh* fifty; *ke~* fifth

lincah ADJ nimble, deft, agile; **kelincahan** N agility

lindas: melindas v to run over, squash; **terlindas** ADJ run over

lindung: berlindung v to (take) shelter; **melindungi** v to protect, shelter; **pelindung** N protective device; **perlindungan** N protection

lingkar N ring, circle, circumference; **lingkaran** N circle; **melingkari** v to circle or surround

lingkung: lingkungan N environment, surroundings, circle

lintah N leech

lintang across, latitude; **melintang** ADJ horizontal, across

lipat fold; *dua kali ~* double, twice; **lipatan** N fold; **kelipatan** N multiple; **melipat** v to fold

lipstik N lipstick

liput: liputan N coverage, reporting; **meliputi** v to include, cover

lisan ADJ oral, verbal

listrik electric, electricity

liter N liter, litre

lobak N radish

logam N metal

logat N accent

logika N logic

lohor ISL the midday prayer

lok, lokomotif N locomotive

lokakarya N seminar, workshop

lokasi N location

lokét N counter, desk, ticket window or office

lokomotif, lok N locomotive

lolong howl; **melolong** v to howl (of dogs)

lolos v to escape; succeed, progress

lomba race, competition, contest; **berlomba** v to compete, race

lombok N chilli

lompat jump, leap; **melompat** v to jump, leapfrog

loncat jump (over something); **meloncat** v to spring, jump

loncéng N bell

longgar ADJ loose, wide

longsor slip; *tanah ~* landslide

lonjong ADJ oval

lontar throw; **melontarkan** v to throw

lontong N cooked, solid slab of rice

loper N newspaper delivery boy

lorong N path; lane, alley

losmén N guest house, accommodation, cheap hotel

loték N a dish of fresh vegetables with peanut sauce

loténg N attic, loft

lotot → melotot, pelotot

lowongan ADJ wanted, vacancy

loyang N cake tin, tray, mould

Lt. *lantai* floor, level

lu SL you

INDONESIAN—ENGLISH

luang ADJ free, empty; **peluang** N chance, opportunity

luap: meluap V to overflow, swell, wash

luar out, external; ~ *biasa* outstanding, extraordinary; ~ *negeri* overseas, abroad; **keluar** go out; be issued; PREP out, outside; **mengeluarkan** V to issue, publish, send out, release

luas wide, broad; space; **luasnya** N width; area

lubang, lobang N hole, passage; ~ *hidung* nostril

lubuk N deep pool

lucu ADJ cute, sweet; funny; odd; **lelucan** N joke

ludah N saliva, spit; **meludah** V to spit

lugu ADJ naive, gullible

luhur ADJ lofty, noble, esteemed; **leluhur** N ancestor

luka wound; injured; **melukai, melukakan** V to hurt or wound

lukis V to paint, draw; **lukisan** N painting, picture, portrait (of a person); **melukis** V to paint, draw; **pelukis** N painter, artist

lulus V to pass; **lulusan** N graduate

lumas: pelumas N lubricant

lumayan ADV, ADJ quite, not bad, fairly

lumba-lumba N dolphin, porpoise

lumpang N pestle, rice pounder

lumpia N spring rolls

lumpuh ADJ paralysed, lame

lumpur N mud

lumur smear; **berlumuran** ADJ smeared, stained

lumut N moss

lunak ADJ soft

lunas ADJ paid off, in full

luncur: meluncurkan V to launch, set in motion

luntur fade, lose color, run

lupa V to forget; **kelupaan** N something forgotten; **melupakan** V to forget something; **terlupakan** *tak* ~ unforgettable

lurah N head of a *kelurahan*, village chief; **kelurahan** N administrative unit, village

lurus ADJ straight; **pelurusan** N straightening

lusa ADV the day after tomorrow; *besok* ~ tomorrow or the day after

lusin N dozen, twelve; **selusin** N a dozen

lutut N knee; **berlutut** to kneel (down)

M

M *Masehi* Christian calendar

m meter

maaf sorry; *minta* ~ apologize, say you're sorry; **memaafkan** V to forgive, pardon

maag, mag N, COLL stomach (disorder); *sakit* ~ weak stomach, gastric pain

mabuk ADJ drunk; ill; motion sickness

macam N kind, sort, model; **macam-macam** ADJ, NEG all sorts; **bermacam-macam** ADJ various; **semacam** ADJ a kind or type of

macan N large spotted cat; N, COLL tiger

macet, macét jammed, blocked; traffic jam; **kemacetan** N (traffic) jam

madrasah N, ISL boarding school, college

madu N honey

madya ADJ medium, middle

magang (do) work experience, apprentice

magrib, maghrib N sunset; sunset (prayer)

mahal ADJ expensive, dear

mahasiswa N (university or college) student; **mahasiswi** N, F (female) student

mahir ADJ expert, skilled

mahkota N crown, crest

main V to play, do (a sport); **main-main** V to joke around, not be serious; **mainan** V toy; **bermain** V to play; **memainkan** V to play something; **pemain** N player, actor; **permainan** N game, match

majalah N magazine

majikan N employer

maju go forward, advance, progress, improve; **kemajuan** N progress, advance

maka CONJ therefore, so, then; **makanya** CONJ that's why, so

INDONESIAN–ENGLISH

M

makam N grave; **memakamkan** V to bury; **pemakaman** N funeral, burial
makan V to eat; ~ *dulu* said when eating first before others; ~ *malam* (eat or have) dinner; **makanan** N food; **memakan** V to eat, consume, take
makanya CONJ that's why, so → maka
makhluk, mahluk N creature
maki, mencaci-maki V to insult, abuse; **memaki, memaki-maki** V to insult, heap abuse on
makin ADV increasingly; ~ *lama*, ~ *besar* the longer, the bigger; **semakin** ADV even more
maklum V to know, be aware
makmur ADJ prosperous
makna N meaning
maknit, magnét N magnet
maksimal maximal(ly); **maksimum** N maximum
maksud N purpose, intention, meaning; **bermaksud** V to intend; **dimaksud(kan)** V to be meant or intended
mal, mol N shopping center, mall
malah, malahan instead, rather, on the other hand
Malaka, Melaka N Malacca
malam N night, evening; ~ *Jumat* Thursday night; *Jumat* ~ Friday night; **malam-malam** ADV late at night; **bermalam** V to spend or stay the night; **kemalaman** ADV too late (at night); after dark; **semalam** ADV last night
malang ADJ unlucky
malas ADJ lazy, can't be bothered; **bermalas-malas(an)** V to lie or laze around, be lazy
Malaysia N Malaysia; *bahasa* ~, *orang* ~ Malaysian
maling N thief
malu ADJ shy, ashamed, embarrassed; **malu-malu** ADJ shy; **kemaluan** N genital, sex organ; **memalukan** ADJ embarrassing
mam, mam-mam V, CH eat
mampet ADJ stuck, blocked, jammed
mampir V to drop in, call on
mampu ADJ able, capable; ADJ well-off; **kemampuan** N ability, capability
mana PRON where, which; ~ *saja* whichever; *dari* ~ from where; *di* ~

where; *ke* ~ where; **mana-mana** *di* ~, *ke* ~ everywhere
mancing → pancing
mancung ADJ straight (of noses)
mancur *air* ~ fountain → pancur
mandek, mandeg stop, cease, get stuck, stagnate
mandi bathe, take a bath, wash (the body); **memandikan** V to wash someone
manfaat N benefit, use; **bermanfaat** ADJ useful, of benefit; **memanfaatkan** V to take advantage of, (draw) benefit from
mangga N mango
manggis N mangosteen
mangkok, mangkuk N bowl
mangsa N prey
manik: manik-manik N beads
manis ADJ sweet; pretty; nice; **manisan** ~ sweets, candy; sugared snacks; **pemanis** ~ *buatan* artificial sweetener
manja spoilt; **memanjakan** V to spoil someone
mantan ADJ former (of people); ~ *Presiden* former President
mantap ADJ stable, steady
mantel N (long) coat, raincoat
mantu N son- or daughter-in-law; V to marry off a son or daughter → menantu
manula N old person, senior citizen → manusia lanjut usia
manusia N human (being); humanity
map N folder
mapan ADJ settled, comfortable
marah ADJ angry; **marah-marah** frequently angry; in a bad mood; **kemarahan** N anger; **memarahi** V to scold, be angry with
Maret *bulan* ~ March
marga N (Batak) family name
mari let's go, come on; please (said when someone begs leave); ~*lah* let us
marinir N Marines
markas N office, headquarters
markisa N kind of passionfruit
marmer N marble
marmot, marmut N guinea pig, marmot
Maroko, Marokko N Morocco

INDONESIAN—ENGLISH

martabak N large fried snack with filling

mas, emas N gold

Mas PRON, M address for elder brother, male person slightly older than yourself, or worker in service industry

masa N time, period

masa, masak no! I can't believe it! it's not possible (expression of disbelief)

masak cook; cooked; **masakan** N food, cooking, dish; **memasak** v to cook

masalah N problem; *~nya* the problem is; **bermasalah** ADJ problem, troublesome

masam, masem ADJ sour; acid

masih ADV still, yet

masing: masing-masing PRON each, respectively

masinis N train driver, engineer

masjid, mesjid N mosque

masker N surgical mask

massa N the masses, the public; **massal** ADJ mass

masuk v to come in, enter; **memasukkan** v to put in, insert, import, enter; **termasuk** ADJ including

masyarakat N society

mata N eye; **mata-mata** N spy

matahari N sun; *bunga ~* sunflower; *~ terbenam* sunset; *~ terbit* sunrise

mata-mata N spy → **mata**

matang ADJ ripe, cooked, mature

matématika N mathematics, maths

matéri N material; **matérial** ADJ material

mati die; go out, be extinguished; *~ lampu* blackout; **kematian** N death, passing; **mematikan** v to kill, extinguish, put out

mau v to want, will; **kemauan** N want, will, desire

maya *dunia ~* cyberspace

mayat N corpse

Mbak PRON, F address for elder sister, female person slightly older than yourself, or worker in service industry

Mbok PRON, F mother; address for female servants

mébel, meubel N furniture

medali, médali N medal

megah ADJ glorious, luxurious, grand

Méi *bulan ~* May

méja N table

Mekah, Mekkah N Mecca

mekar v to blossom

Méksiko N Mexico

melacak v to trace → **lacak**

melafalkan v to pronounce → **lafal**

melahirkan v to give birth to; to create → **lahir**

melainkan CONJ rather, instead

Melaka, Malaka N Malacca

melakukan v to do, perform, carry out → **laku**

melalui v to pass through; CONJ through, via → **lalu**

melamar v to apply → **lamar**

melambaikan v to wave something; *~ tangan* to wave goodbye → **lambai**

melambatkan v to slow down → **lambat**

melambung v to bounce → **lambung**

melampirkan v to attach, enclose

melamun v to day-dream, fantasize → **lamun**

melanggar v to disobey, offend → **langgar**

melangkah v to step → **langkah**

melanjutkan v to continue something → **lanjut**

melapor v to report; **melaporkan** v to report, inform → **lapor**

melarang v to ban, prohibit, forbid → **larang**

melarikan v to run off with, abduct, kidnap → **lari**

melati N jasmine

melatih v to train → **latih**

melawan v to oppose, resist → **lawan**

melayani v to serve → **layan**

melayat v to visit a house in mourning, to pay your respects → **layat**

Melayu Malay; Indonesian; *bahasa ~, orang ~* Malay

melébarkan v to widen → **lébar**

melebihi v to exceed, surpass → **lebih**

meledak v to explode → **ledak**

meledék N to tease, provoke → **ledék**

melégalisasi, melégalisir v to legalize → **légalisasi**

melék awake, eyes open

INDONESIAN–ENGLISH

melekat v to stick → lekat

melelahkan ADJ tiring → lelah

meléléh v to drip, run → léléh

melémpar v to throw → lémpar

meléncéng v to deviate, go out of your way → léncéng

melengkapi v to furnish, supply → lengkap

melepaskan v to release, let free → lepas

melését v to slip, skid; to miss the target → lését

meletakkan v to put in place, set down → letak

meletus v to erupt → letus

meléwati v to pass or go through → léwat

melibatkan v to involve, include → libat

melihat v to see, look; melihat-lihat v to look around, have a look → lihat

melindas v to run over, squash → lindas

melindungi v to protect, shelter → lindung

melingkari v to circle or surround → lingkar

melintang ADJ horizontal, across → lintang

melipat v to fold → lipat

meliputi v to include, cover → liput

melolong v to howl (of dogs) → lolong

melompat v to jump, leapfrog → lompat

mélon N rockmelon, cantaloupe

meloncat v to spring, jump (over something) → loncat

melontar, melontarkan v to throw → lontar

melotot v to stare or gape at, with bulging eyes → lotot

meluap v to overflow, swell, wash → luap

meludah v to spit → ludah

melukai, melukakan v to hurt or wound → luka

melukis v to paint, draw → lukis

meluncurkan v to launch, set in motion → luncur

melupakan v to forget something → lupa

memaafkan v to forgive, pardon → maaf

memadukan v to combine, unite → padu

memahami v to understand, comprehend → paham

memahat v to sculpt, chisel → pahat

memainkan v to play something → main

memakai v to wear; to use → pakai

memakamkan v to bury → makam

memakan v to eat, consume, take → makan

memaki, memaki-maki v to insult, heap abuse on → maki

memaksa v to force → paksa

memalsukan v to falsify, forge → palsu

memalukan ADJ embarrassing → malu

memanaskan v to heat (up) → panas

memancing v to fish (with hook and line) → pancing

memandang v to view, consider → pandang

memandikan v to wash someone → mandi

memandu v to guide → pandu

mémang CONJ émang COLL indeed

memanggang v to roast, bake, toast → panggang

memanggil v to call → panggil

memanjakan v to spoil someone → manja

memanjat v to climb

memantau v to observe, watch → pantau

memar ADJ bruised

memarahi v to scold, be angry with → marah

memasak v to cook → masak

memasang v to put up, attach, fix → pasang

memastikan v to confirm, make sure, ascertain → pasti

memasukkan v to put in, insert, import, enter → masuk

mematahkan v to break → patah

mematikan v to kill, extinguish, put out → mati

mematuhi v to obey → patuh

INDONESIAN—ENGLISH

M

membaca v to read → baca
membagi v to divide, distribute → bagi
membahas v to discuss, debate → bahas
membaik v to improve → baik
membajak v to hijack; to copy illegally → bajak
membajak v to plough → bajak
membakar v to burn → bakar
membalap v to race → balap
membalas v to reply, respond → balas
membalik v to return, reverse, turn over; **membalikkan** v to turn something over → balik
membandingkan v to compare something → banding
membangun v to build or create
membangunkan v to wake someone up → bangun
membantah v to deny, dispute → bantah
membantai v to slaughter, kill viciously → bantai
membanting v to throw down (with a bang) → banting
membantu v to help (someone) → bantu
membasahi v to moisten, wet → basah
membatalkan v to cancel, repeal → batal
membatik N to apply wax onto fabric → batik
membawa v to take, bring, carry; conduct → bawa
membayar v to pay → bayar
membédakan v to discriminate, differentiate between, consider as different → béda
membeku v to freeze → beku
membéla v to defend → béla
membelah v to split in two → belah
membeli v to buy, purchase → beli
membélok v to bend, turn → bélok
membenarkan v to confirm, verify; justify → benar
membenci v to hate → benci
membentuk v to form, set up something (eg. committee) → bentuk
memberantas v to wipe out, fight against → berantas

memberéskan v to clear up, make ready → bérés
memberhentikan v to stop (a vehicle); dismiss
memberi v to give → beri
memberitahu v to advise, inform, tell → beri tahu
memberitakan v to report → berita
memberontak v to rebel, revolt → berontak
membersihkan v to clean; wipe out (eg. disease) → bersih
membesarkan v to bring up, raise (children) → besar
membetulkan v to correct, repair → betul
membiarkan v to let, allow, permit → biar
membicarakan v to discuss → bicara
membilas v to rinse → bilas
membimbing v to lead, guide, coach → bimbing
membina v to build up, found → bina
membingungkan ADJ confusing → bingung
membintangi v to star (in) → bintang
membisik v to whisper → bisik
membius v to drug, anesthetize → bius
memblokir v to block → blokir
membocorkan v to leak something → bocor
membohong v to lie → bohong
memboikot v to boycott something → boikot
membolos v skip, be absent, play truant, wag, skive → bolos
membongkar v to pull apart, dismantle; to unpack; to unearth → bongkar
memborong v to buy up, buy in bulk → borong
membosankan ADJ boring, tiresome → bosan
membuang v to throw out; to waste; to exile → buang
membuat v to make → buat
membubarkan v to break something up → bubar
membujuk v to coax → bujuk

INDONESIAN–ENGLISH

M

membuka v to open → buka
membuktikan v to prove → bukti
membumihanguskan v to conduct a searched-earth policy
membungkus v to wrap; ~ *kado* wrap a gift → bungkus
membunuh v to kill → bunuh
membunyikan v to sound, ring something → bunyi
memburu v to hunt, chase → buru
membutuhkan v to need something → butuh
memecah ~ *belah* to break into fragments, cause division; **memecahkan** v to break; to solve → pecah
memecat v to fire, dismiss → pecat
memedulikan v to care or be bothered about → peduli
memegang v to hold, grasp → pegang
memelésétkan v to up-end, send off-course; change → pelését
memelihara v to take care of, look after, cultivate → pelihara
memeluk v to hug or embrace → peluk
memencét v to press (a button, key) → pencét
memengaruhi v to influence, affect → pengaruh
memenjara, memenjarakan v to put in prison, imprison → penjara
meménsiunkan v to pension off → pénsiun
mementingkan v to make important, emphasize → penting
memenuhi v to fulfill, meet requirements → penuh
memerankan v to portray, play the role of → peran
memeras v to squeeze, press; to blackmail, extort → peras
memercayai v to trust someone; **memercayakan** v to entrust with → percaya
memeriahkan v to liven up, enliven → meriah
memeriksa v to examine or investigate → periksa
memerkosa v to rape → perkosa
memerlukan v to need, require → perlu

memesan v to order → pesan
memetik v to pick; to strum → petik
memfokuskan v to focus something → fokus
memicu v to trigger, set off → picu
memijat v to massage → pijat
memikirkan v to think about → pikir
memilih v to choose or select; to elect or vote (for) → pilih
memiliki v to own, possess → milik
memimpikan v to dream of → mimpi
memimpin v to lead → pimpin
memindahkan v to move, transfer → pindah
meminjam v to borrow; **meminjami** v to lend someone; **meminjamkan** v to lend something → pinjam
meminta v to ask for, request; **meminta-minta** v to beg, ask for money → minta, pinta
memisahkan v to separate something → pisah
memompa v to pump → pompa
memotong v to cut, deduct; to slaughter, amputate; to interrupt → potong
memotrét v to photograph → potrét
mempelai ~ *pria* groom; ~ *wanita* bride
mempelajari v to study something in depth → ajar
memperbaiki v to repair, fix → baik
memperbesar v to enlarge something → besar
memperboléhkan v to allow, permit → boléh
mempercepat v to speed up, accelerate → cepat
memperhatikan v to notice, pay attention to → hati
memperingati v to commemorate → ingat
memperkenalkan v to introduce → kenal
memperkirakan v to estimate, calculate → kira
memperoléh v to obtain, get → oléh
memperpanjang v to extend, make longer → panjang
mempersatukan v to unite various things → satu
mempersembahkan v to offer (up), present → sembah

INDONESIAN–ENGLISH

M

mempersiapkan v to prepare something, get something ready → **siap**
mempersilakan v to invite someone to do something → **sila**
mempersoalkan v to question, discuss → **soal**
mempertahankan v to defend or maintain → **tahan**
mempertanggungjawabkan v to account for → **tanggung jawab**
mempertanyakan v to query → **tanya**
mempertimbangkan v to consider → **timbang**
mempraktékkan v to put into practice → **prakték**
memprihatinkan ADJ worrying → **prihatin**
memprioritaskan v to prioritize → **prioritas**
memproduksi v to produce → **produksi**
mempromosikan v to promote → **promosi**
memprotés v to (make a) protest → **protés**
mempunyai v to have, own, possess → **punya**
memuaskan ADJ satisfactory → **puas**
memuat v to contain → **muat**
memuja v to worship → **puja**
memuji v to praise
memukul v to hit, beat, strike → **pukul**
memulai v to start or begin something → **mula, mulai**
memulangkan v to give back; to send back, repatriate → **pulang**
memungkinkan ADJ conducive; v to enable, make possible → **mungkin**
memungut v to pick up, collect → **pungut**
memusatkan v to focus → **pusat**
memusuhi v to fight against, antagonize, make an enemy of → **musuh**
memutar v to wind; to rotate; **perputaran** N rotation → **putar**
memutuskan v to terminate or break; to decide → **putus**
menabrak v to collide with → **tabrak**
menabuh v to beat (a drum) → **tabuh**

menabung v to save or deposit money → **tabung**
menahan v to bear, endure; to detain → **tahan**
menaiki v to ride, mount, get on; **menaikkan** v to raise, hoist → **naik**
menakutkan v, ADV frightening; to frighten or scare → **takut**
menambah v to add to or increase; **menambahi** v to increase something; **menambahkan** v to add something to → **tambah**
menambal v to mend, patch, darn → **tambal**
menampar v to slap → **tampar**
menanam v to plant or grow; to invest → **tanam**
menandai v to mark → **tanda**
menandatangani v to sign something → **tanda tangan**
menang v to win; **kemenangan** N victory; **pemenang** N winner, victor
menangani v to handle → **tangan**
menanggapi v to respond, reply → **tanggap**
menanggung v to guarantee, be responsible → **tanggung**
menangis v to cry → **tangis**
menangkap v to catch, capture → **tangkap**
menanjak ADJ rising, climbing, steep → **tanjak**
menantang v to challenge; ADJ challenging → **tantang**
menanti-nanti v to wait for a long time; **menantikan** v to wait for → **nanti**
menantu N son- or daughter-in-law → **mantu**
menanyakan v to ask about → **tanya**
menara N tower; minaret (of a mosque)
menari v to dance, perform a traditional dance; **menari-nari** v to dance about → **tari**
menarik v to pull or draw; ADJ interesting, attractive → **tarik**
menaruh v to put (away) → **taruh**
menasihati v to advise → **nasihat**
menawar v to bargain; **menawarkan** v to offer or bid → **tawar**
mencabut v to pull out, remove → **cabut**

INDONESIAN–ENGLISH

M

mencair v to melt, turn into liquid → cair

mencakar v to scratch → cakar

mencalonkan v to nominate someone → calon

mencambuk v to whip → cambuk

mencampuradukkan v to mix up, confuse → campur

mencapai v to reach, attain → capai

mencari v look or search for, seek; mencari-cari v to search repeatedly, everywhere → cari

mencatat v to note (down) → catat

mencegah v to prevent, fight against → cegah

mencekik v to strangle → cekik

mencemari v to dirty, pollute → cemar

mencengkeram v to grip, squeeze → cengkeram

mencerai, menceraikan v to divorce someone → cerai

menceritakan v to describe, relate → cerita

mencerminkan v to reflect → cermin

mencerna v to digest → cerna

mencétak v to print → cétak

mencicil v to pay by instalments → cicil

mencicipi v to try, taste something → cicip

mencintai v to love someone → cinta

mencipta, menciptakan v to create, make → cipta

mencium v to smell; to kiss → cium

mencoba v to try, attempt → coba

mencoblos v to vote, pierce → coblos

mencocokkan v to match → cocok

mencopét v to pick someone's pocket → copét

mencorét v to scratch, cross out → corét

méncrét v to have diarrhea

mencubit v to pinch → cubit

mencuci v to wash, clean → cuci

mencukur v to shave → cukur

menculik v to kidnap → culik

mencuri v to steal → curi

mencurigakan ADJ suspicious, suspect → curiga

mendadak ADJ sudden → dadak

mendaftar v to register; mendaftarkan v to register something → daftar

mendahului v to precede, overtake → dahulu

mendaki v to climb, ascend; ~ *gunung* (to go) mountaineering, bushwalking → daki

mendalam ADJ deep → dalam

mendalangi v to orchestrate (events) → dalang

mendamaikan v to reconcile, pacify → damai

mendampingi v to accompany, flank → damping

mendandani v to decorate, dress, adorn → dandan

mendapat v to obtain, receive; mendapatkan v to obtain; discover → dapat

mendarat v to land → darat

mendatang ADJ coming, next; mendatangkan v to bring, import → datang

mendatarkan v to make flat, level → datar

mendaur-ulang v to recycle → daur ulang

mendayung v to stroke (an oar), row; to pedal → dayung

mendébet v to debit → débet

mendekati v to approach → dekat

mendémo v to protest against → démo

mendenda v to fine → denda

mendengar v to hear; mendengarkan v to listen → dengar

mendengkur v to snore; to purr (of a cat) → dengkur

menderita v to suffer, endure → derita

mendesak ADJ pressing, urgent; v to press, urge, push → desak

mendidih ADJ boiling → didih

mendidik v to educate, bring up, teach → didik

mending, mendingan ADJ, COLL better, better off

mendirikan v to build, establish, erect → diri

mendiskriminasi, mendiskriminasikan v to discriminate against → diskriminasi

INDONESIAN—ENGLISH

mendoakan v to pray for → doa

mendorong v to push, encourage → dorong

menduduki v to sit on something; to occupy → duduk

mendukung v to support → dukung

mendung ADJ cloudy, overcast

menebak v to guess → tebak

menebang v to fell, cut down → tebang

menegakkan v to erect; to uphold or maintain → tegak

menegangkan ADJ tense, stressful → tegang

menegaskan v to clarify, point out, affirm → tegas

meneguk v to gulp or guzzle → teguk

menegur v to speak to, address; to warn, rebuke, tell off → tegur

menekan v to press; **menekankan** v to stress, emphasize → tekan

menelan v to swallow something → telan

menélépon v to ring (up), call, (tele)phone → télépon

menemani v to accompany → teman

menémbak v to shoot → témbak

menembus v to pierce, stab → tembus

menempati v to occupy, take a place → tempat

menémpél v to stick or adhere to; **menémpélkan** v to stick, paste or glue something → témpél

menempuh v to endure, go through; to take on, take up → tempuh

menemui v to meet up with, arrange to meet; **menemukan** v to discover → temu

menenangkan v to calm someone (down) → tenang

menendang v to kick → tendang

menengah ADJ intermediate → tengah

menéngok v to look or see; to look in on someone → téngok

menentang v to oppose, resist → tentang

menénténg v to carry dangling from the hand → ténténg

menentukan v to decide, determine, stipulate → tentu

menenun v to weave → tenun

menerangkan v to explain → terang

menerapkan v to apply something → terap

menerbangkan v to fly something → terbang

menerbitkan v to publish, issue → terbit

menerima v to receive, accept → terima

menerjemahkan v to translate (writing); to interpret (speaking) → terjemah

menertawakan v to laugh at → tawa

menertibkan v to keep order, discipline → tertib

meneruskan v to continue, keep doing something → terus

menetap v to stay; **menetapkan** v to appoint, fix, stipulate → tetap

menéwaskan v to kill someone → téwas

mengacaukan v to mix or mess up → kacau

mengadakan v to create, organize, make available; ~ *kampanye* to run a campaign → ada

mengadu v to complain, report → adu

mengaduk v to stir, mix → aduk

mengagumi v to admire → kagum

mengaitkan v to link, connect, join → kait

mengajak v to invite, ask out; to urge; ~ *jalan-jalan* to ask out; ~ *kawin*, ~ *nikah* to ask someone to marry you → ajak

mengajar v to teach; **mengajari** v to teach someone → ajar

mengaji v to recite or read the Koran → kaji

mengakhiri v to end, finish something → akhir

mengaku v to admit, confess, acknowledge; to claim; ~ *salah* to admit guilt → aku

mengalahkan v to conquer, defeat → kalah

mengalami v to experience → alam

mengalir v to flow → alir

mengamankan v to make safe, restore order; to place in custody → aman

M

INDONESIAN–ENGLISH

M

mengambil v to take, get, fetch → **ambil**

mengamén v ngamén coll to sing in the street for money, busk → **amén**

mengamuk v to run amok, go berserk → **amuk**

mengancam v to threaten, intimidate → **ancam**

mengandung v to contain, carry; to be pregnant → **kandung**

mengangguk v to nod → **angguk**

mengangkat v to lift or pick up, raise; to appoint; to remove, amputate → **angkat**

menganjurkan v to suggest, propose → **anjur**

mengantar v to take, escort, accompany; **mengantarkan** v to take someone or something → **antar**

mengantri v to queue → **antré, antri**

mengantuk ADJ sleepy → **kantuk**

menganut v to follow → **anut**

menganyam v to weave, plait, braid → **anyam**

mengapa why → **apa**

mengapung v to float, be suspended → **apung**

mengarang v to write, compose → **karang**

mengatakan v to say → **kata**

mengatasi v to overcome → **atas**

mengatur v to arrange, organize, regulate → **atur**

mengawasi v to supervise → **awas**

mengawinkan ~ *anak* to marry off a son or daughter → **kawin**

mengayuh v to paddle or pedal something; ~ *sepeda* to ride a bicycle → **kayuh**

mengebom v to bomb something → **bom**

mengecap v to brand → **cap**

mengecas v to charge (electrical equipment) → **cas, charge**

mengecat v to paint, dye → **cat**

mengecék v to check, confirm → **cék**

mengecéwakan v to disappoint; ADJ disappointing → **kecéwa**

mengecilkan v to make smaller, decrease → **kecil**

mengéjék v to tease, mock, ridicule → **éjék**

mengejutkan ADJ surprising, startling; v to surprise or startle → **kejut**

mengékspor v to export → **ékspor**

mengelap v to wipe, mop → **lap**

mengelas v to weld → **las**

mengelilingi v to circle, go around → **keliling**

mengelola v to manage, run → **kelola**

mengeluarkan v to issue, send out, release → **keluar**

mengeluh v to complain → **keluh**

mengelupas v to peel, come off (of a skin) → **kelupas**

mengelus v to caress, stroke or pat (an animal) → **elus**

mengembalikan v to give or send back, return → **kembali**

mengembangkan v to develop something → **kembang**

mengemis v to beg → **emis, kemis**

mengemudikan v to drive, steer → **kemudi**

mengemut v to suck on (sweets etc) → **emut, kemut**

mengenai CONJ about, over, on, concerning → **kena**

mengenal v to know, be acquainted with, recognize; **memperkenalkan** v to introduce → **kenal**

mengencangkan v to tighten → **kencang**

mengendalikan v to control → **kendali**

mengepak v to pack → **pak**

mengepél v to mop (up) → **pél**

mengeraskan v to make something harder, louder → **keras**

mengerém v to brake → **rém**

mengerikan ADJ terrifying, horrifying → **ngeri**

mengeringkan v to dry something → **kering**

mengerjakan v to do, carry out → **kerja**

mengeroyok v to beat savagely in a mob → **keroyok**

mengerti v to understand; **dimengerti** v to be understood; **pengertian** N understanding → **arti**

mengesahkan v to validate, ratify, legitimize, legalize → **sah**

mengesankan ADJ impressive → **kesan**

INDONESIAN–ENGLISH

mengetahui v to know something, have knowledge of → **tahu**

mengetik v to type → **ketik**

mengetuk v to knock → **ketuk**

menggabungkan v to connect, combine, fuse → **gabung**

menggadaikan v to pawn something → **gadai**

menggaji v to pay, remunerate, employ → **gaji**

menggali v to dig → **gali**

menggambar v to draw, depict; **menggambarkan** v to describe, illustrate → **gambar**

mengganggu v to bother, disturb → **ganggu**

mengganti v to change, substitute, replace; **menggantikan** v to substitute or replace someone/something → **ganti**

menggantung v to hang, suspend → **gantung**

menggaruk v to scratch, scrape → **garuk**

menggelar, menggelarkan v to hold (an event) → **gelar**

menggéléng to shake your head → **géléng**

menggelikan ADJ funny, comic; off-putting → **geli**

menggelitik v to tickle → **gelitik**

menggembirakan ADJ exciting, happy → **gembira**

menggembok v to padlock → **gembok**

menggenggam v to grip, grasp → **genggam**

menggerakkan v to move, shift something → **gerak**

menggésék v to rub, scrape → **gésék**

menggésér v to move aside or over → **gésér**

menggigil v to shiver → **gigil**

menggigit v to bite → **gigit**

menggoda v to tempt → **goda**

menggoncangkan v to rock or make something move → **goncang**

menggoréng v to fry → **goréng**

menggorés v to scratch, make a stroke → **gorés**

menggosok v to rub, polish → **gosok**

menggotong v to carry together → **gotong**

menggoyangkan v to shake or rock something → **goyang**

menggugat v to sue, accuse → **gugat**

menggunakan v to use → **guna**

mengguncangkan v to rock or make something move → **guncang**

menggunting v to cut (out) → **gunting**

menggusur v to evict, sweep aside, forcibly remove → **gusur**

menghabiskan v to finish, use up, spend → **habis**

menghadap v to face, appear before; **menghadapi** v to face someone or something → **hadap**

menghadiri v to attend → **hadir**

menghafalkan v to learn by heart → **hafal**

menghambat v to obstruct, impede, hamper → **hambat**

menghancurkan v to smash, crush, destroy → **hancur**

mengharapkan v to expect → **harap**

menghargai v to appreciate → **harga**

mengharukan ADJ moved, touched (emotionally) → **haru**

menghasilkan v to produce → **hasil**

menghéla v to draw, drag → **héla**

menghémat v to save on or economize → **hémat**

menghembus v to blow → **hembus**

menghendaki v to want → **hendak**

menghentikan v to stop something → **henti**

menghérankan ADJ astonishing, astounding → **héran**

menghiasi v to adorn, decorate something → **hias**

menghibur v to entertain; to comfort, console → **hibur**

menghidupkan v to bring to life, start or turn on (a device) → **hidup**

menghilang v to disappear, vanish; **menghilangkan** v to remove → **hilang**

menghinakan v to humiliate, insult → **hina**

menghindar v to steer clear, avoid; **menghindari** v to avoid something → **hindar**

menghirup v to breathe in → **hirup**

INDONESIAN–ENGLISH

M

menghitung v to count, calculate, reckon; **menghitungkan** v to count or calculate something → hitung

menghormat, menghormati v to honor or respect

menghubungi v to contact someone; **menghubungkan** v to connect, join, link different parts → hubung

menghukum v to punish, sentence, condemn → hukum

mengidam v to crave (esp of pregnant woman) → idam

mengijinkan v to permit, allow → ijin, izin

mengikat v to tie, fasten → ikat

mengikut v to follow, accompany; **mengikuti** v to follow, join, participate in → ikut

mengimpor v to import → impor

menginap v to stay the night, stay over → inap

mengingat v to remember, bear in mind; **mengingatkan** v to remind someone about something → ingat

menginjak v to step, tread, or stamp on → injak

menginterviu v to interview → interviu

mengintip v to peep at, spy on → intip

mengira v to assume, think → kira

mengirim v to send → kirim

mengisap v to suck; to smoke → isap

mengisi v to fill, load → isi

mengizinkan v to permit, allow → izin, ijin

mengkhianati v to betray someone → khianat

mengkilap v to shine, gleam → kilap

mengobati v to treat, cure → obat

mengobral v to put on sale → obral

mengobrol v to chat → obrol

mengolés v to grease, spread, lubricate; **mengoléskan** v to smear with something → olés

mengomél v to complain, grumble, whinge, whine → omél

mengompol v to wet your pants, the bed → ompol

mengorbankan v to sacrifice → korban

mengorék v to scrape, scratch

mengoréksi v to correct → koréksi

mengosongkan v to empty → kosong

menguap v to yawn → kuap

menguasai v to control, have power over → kuasa

menguatirkan v to worry about something → kuatir

mengubah v to change or alter → ubah

menguburkan v to bury → kubur

mengucap, mengucapkan v to say or express something → ucap

menguji v to examine or test → uji

mengukir v to carve or engrave → ukir

mengukur v to measure → ukur

mengukus v to steam (food) → kukus

mengulang v to repeat, do again; **mengulangi** v to repeat something → ulang

mengumpat v to curse, swear → umpat

mengumpet v to hide or conceal yourself → umpet

mengumpulkan v to collect, gather → kumpul

mengumumkan v to announce or declare → umum

mengunci v to lock (up) → kunci

mengundang v to invite (formally) → undang

mengundi v to conduct a draw or lottery → undi

mengundurkan v to postpone → undur

mengungkap v to uncover; **mengungkapkan** v to express → ungkap

mengungsi v to evacuate or flee → ungsi

mengunjungi v to visit a place → kunjung

menguntungkan v to profit; ADJ profitable → untung

mengupas v to peel; to analyze → kupas

menguping v to eavesdrop, listen in → kuping

mengurangi v to take from, subtract, minus → kurang

INDONESIAN–ENGLISH

M

mengurung v to cage, put in a cage, lock up → **kurung**

mengurus v to arrange, organize, manage → **urus**

mengurut v to massage → **urut**

mengusahakan v to try, endeavor to → **usaha**

mengusir v to drive away or out, chase away, expel → **usir**

mengusulkan v to propose or suggest → **usul**

mengutak-atik, mengutak-ngatik-kan v to work on or tinker with → **kutak, utak-atik**

mengutamakan v to give preference or priority to → **utama**

mengutip v to quote, cite an extract → **kutip**

mengutuk v to curse → **kutuk**

menidurkan v to put to sleep → **tidur**

menikah v to marry, get married; **menikahi** v to marry someone → **nikah**

menikam v to stab → **tikam**

menikmati v to enjoy → **nikmat**

menilai v to evaluate, appraise

menimbulkan v to give rise, bring to the surface → **timbul**

menindaklanjuti v to take a step or measure → **tindak lanjut**

meninggal ~ *(dunia)* to die; **meninggalkan** v to leave (behind), abandon → **tinggal**

meningkat v to rise, increase, improve; **meningkatkan** v to increase or raise the level of something → **tingkat**

meninjau v to observe, view → **tinjau**

menipu v to trick, deceive → **tipu**

meniru v to copy or imitate → **tiru**

menit N minute

menitip v to leave in someone's care, entrust → **titip**

meniup v to blow → **tiup**

menjadi v to be or become → **jadi**

menjaga v to guard, keep watch → **jaga**

menjahit v to sew → **jahit**

menjajah v to colonize, rule another country → **jajah**

menjalankan v to operate, run, set in motion → **jalan**

menjalin v to forge links, network → **jalin**

menjamin v to guarantee, promise → **jamin**

menjanjikan v to promise something → **janji**

menjaring v to fish with a net; to filter or sift → **jaring**

menjatuhkan v to fell, let drop → **jatuh**

menjawab v to answer, reply → **jawab**

menjebak v to trap → **jebak**

menjelajahi v to travel through or explore a place → **jelajah**

menjelang v to approach (usu time) → **jelang**

menjelaskan ADJ to explain, clarify → **jelas**

menjemput v to pick up → **jemput**

menjemur v to air, dry in the sun → **jemur**

menjeprét v to snap, staple → **jeprét**

menjerit v to scream, shriek → **jerit**

menjijikkan ADJ disgusting, revolting, foul → **jijik**

menjilat v to lick; SL to suck up, flatter → **jilat**

menjodohkan v to set up, match → **jodoh**

menjual v to sell → **jual**

menodong v to threaten or hold up at knifepoint → **todong**

menolak v to refuse, reject → **tolak**

menolong v to help or assist → **tolong**

menonjok v to punch, hit → **tonjok**

menonjol v to stick out, protrude; ADJ prominent → **tonjol**

menonton v to watch, look on → **tonton**

méns COLL period, menstruation

mensukséskan v to make something succeed → **suksés**

mensyukuri v to appreciate, be thankful → **syukur**

mentah ADJ raw, uncooked, not ripe

méntal, méntalitas N way of thinking, mentality

mentéga N butter

menteri N minister; **kementerian** N ministry, department, office

INDONESIAN–ENGLISH

M

mentimun, timun N cucumber

mentraktir v to invite out, shout, treat, pay for another → **traktir**

menuding v to accuse, point the finger → **tuding**

menuduh v to accuse → **tuduh**

menugaskan v to assign someone, give a task to → **tugas**

menuju v to approach, go towards → **tuju**

menukar v to change; **menukarkan** v to change something → **tukar**

menular v to infect; ADJ contagious, infectious → **tular**

menulis v to write → **tulis**

menumpahkan v to spill something → **tumpah**

menumpang v to make use of someone else's facilities; to get a lift or ride → **tumpang**

menunda v to delay, put off, postpone; **menundakan** v to delay or postpone something → **tunda**

menunduk v to bow your head; **menundukkan** v to bow or lower something; to defeat → **tunduk**

menunggang v to ride → **tunggang**

menunggu v to wait for something; **menunggu-nunggu** v to wait a long time for → **tunggu**

menunjuk v to indicate, point out, refer to; **menunjukkan** v to show, point out → **tunjuk**

menuntut v to claim or demand → **tuntut**

menurun v to fall, drop, decline; **menurunkan** v to lower or reduce → **turun**

menurut CONJ according to → **turut**

menutup v to close or shut; **menutupi** v to cover (up) → **tutup**

menyadari v to realize, be aware of → **sadar**

menyahut v to answer, reply, respond → **sahut**

menyajikan v to serve, present, offer → **saji**

menyakiti v to hurt, treat badly; **menyakitkan** ADJ painful → **sakit**

menyaksikan v to witness → **saksi**

menyala v to burn, blaze; **menyalakan** v to light, set fire to → **nyala**

menyalami v to greet → **salam**

menyalin v to copy → **salin**

menyalip v overtake, slip past → **salip**

menyamar v to be in disguise → **samar**

menyambung v to join, continue; **menyambungkan** v to connect to (something else) → **sambung**

menyambut v to welcome or receive → **sambut**

menyampaikan v to deliver, hand over, pass on → **sampai**

menyandar v to lean → **sandar**

menyangka v to suspect, suppose, presume; *tidak* ~ never thought → **sangka**

menyanyi v to sing; **menyanyikan** v to sing something → **nyanyi**

menyapu v to sweep or wipe → **sapu**

menyarankan v to suggest → **saran**

menyatakan v to declare, state, certify → **nyata**

menyatukan v to unite various things → **satu**

menyayangi v to love → **sayang**

menyebabkan v to cause → **sebab**

menyebalkan ADJ annoying, tiresome → **sebal**

menyebarkan v to spread something → **sebar**

menyeberang v to cross → **seberang**

menyebut v to mention, name, say → **sebut**

menyediakan v to prepare, get ready → **sedia**

menyedihkan ADJ depressing, sad → **sedih**

menyedot v to suck (up) → **sedot**

menyegarkan ADJ refreshing → **segar**

menyelam v to dive → **selam**

menyelamatkan v to save, rescue → **selamat**

menyelenggarakan v to run, hold, organize → **selenggara**

menyelesaikan v to finish, end, settle → **selesai**

menyelidiki v to investigate → **selidik**

menyelundupkan v to smuggle (in) → **selundup**

menyembah v to pay homage to, worship → **sembah**

INDONESIAN–ENGLISH

menyembelih v to slaughter, butcher → **sembelih**

menyembuhkan v to cure, heal → **sembuh**

menyembunyikan v to hide or conceal something → **sembunyi**

menyempit v to (become) narrow → **sempit**

menyemprot v to spray; **menyemprotkan** v to spray with something → **semprot**

menyenangkan ADJ pleasing, agreeable → **senang**

menyengat v to sting → **sengat**

menyénggol v to bump, brush, tweak → **sénggol**

menyentuh v to touch → **sentuh**

menyépak v to kick (out) → **sépak**

menyepakati v to agree to → **sepakat, pakat**

menyerah v to surrender, give in, give up; **menyerahkan** v to hand over → **serah**

menyerang v to attack → **serang**

menyerap v to absorb, soak up → **serap**

menyérét v to drag → **sérét**

menyerobot v to push in front → **serobot**

menyesal v to regret; **menyesalkan** v to feel bad about, regret (another's action) → **sesal**

menyesatkan ADJ misleading, confusing → **sesat**

menyesuaikan v to adapt, bring into line → **sesuai**

menyetél v to tune, set, adjust → **setél**

menyetir v to drive → **setir**

menyetor v to pay in, deposit → **setor**

menyetrika v to iron → **setrika**

menyetujui v to agree to, approve, ratify → **tubuh, setubuh**

menyéwa v to rent, hire; **menyéwakan** v to let (a house), hire out, lease → **séwa**

menyiapkan v to prepare something, get something ready → **siap**

menyikat v to brush → **sikat**

menyiksa v to torture → **siksa**

menyimpan v to keep, save up, store → **simpan**

menyimpulkan v to conclude or summarize → **simpul**

menyindir v to insinuate, allude → **sindir**

menyinggung v to touch on → **singgung**

menyingkatkan v to abbreviate, shorten → **singkat**

menyingkirkan v to remove, brush aside → **singkir**

menyiram v to pour, water (plants) → **siram**

menyisir v to comb, check thoroughly → **sisir**

menyobék v to tear off → **sobék**

menyogok v to bribe → **sogok**

menyonték v to copy, cheat → **conték, sonték**

menyoroti v to light up, illuminate, focus on → **sorot**

menyuap v to feed by hand; to bribe → **suap**

menyucikan v to purify, cleanse → **suci**

menyudutkan v to push into a corner, deflect → **sudut**

menyukai v to like → **suka**

menyulam v to embroider → **sulam**

menyulap v to conjure up; to make something vanish or change → **sulap**

menyumbang v to contribute, make a donation → **sumbang**

menyumbat v to plug, stop → **sumbat**

menyunatkan v to have someone circumcised → **sunat**

menyuntik v to inject or vaccinate → **suntik**

menyupir v to drive → **supir**

menyurati v to write a letter to → **surat**

menyuruh v to command, order → **suruh**

menyusahkan v to bother, make difficult → **susah**

menyusui v to feed → **susu**

menyusul v to follow, go after → **susul**

menyusun v to heap or pile; to arrange, organize, compile → **susun**

mépét ADJ tight, squeezed

INDONESIAN–ENGLISH

M

meraba v to feel or grope something → raba

meracuni v to poison → racun

meradang v to become inflamed → radang

meragukan v to doubt something → ragu

mérah ADJ red; ~ *jambu* pink

merahasiakan v to keep secret → rahasia

merajut v to knit; to crochet → rajut

merak N peacock

merakit v to assemble → rakit

meralat v to correct a mistake → ralat

meramaikan v to liven up, enliven → ramai

meramal v to tell fortunes; meramalkan v to predict, foretell → ramal

merampok v to rob, hold up → rampok

merancang v to plan, design → rancang

merangkak v to crawl → rangkak

merantai v to chain up → rantai

merasa v to think, feel; merasakan v to feel something → rasa

meratakan v to level, flatten → rata

merawat v to nurse, care for; to maintain, look after → rawat

merayakan v to celebrate → raya

merayap v to crawl, creep → rayap

merayu v to tempt, flatter, seduce → rayu

mercon N fireworks

mercu ~ *suar* lighthouse

merdéka ADJ free, independent; kemerdékaan N freedom, independence, liberty

merdu ADJ sweet, melodious, honeyed

merebus v to boil (in) water → rebus

merebut v to snatch, capture; merebutkan v to snatch something → rebut

mérek N brand, label (clothes), make (vehicle); bermérek v to have a label, branded

meréka PRON, PL they, them, their; ~ *punya* theirs

merekam v to record → rekam

merekrut v to recruit → rekrut

merem be asleep, eyes shut

merembes v to seep in, leak, ooze → rembes

meréméhkan v to belittle, treat as unimportant → réméh

merencanakan v to plan → rencana

merendahkan v to lower; to humiliate → rendah

meréngék v to whimper, whine → réngék

merenggut v to snatch, tug → renggut

merenung v to daydream → renung

merépotkan v to make someone busy or go to some trouble → répot

meresap v to be absorbed, penetrate, seep into → resap

meresépkan v to write a prescription for a drug → resép

meresmikan v to formalize, make official → resmi

merestui v to agree to, give your blessing to → restu

meriah ADJ merry, lively; memeriahkan v to liven up, enliven

meriam N cannon

merica N pepper

merinding v to have goose-bumps or an eerie feeling, be spooked → rinding

merindukan v to miss, long for → rindu

mérk → mérek

merobék v to tear up, shred → robék

merokok v to smoke → rokok

merombak v to pull down, demolish; to reorganize → rombak

merosot v to fall down, descend, plummet → rosot

merpati N pigeon, dove

mertua N parents-in-law

merubah → mengubah

merugikan v to hurt, harm, injure → rugi

meruntuhkan v to destroy overthrow → runtuh

merupakan v to be, form, constitute → rupa

merusak v to spoil, damage; merusakkan v to level, break → rusak

méses N chocolate sprinkles

mesin N machine, engine

INDONESIAN—ENGLISH

mesjid, masjid N mosque
meski, meskipun CONJ although, even though
mesra ADJ intimate, close
mesti, musti V, AUX should; ~*nya* should; *semestinya* should have (been)
méter N meter; metre; **méteran** N tape measure
meterai, méterai N seal
métode N method
méwah N luxurious; **keméwahan** N luxury
mewakili V to represent → **wakil**
mewarisi V to inherit → **waris**
mewarnai V to color (in) → **warna**
mewawancarai V to interview → **wawancara**
mewujudkan V to make something real, realize something → **wujud**
meyakini V to convince someone; **meyakinkan** ADJ convincing, believable → **yakin**
mi, mie N noodles; ~ *goreng* fried noodles
migrasi N migration
migrén N migraine
mik, mikrofon N microphone, mike
mili, miliméter N millimeter
miliar, milyar N billion → **milyar**
milik N property, possession; **memiliki** V to own, possess; **pemilik** N owner
milis N mail list
militér N military
milyar, miliar N billion; **milyarder** N billionaire
mimbar N pulpit, platform, forum
mimisan nose bleed, blood nose
mimpi dream; **bermimpi** V to dream; **memimpikan** V to dream of → **impi**
min → **minus**
minal aidin (wal faidzin) greeting at Idul Fitri
Minang, Minangkabau ethnic group of West Sumatra
minder to lack confidence, low self-esteem; to feel inferior
minggir V, COLL to move to one side, pull over (on the road) → **pinggir**
minggu N week; Sunday; *malam* ~ Saturday night; **berminggu-**

minggu ADV for weeks; **seminggu** ADJ a week
miniatur ADJ miniature
minoritas N minority
minta V to ask, beg, request; to apply for; **minta-minta** V to beg (alms); **meminta** V to ask for, request; **permintaan** N request
minum drink; **minuman** N drink
minyak N oil; ~ *wangi* perfume; **berminyak** ADJ oily, greasy; **perminyakan** N oil and gas
miring ADJ sloping, slanting; not straight
misa N, CATH mass
misal N example; **misalnya, misalkan** for example, for instance
miskin ADJ poor, lacking in; **kemiskinan** N poverty
mistéri N mystery; **mistérius** ADJ mysterious
mistik, mistis ADJ mystical
mitos N myth
mitra N partner, friend
mobil N car
mode N fashion, trend
moga: moga-moga, semoga may, hopefully
mogok strike; break down
mohon V to request, ask, beg; please; **permohonan** N request, application → **pohon**
molék ADJ pretty, charming
molor stretch, become longer
Monas N National Monument in Central Jakarta → **Monumén Nasional**
moncong N muzzle, nose
mondar-mandir V to go back and forth, to and fro
mondok V, COLL to board, stay → **pondok**
montir N mechanic
monumén N monument
monyét N monkey; DEROG term of abuse
motif N design, pattern, motif; **bermotif** V to have a design
moto N MSG, monosodium glutamate → **Ajinomoto**
moto N motto, chant
motor N motorcycle, (motor)bike
-mu PRON, POSS, s your; *buku~* your book → **kamu**

INDONESIAN–ENGLISH

M

mua N eel
muak loathe; disgusted, fed up
mual ADJ nauseous, queasy, sick
muara N mouth (of a river); **bermuara** v to have a mouth, empty into
muat contain; **muatan** N load, cargo; **memuat** v to contain
muda ADJ young; *hijau ~* light green; **pemuda** N youth; young man
mudah ADJ easy; **mudah-mudahan** ADV hopefully; **kemudahan** N ease, facility
mudik v to go upstream, back to the village
muka N face, front, surface; *ke ~* to the front, forward; **terkemuka** ADJ prominent; **bermuka** v to have a face; *~ dua* two-faced; **permukaan** N surface
mukim: permukiman N housing, residential area
mula beginning, start; **bermula** v to start, begin; **memulai** v to start or begin something; **pemula** N beginner; **semula** ADV originally
mulai v to begin, start; **memulai** v to start or begin something → **mula**
mulas (stomach) cramp
mulia ADJ honorable, noble
mulus ADJ smooth, flawless
mulut N mouth
mumpung v to make the most of, capitalize on
muncrat v to spurt, spray
muncul v to appear, turn up
mundur v to go backwards, reverse, retreat; to resign → **undur**
mungkin CONJ maybe, possibly; **kemungkinan** N possibility; **memungkinkan** ADJ conducive; v to enable, make possible
muntah v to vomit, throw up
mur N nut
murah ADJ cheap
murid N pupil, student
murni ADJ pure; only
murung ADJ gloomy, despondent
musang N civet cat
mushola, musholla, mushalla N, ISL small prayer-house
musibah N disaster, calamity
musik N music; **pemusik, musikus, musisi** N musician

musim N season; *~ bunga, ~ semi* spring; *~ dingin* winter; *~ gugur* autumn, fall; *~ panas* summer
musium, muséum N museum
Muslim ADJ, ISL Muslim → **Islam**
musnah ADJ destroyed
mustahil ADJ impossible
musuh N enemy; **memusuhi** v to fight against, antagonize, make an enemy of
musyawarah: bermusyawarah v to deliberate, discuss
mutakhir ADJ modern, latest
mutiara N pearl
mutu N quality; **bermutu** ADJ quality
Myanmar N Myanmar, Burma

N

nabati ADJ vegetable, plant
nabi N, ISL, CHR prophet
nada N note, tone, sound; *~ dering* ringtone
nadi N pulse
nafas, napas breath, breathe; **bernafas** v to breathe; **bernafaskan** v with a breath of; **pernafasan** N breathing, respiration
nafsu N desire; **bernafsu** ADJ passionate, lusty
naga N dragon
nah, na well, well then; look!
naik go up, climb, rise, ascend; *~ haji* to go on the pilgrimage to Mecca; *~ pesawat* to board, boarding; **kenaikan** N rise, raise; **menaiki** v to ride, mount, get on; **menaikkan** v to raise, hoist
nakal ADJ naughty
naluri N instinct
nama N name; *~ depan* first name; *~ kecil* everyday name, nickname; **bernama** ADJ named; **menamakan** v to call, name; **ternama** ADJ famous, well-known
nampak → **tampak**
namun CONJ however, yet
nanah N pus
nanas, nenas N pineapple
nangka N jackfruit
nanti ADV later; **menanti** v to wait; **menanti-nanti** v to wait for a long time; **menantikan** v to wait for

INDONESIAN–ENGLISH

N

napas, nafas breath, breathe; **bernapas** v to breathe; **bernapaskan** v with a breath of; **pernapasan** N breathing, respiration

narkoba N (illegal) drugs, narcotics and other banned substances → narkotik, psikotropika dan obat terlarang

nasabah N (bank) customer

naséhat → nasihat

nasi N (cooked) rice; ~ *goreng* fried rice

nasib N fate, lot, destiny

nasihat, naséhat N advice; **menasihati** v to advise; **penasihat** N adviser

nasional N national; **nasionalis** N nationalist; **nasionalisme** N nationalism

naskah N manuscript, original (text); *penulis* ~ script writer

Natal Christmas; **natalan** v, COLL to celebrate Christmas

ndak, nggak, enggak COLL no, not → tidak

negara N state, country; **negarawan** N statesman

negeri N country, land

nékad, nékat reckless; stubborn; **kenékatan** N determination, resolve, recklessness

nelayan N fisherman

nenas → nanas

nénék N, PRON grandmother; great-aunt; female relative of grandmother's generation

népotisme N nepotism

neraka N hell

nétral ADJ neutral

ngaji v, COLL to recite or read the Koran → kaji

ngantor v, COLL to go to work → kantor

ngantuk ADJ, COLL sleepy → antuk

ngarang v, COLL to make something up (off the top of your head) → karang

ngeri ADJ terrified; **mengerikan** ADJ terrifying, horrifying

ngetrén, ngetrénd ADJ, COLL trendy, fashionable → trénd

ngetwit v to tweet (on Twitter)

nggak, enggak, ndak COLL no, not → tidak

ngilu ADJ painful (of teeth), smarting; *rasa* ~ pain

ngobrol v, COLL to chat → obrol

ngomong v, COLL to speak, talk; **ngomong-ngomong** ADV by the way

ngompol v, COLL to wet your pants, the bed → ompol

ngorok v, COLL to snore; to sleep

niaga N commerce; **perniagaan** N commerce, trade, business

niat N intention; **berniat** v to intend

nikah POL marry; **menikah** v to marry, get married; **menikahi** v to marry someone; **pernikahan** N wedding

nikmat ADJ enjoyable, delicious; **menikmati** v to enjoy

nilai N value, worth; mark, grade (at school); **menilai** v to evaluate, appraise

ninabobo lullaby; sing to sleep

nir- PREF without; **nirlaba** ADJ non-profit, not for profit

nisan N headstone, gravestone

noda N stain

nol ADJ zero, nil

nomor, nomer N number; event, match; **menomersatukan** v to put first, give priority

non- PREF not; non-; **nonaktif** ADJ not in active service; **menonaktifkan** v to release from active service, non-activate

Non, Nona PRON Miss

nonaktif ADJ not in active service

nongkrong → tongkrong

nonton v, COLL to watch, look on → tonton

Nopémber → November

norit N diarrhea tablets, made from black carbon

Norwégia N Norway

notaris N notary

Novémber, Nopémber *bulan* ~ November

nuansa N touch, nuance

nuklir ADJ nuclear

numpang → tumpang

nurani ADJ inner

nuri *burung* ~ parrot

nusa N island; ~ *Tenggara* the Lesser Sunda Islands; **Nusantara** N Indonesia

INDONESIAN–ENGLISH

N

Ny. ABBREV *Nyonya* Madam, title for married woman, especially a non-Indonesian

-nya SUF, POSS added to words to indicate possession; the

nyala flame, blaze, burn; **menyala** v to burn, blaze; **menyalakan** v to light, set fire to

nyaman ADJ comfortable, pleasant; **kenyamanan** N comfort

nyamuk N mosquito

nyanyi sing; **nyanyian** N song; **bernyanyi, menyanyi** v to sing; **menyanyikan** v to sing something; **penyanyi** N singer, vocalist

nyaring ADJ clear, loud, shrill

nyata ADJ clear, obvious, plain; **kenyataan** N fact; **menyatakan** v to declare, state, certify; **pernyataan** N statement, declaration

nyawa N soul, life

nyekar v, COLL to strew flower petals on a grave; to visit a grave → sekar

nyenyak ADJ sound asleep

Nyepi N Balinese Day of Seclusion

nyeri N pain

nyiur N coconut palm

nyonya PRON, F term of address for a married woman, Madam; Mrs

O

o EXCL oh; ~ *ya* oh yes, by the way

obat N medicine; **berobat** v to go to the doctor, seek medical advice; **mengobati** v to treat, cure; **pengobatan** N treatment

obral N sale; **mengobral** v to put on sale

obrol: mengobrol v ngobrol COLL to chat; **obrolan** N chat

obyék N object; ~ *wisata* tourist destination, sight

obyék: mengobyék, ngobyék v, COLL to have a job on the side, moonlight

odol N, ARCH toothpaste

ogah ADJ, SL unwilling, reluctant

ojék, ojég N motorcycle taxi

oké SL okay, OK

oksigén N oxygen

Oktober *bulan* ~ October

olah: olahan ADJ processed; **pengolahan** v processing

olahraga v sport; **berolahraga** v to do or play sport; **olahragawan** N, M sportsman

oléh CONJ by, through; **oléh-oléh** N souvenir; **memperoléh** v to obtain, get; **peroléhan** N acquisition

oléng ADJ on a lean, leaning to one side

olés: olésan N smear; **mengolés** v to grease, spread, lubricate; **mengoléskan** v to smear with something

oli, olie N (engine) oil

Olimpiade N the Olympics, the Olympic Games

Om, Oom PRON Uncle; term of address to extended family, parents' friends, friends' parents etc

ombak N wave; **berombak** ADJ wavy

omél: mengomél v to complain, grumble, whinge, whine → **omél**

omong chat, talk, speak; **omongan** N chat; gossip; **ngomong** v, COLL to speak, talk; **ngomong-ngomong** by the way

ompol: mengompol v to wet the bed, wet your pants

ompong ADJ toothless

oncom N fermented soybean cake

ondé: ondé-ondé N small round cakes made of green peanuts, covered in sesame seeds

onderdil N (automotive) spare part

ongkos N cost (for a service), expense, charge

ons ounce

operasi N operation

opini N opinion

opname go into hospital, hospitalization; **diopname** v to be admitted to hospital, be hospitalized

opor ~ *ayam* chicken in coconut sauce

optik optician; optical

orang N person, human; ~ *Barat* Westerner; ~ *Cina*, ~ *Tionghoa* (ethnic) Chinese; ~ *gila* tramp; mentally-ill person; ~ *Islam* Muslim; ~ *kulit putih* white person; ~ ~ *tua* parents; **perorangan** ADJ personal, individual; **seorang** a (person); counter for people;

INDONESIAN—ENGLISH

P

perseorangan ADJ individual;
seseorang N a certain person,
somebody
oranye ADJ orange
orgel, organ N organ
orkés N orchestra
ormas N social or people's organization → organisasi masyarakat
orok N (newborn) baby
oséng: oséng-oséng N stir-fried
vegetables
otak N brain
otak: otak-otak N steamed fish
cakes, baked in banana leaves
otda N regional autonomy → otonomi daérah
otomatis ADJ automatic
otomotif ADJ automotive
otonomi N autonomy
otorita, otoritas N authority
otot N muscle; berotot ADJ muscular
oven N oven, kiln
overdosis, OD overdose
oya, o ya oh yes, by the way

P

pabrik factory
pacar N boyfriend, girlfriend;
pacaran V, COLL to be going out,
to go out, date
pada PREP in, at, on (expressing
time); to
pada COLL, PL pluralizing word
sudah ~ pulang everybody's going
home
padahal CONJ whereas, however
padam put out, extinguish; pemadam pasukan ~ kebakaran fire
brigade
padang N field, plain
padat ADJ dense, full, crammed
padi N (unhusked) rice
padu: memadukan V to combine,
unite; terpadu ADJ integrated
pagar N fence; hedge
pagi N morning; pagi-pagi ADV
(very) early
paha N thigh
pahala N reward, merit
paham, faham V to understand,
know; memahami V to understand,
comprehend

pahat chisel; memahat V to sculpt,
chisel
pahit ADJ bitter
pahlawan N hero
pai N pie
pajak tax
pajang: pajangan N display
pak: mengepak V to pack
Pak, Bapak PRON Father; term of
address to older, respected men
pakai, paké SL wear; use; pakaian N
clothes, dress; ~ dalam underwear;
berpakaian ADJ dressed in;
memakai V to wear; to use;
pemakai N user; pemakaian N use,
usage; terpakai ADJ used, in use
pakar N expert, authority
pakat: sepakat V to agree; kesepakatan N agreement; menyepakati V
to agree to
pakét N packet, package, promotion
pakis N fern
paksa force; memaksa V to force;
terpaksa ADJ forced
paku N nail
pala buah ~ nutmeg
palang N barrier, bar, cross; ~ Merah
Red Cross
palem N palm
Palestina N Palestine
paling ADV most; at the most; ~ baik
the best
palsu ADJ false, forged; memalsukan V to falsify, forge
paman N uncle, male relative of
parents' generation
pamér show off; paméran N exhibition
pamit, pamitan, berpamit V to take
leave
panah N bow; panahan N archery;
pemanah N archer
panas ADJ hot, warm; hot and dry;
kepanasan N heat; ADJ too hot;
memanaskan V to heat (up)
panca ADJ five; Pancasila N Indonesian state philosophy of five principles
pancaroba N change of season
Pancasila N Indonesian state philosophy of five principles
panci N saucepan, pan
pancing: memancing V to fish

INDONESIAN—ENGLISH

P

(with hook and line); **terpancing**
ADJ hooked, caught up; involved
pancur: pancuran, pancoran N
fountain; shower
pandai ADJ clever; ~ *besi* smith
pandan *daun* ~ pandanus leaf, used
for green coloring in food
pandang see, gaze; **pandangan** N
view, sight; **memandang** V to view,
consider; **pemandangan** N view
pandu guide, scout, pilot;
memandu V to guide
panén N harvest, windfall
pangan N food
pangéran N prince
panggang N roast, bake, toast;
ayam ~ roast chicken;
memanggang V to roast, bake,
toast; **pemanggangan** N spit
panggil call; **panggilan** N call, sum-
mons; **memanggil** V to call
panggul N hip
panggung N stage
pangkal N base; **pangkalan** N terminal, base; ~ *udara (lanud)* air base
pangkas cut; ~ *rambut* barber
pangkat N rank, class; to the power
of; **berpangkat** V to have the rank of
pangku lap; **pangkuan** N lap
panglima N commander
pangsit N wonton, dumpling
panik N panic
panitia N committee, board
panjang ADJ long; ~*nya* length;
~ *lebar* detailed; *(empat) persegi* ~
rectangle; ~ *umur* long life; **kepanjangan** ADJ too long; **memperpanjang** V to extend, make longer;
sepanjang CONJ, ADJ as long as
panjat climb; **memanjat** V to climb;
memanjatkan V to send up
pantai N beach, coast; ~ *batu* pebble
beach
pantas ADJ proper, decent, right;
sepantasnya ADV proper, rightly
pantat N bottom, backside
pantau: pantauan N observation;
memantau V to observe, watch;
pemantau N observer, monitor
panti N building; ~ *asuhan* orphanage
pantul: memantulkan V to reflect
something

pantun N traditional poem (of four
lines)
papan N plank, board, bench; ~ *tulis*
blackboard, whiteboard
papaya → pepaya
paprika N red or green pepper, paprika
Papua Nugini N Papua New
Guinea, PNG
para pluralizes the following word;
~ *pemirsa* viewers
parabola N satellite dish; parabola;
TV ~ satellite TV
paraf N initials
parah ADJ grave, serious, bad
parang N chopper, machete
parasut N parachute → payung
parau ADJ hoarse
paré, paria, peria N kind of bitter
gourd or squash
parfum N perfume
paria → paré
parit N (roadside) ditch
pariwisata N tourism
parkir park (a vehicle); *tempat* ~ car
park, parking lot
parkit *burung* ~ parakeet
parpol N (political) party → partai
politik
partai N party; ~ *politik (parpol)*
political party
paru, paru-paru N lung
paruh, paro N half, part; *kerja* ~
waktu work part-time; **separuh** N
half
paruh N bill, beak
parut grater
pas exact, just (as); fit; *kamar* ~
changing room
pasal N, LEG paragraph, section
pasang N pair, couple; **pasangan** N
pair; **sepasang** N a pair of
pasang, memasang V to put up,
attach, fix; **pemasangan** N installation
pasang ~ *surut* rise and fall, ebb
and flow
pasar N market, bazaar; **pemasaran**
N marketing
pasca PREF [pasca, paska] after, post-;
pascasarjana ADJ post-graduate
pasfoto N passport(-sized) photo
pasién N patient
pasir N sand

INDONESIAN–ENGLISH

Paskah n Easter
pasok: pasokan n supply
paspor n passport
pasrah adj accepting, fatalistic; **kepasrahan** n submission
pasta n paste; pasta, spaghetti; ~ *gigi* toothpaste
pastél n samosa, small pasty containing vegetables, egg and vermicelli noodles
pasti sure, certain, definite; **kepastian** n certainty; **memastikan** to confirm, make sure, ascertain
pastor n, cath priest
pasuk: pasukan n troops
patah break, fracture (of bones); **mematahkan** v to break
patok: patokan n standard, peg
patri solder
patroli n patrol
patuh adj loyal, obedient; **mematuhi** v to obey
patung n statue, figurine; **pematung** n sculptor
patungan v to pay together; to work together
patut adj decent, proper, deserving
paus *ikan* ~ whale
Paus Pope
paut: terpaut adj fastened, bound; separated
pavilyun, paviliun n smaller house attached to a larger one
payah adj difficult, serious; tired
payudara n, f breast
payung n umbrella; parachute
Pébruari → Fébruari
pecah break, smash; curdled (of milk); **pecahan** n piece, fragment; fraction; **memecahkan** v to break; to solve
pecat sacked, dismissed, fired; **memecat** v to fire, dismiss
pecel ~ *lele* catfish with rice and side-dishes; *nasi* ~ rice and salad with peanut sauce
péci n black, flat-topped cap worn by men, also with national dress
Pecinan n Chinatown → Cina
pecinta n lover → cinta
pedagang n merchant → dagang
pedanda n Balinese priest
pedang n sword

pedas adj spicy, hot; **kepedasan** adj too hot or spicy
pédé, PD sl self-confidence; → percaya diri
pedésaan n country(side), rural areas → désa
pedih, perih smart, sting
pédikur n pedicure
peduli v perduli coll to care, bother; **memedulikan** v to care or be bothered about
pegadaian n pawnshop → gadai
pegal adj sore, cramped, stiff
pégang, pegang hold, grip, grasp; **berpegang** v to hold onto; **memegang** v to hold, grasp
pegas n spring
pegawai n official, employee; ~ *negeri* public or civil servant
pegunungan n mountain range → gunung
pejabat n (government) official → jabat
pekan n week; market; *akhir* ~ weekend
pekat adj thick, strong, concentrated; **kepekatan** n thickness, viscosity
pekerja n worker, laborer; **pekerjaan** n work, profession → kerja
pél *kain* ~ rag for mopping the floor; **mengepél** v to mop (up); **dipél** v to be mopped, cleaned
pelabuhan port, harbor → labuh
pelacur n prostitute → lacur
pelajar n pupil, student; **pelajaran** n lesson → ajar
pelampung n floater, flotation device → lampung
pelan, perlahan: pelan-pelan, perlahan-lahan adv slowly, softly
pelana n saddle
pelanggan n subscriber, customer → langgan
pelangi n rainbow
pelan-pelan adv slowly, softly → pelan
pelantikan n inauguration → lantik
pelari n runner → lari
pelat n plate; ~ *polisi* (vehicle) number plate, license plate
pelatih n coach, trainer; **pelatihan** n training → latih
pelaut n sailor, seaman → laut

INDONESIAN–ENGLISH

P

pelawak N comedian, comic, clown → lawak

pelayan N waiter; M waitress; F attendant; **pelayanan** N service → layan

pelayaran N voyage → layar

pelbagai, berbagai ADJ all kinds or sorts of, various → bagai

pélek N rim of wheel → vélg

pelekat *bahan* ~ adhesive → lekat

pelembab, pelembap N moisturizer → lembab

pelését: memelésétkan V to up-end; to send off-course; **terpelését** ADJ slipped, skidded; tripped → lését

pelihara take care of; **peliharaan** *hewan* ~ pet; **memelihara** V to take care of, look after; to cultivate; **pemeliharaan** N care, maintenance, cultivation; **terpelihara** ADJ well cared-for, well-maintained → piara

pelindung N protective device → lindung

pelipis N temple (on head)

Pélni N National Shipping Line, state passenger shipping service → Pelayaran Nasional Indonésia

pelopor N pioneer, leader, forerunner

pelosok N remote place

pelotot: melotot V to stare, have bulging eyes → lotot

peluang N opportunity; **berpeluang** V to have an opportunity, a chance → luang

peluit, pluit N whistle

peluk hug; **pelukan** N embrace; **memeluk** V to hug or embrace; **pemeluk** N follower, adherent

pelukis N painter, artist → lukis

pelumas N lubricant → lumas

peluntur N laxative → luntur

peluru N bullet

pemadam *pasukan* ~ *kebakaran* fire brigade → padam

pemain N player, actor → main

pemakai N user; **pemakaian** N use, usage → pakai

pemakaman N funeral, burial → makam

pemandangan N view → pandang

pemanggangan N spit → panggang

pemanis ~ *buatan* artificial sweetener → manis

pemasangan N installation → pasang

pemasaran N marketing → pasar

pematung N sculptor → patung

pembaca N reader → baca

pembalut N sanitary pad → balut

pembangunan N development → bangun

pembantu N servant, maid; assistant → bantu

pembayaran N payment → bayar

pembelian N purchase → beli

pemberitahuan N announcement, notice → beri tahu

pemberontakan N rebellion, revolt, mutiny → berontak

pembersih N cleaning agent → bersih

pembicaraan N discussion → bicara

pembohong N liar → bohong

pemborong N developer, contractor → borong

pembuat N producer; maker; **pembuatan** N production, manufacture → buat

pembunuh N murderer, killer; **pembunuhan** N murder, killing → bunuh

pemburu N hunter → buru

Pémda N Regional Government → Pemerintah Daérah

pemeliharaan N care, maintenance, cultivation → pelihara

pemeluk N follower, adherent → peluk

pemenang N winner, victor → menang

pementasan N staging, production → pentas

pemeriksa N examiner; **pemeriksaan** N examination, investigation → periksa

pemesanan N order, request → pesan

pemicu N trigger → picu

pemikir N thinker; **pemikiran** N thinking, consideration → pikir

pemilihan N election; ~ *umum* (*pemilu*) general election → pilih

pemilik N owner → milik

INDONESIAN–ENGLISH

P

pemilu N general election → pemilihan umum

pemimpin N leader → pimpin

pemindahan N transfer, shifting, removal → pindah

pemirsa N television audience, viewer → pirsa

permohonan N request, application → mohon

pémpék, mpék mpék N fried fishcakes, a specialty of Palembang

pemuda N youth; young man → muda

pemugaran N restoration, renovation → pugar

pemula N beginner → mula

pemusik N musician → musik

pemutih N bleach → putih

péna N (fountain) pen, quill

penakut N coward → takut

penampilan N performance → tampil

penangkapan N capture, arrest → tangkap

penari N dancer → tari

penasaran ADJ curious, inquisitive, impatient

penasihat N adviser → nasihat

penawaran N offer, bid → tawar

pencahar N laxative → cahar

pencak ~ *silat* traditional self-defense

pencemaran N pollution → cemar

pencernaan N digestion → cerna

pencét press; **memencét** v to press (a button, key); **terpencét** ADJ accidentally pressed

pencil: terpencil ADJ isolated, remote

pencinta N lover → cinta

penculikan N kidnapping → culik

pencuri N thief, burglar → curi

pendaftaran N enrollment, registration → daftar

pendamping N companion → damping

pendapat N opinion, point of view; **pendapatan** N income, revenue → dapat

pendarahan N bleeding → darah

pendatang N immigrant, migrant; newcomer → datang

péndék ADJ short; ~ *kata* in short; ~*nya* in a word; **kepéndékan** N abbreviation; **meméndékkan** v to shorten

pendekatan N approach; getting to know → dekat

pendengar N listener; **pendengaran** N hearing → dengar

pendéta N, CHR minister, clergyman, vicar; HIND priest

pendopo, pendapa N traditional large roofed verandah in front of an official residence

penduduk N inhabitant, citizen, resident; **pendudukan** N occupation → duduk

pendukung N supporter → dukung

penebangan N logging; ~ *liar* illegal logging → tebang

peneliti N researcher; **penelitian** N research → teliti

penémbak N marksman, gunman → témbak

penemu N inventor, discoverer; **penemuan** N invention, discovery → temu

penerbang N pilot, aviator; **penerbangan** N flight; aviation → terbang

penerbit N publisher → terbit

penerjemah N translator; **penerjemahan** N translation → terjemah

penerjun ~ *(payung)* parachutist, sky diver → terjun

penerus N successor; someone who continues another's work → terus

penetapan N appointment → tetap

pengacara N lawyer, solicitor → acara

pengadilan N court of justice or law; trial → adil

pengaduan N complaint; *surat* ~ letter of complaint → adu

pengait N catch

pengajar N teacher → ajar

pengalaman N experience → alam

pengamat N observer; **pengamatan** N observation, monitoring → amat

pengamén N street singer, busker → amén

pengangguran N unemployment, unemployed person → anggur

pengantin, pengantén N, F bride; N, M (bride)groom; marrying couple; ~ *baru* newlyweds; ~ *pria* (bride)groom; ~ *wanita* bride

INDONESIAN–ENGLISH

P

penganut N follower, believer → anut

pengap ADJ stuffy; stale, musty

pengarang N author, writer, composer → karang

pengaruh N influence; ~ *obat* effect of medicine or drugs; ber-pengaruh ADJ influential; memengaruhi V to influence, affect; terpengaruh ADJ affected or influenced

pengasuh N carer; ~ *anak* nurse-maid, babysitter → asuh

pengawal N (body)guard, sentry → kawal

pengecut N coward → kecut

pengelolaan N management → kelola

pengemudi N driver → kemudi

péngén, pingin, kepéngén, ke-pingin V, COLL to really want to

pengeras ~ *suara* loudspeaker → keras

pengertian N understanding → erti, arti

pengetahuan N knowledge → tahu

penggalian N digging → gali

pengganti N replacement, substitute, successor → ganti

penggaris N ruler → garis

penggemar N fan, enthusiast → gemar

penggoréngan N wok, frying pan; process of frying → goréng

pengguna N user → guna

penghargaan N appreciation, award → harga

penghasil N producer → hasil

penghinaan N insult, libel (written), slander (spoken) → hina

penghuni N occupant, resident → huni

pengimpor N importer → impor

penginapan N accommodation, hotel → inap

pengirim N sender; pengiriman N dispatch, forwarding → kirim

pengkhianat N traitor → khianat

pengobatan N treatment → obat

pengolahan V processing → olah

penguji N examiner → uji

pengukuran N measuring, measurement → ukur

pengumuman N notice, announcement → umur

pengunduran N postponement, delay → undur

pengungsi N refugee, evacuee; pengungsian N evacuation → ungsi

pengurus N manager, organizer → urus

pengusaha N, M businessman; F businesswoman → usaha

penindasan N oppression → tindas

pening ADJ dizzy

peningkatan N rise, increase → tingkat

peninjau N observer → tinjau

penipu N con man, trickster; peni-puan N deception → tipu

peniti N safety-pin; brooch

penitipan N care → titip

penjahat N criminal

penjajah N colonizer, ruler, colonial power → jajah

penjara N prison, jail; memenjara-(kan) V to put in prison, imprison

penjelasan N explanation → jelas

penjual N seller, dealer; penjualan N sale, sales → jual

penolakan N refusal, rejection → tolak

penonton N spectator, audience → tonton

pénsil N pencil

pénsiun pension, retired; pénsiun-an N pensioner meménsiunkan V to pension off

pentas stage; pementasan N staging, production

péntil N valve

penting ADJ important; kepentingan N importance, interest

pentol: pentolan N boss, big shot

penuh ADJ full; memenuhi V to fulfill, meet requirements; sepe-nuhnya ADV fully, completely; terpenuhi ADJ satisfied, fulfilled

penulis N author, writer → tulis

penumpang N passenger → tumpang

penutup N stopper, lid; end → tutup

penutur N speaker → tutur

penyair N poet → syair

penyakit N disease, illness, complaint → sakit

INDONESIAN—ENGLISH

penyanyi N singer, vocalist → nyanyi

penyebab N cause → sebab

penyeberangan N crossing → seberang

penyelam N diver → selam

penyelamatan N rescue (operation) → selamat

penyelenggara N organizer → selenggara

penyelesaian N solution, settlement → selesai

penyelidik N investigator, detective; **penyelidikan** N investigation → selidik

penyerahan N handing over, hand-over → serah

penyiar N announcer → siar

penyidikan N investigation → selidik, sidik

penyihir N wizard, witch, sorcerer → sihir

pényok, péyot, péot ADJ dented

penyu N turtle

penyulap N magician, conjurer → sulap

penyulihan ~ *suara* dubber

penyunting N editor → sunting

penyusun N compiler, author → susun

pepatah N proverb, saying

pepaya, papaya N pawpaw, papaya

peperangan N battle → perang

pépés method of cooking by steaming or roasting in banana leaves

pér N spring

perabot N tools; **perabotan** N furnishings

peraga N visual aid; **peragawati** N, F model

perahu N (sail) boat

perajin N craftsman, artisan → rajin

pérak N silver; silver coin; *seratus* ~ one hundred rupiah

perakitan N assembly → rakit

peralatan N equipment → alat

perampok N robber; **perampokan** N robbery → rampok

peran N part, role; **berperan** v to play the role or part; **memerankan** v to portray, play the role of; **pemeran** N actor, actress

peranakan ADJ of mixed Chinese and Indonesian blood, Straits Chinese → anak

perancang N designer, planner → rancang

Perancis, Prancis N France

perang N war; ~ *Dunia Kedua* World War II; ~ perang-perangan N war games; paintball; **berperang** v to wage war, go to war; **peperangan** N battle

perangkap N trap; **terperangkap** ADJ trapped, caught

perangko, prangko N (postage) stamp

perang-perangan N war games; paintball → perang

perantara N broker, intermediary, go-between → antara

peranti, piranti N apparatus, equipment; ~ *lunak* software

perapian N fireplace, oven → api

peras, memeras v to press, squeeze; to blackmail, extort

perasaan N feeling → rasa

peraturan N rule, regulation → atur

perawan N virgin

perawat N nurse, sister; **perawatan** treatment; maintenance, upkeep → rawat

perayaan N celebration → raya

perbaikan N repair, improvement → baik

perban N bandage, dressing; **diperban** v to be bandaged

perbandingan N comparison, ratio → banding

perbankan ADJ banking

perbatasan N border, frontier → batas

perbédaan N difference → béda

perbelanjaan *pusat* ~ shopping center, mall → belanja

perbuatan N act, deed → buat

percakapan N conversation → cakap

percaya trust, believe; **kepercayaan** N belief, faith; **memercayai** v to trust someone; **memercayakan** v to entrust with; **terpercaya** ADJ trusted, reliable

perceraian N divorce → cerai

percobaan N experiment, test → coba

INDONESIAN–ENGLISH

P

percuma in vain
perdagangan N commerce, trade → dagang
perdamaian N peace, reconciliation → damai
perdana ADJ first, starter; ~ *Menteri* Prime Minister
perdebatan N debate, discussion → debat
perekat N glue, adhesive → rekat
perempat N quarter; **perempatan** N crossroads, intersection → empat
perempuan N woman, female
perenang N swimmer → renang
peresmian N formal ceremony, inauguration → resmi
pergaulan N mixing, social intercourse; association → gaul
pergelangan ~ *kaki* ankle; ~ *tangan* wrist → gelang
pergi go, leave; **bepergian** V to travel, be away; **kepergian** N departure
perguruan ~ *tinggi* university → guru
perhatian N attention → hati
perhiasan N jewelery → hias
perhitungan N calculation → hitung
perhotélan N hotel studies, hospitality → hotél
perhubungan N communications, connection → hubung
peri- PREF concerning; **perihal** N subject; CONJ about, concerning
peri N fairy godmother
perih, pedih smart, sting
perihal N subject; CONJ about, concerning
perikanan N fisheries → ikan
periksa investigate, check; **memeriksa** V to examine or investigate; **pemeriksa** N examiner; **pemeriksaan** N examination, investigation
perincian N details, detailed explanation → rinci
perintah order, command; **pemerintah** N government
perintis N pioneer → rintis
perisai N shield
peristiwa N incident, occurrence, happening

periuk N cooking pot
perjalanan N journey, trip → jalan
perjanjian N agreement, contract → janji
perjuangan N battle, fight, struggle → juang
perkakas N tool, instrument
perkantoran N office block → kantor
perkapalan N shipping → kapal
perkara N matter, case, affair
perkasa ADJ powerful; manly, virile
perkawinan N marriage, wedding → kawin
perkedél N (potato) patty, croquette; ~ *jagung* corn patty
perkémahan N camping, camp → kémah
perkembangan N development → kembang
perkenalan N introduction → kenal
perkiraan N estimate, guess → kira
perkosa: memerkosa V to rape, violate; **perkosaan** N rape
perkotaan N metropolitan area → kota
perkumpulan N association, club; assembly → kumpul
perkutut *burung* ~ turtledove
perlahan, pelan, perlahan-lahan, pelan-pelan ADV slowly, softly
perlawanan N opposition, resistance → lawan
perlengkapan N outfit, equipment → lengkap
perlindungan N protection → lindung
perlu need, necessary; **keperluan** N needs, requirements; **memerlukan** V to need, require
permadani N carpet
permainan N game, match → main
permak, vermak alteration to clothes; **dipermak** ADJ altered, shortened
permén N sweet, lolly, candy
permintaan N request; *atas* ~ by request → minta
perminyakan N oil and gas → minyak
permisi excuse me
permohonan N request, application → mohon

INDONESIAN–ENGLISH

P

permukaan N surface → muka
permukiman N housing, residential area → mukim
pernafasan, pernapasan N breathing, respiration → nafas
pernah ADV ever; once; have + past perfect form of verb; ~ *makan bebek?* Have you ever eaten duck?
pernikahan N wedding → nikah
pernis N varnish
pernyataan N statement, declaration → nyata
peroléhan N acquisition → oléh
perompak N pirate → rompak
péron N platform
perona ~ *mata* eyeshadow; ~ *pipi* rouge → rona
perosotan N (children's) slide → rosot
perpisahan N parting, farewell → pisah
perpustakaan N library → pustaka
pérs N press, media
persaingan N competition → saing
persalinan N childbirth → salin
persamaan N similarity, likeness, resemblance; equation → sama
persatuan N union, association → satu
persediaan N stock, supply → sedia
persegi ADJ square; sided → segi
perselingkuhan N affair → selingkuh
persembunyian N hiding place, hideout → sembunyi
persén N percent; *seratus* ~ one hundred percent; **persénan** N tip; **perséntase, proséntase** N percentage
perserikatan N federation → serikat
perséro ADJ proprietary limited (Pty Ltd) → séro
persetujuan N agreement, approval → tuju, setuju
persiapan N preparations → siap
persimpangan N intersection → simpang
persis ADV exactly
persoalan N problem, issue, matter → soal
personalia, personél ADJ personnel, staff
pertahanan N defense

pertama ADJ first; **pertama-tama** ADV first of all
pertambahan N increase → tambah
pertambangan N mining → tambang
Pertamina N state-run national oil and gas company
pertandingan N contest, competition, match → tanding
pertanian N agriculture → tani
pertanyaan N question → tanya
pertempuran N battle → tempur
pertemuan N meeting → temu
pertengkaran N quarrel → tengkar
pertigaan N T-junction → tiga
pertimbangan N consideration → timbang
pertokoan N shopping center or complex, mall → toko
pertolongan N help, assistance, aid → tolong
pertukaran N exchange → tukar
pertumbuhan N growth, development → tumbuh
pertunangan N engagement → tunang
pertunjukan N show, performance → tunjuk
perubahan N change, alteration → ubah
perumahan N housing (complex) → rumah
perundingan N discussion → runding
perunggu N bronze
perusahaan N company → usaha
perut N stomach, belly
perwakilan N representation, delegation → wakil
perwira N officer
pesan message, instruction, order; **pesanan** N order; **memesan** V to order; **pemesanan** N order, request
pesantrén N Islamic boarding school → santri
pesat ADJ fast, rapid
pesawat N machine; ~ *(terbang)* aeroplane, airplane
pésék ADJ flat-nosed
peserta N participant → serta
pesiar N trip, cruise; *kapal* ~ cruise ship, pleasure craft
pesindén N, F singer accompanying a gamelan orchestra

INDONESIAN–ENGLISH

P

pesing *bau* ~ stink of urine
pesisir N coast
pésta N party, celebration; ~ *perkawinan*, ~ *pernikahan* wedding reception; **berpésta** V to (have a) party
pesuruh N messenger, errand boy → **suruh**
peta N map, chart; ~ *dunia* world map; *buku* ~ atlas; *buku* ~ *jalan* road atlas, street directory
petani N farmer → **tani**
petas: petasan N firecracker, fireworks
peté, petai N stinkbean
peténis N tennis player → **ténis**
peternakan N cattle farm, ranch → **ternak**
peti N chest, case, box; ~ *es* ice-box
petik pluck; **petikan** N extract, quotation; **memetik** V to pick; to strum
petinju N boxer → **tinju**
petir N thunder, lightning
petis *tahu* ~ fried tofu with a spicy sauce
pétromaks *lampu* ~ kerosene lantern
petunjuk N instruction, direction → **tunjuk**
pewarna N dye, stain → **warna**
péyot, péot, pényok ADJ dented
piala N trophy, cup
piano N piano; **pianis** N pianist
picu N trigger; **memicu** V to trigger, set off; **pemicu** V trigger
pidato N speech, address; **berpidato** V to make a speech, give an address
pigura N picture frame
pihak N party; side; **berpihak, sepihak** ADJ unilateral
pijak: pijakan N foothold, something to stand on
pijar *lampu* ~ light bulb
pijat, pijit massage; **memijat** V to massage
pikir, fikir V to think; **pikiran** N thought, idea; **berpikir** V to think; **memikirkan** V to think about; **pemikir** N thinker; **pemikiran** N thinking, consideration
piknik N picnic
pikun ADJ senile, dotty

pil N (contraceptive) pill, tablet
pilek sniffle, have a cold or runny nose
pilem → **film**
pilih choose; **pilihan** N choice, selection; ADJ select; **memilih** V to choose or select; to elect or vote (for); **pemilihan** N election; ~ *umum (pemilu)* general election
pimpin, memimpin V to lead; **pemimpin** N leader
pincang ADJ crippled, lame
pindah move; change; **berpindah** V to move; **memindahkan** V to move, transfer; **pemindahan** N transfer, shifting, removal
pinggang N waist
pinggir N edge, border; **pinggiran** N edges, outskirts; **minggir** V, COLL to move to the side, pull over; **terpinggirkan** ADJ cast aside, marginalized
pingpong N table tennis, pingpong; **dipingpong** V to be sent here and there, messed about
pingsan faint, collapse; unconscious
pinisi, phinisi *kapal* ~ Buginese cargo boat
pinjam borrow; **pinjaman** N loan; **meminjam** V to borrow; **meminjami** V to lend someone; **meminjamkan** V to lend something
pinsét N tweezers
pinta: (me)minta V to request, ask for; **(me-)minta-minta** V to beg, ask for money; **permintaan** N request; *atas* ~ by request
pintar ADJ pinter COLL clever
pintu N door, gate; ~ *darurat* emergency exit; ~ *keluar* exit; ~ *masuk* entrance
pipa N pipe, tube
pipi N cheek
pipis N, CH wee, pee, go to the toilet
pirang ADJ, M blond, F blonde, fair-haired
piranti, peranti N apparatus, equipment; ~ *lunak* software
piring N plate, dish; *mencuci* ~ to wash the dishes; **piringan** N plate-shaped object
pirsa: pemirsa N television audience, viewer

INDONESIAN—ENGLISH

pisah separate, split; ~ *ranjang* separate (of a couple); **berpisah** v to part, separate; **memisahkan** v to separate something; **perpisahan** N parting, farewell; **terpisah** ADJ separated

pisang N banana

pisau N knife

pita N ribbon

piton N *(ular)* ~ python

piyama N pyjamas, pajamas

plafon N ceiling

plagiat N plagiarism; **plagiator** N someone who copies or commits plagiarism

plakat N placard, poster

plastik ADJ plastic; N plastic bag, carrier bag

platina N platinum

pléster N sticking plaster, bandaid

plong ADJ relieved

PLTA ABBREV *Pembangkit Listrik Tenaga Air* hydro-electric power station

pluit → peluit

plus ADJ plus, added; *kacamata* ~ long-sighted glasses

PMI ABBREV *Palang Merah Indonesia* Indonesian Red Cross

PNG ABBREV *Papua Nugini* Papua New Guinea

poci N teapot

poco-poco N line dance from North Sulawesi

pohon N tree

poin N point, mark

pojok N corner; **pojokan** N, SL corner

pokok N main; ~*nya* basically, the main thing is; *gaji* ~ base salary

pola N pattern

Polandia N Poland

Polda N Regional Police → **Polisi Daérah**

polés polish

poligami N polygamy

poliklinik, poli N polyclinic, doctor's surgery; ~ *umum* GP's surgery, doctor's surgery

polisi N police; ~ *wanita (polwan)* policewoman; *kantor* ~ police station

politik N politics; **politikus** N **politisi** PL politician; **politis** ADJ political

polos ADJ plain, unpretentious; smooth; *baju* ~ plain shirt

Polri N Indonesian police force

polsék N local police station → **polisi séktor**

polusi N pollution; ~ *udara* air pollution

Polwan N policewoman → **polisi wanita**

pompa pump; ~ *bensin* petrol station, gasoline pump, service station; **memompa** v to pump

pon N pound

pondok N hut, cottage; **mondok** v, COLL to board, lodge, stay

poni N fringe, bangs

popok N napkin, diaper

populér ADJ popular; **popularitas** N popularity

porno ADJ pornographic; **pornoaksi** N pornographic actions; **pornografi** N pornography

porsi N serve, portion

portal N iron gateway into a building complex; barrier blocking access into a complex; **diportal** v to be blocked by a barrier, have a barrier lowered

Portugal, Portugis N Portugal

pos N post; ~ *penjagaan*, ~ *satpam* security post; ~ *udara* airmail

pose N pose (for a photograph); **berpose** v to pose for a photograph

posisi N position

positif ADJ positive; *berpikir* ~ to think positive

posko N post (for a political party or fund-raising effort) → **pos koordinasi**

posyandu N all-in-one government administrative office → **pos pelayanan terpadu**

pot N pot, vase; ~ *bunga* vase (indoors), flowerpot (outdoors)

potong piece, cut; ~ *rambut* cut your hair, get your hair cut; hairdresser, barber (for men); **potongan** N discount, reduction; cut (of clothes); **memotong** v to cut, deduct; to slaughter, amputate; to interrupt; **terpotong** ADJ cut (off)

potrét N portrait; photograph of a person; **memotrét** v to photograph

INDONESIAN–ENGLISH

P

PP ABBREV *pulang pergi* there and back, shown on public transport

PR ABBREV *pekerjaan rumah* homework

pra- PREF pre-, before; *~sangka* prejudice

prajurit N soldier

prakték, praktik N practice; practical; **mempraktékkan** V to put into practice; **praktis** ADJ practical

pramugara N, M steward; cabin crew; **pramugari** N, F stewardess, air hostess; cabin crew

Pramuka N Scouts

prapatan, perapatan N, COLL crossroads, intersection

prasangka N prejudice

prasmanan ADJ buffet-style

préman N thug

préséntasi N (oral) presentation

présiden N president

préstasi N performance, achievement; **berpréstasi** ADJ prestigious; successful

pria N male, man

pribadi N self, individual, personality; **kepribadian** N personality

pribumi N pri COLL native inhabitant, indigenous Indonesian; **non-pri** COLL ethnic Chinese

prihatin concerned, worried; **memprihatinkan** ADJ worrying

prinsip N principle

prioritas N priority; **memprioritaskan** V to prioritize

priyayi N upper class, esp in colonial era

problém, problim N problem

produk N product; **produksi** N production; **memproduksi** V to produce

profési N profession; **profésional** ADJ professional

profil N profile, outline

proklamasi N proclamation (of independence)

promosi N promotion; **mempromosikan** V to promote

propinsi N province

prosédur N procedure; **prosédural** ADJ procedural

prosés N process; court case; **memproséskan** V to process

protés protest; **memprotés** V to (make a) protest

Protéstan N Protestant → **Kristen**

provokasi N provocation; **provokator** N trouble-maker, provocateur

proyék N project, scheme

psikiater N [sikiater] psychiatrist → **jiwa**

psikolog [sikolog] N psychologist; **psikologi** N psychology → **jiwa**

puas ADJ satisfied, content; **memuaskan** ADJ satisfactory

puber N puberty

pucat ADJ pale; ADJ, COLL scared

pucuk N shoot, sprout

pudar faded, washed-out; **memudar** V to fade

puding N pudding, dessert

pugar: pemugaran N restoration, renovation

puing N ruins; rubble

puisi N poetry (esp Western); **puitis** ADJ poetic

puja worship; **pujaan** N something worshipped or idolized; **memuja** V to worship

pujaséra N food court, collection of food stalls → **pusat jajan serba rasa**

puji praise; **pujian** N praise; **memuji** V to praise; **terpuji** ADJ highly-praised

pukul strike; FORM hour; *~ tiga belas* 1 pm; **pukulan** N strike, beat, hit; **memukul** V to hit, beat, strike; **terpukul** ADJ hard-hit

pula ADV also, too; again

pulang V to go home, return; *~ hari* to return on the same day, not stay overnight; *~ pergi (PP)* there and back, both ways; **memulangkan** V to give back; to send back, repatriate

pulau N island; *~ Seribu* the Thousand Islands; **kepulauan** N archipelago, chain

pulih recovered

pulpén N fountain pen

pulsa N credit (for a telephone)

puluh *dua ~* twenty; **puluhan** N dozens; *tahun delapan ~* the eighties; **sepuluh** N ten

pun emphasizing particle; too, also; even; then

INDONESIAN—ENGLISH

R

punah ADJ extinct
puncak N peak, summit, top
pundak N shoulder
pundi N piggybank, purse
punggung N back
pungut pick up (off ground);
  memungut v to pick up, collect
puntung ~ *rokok* cigarette butt
punya have, own; *yang* ~ the
  owner; **kepunyaan** N possession,
  belonging; **mempunyai** v to have,
  own, possess
pupuk N fertilizer
pura N Balinese or Hindu temple
pura-pura pretend, fake
purba ADJ ancient; **purbakala** N
  ancient times
puri N palace, castle
purna- PREF post-, after
pus N, COLL pussycat
pusaka N heirloom, inheritance
pusar N navel, belly button; **pusaran**
  N vortex; ~ *angin* whirlwind; **berpusar** v to revolve, whirl
pusat N center; **berpusat** ~ *pada* to
  focus or center on; **memusatkan** v
  to focus
pusing ADJ dizzy; ~ *kepala* headache
puskésmas N clinic, public health
  center → **pusat keséhatan
  masyarakat**
pustaka N, LIT book; *daftar* ~ list of
  references; **perpustakaan** N
  library; **pustakawan** N librarian
putar turn around, rotate; **putaran** N
  round, revolution; **berputar** v to
  rotate, turn; **memutar** v to wind; to
  rotate; **seputar** ADJ around, about
putih ADJ white; ~ *telur* albumen,
  egg white; *merah* ~ red and white;
  keputihan N thrush, vaginal itching
  (white discharge); **memutihkan** v
  to whiten, bleach; **pemutih** N
  bleach
puting N nipple
putra, putera N, POL son; ~ *mahkota*
  crown prince; ~-*putri* children, sons
  and daughters
putri, puteri N, POL daughter
putus broken off; ~ *asa* give up
  hope; **keputusan** N decision,
  decree; **memutus** v to break;
  memutuskan v to terminate or

break; to decide; **terputus** ADJ cut
off; **terputus-putus** v to keep cutting out
puyuh *burung* ~ quail
puyung hai → **fuyung hai**

Q

Quran *al-*~ the Koran

R

raba: meraba v to feel or grope
  something
Rabu, Rebo *hari* ~ Wednesday
rabun ADJ blurry; ~ *jauh* short-
  sighted
racik: racikan N blend, concoction;
  prescription
racun N poison (not from animals);
  beracun ADJ poisonous, containing
  poison; **keracunan** ADJ poisoned;
  meracuni v to poison
rada ADV, COLL quite, rather
radang ADJ inflamed; **meradang** v
  to become inflamed
radio N radio; ~ *Republik Indonesia
  (RRI)* Indonesian state radio
rafia *tali* ~ plastic twine
raga N body; **peraga** N visual aid;
  peragawati N, F model
ragam N manner, way; kind;
  beragam ADJ various; **seragam** N
  uniform
ragu doubt, doubtful; **ragu-ragu** ADJ
  doubtful, unsure; **keragu(-ragu)an**
  N doubt, uncertainty; **meragukan** v
  to doubt something
rahang N jaw
rahasia N secret, mystery; **merahasiakan** v to keep secret
rahim N uterus, womb
raib vanished, disappeared
raja N king; **kerajaan** N kingdom
rajaléla: merajaléla v to be out of
  control; to act violently
rajin ADJ diligent, hard-working,
  industrious; **kerajinan** N crafts;
  perajin N craftsman, artisan
rajungan N kind of small edible crab
rajut: rajutan N knitting, crochet
  work; **merajut** v to knit; to crochet
rak N shelf; ~ *buku* bookshelf

INDONESIAN—ENGLISH

R

rakét N racquet, racket
rakit N raft; **merakit** v to assemble; **perakitan** N assembly
raksasa giant
rakus ADJ greedy
rakyat N people
ralat N correction, errata; **meralat** v to correct a mistake
Ramadan Muslim fasting month
ramah ADJ friendly; **keramahan** N friendliness
ramai, ramé ADJ busy, lively; crowded; **ramai-ramai** ADV in a group, together; **keramaian** N noise, din; lively atmosphere; **meramaikan** v to liven up, enliven
ramal: ramalan N prediction, prophecy, forecast; **meramal** v to tell fortunes; **meramalkan** v to predict, foretell
rambut N hair; **rambutan** N rambutan, fruit with hairy red skin; **berambut** ADJ hairy; v to have hair
ramé → ramai
rami N hemp, jute
ramping ADJ slender
rampok, merampok v to rob, hold up; **perampok** N robber; **perampokan** N robbery
ramu: ramuan N mixture
rancang: rancangan N plan, design; **merancang** v to plan, design; **perancang** N designer, planner
rangka N skeleton, framework → kerangka
rangkai: rangkaian N combination, series
rangkak: merangkak v to crawl
rangkap multiple; *tiga* ~ three copies, in triplicate
ranjang N bed
ranjau N mine
ransel N backpack
rantai N chain; **merantai** v to chain up
rantau N abroad, across the sea
rapat ADJ close to; tight
rapat N meeting, meet
rapi ADJ neat, tidy, organized
rapot, rapor N (school) report
ras N breed; pure-bred
rasa feel, feeling; sense; taste; ~*nya* it appears, it seems; **kerasan** COLL

feel at home; **merasa** v to think, feel; **merasakan** v to feel something; **perasaan** N feeling; **terasa** v to be felt
rata ADJ flat, even, level; **rata-rata** ADV equally; on average; **meratakan** v to level, flatten
ratu N queen
ratus *dua* ~ two hundred; **seratus** ADJ one hundred, a hundred
raut: rautan ~ *pensil* pencil sharpener
rawa N swamp, marsh
rawan ADJ vulnerable, troubled, unsafe
rawat: merawat v to nurse, care for; to maintain, look after; **perawat** N nurse, sister; **perawatan** N treatment; maintenance, upkeep
rawon N black meat soup from East Java
raya ADJ great, greater; *hari* ~ holiday, feast day; Idul Fitri; *Indonesia* ~ the national anthem; **merayakan** v to celebrate; **perayaan** N celebration
rayap N termite, white ant; *kena* ~, *dimakan* ~ eaten by termites; **merayap** v to crawl, creep
rayu: merayu v to tempt, flatter, seduce
razia N raid, spot-check
réaksi N reaction; **beréaksi** v to react
rebab N two-stringed musical instrument
rebana N tambourine
rebus v boil, boiled; **merebus** v to boil in water
rebut, merebut v to snatch, capture; **rebutan** v fighting for something; **berebut** v to fight for; **berebutan** v to fight each other for; **merebutkan** v to snatch something
redaksi N editors, editorial staff; **redaktur** N editor
redup dim, go out
réformasi N reform (esp after 1998); **réformis** ADJ reformist, pro-reform
rejeki, rezeki, rizki N fortune, luck; livelihood, living
rekam: rekaman N recording; **merekam** v to record
rekan N colleague, partner, associate; **rekanan** N regular service provider

INDONESIAN–ENGLISH

rekat: perekat N glue, adhesive
rékayasa N engineering
rékening N (bank) account
réklamasi N reclamation
rékoméndasi N recommendation
rékor N record; ~ *dunia* world record
rékréasi N recreation, relaxing, fun
rekrut recruit; **merekrut** v to recruit
réktor N vice-chancellor, rector; **réktorat** N vice-chancellor's office
rél N rail; ~ *kereta api* railway line, railroad, train tracks
réla, réd(h)a, ridha, ridho willing; **relawan** N volunteer
rélatif ADJ relative
rém N brake; **mengerém** v to brake
remaja N teen, adolescent, young single person, youth
rématik N rheumatism
rembes: merembes v to seep in, leak, ooze
réméh ADJ small, unimportant, trifling; **meréméhkan** v to belittle, treat as unimportant
rempah N spice; **rempah-rempah** N spices
rempéyék, péyék N peanut crisps
renang swimming; **berenang** v to swim; **perenang** N swimmer
rencana N plan, program, draft; **berencana** v to plan; **merencanakan** v to plan
rénda N lace
rendah ADJ low, humble; ~ *hati* humble; **merendahkan** v to lower; to humiliate; **terendah** ADJ lowest
rendam soak; **terendam** ADJ inundated, flooded, soaked
rendang N meat cooked in coconut milk
réngék: meréngék v to whimper, whine
renggut: merenggut v to snatch, tug
renta ADJ worn
rentak: serentak ADJ all at once, simultaneous, at the same time
rentan ADJ susceptible
renung: renungan N reflection, musing, contemplation; **merenung** v to daydream
renyah ADJ crisp, crispy

réog N trance dance, most famously in Ponorogo, East Java
réparasi N repair(s) → baik
répot very busy; bothered; **répot-répot** v to go to great trouble; **merépotkan** v to make someone busy or go to some trouble
reruntuhan, runtuhan N ruins → runtuh
resah ADJ restless
resap: meresap v to be absorbed; to penetrate, seep into
résénsi, risénsi N review
resép N recipe; prescription; **meresépkan** v to write a prescription for a drug
resépsi N reception; ~ *perkawinan*, ~ *pernikahan* wedding reception; **resépsionis** N receptionist
resérse N detective, forensic
resik ADJ clean
resmi ADJ official, formal; **meresmikan** v to formalize, make official; **peresmian** N formal opening, inauguration
résto N upmarket restaurant
réstoran N restaurant
réstorasi N restoration
restu N blessing; **merestui** v to agree to, give your blessing to
retak ADJ cracked; **retakan** N crack, fissure
réuni N (school) reunion
révolusi N revolution
réwél ADJ fussy, troublesome, difficult
RI ABBREV *Republik Indonesia* Republic of Indonesia
riam N (river) rapids
rias *meja* ~ dressing table; **riasan** N make-up
ribu N thousand; *sepuluh* ~ ten thousand; **beribu(-ribu)** ADJ thousands of; **seribu** ADJ one thousand, a thousand
ribut noise; noisy
ricuh ADJ chaotic, out of control; **kericuhan** N chaos
rilék, riléks, rélaks relax, relaxed
rimba N jungle, forest
rinci detail; **rincian** N details; **perincian** N details, detailed explanation
rindang ADJ leafy, shady

INDONESIAN—ENGLISH

rinding: merinding v to have goose-bumps or an eerie feeling, be spooked

rindu longing; **kerinduan** N longing, craving; **merindukan** v to miss, long for

ring N (boxing) ring

ringan ADJ light, easy

ringgit N ringgit, Malaysian currency (100 cents)

ringkas: ringkasan N summary, synopsis

rintang: rintangan N obstacle; barricade

rintis: perintis N pioneer

risau ADJ uneasy, anxious

risét N research

risih, risi, résé feel uncomfortable

risik: berisik ADJ noisy, loud; v to rustle

risiko N risk; **berisiko** ADJ risky

risték N research and technology → **risét dan téknologi**

riwayat N story, tale

robah, rubah → **ubah**

robék ADJ torn (of cloth), holey; **merobék** v to tear up, shred

roboh, rubuh collapse; **merobohkan** v to knock down, demolish

roda N wheel; **beroda** ADJ wheeled

rogoh: merogoh v to grope around, search for (inside something else)

roh N spirit, ghost; **rohani** ADJ spiritual, religious

rok N skirt; dress; ~ *mini* miniskirt

rokok N cigarette; **merokok** v to smoke

romansa N romance; **romantik** ADJ romantic

Romawi, Rumawi ADJ Roman; *huruf* ~ Roman letters or numerals

rombak: merombak v to pull down, demolish; to reorganize

rombong: rombongan N group, party

romo, Romo N, PRON, CATH (Catholic) priest, Father

rompak: perompak N pirate

rompi N waistcoat, vest

rona N color, shade; **perona** ~ *mata* eyeshadow; ~ *pipi* rouge

ronda patrol; ~ *malam* night watch, night patrol

rondé *wedang* ~ Javanese warm drink

rongga N cavity, hollow, hole

rongkong → **kerongkongan**

ronsen → **rontgen**

ronta: meronta(-ronta) v to struggle, squirm to get loose

rontak → **berontak**

rontgen [ronsen], **ronsen** N x-ray; **dironsen** v to be x-rayed

rontok fall out, shed

rosot: merosot v to fall down, descend, plummet; **perosotan** N (children's) slide

rotan N rattan

roti N bread, bun; ~ *gandum* (brown or wholemeal) bread

Rp. *rupiah* rupiah, Indonesian currency

RRC ABBREV *Republik Rakyat Cina* People's Republic of China

RS ABBREV *rumah sakit* hospital

RT/RW ABBREV *Rukun Tetang-ga/ Rukun Warga* neighborhood association/citizens' association

ruang N space, room; ~ *makan* dining room; **ruangan** N room; hall

ruas N space between joints

rubuh collapse, fall down → **roboh**

rudal N guided missile → **peluru kendali**

rugi loss, lose out; **kerugian** N loss; damage; **merugikan** v to hurt, harm, injure

rujak N fruit salad with spicy sauce

rujuk: rujukan N reference

rukan N office with a dwelling upstairs, shophouse → **rumah kantor**

ruko N shophouse → **rumah toko**

rukun ADJ harmonious

rukun N pillar, principle

rumah N house; ~ *makan* restaurant; ~ *sakit* hospital; *di* ~ at home; ~ *tangga* household, family; **perumahan** N housing (complex)

rumpun: serumpun ADJ related, of one family; *bahasa* ~ languages related to Indonesian

rumput N grass, lawn

rumus N formula

runcing ADJ sharp, pointed; *bambu* ~ bamboo spear

runding: perundingan N discussion

INDONESIAN–ENGLISH

runtuh fall down, collapse; **runtuhan, reruntuhan** N ruins; **meruntuhkan** v to overthrow

rupa shape, appearance, look; *~nya* it seems, appears; **rupa-rupa** ADJ all kinds of; **berupa** ADJ in the shape or form of; **merupakan** v to be; to form, constitute; **serupa** ADJ similar

rupiah N rupiah, Indonesian currency

rusa N deer

rusak ADJ broken, damaged, destroyed, spoilt; *~ parah* badly damaged; **kerusakan** N damage; **merusak** v to spoil, damage; **merusakkan** v to destroy, break

Rusia N Russia; *bahasa ~, orang ~* Russian

rusuh restless, disturbed; **kerusuhan** N riot, disturbance

rute N route

ruwet ADJ complicated

S

saat N moment, time

sabar ADJ patient; **bersabar** v to be patient; **kesabaran** N patience

sabit N sickle

sablon N screen-printed cloth banner; screen-printing

Sabtu *hari ~* Saturday

sabuk N belt, sash

sabun N soap; *~ cuci piring* dishwashing liquid

sabung *~ ayam* cock fighting

sabut *~ kelapa* coconut fiber

sadar conscious, aware; **kesadaran** N consciousness, awareness; **menyadari** v to realize, be aware of

sado N two-wheeled horse carriage

safir *batu ~* sapphire

sagu N sago

sahabat N friend; **bersahabat** ADJ to be friends

saham N share

sahur, saur N, ISL meal before dawn during fasting month

sahut, menyahut v to answer, reply, respond

saing: bersaing v to compete; *harga ~* competitive price; **persaingan** N competition

saja, aja ADV only, just; *-ever*; *itu ~* just that → **sahaja**

sajadah, sejadah N, ISL prayer mat or rug

sajak N rhyme; poem

saji serve; **sajian** N dish; offering; **sesajén** N ritual offering; **menyajikan** v to serve, present, offer; **penyajian** N presentation

Saka *Tahun ~* Balinese calendar

saking CONJ, COLL all because of, due to, as a result of

sakit sick, ill; pain, ache; *~ perut* stomach ache, upset stomach; *~-sakitan* often ill, frequently unwell; **kesakitan** ADJ in pain; **menyakiti** v to hurt, treat badly; **menyakitkan** ADJ painful; **penyakit** N disease, illness, complaint

sakral ADJ holy, sacred

saksi witness; **kesaksian** N evidence, testimony; **menyaksikan** v to witness

sakti ADJ magically or supernaturally powerful

saku N pocket

salah ADJ wrong, mistaken, faulty; *~ satu* one of; **bersalah** ADJ guilty; **kesalahan** N mistake

salak *buah ~* fruit with a hard brown skin like a snake, snakefruit

salam peace; *~ alaikum* ISL peace be upon you; *~ hormat* respectfully yours, yours sincerely; *~ saya* best wishes, regards; **menyalami** v to greet

saldo N balance; *~ terakhir* current balance

saléh → **soléh**

salep N ointment, cream

salib N cross

salin copy, duplicate; *baju ~* change of clothes, spare clothes; **salinan** N copy; **bersalin** v to give birth; **menyalin** v to copy; **persalinan** N childbirth

saling PRON each other, mutual; *~ mencintai* to love each other

salip, menyalip v to overtake, slip past

salju N snow; **bersalju** ADJ snowy, snow-covered

salon N beauty salon, hairdresser's

INDONESIAN–ENGLISH

S

salto N somersault
salur: saluran N channel
salut V, COLL to admire, salute
sama ADJ, ADV same, both; ~ *sekali*
NEG completely; **sama-sama**
you're welcome; ADV both, equally;
bersama ADV together; jointly;
persamaan N similarity, likeness,
resemblance; equation; **sesama**
ADJ fellow, another
sama-sama you're welcome; ADV
both, equally → **sama**
sambal, sambel N chilli sauce
sambil V, AUX while, at the same
time; ~ *lalu* in passing
sambung connect; **sambung-
menyambung** ADJ continuously;
sambungan N connection; **bersambung** ADJ in parts; to be continued; **menyambung** V to join,
continue; **menyambungkan** V to
connect to (something else); **tersambung** ADJ connected
sambut welcome; **sambutan** N
reception, welcome; **bersambut,
menyambut** V to welcome or
receive
sampah N rubbish, garbage, trash,
waste; *tempat* ~ rubbish bin, garbage can, trashcan; *tukang* ~ garbage man
sampai, sampé arrive, reach; until;
~ *jumpa*, ~ *nanti* see you later;
kesampaian ADJ achieved, reached,
realized; **menyampaikan** V to
deliver, hand over, pass on
samping N side; *di* ~ next to,
beside(s); **sampingan** N side-job,
extra work; **bersampingan** ADJ
next to each other
sampo N shampoo; ~ *anti-ketombe*
anti-dandruff shampoo
sampul N cover, folder, envelope
samudera, samudra N ocean; ~
Hindia, ~ *Indonesia* Indian Ocean
sana ADV yonder, over there (far
from speaker and listener); *di* ~
over there (far from both speaker
and listener); ~*-sini* here and there
sandal N sandals (open-toed shoes);
~ *jepit* thongs, flip flops
sandar: sandaran N support, prop;
bersandar, menyandar V to lean

sandera N hostage
sandi N code, cipher; *kata* ~ password
sandiwara N drama, play
sangat ADV very, extremely
sanggar N workshop, studio
sanggul N bun (worn with women's
national costume)
sanggup V, AUX to be able to, to be
capable of
sangka V to guess, suspect; **sangkaan** N suspicion; **bersangka** V to
suspect or think; **menyangka** V to
suspect, suppose, presume; *tidak* ~
never thought; **tersangka** N *(yang)*
~ suspect
sangkar N cage
sangkut ~ *paut* connection, link;
bersangkutan ADJ concerned,
involved; **tersangkut** ADJ involved;
caught, snagged
sanksi N disciplinary action, sanc-
tion
santai ADJ relaxed, easy-going,
informal
santan N coconut milk (used in
cooking)
santer ADJ strong, rife
santri N student at an Islamic school
(esp a boarder); strict Muslim;
pesantrén N Islamic boarding
school
santun ADJ polite, well-mannered;
santunan N benefit, compensation
(from insurance)
sapa greet; **sapaan** N greeting
sapi N cow; *susu* ~ cow's milk
sapu broom; ~ *tangan* handerchief,
hanky; **menyapu** V to sweep or
wipe
saput: tersaput ~ *awan* clouded
over
SARA ADJ communal, sectarian;
related to ethnicity, religion, race
or socioeconomic group → **suku
agama ras antargolongan**
saraf N nerve
saran N suggestion; **menyarankan** V
to suggest
sarana N facility, means; ~ *umum*
public amenity; *pra*~ infrastructure
sarang N nest
sarap: sarapan N breakfast

INDONESIAN—ENGLISH

sardin, sardén *ikan* ~ sardine
sari N essence, extract; flower; ~ *bunga* pollen
sariawan, seriawan (mouth) ulcer, have an ulcer
saring filter; **saringan** N filter, sieve
sarjana N university graduate; ~ *muda* undergraduate
sarung N sarong; cover, case; ~ *bantal* pillowcase, pillowslip
Sasak ethnic group of Lombok
sasando N harp-like musical instrument from Timor
sasar: sasaran N target; **kesasar** V, COLL to lose your way, (get) lost
sastra N literature; ~ *Indonesia* Indonesian literature; **sastrawan** N literary figure
sate, satai N satay, kebab; ~ *ayam* chicken satay; ~ *kambing* goat satay
satpam N security guard → **satuan pengamanan**
satu ADJ one; **satu-satu** ADV one by one, individually; **satuan** N unit; **bersatu** V to be united; **menyatu-kan, mempersatukan** V to unite various things; **pemersatu** N unifying agent, unifier; **persatuan** N union, association
satwa N animal, fauna
saudara N family (member); sibling, brother, sister; PRON you; brother, sister; ~ *perempuan* sister; **bersaudara** V to be related; to have brothers and sisters; **saudari** PRON, F you, sister; *saudara-*~ brothers and sisters
sauh N anchor
sauna N sauna; small steaming box in a salon
saung N open-air restaurant by a fish-pond, esp in West Java
saus N sauce, gravy; ~ *tomat* tomato sauce
sawah N (irrigated or wet) rice paddy, ricefield
sawi N bok choy, mustard greens; green leafy vegetable
sawo N brown, sweet fruit; sapodilla
saya PRON I, me, my; ~ *sendiri* I (myself); *kepada* ~ to me
sayang pity, regret; love; PRON darling; ~*ku* my darling; ~ *sekali* what

a pity; **kesayangan** favorite, pet; **menyayangi** V to love
sayap N wing; **bersayap** ADJ winged
sayat: sayatan N slice
sayembara N contest, competition
sayur N vegetable; ~ *asem* sour vegetable soup; ~ *mayur* (all kinds of) vegetables; **sayur-sayuran** N vegetables
SD ABBREV *Sekolah Dasar* primary/elementary school
seadanya ADJ what's there → **ada**
seandainya CONJ supposing, if → **andai**
sebab N reason, cause; CONJ because; ~*nya* the reason is, the reason being; **menyebabkan** V to cause; **penyebab** N cause
sebagai CONJ like, as
sebagian N some, a section of → **bagi**
sebaiknya ADV preferably, it's best if → **baik**
sebal ADJ fed up, annoyed, cheesed off; **menyebalkan** ADJ annoying, tiresome
sebaliknya ADV on the contrary, on the other hand → **balik**
sebar: menyebarkan V to spread, distribute
sebelah PREP next to; N half, side; *(di)* ~ *kanan* on the right (side) → **belah**
sebelas ADJ eleven → **belas**
sebelum PREP before; **sebelumnya** ADV previously, before(hand) → **belum**
sebenarnya ADV in fact, actually → **benar**
sebentar N a moment, minute, while
seberang across, other side; **menyeberangi** V to cross; **penye-berangan** N crossing
sebetulnya ADV in fact, actually → **betul**
sebisanya, sebisa-bisanya ADV as well as you can, to the best of your ability → **bisa**
sebuah ADJ a, one (generic counter); ~ *kursi* a chair → **buah**
sebut mention; ~ *saja* take (for instance); **sebutan** N mention; **menyebut** V to mention, name,

INDONESIAN–ENGLISH

S

say; **tersebut** ADJ (afore)mentioned, said

secara ADV in a way; used to form adverbs → cara

secepat CONJ as fast as; ~ *mungkin*, **secepat(-cepat)nya** ADV as fast as possible → cepat

secukupnya ADJ sufficient, adequate → cukup

sedak: tersedak ADJ choking

sedang ADJ medium, moderate

sedang AUX while, -ing; ~ *tidur* sleeping; **sedangkan** CONJ whereas, while

sedap ADJ delicious, tasty

sedapatnya ADV what you can get → dapat

sedekah N alms, charity, handout

sederhana ADJ simple, plain

sedia ready, prepared; willing; **bersedia** V to be prepared or willing; **menyediakan** V to prepare, get ready; **persediaan** N stock, supply; **tersedia** ADJ available, prepared

sedih ADJ sad; **bersedih** V to be or feel sad; **kesedihan** N sadness, sorrow; **menyedihkan** ADJ depressing, sad

sedikit ADJ a little, a few, a bit

sedot suck; **sedotan** N straw; **menyedot** V to suck (up)

sedu sob

seénaknya ADV, NEG just how you like, at will → énak

segala ADJ all, every; **segala-galanya** N everything, the lot

segan ADJ reluctant, averse

segar ADJ fresh; ~ *bugar* fit and healthy; **menyegarkan** ADJ refreshing

ségel seal, stamp

segera ADV immediately, directly; soon; *dengan* ~ express, immediately

segi N side, angle; point of view; ~ *empat* square, rectangle; ~ *tiga* triangle; **persegi** ADJ square, rectangular

segini ADJ this much → ini

segitu ADJ that much → itu

sehabis CONJ after → habis

sehari-hari ADV every day, daily; **seharian** ADV, COLL all day → hari

seharusnya should → harus

séhat ADJ healthy; **keséhatan** N health

sehingga CONJ until, to the point that, as far as; so that → hingga

seimbang ADJ balanced, well-proportioned → imbang

sejahtera ADJ prosperous; **kesejahteraan** N welfare

sejak CONJ since, from the time when

sejarah N history; **bersejarah** ADJ historic, historical

sejati ADJ original, genuine, real → jati

sejenis ADJ of the same type or species → jenis

sejuk ADJ cool

sekadar ADJ just; ~*nya* as necessary → kadar

sekali ADV very; *indah* ~ very beautiful

sekali ADV once; *jangan* ~-*kali* never (do this); **sekali-sekali**, **sesekali** ADV every now and then, occasionally

sekalian ADV all together, all at once; ADV, COLL at the same time → kali

sekaligus ADV all at once → kali

sekalipun CONJ even though → kali

sekali-sekali ADV every now and then, occasionally → kali

sekarang ADV now, at present

sekat bar, block, partition

sekejap N moment, flash, blink → kejap

sekian ADV so much, this much → kian

sekilas N flash, glance → kilas

sekitar PREP around; ADV around; near; **sekitarnya** *di* ~ around (a place) → kitar

sékjén N secretary-general → sékretaris jénderal

sekolah N school; institute of learning; ~ *Dasar (SD)* primary school, elementary school; *menengah* secondary school, high school; **bersekolah** V to go to school

sekongkol, persekongkolan N plot, intrigue, conspiracy → kongkol

sekop, skop N spade, shovel; spades (in cards)

sékretariat N secretariat; **sékretaris** N secretary

INDONESIAN—ENGLISH

sekrup N screw

séks N sex; *hubungan* ~ sexual relations, sexual intercourse; **seksi** ADJ sexy; **séksual** ADJ sexual

séksi N section

séksi ADJ sexy → seks

sékte N sect

séktor N sector

sekurangnya, sekurang-kurangnya ADV at least → kurang

sekutu N partner, ally; **persekutuan** N alliance, partnership

sél N cell

sela N gap, pause

selada, salada, salat N salad; lettuce

selai N jam; ~ *jeruk* marmalade; ~ *kacang* peanut butter

selain CONJ except, besides, apart from → lain

selalu ADV always → lalu

selam diving; **menyelam** V to dive; **penyelam** N diver

selama CONJ during, as long as; **selamanya** ADV always, forever → lama

selamat safe; congratulations; ~ *datang* welcome; ~ *jalan* goodbye; bon voyage, have a safe trip; ~ *malam* good evening; ~ *sore* good afternoon; **selamatan** N (thanksgiving) feast; **keselamatan** N safety; salvation; **menyelamatkan** V to save, rescue; **penyelamatan** N rescue (operation)

selambat-lambatnya ADV at the latest → lambat

selancar *papan* ~ surfboard; **berselancar** V to surf, go surfing → lancar

Sélandia Baru N New Zealand

selang N interval; ~ *sehari* every other day, every second day

selang N hose

selanjutnya ADV then, after that → lanjut

Selasa *hari* ~ Tuesday

selat N strait

selatan ADJ south

sélébritis, séléb N celebrity

selédri N celery

seléndang, sléndang N shawl; sash worn over the shoulder with women's national costume

selenggara: menyelenggarakan V to run, hold, organize; **penyelenggara** N organizer

seléra N appetite, taste

selesai finished, over; **menyelesaikan** V to finish, end, settle; ~ *masalah* to overcome a problem; **penyelesaian** N solution, settlement

selesma, selésma having a cold; cold

selidik: menyelidiki V to investigate; **penyelidik** N investigator, detective; **penyelidikan** N investigation

selimut N blanket

selingkuh, berselingkuh V to have an affair; **perselingkuhan** N affair

selip: terselip ADJ fallen or slipped into

selisih N difference

selok: selokan N ditch, trench

selonjor sit with legs sticking out in front

selop N slipper

sélotip N sellotape, adhesive or sticky tape

seluk ~ *beluk* ins and outs, details

selundup: selundupan *barang* ~ contraband, smuggled goods; **menyelundupkan** V to smuggle (in)

seluruh ADJ entire, whole; **seluruhnya** ADV completely; ADJ all; **keseluruhan** *secara* ~ totally, completely

selusin N a dozen → lusin

semak shrub, bush

semakin ADV even more → makin

semalam ADV last night → malam

semangat N spirit, enthusiasm; **bersemangat** ADJ spirited, enthusiastic

semangka N watermelon

sembah N homage, tribute, respect; **menyembah** V to pay homage to, worship; **mempersembahkan** V to offer (up), present

sembahyang pray, prayer; **bersembahyang** V to pray, perform a prayer

sembako N nine daily necessities → sembilan bahan pokok

sembarang ADJ any, whichever; **sembarangan** ADJ arbitrary, random

sembelih: menyembelih V to slaughter, butcher

INDONESIAN–ENGLISH

S

sembelit constipation, constipated
sembilan ADJ nine; ~ *belas* nineteen; ~ *puluh* ninety
semboyan N motto, slogan
sembuh recovered, better; *cepat* ~ get well soon; **menyembuhkan** V to cure, heal
sembunyi hide, conceal; **sembunyi-sembunyi** ADV secretly, in secret; **bersembunyi** V to hide (yourself); **menyembunyikan** V to hide or conceal something; **persembunyian** N hiding place, hideout
semenanjung N peninsula
sementara CONJ during; ADJ temporary; ~ *itu* in the meantime, meanwhile
semestinya should have (been) → **mesti**
seminggu ADJ a week → **minggu**
semir polish; ~ *sepatu* shoe polish
semoga may, hopefully → **moga**
sempat chance, opportunity; **kesempatan** N opportunity
sempit ADJ narrow; **menyempit** V to (become) narrow
semprot squirt; spurt; **semprotan** N spray-gun; **menyemprot** V to spray; **menyemprotkan** V to spray with something
sempurna ADJ perfect, complete
semrawut ADJ haphazard, uncontrolled
semua ADJ all; ~*nya* all, everyone
semula ADV originally → **mula**
semut N ant; **kesemutan** V to have pins and needles
sén cent
senam N gymnastics, aerobics; exercise; ~ *hamil* pre-natal exercises; ~ *pagi* morning exercise; *baju* ~ leotard
senang ADJ happy, content; V to like; **bersenang-senang** V to enjoy yourself, have fun; **kesenangan** N amusement, hobby; **menyenangkan** ADJ pleasing, agreeable
senapan N rifle
senda ~ *gurau* joke; **bersenda** ~ *gurau* to joke around
sendawa: bersendawa V to burp, belch
sendi N joint

sendiri ADV alone; PRON self; **sendirian** ADV alone, single-handedly; **tersendiri** ADJ its own; apart, separate → **diri**
séndok N spoon; ~ *garpu* spoon and fork
séng N zinc
sengaja ADV deliberately, on purpose; *tidak* ~ unintentionally
sengat sting; **sengatan** N sting, bite; **menyengat** V to sting
sénggol brush, bump; **menyénggol** V to bump, brush, tweak; **tersénggol** ADJ bumped, brushed
sengkéta N dispute; *tanah* ~ disputed land
sengsara misery
seni N art; ~ *lukis* painting; **kesenian** N art (form); **seniman** N, M **seniwati** N, F artist
Senin, Senén *hari* ~ Monday
sénior N person in higher class or of higher position
senja N twilight, dusk
senjata N weapon; ~ *api* firearm, gun; **senjata** ADJ armed
sénsor N censor; *kena* ~, *disensor* censored
sénsus N census
sénter N *(lampu)* ~ flashlight, torch
sénti N centimeter, centimetre; *berapa* ~ how many centimeters, how long → **séntiméter**
sentil: sentilan N flick, nudge
sentimétér, sénti N centimeter, centimetre
séntral central
sentuh touch; **sentuhan** N touch; **menyentuh** V to touch; **tersentuh** ADJ touched
senyap ADJ quiet, still
senyum, tersenyum V to smile
seorang a (person); counter for people; ~ *Arab* an Arab → **orang**
sépak kick; ~ *bola* soccer, football; ~ *takraw* game played with a rattan ball; **menyépak** V to kick (out)
sepakat V to agree; **kesepakatan** N agreement; **menyepakati** V to agree to → **pakat**
sepanjang CONJ, ADJ as long as → **panjang**
séparatis separatist

INDONESIAN—ENGLISH

S

separo, separuh N half → paruh

sepasang N a pair of → pasang

sepatu N shoe(s); ~ *sandal* sandals; **bersepatu** ADJ in shoes

sepéda N bicycle, (push)bike; ~ *motor* motor bike; *naik* ~ to ride a bike; **bersepéda** v to ride a bicycle

sepenuhnya ADV fully, completely → penuh

seperempat N one quarter → empat

seperti CONJ like; ~*nya* it seems

sepertiga ADJ one-third → tiga

sepi ADJ quiet, still, lonely; **kesepian** N loneliness, solitude

sepihak ADJ unilateral → pihak

sepoi: sepoi-sepoi *angin* ~ breeze, zephyr

seprei, seprai N (bed)sheet

Séptémber *bulan* ~ September

sepuluh N ten → puluh

sepupu N cousin

sepur N, COLL railway (line); rail; platform

seputar ADJ around, about → putar

seragam N uniform → ragam

serah hand over, transfer; **menyerah** v to surrender, give in, give up; **menyerahkan** v to hand over; **penyerahan** N handing over, handover; **terserah** ADJ it depends; up to you

serai, séréh N lemongrass, citronella

serak ADJ hoarse

serakah ADJ greedy

seram ADJ weird, creepy

serambi N verandah

serang, menyerany v to attack; **serangan** N attack

serangga N insect, bug

serap absorb; **menyerap** v to absorb, soak up

serat N fiber, fibre

seratus ADJ one hundred, a hundred → ratus

serba ADJ all kinds of, various

serbét N serviette, table napkin

serbu: menyerbu v to attack (as a group), charge, invade

serbuk N powder

séréal N (breakfast) cereal

séréh, serai N lemongrass, citronella

serentak ADJ all at once, simultaneous, at the same time

sérét, menyérét v to drag

seri N draw, tie

séri N series

seribu ADJ one thousand, a thousand → ribu

serigala N wolf

serikat union, united; **perserikatan** N federation

sérius ADJ serious

séro: perséroan N company

serobot push in front; **menyerobot** v to push in front

sérong ADJ on an angle, oblique

serpih, serpihan N shred, bit, piece; ~ *kayu* wood chip

serta CONJ (together) with; **beserta** CONJ along with, and; **peserta** N participant

seru ADJ exciting, great

seruling, suling N flute

serumpun ADJ related, of one family; *bahasa* ~ related languages → rumpun

serupa ADJ similar → rupa

sérvis N repairs, service, maintenance; **disérvis** v to be serviced

sesajén N ritual offering → saji

sesak ADJ close, dense, crowded

sesal regret; **menyesal** v to regret; **menyesalkan** v to feel bad about, regret (another's action)

sesama ADJ fellow, another → sama

sesat lost; **menyesatkan** ADJ misleading, confusing; **tersesat** ADJ lost

sesekali ADV every now and then, occasionally → kali

seseorang N somebody, a certain person → orang

sesuai ADJ in accordance with, appropriate; **menyesuaikan** v to adapt, bring into line → suai

sesuatu N something → suatu

sesudah PREP after; ~ *itu*, sesudahnya after that, then → sudah

sesungguhnya ADV actually, really → sungguh

setahu CONJ as far as is known → tahu

sétan, syaitan N devil, demon

setasiun, stasiun, setasion N (railway) station

setél N set; **setélan** N set, suit

INDONESIAN–ENGLISH

S

setél, menyétel v to tune, set, adjust; ~ *mesin mobil* to tune an engine

setelah PREP after → **telah**

setempat ADJ local → **tempat**

setengah ADJ half; *jam* ~ *dua* half past one; **setengah-setengah** ADV half-heartedly → **tengah**

seterusnya ADV after that, henceforth → **terus**

setia ADJ faithful

setiap ADJ each, every; ~ *saat* any time → **tiap**

setidaknya, setidak-tidaknya ADV at least → **tidak**

setinggi ADJ as high as → **tinggi**

setir: menyetir v to drive

setop: setopan N, COLL traffic lights

setor: setoran (make a) deposit; **menyetor** v to pay in, deposit

setrika, seterika iron; **setrikaan** N (clothes for) ironing; **menyetrika** v to iron

setrip, strip N (diagonal) slash; strip; section of a mobile phone battery symbol

setrum N current; **kesetrum** v, COLL to receive an electric shock

setuju agree, agreed; **menyetujui** v to agree to, approve, ratify; **persetujuan** N agreement, approval → **tuju**

seumpamanya CONJ for instance → **umpama**

seumur ADJ the same age; lifelong → **umur**

séwa hire, rent; **menyéwa** v to rent, hire; **menyéwakan** v to let (a house), hire out, lease

shio N Chinese horoscope, based on year born

sholat, shalat, solat ISL (perform) one of the five daily prayers

si PREF used before the name of a familiar third party

sia: sia-sia ADJ pointless, useless

siaga ADJ alert, on guard, ready

sial unlucky; **sialan** EJAC damn! hell!

siang N day; late morning, early afternoon (usu between 10 am and 3 pm); *makan* ~ lunch; **kesiangan** ADJ late, too late in the day

siap ready; **bersiap** v to get ready; **bersiap-siap** v to make preparations; **menyiapkan, mempersiap-**

kan v to prepare something, get something ready; **persiapan** N preparations

siapa INTERROG, PRON who; ~ *namanya?* what's your name?; ~ *saja* anybody; **siapa-siapa** PRON, NEG nobody

siar: siaran N telecast, broadcast; **penyiar** N announcer

siar: pesiar N trip, cruise; *kapal* ~ cruise ship; pleasure craft

sia-sia ADJ pointless, useless

sibuk ADJ busy; engaged (of phones); **kesibukan** N activity, fuss, bustle, business

sidang N session, meeting; hearing

sidik ~ *jari* fingerprints; **penyidikan** N investigation → **selidik**

sifat N quality, nature, character; **bersifat** v to have the quality of

sih used as a filler; *saya* ~ *tidak keberatan* I myself have no objection

sihir N spells, witchcraft; **penyihir** N wizard, witch, sorcerer

sikap N attitude; **bersikap** v to display an attitude

sikat brush; **menyikat** v to brush

siklus N cycle

siksa torture; **menyiksa** v to torture; **tersiksa** ADJ tortured

siku N elbow; bracket

sila: silakan, silahkan please (when offering); ~ *masuk* please come in; **mempersilakan** v to invite someone to do something

silang cross, across

silat traditional self-defense

silaturahmi N good relations, friendship; **bersilaturahmi** v to maintain good relations, visit or meet friends

silau ADJ blinded, dazzled

silét N razor, scalpel

silsilah N family tree, pedigree (of an animal)

SIM N driver's license, driving license → **Surat Izin Mengemudi**

simpan v to keep, put; **simpanan** N something kept; *uang* ~ savings, deposit; **menyimpan** v to keep, save up, store

simpang cross; ~ *tiga* T-junction; **persimpangan** N intersection

simpul N knot; **kesimpulan** N con-

INDONESIAN—ENGLISH

clusion; **menyimpulkan** v to conclude or summarize

sinar n ray, beam; **bersinar** v to
shine, gleam

sindir, menyindir v to insinuate,
allude; **sindiran** n allusion, insinu-
ation

sinéas n cinematographer; **sinétron**
n local TV comedy or drama →
sinéma éléktronik

singa n lion

Singapura n Singapore

singgah v to drop by, call at, stop
over

singgung, menyinggung v to touch
on; **tersinggung** adj offended, hurt

singkat adj short, brief, concise;
~nya in brief; **singkatan** n abbreviation; **menyingkatkan** v to
abbreviate, shorten

singkir: menyingkirkan v to
remove, brush aside; **tersingkir** adj
eliminated, swept aside

singkong n cassava

sini adv here; di ~ here → ini

sinsé, sin shé n Chinese doctor,
practitioner of Chinese medicine or
acupuncture

sinyal n signal

siomay, sio may n fishcakes eaten
with peanut sauce

sipil adj civil

sipit adj narrow, slanting (of eyes)

siput n snail

siram v to pour; **siraman** n bathing
ceremony before a wedding;
menyiram v to pour, water (plants)

siréne n siren

sirih n betel; makan ~ chew betel

sirip n fin

sirkuit n (racing) circuit, race track

sirkus n circus

sirop n syrup, cordial

sirsak n soursop, green-skinned
fruit with white fleshy interior

sisa n rest, remainder, remains;
tersisa adj leftover

sisi n side

sisik n scale (of fish)

sisir n comb; hand (of bananas);
se~ pisang a bunch of bananas;
menyisir v to comb, check thoroughly

sistém, sistim n system

siswa n pupil; **siswi** n, f pupil

situ di ~ there (close to listener) →
itu

situasi n situation

situs n site; ~ internet website

siul: bersiul v to whistle

skala n scale; **berskala** v to be on a
scale

skétsa n sketch

skor n score

Skotlandia n Scotland

SLI abbrev Sambungan Langsung
Internasional international direct
dialling

SLJJ abbrev Sambungan Langsung
Jarak Jauh long-distance direct
dialling

SMA abbrev Sekolah Menengah
Atas Senior High School

SMP abbrev Sekolah Menengah
Pertama Junior High School

soal n question, issue, problem,
matter; conj on the topic of; ~nya
the problem is; **mempersoalkan** v
to question, discuss; **persoalan** n
problem, issue, matter

sobat n friend, comrade

sobék torn (esp of paper);
menyobék v to tear

soda air ~ soda water; **bersoda** adj
carbonated; minuman ~ carbonated
drink

sofbol n softball

sogok uang ~ bribe; **sogokan** n
bribe; **menyogok** v to bribe

sohun, so'un n vermicelli noodles

sok coll pretend; as if; ~ tahu be a
know-all

sol ~ sepatu (shoe) sole

solar n diesel fuel

soléh, saléh adj pious, religious

solusi n solution

sombong adj arrogant, stuck-up

songkét n (kain) ~ woven cloth,
often with gold thread

sop n (western-style) soup

sopan adj polite, well-mannered;
kesopanan n manners, politeness;
kesopan-santunan n manners,
etiquette

sorak cheer, shout; applause; **bersorak** v to cheer, shout

INDONESIAN–ENGLISH

S

soré (late) afternoon, early evening; ~ *hari* late in the day; **kesoréan** ADV too late

sorot N beam of light; **sorotan** N focus; **menyoroti** v to light up, illuminate, focus on

sosial ADJ social

sosis N sausage

sosok N figure

soto N clear soup; ~ *ayam* chicken soup

sotong *ikan* ~ cuttlefish, squid

spanduk N large banner

Spanyol N Spain

spasi N space, spacing

spérma N sperm

spidol N felt-tip marker or pen, texta; whiteboard marker

spion N spy

spontan ADJ spontaneous

srikaya, serikaya N custard-apple

stabil ADJ stable

stabilo N highlighter, fluorescent marker

stadion N (sports) stadium

stadium N stage (of an illness); ~ *tiga* advanced

status N (marital) status

stémpel, setémpel N official stamp

stopkontak N power point, electricity socket

stréng ADJ strict, harsh, disciplinarian

strés, setrés stress(ed)

stupa N stupa, bell-shaped dome covering a Buddha statue

suai: sesuai ADJ in accordance or keeping with; **menyesuaikan** v to adapt

suaka N asylum; *pencari* ~ asylum seeker

suami N husband; **bersuami** ADJ, F married

suap N mouthful; bribe; **suapan** N bribe; **menyuap** v to feed by hand; to bribe

suara N voice

suasana N atmosphere

suatu ADJ a (certain); ~ *hari* one day; **sesuatu** N something

subuh N, ISL dawn

subur ADJ fertile

subyék N subject

suci ADJ pure, holy; **menyucikan** v to purify, cleanse

sudah AUX udah COLL already; indicates past time; **sesudah** PREP after; **sesudahnya** after that, then

sudut N corner, angle, perspective, point of view; **menyudutkan** v to push into a corner, deflect

suguh: suguhan N something offered or presented

suhu N temperature

suit whistling sound; **suitan** N whistle

suka v to like; ADV often; **kesukaan** N hobby; enjoyment; **menyukai** v to like

sukar ADJ difficult, hard; **kesukaran** N difficulty

sukaréla ADJ voluntary; **sukarélawan** N volunteer → *réla*

suksés N success; *semoga* ~ good luck, every success; **mensukséskan** v to make something succeed

suku N tribe; part; ~ *bangsa* ethnic group

sulam: sulaman N embroidery; **menyulam** v to embroider

sulang: bersulang v to toast, drink to

sulap magic, conjure; **sulapan** N conjuring, magic; **menyulap** v to conjure up; to make something vanish or change; **penyulap** N magician, conjurer

Sulawési, Sulawesi *(pulau)* ~ Sulawesi, Celebes

sulit ADJ difficult, hard

Sulsel N South Sulawesi → Sulawési Selatan

Sulteng N Central Sulawesi → Sulawési Tengah

Sultra N Southeast Sulawesi → Sulawési Tenggara

Sulut N North Sulawesi → Sulawési Utara

Sumatera, Sumatra *(pulau)* ~ Sumatra

sumbang: sumbangan N contribution, donation; **menyumbang** v to contribute, make a donation

Sumbar N West Sumatra → Sumatera Barat

sumbat plug; cork, stopper; **menyumbat** v to plug, stop

INDONESIAN–ENGLISH

sumber N source; well
sumpah curse; oath; **bersumpah** v to swear
sumpek ADJ crowded, stuffy
sumpit N chopsticks
Sumsel N South Sumatra → Sumatera Selatan
sumsum N bone marrow
sumur N well
Sumut N North Sumatra → Sumatera Utara
sun peck on the cheek, kiss
sunat: sunatan N circumcision (celebration); **disunat** v to be circumcised; **menyunatkan** v to have someone circumcised
Sunda *bahasa ~, orang ~* Sundanese
sungai N river
sungguh ADJ real, true; **sungguh-sungguh** ADJ serious; **sesungguhnya** ADV actually, really
suntik: suntikan N vaccination, injection; needle; **menyuntik** v to inject or vaccinate
sunting: penyunting N editor
sunyi ADJ lonely, still, quiet
supaya CONJ in order that, so (used before nouns)
supir, sopir N driver, chauffeur; **menyupir** v to drive
suram ADJ gloomy, dark
surat N letter; certificate, card; *~ kabar* newspaper; **menyurati** v to write a letter to
surga, syurga, sorga N heaven, paradise
Suriah N Syria; *orang ~* Syrian
Suriname N Surinam
suruh order, ask; tell; **suruhan** N messenger, errand-boy; **menyuruh** v to command, order; **pesuruh** N messenger, errand boy
surut v to recede; *air ~* low tide
surya *tenaga ~* solar energy
susah difficult; trouble, sorrow; **kesusahan** N trouble, difficulty; **menyusahkan** v to bother, make difficult
suster N nurse(maid); N, CATH nun
susu N milk; N, SL breast; *~ kaleng* condensed milk; **menyusui** v to feed

susul: menyusul v to follow, go after
susun heap, pile; *rumah ~ (rusun)* block of flats, apartment block; **susunan** N arrangement, organization, system; **menyusun** v to heap or pile; to arrange, organize, compile; **penyusun** N compiler, author
sutera, sutra N silk
sutradara N director
swa- PREF self-; *~layan* self-serve, supermarket
Swédia N Sweden
Swis N Switzerland
switer N jumper, pullover, sweater
syair N poem; **penyair** N poet
syal N shawl, scarf
syarat, sarat N condition, terms; *dengan ~* on condition; **bersyarat** ADJ conditional
syariah *hukum ~* Islamic law
syukur, sukur thanks, thanksgiving; thank goodness; **bersyukur** ADJ grateful; **mensyukuri** v to appreciate, be thankful

T

taat ADJ obedient; religious
tabel N table, chart
tabir N curtain, screen; *~ surya* sunscreen, sunblock
tabrak collide; **tabrakan** N collision, accident; **menabrak** v to collide with; **tertabrak** ADJ to be hit
tabu taboo
tabuh N drum; drumstick; **menabuh** v to beat (a drum)
tabung N container, tube; **tabungan** N savings; **menabung** v to save or deposit money
tabur scatter, sprinkle; **bertaburan** ADJ scattered over
tadi ADV just now; *~nya* originally, at first; *~ pagi* this morning; *~ malam* last night
tagih: tagihan N amount due, bill; **ketagihan** ADJ addicted to
tahan bear, stop, last; *tidak ~* can't bear; **tahanan** N prisoner, detainee; custody, detention; **menahan** v to bear, endure; to detain; **mempertahankan** v to defend or maintain;

INDONESIAN—ENGLISH

T

pertahanan N defense; **tertahan** ADJ held back, prevented

tahap N stage, phase; **bertahap** ADJ in stages

tahi N shit, feces; ~ *lalat* mole

tahu V [tau] to know; **tahu-tahu** ADV suddenly, unexpectedly; **ketahuan** V to be found out; **mengetahui** V to know something, have knowledge of; **pengetahuan** N knowledge; **setahu** CONJ as far as is known

tahu N tofu

tahun N year; ~ *Baru* New Year; ~ *Baru Cina*, ~ *Baru Imlek* Chinese New Year; **tahunan** ADJ annual, yearly

tahu-tahu ADV suddenly, unexpectedly → **tahu**

Taiwan N Taiwan

tajam ADJ sharp

taji N spur (of a cock)

tajuk N crown; editorial

tak no, not; ~ *kan*, ~*kan* will not, won't → **tidak**

takar: takaran N measuring container or spoon

takkan will not, won't → **tak kan**

takraw N small rattan ball

taksi N taxi

takut ADJ scared, afraid; *rasa* ~ fear; **ketakutan** ADJ frightened, terrified, scared; **menakutkan** V, ADV frightening; to frighten or scare; **penakut** N coward

talang N (roof) gutter

talenan N chopping or cutting board

tali N rope, cord, tie; ~ *sepatu* shoelace

taman N garden, park; ~ *budaya* cultural center; ~ *kanak-kanak (TK)* kindergarten

tamasya V view; spectacle; excursion

tamat end, finish; ~ *sekolah* graduate; **tamatan** N graduate

tambah add; **tambahan** N addition, increase; **bertambah** V to increase; **menambah** V to add to or increase; **menambahi** V to increase something; **menambahkan** V to add something to; **pertambahan** N increase

tambak N dam, pond; dike, levee, embankment

tambal N patch; ~ *ban* tire repair; **tambalan** N patch, darn (on a sock); **menambal** V to mend, patch, darn

tambang N mine; ~ *emas* gold mine; **pertambangan** N mining

tambat tie up, tether

tambur N drum

taméng N shield

tampak visible, appear

tampan ADJ, M handsome

tampang N appearance; COLL face

tampar slap, smack; **menampar** V to slap

tampil V to appear; **penampilan** N performance

tamu N guest, visitor; *ruang* ~ front room, living room; room for receiving guests

tanah N earth, ground, land, soil; country; ~ *air* Indonesia; *minyak* ~ kerosene

tanam: tanaman N plant; **menanam** V to plant or grow; to invest

tancap *layar* ~ open-air makeshift cinema; ~ *gas* step on the gas, accelerate

tanda N sign, mark, symbol; ~ *tangan* signature; **bertanda** ADJ marked; **menandatangani** V to sign something; **menandai** V to mark

tanding N match, equal; **bertanding** V to compete, play; **pertandingan** N contest, competition, match

tanduk N horn

tandus ADJ infertile, barren

tangan N hand, arm; sleeve; **menangani** V to handle

tangga N ladder, stair(case)

tanggal N date; ~ *lahir* date of birth; **tertanggal** ADJ dated

tanggap: tanggapan N response, reaction; **menanggapi** V to respond, reply

tanggul N dike, levee, embankment

tanggung ADJ guaranteed; ~ *jawab* responsibility; **bertanggung jawab** V to be responsible; **mempertanggung jawabkan** V to account for; **tanggungan** N dependent; responsibility; **menanggung** V to guarantee, be responsible

tangis *isak* ~ crying; **tangisan** N weeping, crying; **menangis** V to cry

INDONESIAN—ENGLISH

tangkai N stem, stalk

tangkap, menangkap V to catch, capture; **penangkapan** N capture, arrest; **tertangkap** ADJ caught

tangkas ADJ agile, adroit, deft

tangki N tank

tani N farmer; **petani** N farmer; **pertanian** N agriculture

tanjak: tanjakan N rise, ascent, climb; **menanjak** ADJ rising, climbing, steep

tanjung N cape; **semenanjung** N peninsula

tanpa PREP, CONJ without

tantang challenge; **tantangan** N challenge; **menantang** V to challenge; ADJ challenging

tante PRON, POL term of address to a familiar but unrelated woman, esp of mother's generation, in Westernized circles

tanya ask; **bertanya** V to ask; **bertanya-tanya** V to wonder, ask yourself; **menanyakan** V to ask about; **mempertanyakan** V to query; **pertanyaan** N question

tapak, telapak ~ *kaki* sole; footprint; ~ *tangan* palm

tapal ~ *kuda* horseshoe

tapé, tapai N fermented rice

tapi → tetapi

taplak ~ *meja* tablecloth

tar, tart *kue* ~ (birthday) cake

taraf N standard, level

tari N (traditional) dance; ~*-tarian* traditional dancing; **tarian** N (traditional) dance; **menari** V to dance, perform a traditional dance; **menari-nari** V to dance about; **penari** N dancer

tarif, tarip N tariff, fare, rate

tarik pull; **menarik** V to pull or draw; ADJ interesting, attractive; **tertarik** ADJ attracted, interested

taring N tusk; fang

taruh V to place, put; **taruhan** bet, wager; **bertaruh** V to bet; **menaruh** V to put (away)

tas N bag; ~ *pinggang* bum bag; ~ *tangan* handbag

tato N tattoo

tauco, taoco N brown sauce made from fermented soybeans

taugé, taogé, togé N bean sprouts

tawa laugh, laughter; **tawaan** N object of fun; **ketawa** COLL **tertawa** V to laugh or smile; **menertawakan** V to laugh at

tawan: tawanan N prisoner of war (POW), detainee

tawar bargain; **menawar** V to bargain; *tawar-~* bargaining; **menawarkan** V to offer or bid; **penawaran** N offer, bid

tawon N bee

tawur: tawuran gang or street fight, often among schoolboys

tayang: tayangan N program, telecast; ~ *langsung* live telecast

téater N theater (building), theater; drama group

tebak guess; **tebakan** N guess; **menebak** V to guess

tebal ADJ thick

tebang fall, be cut down (of trees); **menebang** V to fell, cut down; **penebangan** N logging; ~ *liar* illegal logging

tebing N cliff, gorge, steep bank

tebu N sugarcane

teduh ADJ shady; quiet, still; **berteduh** V to take shelter

téga V to have the heart to, dare to; *~nya* how could you have the heart

tegak ADJ upright, erect; **menegakkan** V to erect; to uphold or maintain

tegang ADJ tense, stressed, strained; **ketegangan** N tension; **menegangkan** ADJ tense, stressful

tegas ADJ clear, distinct; **menegaskan** V to clarify, point out, affirm

tégel N, ARCH (floor) tile → ubin

teguh ADJ firm, fast, strong, solid

teguk N gulp, swallow, draft; **tegukan** N swallow, gulp; **meneguk** V to gulp or guzzle

tegur speak; rebuke; ~ *sapa* say hello; **teguran** N warning, rebuke; greeting; **menegur** V to speak to, address; to warn, rebuke, tell off

téh N tea; ~ *tawar* black tea no sugar; *kantong ~, celup* ~ teabag

tékad will, determination

tekan press; **tekanan** N pressure, stress; **menekan** V to press; **mene-**

INDONESIAN–ENGLISH

T

kankan v to stress, emphasize; **tertekan** ADJ stressed, pushed, pressured

teka-teki N riddle, puzzle

téken v to sign, initial

téknik, téhnik N engineering; ADJ technical

téknis ADJ technical; **téknisi** N technician

téko N kettle, teapot

téks N text; subtitle

tekuk ~ *lutut* bend your knee

tekun ADJ hard-working

teladan N example, model

telaga N lake

telah ADV already; **setelah** CONJ after

telan v to swallow; **menelan** v to swallow something; **tertelan** v accidentally swallowed

telanjang ADJ naked, nude, bare

telanjur ADV too late, already → lanjur

telantar, terlantar ADJ neglected, abandoned

telapak, tapak ~ *kaki* sole; footprint; ~ *tangan* palm

telat ADV, COLL (too) late

telatén ADJ patient, persevering

telédor ADJ careless

téléfon → télepon

télékomunikasi N telecommunications; *warung* ~ *(wartel)* small office where you can make calls and send faxes

telentang ADJ on your back, prone → lentang

télepon, télépon, téléfon telephone; ~ *seluler (ponsel)* mobile phone; **menélépon** v to ring (up), call, (tele)phone

télér ADJ drunk, intoxicated; exhausted

télévisi, tévé, tivi N television, TV

telinga N ear

teliti ADJ accurate, careful, meticulous; **peneliti** N researcher; **penelitian** N research

teluk N bay, gulf

telur, telor N egg; ~ *ayam* egg

téma N theme

teman N friend; **berteman** v to be friends; **menemani** v to accompany

tembaga N copper

témbak shoot, fire; **témbakan** N shot, shooting; **menémbak** v to shoot; **penémbak** N marksman, gunman; **tertémbak** ADJ shot (accidentally)

tembakau N tobacco

témbok N (concrete or outer) wall

tembus pierce, penetrate; **menembus** v to pierce, stab

tempat N place; ~ *lahir* birthplace, place of birth; ~ *tidur* bed; ~ *tinggal* home, residence; **menempati** v to occupy, take a place; **setempat** ADJ local

témpé N unrefined soybean curd

témpél stick to; **menémpél** v to stick or adhere to; **menémpélkan** v to stick, paste or glue something

témpo N time, pace; ~ *hari* the other day, recently

tempuh: menempuh v to endure, go through; to take on, take up; ~ *ujian* to do an exam

tempur fight, combat; *pesawat* ~ fighter; **pertempuran** N battle

tempurung N coconut shell

temu find, locate; **temuan** N find, discovery; **bertemu** v to meet; *sampai* ~ *lagi* see you later, so long; **ketemu** v, COLL to meet; **menemui** v to meet up with, arrange to meet; **menemukan** v to discover; **penemu** N inventor, discoverer; **penemuan** N invention, discovery; **pertemuan** N meeting

tenaga N energy, power

tenang ADJ calm, still, quiet; **menenangkan** v to calm someone (down)

tenar ADJ well-known, popular

ténda N tent

tendang kick; **tendangan** N kick; **menendang** v to kick

tengah middle, in the middle of, half; **tengah-tengah** PREP middle; **menengah** ADJ intermediate; *kaum* ~ middle class; **setengah** ADJ half; *jam* ~ *dua* half past one; **setengah-setengah** ADV half-heartedly

tenggara ADJ southeast

tenggelam sink, sunken; drown

tenggiling N anteater

tenggiri *ikan* ~ mackerel

tenggorok, tenggorokan N throat

INDONESIAN – ENGLISH

T

tengkar: bertengkar v to quarrel; **pertengkaran** n quarrel

tengkorak n skull

tengkurap, tengkurup ADV on your front or face

téngok, menéngok v to look or see; to look in on someone

ténis n tennis; **peténis** n tennis player

ténsi n blood pressure

tentang CONJ about, concerning; **bertentangan** ADJ contradictory, contrary, opposing; **menentang** v to oppose, resist

tentara n soldier

ténténg, menénténg v to carry dangling from the hand

tentu ADJ certain, sure, definite; ~*nya*, ~ *saja* of course; **ketentuan** n condition, stipulation; **menentukan** v to decide, determine, stipulate; **tertentu** ADJ definite, fixed, certain

tenun *kain* ~ woven cloth; **tenunan** n weaving, woven fabric; **menenun** v to weave

tepat ADJ precise, exact

tepi edge, side; ~ *jalan* side of the road; ~ *laut* seaside

tepuk ~ *tangan* applause, clap; **bertepuk tangan** v to applaud, clap

tepung n flour; ~ *beras* rice flour; ~ *terigu* flour

ter- PREF (before adjectives) the most; **terbaik** ADJ the best; **tertinggi** ADJ the highest

tér n tar

terakhir ADJ last, final, latest → **akhir**

terang ADJ clear; **terang-terangan** ADJ frank, open; **keterangan** n explanation; **menerangkan** v to explain

terap: terapan ADJ applied; **menerapkan** v to apply something

térapi n therapy; *fisio*~ physiotherapy

téras n balcony, terrace

terasa v to be felt → **rasa**

terasi n shrimp paste

teratai *(bunga)* ~ lotus

teratur ADJ organized, regular → **atur**

terbaik ADJ the best → **baik**

terbakar ADJ burnt → **bakar**

terbalik ADJ overturned, upside-down, opposite → **balik**

terbang v fly; **menerbangkan** v to fly something; **penerbang** n pilot, aviator; **penerbangan** n flight; aviation

terbaru ADJ latest, newest → **baru**

terbatas ADJ limited → **batas**

terbayang ADJ imagine, conceivable → **bayang**

terbentuk ADJ formed, shaped, created → **bentuk**

terbesar ADJ largest, biggest → **besar**

terbit v to rise, appear; **terbitan** n publication, edition; **menerbitkan** v to publish, issue; **penerbit** n publisher

terbuka ADJ open → **buka**

terbukti ADJ proven → **bukti**

terbunuh ADJ killed → **bunuh**

terburu-buru ADJ in a hurry → **buru**

tercantum ADJ attached, included, inserted → **cantum**

tercapai ADJ achieved → **capai**

tercatat ADJ registered; *surat* ~ registered mail → **catat**

tercemar ADJ polluted → **cemar**

tercepat ADJ fastest → **cepat**

tercinta ADJ dear, beloved → **cinta**

terdaftar ADJ registered, enrolled → **daftar**

terdakwa n the accused → **dakwa**

terdekat ADJ closest, nearest → **dekat**

terdiri ~ *atas*, ~ *dari* to consist of, be based or founded on → **diri**

terdorong ADJ pushed, shoved → **dorong**

terendah ADJ lowest → **rendah**

terendam ADJ inundated, flooded, soaked → **rendam**

terganggu ADJ bothered, disrupted, disturbed → **ganggu**

tergantung ADJ depending (on), it depends; **ketergantungan** n dependency → **gantung**

tergelincir ADJ skidded, slipped → **gelincir**

tergenang ADJ flooded → **genang**

tergesa-gesa ADJ in a hurry or rush → **gesa**

tergoda ADJ tempted → **goda**

INDONESIAN–ENGLISH

tergolong ADJ to include, be part of or considered → **golong**

tergorés ADJ scratched → **gorés**

terhadap CONJ regarding, against, with respect to → **hadap**

terhalang ADJ blocked, prevented → **halang**

terharu ADJ moved, touched → **haru**

terhormat ADJ respected → **hormat**

teriak scream, yell; **berteriak** V to scream or shout

terigu N wheat

terima menerima V to accept, ~ *kasih* thank you, thanks; **berterima kasih** V to be grateful or thankful

teripang, tripang N sea slug, sea cucumber, *trepang*

terisak, terisak(isak) ADJ sobbing → **isak**

terjadi V to happen, become → **jadi**

terjal ADJ very steep, precipitous

terjamin ADJ guaranteed → **jamin**

terjatuh ADJ (accidentally) fallen → **jatuh**

terjawab ADJ answered → **jawab**

terjebak ADJ trapped, caught → **jebak**

terjemah: terjemahan N translation; **menerjemahkan** V to translate (writing); to interpret (speaking); **penerjemah** N translator; **penerjemahan** N translation

terjepit ADJ pinched, caught in an uncomfortable situation → **jepit**

terjual ADJ sold; *habis* ~ sold out → **jual**

terjun dive, fall; go down; **penerjun** ~ *(payung)* parachutist, sky diver

terkecuali *tidak* ~, *tanpa* ~ without exception → **kecuali**

terkejut ADJ surprised → **kejut**

terkenal ADJ well-known → **kenal**

terkendali ADJ controlled → **kendali**

terkesan ADJ impressed; seemed → **kesan**

terkilir ADJ twisted, sprained → **kilir**

terkira *tak* ~ unsuspected, not thought of → **kira**

terkirim ADJ sent → **kirim**

terkubur ADJ buried in an accident → **kubur**

terkutuk ADJ cursed, accursed → **kutuk**

terlahir ADJ born → **lahir**

terlalu ADV too; **keterlaluan** N excess, too much → **lalu**

terlambat ADJ (too) late, delayed; **keterlambatan** N delay → **lambat**

terlampir ADJ attached, enclosed → **lampir**

terlanjur, telanjur ADJ too late, already → **lanjur**

terlarang ADJ forbidden, banned → **larang**

terlémpar ADJ thrown, flung → **lémpar**

terletak ADJ situated, located → **letak**

terlibat ADJ involved, implicated; **keterlibatan** N involvement, association → **libat**

terlilit ADJ caught up, twisted → **lilit**

terlindas ADJ run over → **lindas**

terlupakan *tak* ~ unforgettable → **lupa**

termasuk ADJ including → **masuk**

términal N (bus) terminal, bus station

ternak N cattle, livestock; **peternakan** N cattle farm, ranch

ternama ADJ famous, well-known → **nama**

terobos break through, pierce; **terobosan** N breakthrough

terompét N trumpet

térong, térung, terung N eggplant, aubergine

teropong N telescope, binoculars

terowong: terowongan N tunnel, shaft

terpadu ADJ integrated → **padu**

terpakai ADJ used, in use → **pakai**

terpaksa ADJ forced → **paksa**

terpancing ADJ hooked, caught up; involved → **pancing**

terpaut ADJ fastened, bound; separated → **paut**

terpelajar ADJ educated → **ajar**

terpelését ADJ slipped, skidded; tripped → **pelését**

terpelihara ADJ well cared-for, well-maintained → **pelihara**

terpencét ADJ accidentally pressed → **pencét**

terpencil ADJ isolated, remote → **pencil**

INDONESIAN–ENGLISH

T

terpengaruh ADJ affected or influenced → pengaruh
terpenuhi ADJ satisfied, fulfilled → penuh
terperangkap ADJ trapped, caught → perangkap
terpercaya ADJ trusted, reliable → percaya
terpisah ADJ separated → pisah
terpotong ADJ cut (off) → potong
terpuji ADJ highly-praised → puji
terpukul ADJ hard-hit → pukul
terputus ADJ cut off; terputus-putus v to keep cutting out → putus
tersambung ADJ connected → sambung
tersangka N (yang) ~ suspect
tersangkut ADJ involved; caught, snagged → sangkut
tersaput ~ awan clouded over → saput
tersebut ADJ (afore-)mentioned, said → sebut
tersedia ADJ available, prepared → sedia
terselip ADJ fallen or slipped into → selip
tersendiri ADJ its own; apart, separate → diri, sendiri
tersenggol ADJ bumped, brushed → senggol
tersentuh ADJ touched → sentuh
tersenyum v to smile → senyum
terserah ADJ it depends; up to you → serah
tersesat ADJ lost → sesat
tersiksa ADJ tortured → siksa
tersinggung ADJ offended, hurt → singgung
tersingkir, tersingkirkan ADJ eliminated, swept aside → singkir
tersisa ADJ leftover → sisa
tertabrak ADJ hit → tabrak
tertahan ADJ held back, prevented → tahan
tertanggal ADJ dated → tanggal
tertarik ADJ attracted, interested → tarik
tertawa v to laugh; menertawakan v to laugh at → tawa
tertekan ADJ stressed, pushed, pressured → tekan

tertelan ADJ accidentally swallowed → telan
tertémbak ADJ shot (accidentally) → témbak
tertentu ADJ definite, fixed, certain → tentu
tertib ADJ orderly, organized, disciplined; menertibkan v to keep order, discipline
tertidur ADJ fallen asleep → tidur
tertolong ADJ saved, rescued → tolong
tertukar ADJ changed by accident → tukar
tertunda ADJ delayed, postponed → tunda
tertutup ADJ closed → tutup
terulang ADJ repeated → ulang
terumbu N coral
terungkap ADJ expressed, revealed → ungkap
terus ADV straight on; continuous, constant; terusan N extension; canal; terus-terusan ADV constantly, continuously; meneruskan v to continue, keep doing something; penerus N successor; someone who continues another's work; seterusnya ADV after that, henceforth
terutama ADV especially, particularly → utama
tetangga N neighbor
tetap ADJ fixed, definite, constant; ADV still; menetap v to stay; menetapkan v to appoint, fix, stipulate; penetapan N appointment
tetapi, tapi CONJ but
tétés drip, drop; tétésan N drip, drop, droplet
tetumbuhan → tumbuh
tévé, tivi N TV → télévisi
téwas v to be killed, die; killed in action; menéwaskan v to kill someone
Thai bahasa ~, orang ~ Thai; Thailand N Thailand
tiada no; there isn't any, there aren't any → tidak ada
tiang N pillar, pole, mast; ~ bendera flagpole
tiap, setiap ADJ each, every; ~ saat any time

INDONESIAN–ENGLISH

T

tiba v to arrive or come; **tiba-tiba** ADV suddenly

tidak, tak, ndak, nggak, enggak no, not; ~ *pasti* uncertain; **setidak-(tidak)nya** ADV at least

tidur sleep; asleep; **tiduran** v to lie down, rest; **ketiduran** v to fall asleep; **menidurkan** v to put to sleep; **tertidur** ADJ fallen asleep

tifa N large drum from Papua

tifus, tipus N typhoid (fever)

tiga ADJ three; ~ *belas* thirteen; **bertiga** ADJ in threes; **ketiga** ADJ the third; **sepertiga** ADJ one-third; **pertigaan** N T-junction

tikai: bertikai v to quarrel or disagree

tikam stab; **tikaman** N stab; **menikam** v to stab

tikar N mat

tikét N (relatively expensive) ticket; ~ *kereta api* (long-distance) train ticket

tikung: tikungan N bend, curve

tikus N (small) mouse, (large) rat; ~ *besar* rat; **tikusan** N (computer) mouse

tilang N traffic fine; **ditilang** v to be fined → **bukti pelanggaran**

tim N team

tim *nasi* ~ steamed rice with chicken

timah N tin; ~ *putih* tin

timbang: timbangan N scales; **ketimbang** CONJ, COLL compared with; **mempertimbangkan** v to consider; **pertimbangan** N consideration

timbel, timbal N lead

timbul emerge; **menimbulkan** v to give rise, bring to the surface

timbun N pile, heap

Timteng N the Middle East → **Timur Tengah**

Timtim N, ARCH East Timor, Timor Loro Sae → **East Timor**

timun, mentimun N cucumber → **mentimun**

timur ADJ east; ~ *laut* northeast; **ketimuran** ADJ Eastern, Oriental

tindak act, deed; ~ *lanjut* follow-up; **menindaklanjuti** v to take a step or measure; **tindakan** N action, measure, step

tindas: penindasan N oppression

tinggal v to live, stay, remain; **meninggal** ~ *(dunia)* to die; **meninggalkan** v to leave (behind), abandon

tinggi ADJ high, tall; ~*nya* height; **ketinggian** N altitude, height; **setinggi** ADJ as high as

tingkah action

tingkat N level, floor, story, grade; **tingkatan** N grade, degree, level; **bertingkat** ADJ having different levels; **meningkat** v to rise, increase, improve; **meningkatkan** v to increase or raise the level of something

tinjau: tinjauan N review; **meninjau** v to observe, view; **peninjau** N observer

tinju N boxing; fist; **bertinju** v to box; **petinju** N boxer

tinta N ink

Tionghoa ADJ, POL Chinese

tipe N type, sort

tipék, tipéks: ditipéks v to white-out, be corrected

tipis ADJ thin

tipu trick, cheat; **menipu** v to trick, deceive; **penipu** N con man, trickster; **penipuan** N deception

tipus, tifus N typhoid (fever)

tirai N curtain

tiri ADJ step-; *adik* ~, *kakak* ~ stepbrother or stepsister

tiru, meniru v to copy or imitate; **tiruan** N imitation, fake

tisu N tissue; ~ *basah* wipe

titik N dot, point; full stop, period

titip, menitip v to leave in someone's care, entrust; **titipan** N parcel, something sent with another person; **penitipan** N care

tiup blow; **meniup** v to blow

tivi, tévé N TV → **télévisi**

TK ABBREV *Taman Kanak-kanak* kindergarten, preschool

TKI ABBREV *Tenaga Kerja Indonesia* Indonesian worker migrant

TNI ABBREV *Tentara Nasional Indonesia* Indonesian National Army/Armed Forces

toalét, toilét N toilet, washroom

todong, menodong v to threaten or hold up at knifepoint

INDONESIAN—ENGLISH

tokék N large gray house gecko

toko N shop, store; **pertokoan** N shopping center or complex, mall

tokoh N figure, character

tol N toll; *jalan ~* toll road

tolak V to refuse, reject; **menolak** V to refuse, reject; **penolakan** N refusal, rejection

tomat N tomato

tombak N spear

tombol N knob, button

tong N drum, barrel, bin

tongkat N stick, cane

tongséng N goat and cabbage curry

tonjok, menonjok V to punch, hit

tonjol: menonjol V to stick out, protrude; ADJ prominent

tonton: tontonan N show, performance; **menonton, nonton** V to watch, look on; **penonton** N spectator, audience

topéng N mask

topi N hat; *~ pet* cap

tosérba N general store; department store → toko sérba ada

tradisi ADJ tradition (not *adat*); **tradisional** ADJ traditional

traktir, mentraktir V to invite out, shout, treat, pay for another

trampil ADJ skilled; **ketrampilan** N skill

transaksi N (bank) transaction

transisi N transition

transmigrasi N transmigration (from Java to other islands)

trén, trénd N trend, fashion; **nge-trén** ADJ, COLL trendy, fashionable

trompét N trumpet

tropis ADJ tropical

trotoar N pavement, sidewalk

truk N truck

tua ADJ old; dark (of colors); **ketua** N chair(person); chief

tuan, Tn PRON master, sir (esp for foréigners)

tuang V to pour

tubuh N body

tuding: tudingan N accusation; **menuding** V to accuse, point the finger

tuduh: tuduhan N charge, accusation; **menuduh** V to accuse

tugas N task, duty, function; **menugaskan** V to assign someone, give a task to

tugu N monument, column

Tuhan N, PRON God, Allah; **tuhan** N god

tuju: tujuan N direction, destination; aim, goal; **menuju** V to approach, go towards; **setuju** agree, agreed; **menyetujui** V to agree to, approve, ratify; **persetujuan** N agreement, approval

tujuh ADJ seven; *~ belas* seventeen; *~ puluh* seventy

tukang N (unskilled) worker; handyman; *~ sepatu* cobbler, shoemaker

tukar V to exchange; *~-menukar* barter; **menukar** V to change; **menukarkan** V to change something; **pertukaran** N exchange; **tertukar** ADJ changed by accident

tulang N bone

tular: ketularan ADJ infected, caught something; **menular** V to infect; ADJ contagious, infectious

tuli ADJ deaf

tulis V to write; **tulisan** N writing, script; **menulis** V to write; **penulis** N author, writer

tulus ADJ sincere

tumbang fall, fallen

tumbuh V to grow; **tetumbuhan, tumbuh-tumbuhan** N plants; **tumbuhan** N a growth; plant; **pertumbuhan** N growth, development

tumis V to stir-fry, sautée

tumpah spill, spilt; **menumpahkan** V to spill something

tumpang: menumpang V to make use of someone else's facilities; to get a lift or ride; **penumpang** N passenger

tumpuk N heap, pile; **bertumpuk** V to be in piles

tumpul ADJ blunt

tuna- PREF without

tunai N cash

tunang: tunangan N, F fiancée; N, M fiancé; V, COLL to be engaged; **pertunangan** N engagement

T

tunda delay; **menunda** v to delay, put off, postpone; **menundakan** v to delay or postpone something; **tertunda** ADJ delayed, postponed

tunduk v to bow to, submit, obey; **menunduk** v to bow your head; **menundukkan** v to bow or lower something; to defeat

tunggal ADJ single, sole

tunggang: menunggang v to ride; ~ *kuda* to ride a horse

tunggu v to wait; **menunggu** v to wait for something; **menunggu-nunggu** v to wait a long time for

tunjang: tunjangan N allowance, bonus

tunjuk, menunjuk v to indicate, point out, refer to; **menunjukkan** v to show, point out; **pertunjukan** N show, performance; **petunjuk** N instruction, direction

tuntas ADJ complete, total

tuntut claim; **tuntutan** N claim, charge; **menuntut** v to claim or demand

tupai N squirrel

tur N tour; **turis** N tourist

Turki N Turkey

turun v to descend, fall, come down; **keturunan** N descendant; **menurun** v to fall, drop, decline; **menurunkan** v to lower or reduce

turut v to take part, join; ~ *berduka cita* express your condolences; **berturut-turut** ADJ consecutive, successive; **menurut** CONJ according to

tusuk skewer, needle; poke; ~ *sate* satay stick

tuts N key, button

tutul ADJ spotted

tutup lid, cover; closed, shut; ~ *botol* bottle-cap; **menutup** v to close or shut; **menutupi** v to cover (up); **penutup** N stopper, lid; end; **tertutup** ADJ closed

tutur speak; **penutur** N speaker

TV ABBREV *teve, tivi, televisi* television

TVRI ABBREV *Televisi Republik Indonesia* Indonesian state-owned television

U

uang N money; ~ *kembali* change; **keuangan** N finance

ubah change; **berubah** v to change; **mengubah** v to change or alter; **perubahan** N change, alteration

uban N (strand of) gray or white hair

ubi N edible tuber or root; sweet potato, yam

ubin N (floor) tile

ubur-ubur N jellyfish

ucap say; **ucapan** N greetings; **mengucap, mengucapkan** v to say or express something

udah → sudah

udang N shrimp

udara N air, atmosphere

udik → mudik

ujar speak, say

uji test; **ujian** N test, exam(ination); **menguji** v to examine or test; **penguji** N examiner

ujung N point, end

ukir, mengukir v to carve or engrave; **ukiran** v carving

ukur measure; **ukuran** N size, measurement; **mengukur** v to measure; **pengukuran** N measuring, measurement

ulang repeat; ~ *tahun* birthday, anniversary; **ulangan** N test; **berulang** v to happen again, recur; **berulang-ulang** ADV again and again, repeatedly; **mengulang** v to repeat, do again; **mengulangi** v to repeat something; **terulang** ADJ repeated

ular N snake

ulat N worm, caterpillar

ultah N birthday, anniversary → ulang tahun

umat N people (of one faith)

umbi N tuber; **umbi-umbian** N tubers

umpama N example; ~*nya* for example; **seumpamanya** CONJ for instance

umpan N bait

umpat, mengumpat v to curse swear; **umpatan** N oath, swear word

umpat, umpet: umpet-umpetan N, COLL hide and seek; **mengumpet** v to hide or conceal yourself

umum ADJ general, public, common;

INDONESIAN–ENGLISH

(pada) ~*nya* generally, in general; **mengumumkan** v to announce or declare; **pengumuman** N notice, announcement

umur N age; **berumur** ADJ aged; **seumur** ADJ the same age; lifelong

undang, mengundang v to invite (formally); **undangan** N invitation; formal event

undang: undang-undang N law, act; ~ *Dasar* constitution

undi N lot; **undian** N lottery; **mengundi** v to conduct a draw or lottery

undur, mundur v to reverse, go back; **mengundurkan** v to postpone; **pengunduran** N postponement, delay

unggul ADJ superior

unggun *api* ~ (camp)fire

ungkap v to express, reveal; **ungkapan** N expression; **mengungkap** v to uncover; **mengungkapkan** v to express; **terungkap** ADJ expressed, revealed

ungsi: mengungsi v to evacuate or flee; **pengungsi** N refugee, evacuee; **pengungsian** N evacuation

ungu ADJ purple

uni N union

unik ADJ unique; **keunikan** N unique thing, uniqueness

univérsitas N university

unjuk ~ *rasa* demonstration

unsur N element

unta, onta N camel; *burung* ~ ostrich

untai string; counter for string-like objects; **untaian** N string, chain

untuk PREP for

untung advantage, gain, profit; luck; **beruntung** ADJ lucky, fortunate; **keuntungan** N advantage, profit; **menguntungkan** v to profit; ADJ profitable

upacara N ceremony

upah N wage, wages

upaya N effort

upil N snot, bogey, nasal mucus

urap N vegetable salad with grated coconut

urat N tendon, vein; muscle; ~ *saraf* nerve

urus organize, arrange; **urusan** N arrangement, dealing, affair;

berurusan v to have dealings with, deal with; **mengurus** v to arrange, organize, manage; **pengurus** N manager, organizer

urut order in a series; **urutan** N order, sequence

urut massage, rub; **mengurut** v to massage

urutan N order, sequence → **urut**

usah *tidak* ~ not necessary

usaha N effort; **berusaha** v to try, make an effort; **mengusahakan** v to try, endeavor to; **pengusaha** N, M businessman; N, F businesswoman; **perusahaan** N company

usia N, POL age; ~ *lanjut* old age; **berusia** v to be (aged)

usir, mengusir v to drive away or out, chase away, expel

usul propose, suggest; motion; **mengusulkan** v to propose or suggest

usus N intestine

utak ~-*atik* fiddle or tinker with → **kutak-katik**

utama ADJ main; **mengutamakan** v to give preference or priority to; **terutama** ADV especially, particularly

utang, hutang N debt; **berutang** v to owe

utara ADJ north

utuh ADJ whole, complete, untouched

V

vaksin N vaccine; **vaksinasi** N vaccination

vakum N vacuum

valas N foreign currency → **valuta asing**

valuta N currency

vanili N vanilla

vas N vase

vélg, véleg, pélek N wheel rim

verboden, perboden no entry

vérsi N version

véspa N moped, motor scooter

vétsin N MSG (monosodium glutamate)

Viétnam N Vietnam

vihara, wihara N Buddhist temple or monastery

INDONESIAN—ENGLISH

vila N villa, holiday house, summer cottage

vital ADJ vital; *alat* ~ vital organs; genitals

vocer, voucer N credit voucher (for mobile phones)

vokal ADJ vocal, outspoken; **vokalis** N vocalist

voli *bola* ~ volleyball

volume N volume, size, bulk

vonis N ruling; sentence; **divonis** v to be sentenced

W

wabah N epidemic, plague

waduk N reservoir; dam

wafat v, POL to pass away or die; ~ *1970* died 1970

wagub N deputy governor → **wakil gubernur**

wah EXCL wow! oh! ADJ amazing, outstanding; fantastic, wonderful

wahana N vehicle, means

Waisak, Wésak N Buddhist New Year

wajah N, POL face

wajan N wok

wajar ADJ natural

wajib compulsory; must, obliged; **kewajiban** N obligation, duty

wajik N diamonds (card suit); diamond-shaped cake of sticky rice

wakil N representative, substitute; ADJ vice; **mewakili** v to represent; **perwakilan** N representation, delegation

waktu N time, hours; CONJ when; *pada ~nya* in due time, at the right time

walaikum ISL ~ *salam* and upon you be peace (said in response to *salam alaikum*)

walau, walaupun CONJ although

walét *burung* ~ swift (bird)

-wan SUF, M -man, one who does something

wangi fragrant; perfume; **wangi-wangian, wewangian** N scents, perfumes

wanita N woman

waprés N vice-president → **wakil présidén**

waras ADJ sane, healthy

warga N citizen; **warganegara** N citizen, national; **kewarganegaraan** N citizenship

waris: warisan N inheritance; **mewarisi** v to inherit

warna N color; ~ *putih* white; ~-*warni* colorful, multicolored; **berwarna** ADJ colored; **mewarnai** v to color (in); **pewarna** N dye, stain

warnét N Internet café → **warung internét**

warpostél N office where you can make calls, and send post and faxes → **warung pos dan télékomunikasi**

warta N news; M **wartawan**, F **wartawati** journalist, reporter

warteg N small, cheap food stall → **warung Tegal**

wartél N small office where you can make calls and send faxes → **warung télékomunikasi**

warung N stall, small local shop; ~ *kopi* coffee stall

waserai N (commercial) laundry

wasir N hemorrhoids

wasit N umpire, referee

waslap N washcloth, flannel

waspada ADJ on guard, careful, cautious

wassalam ISL and upon you be peace

wastafel N basin, sink (in bathroom)

watak N nature, character

-wati SUF, F -woman, one who does something

wawancara N interview; **mewawancarai** v to interview

wawas: wawasan N outlook, view, concept

wayang N puppet; ~ *golek* wooden, three-dimensional puppet; ~ *kulit* shadow puppet (performance)

WC N [wé sé] toilet, bathroom, lavatory

wédang N warm Javanese beverage

wéker N alarm; *jam* ~ alarm clock; *memasang* ~ to set the alarm

wenang: kewenangan, wewenang N authority; **sewenang-wenang** ADV tyrannically, arbitrarily

wewangian → **wangi**

wewenang N authority → **wenang**

INDONESIAN–ENGLISH

WIB ABBREV *Waktu Indonesia Barat* Western Indonesian time

wihara, vihara N Buddhist temple or monastery

wilayah N area, territory

windu N eight-year cycle

wingko ~ *babat* small coconut slice, a specialty of Semarang

wira-: wirausaha N business; **wiraswasta** N, M businessman F businesswoman

wisata N tourism, travel; *biro* ~ travel agent; **wisatawan** N tourist

wiski N whisky, whiskey

wisma N house, building

wisuda graduate

WIT ABBREV *Waktu Indonesia Timur* Eastern Indonesian time

WITA ABBREV *Waktu Indonesia Tengah* Central Indonesian time

WNA ABBREV *warga negara asing* foreign national

WNI ABBREV *warga negara Indonesia* Indonesian national

wol N wool

wortel N carrot

wujud N existence; **mewujudkan** V to make something real, realize something

wulan *catur* ~ trimester, term

X

X *sinar* ~ X-ray

Y

ya, iya yes

ya EJAC oh, O

Yahudi ADJ Jewish; *orang* ~ Jewish, Jew

yaitu CONJ namely, that is

yakin ADJ sure, convinced; **keyakinan** N belief, conviction, faith; **meyakini** V to believe, be convinced; **meyakinkan** ADJ convincing, believable

Yaman N Yemen

yang CONJ that, which, who; ~ *biru* the blue one; ~ *lalu* in the past

yatim N orphan, fatherless child; ~ *piatu* orphan

yayasan N foundation (not for profit)

Yordania N Jordan

yth. *yang terhormat* the respected, used when addressing letters

yuk → ayo

Yunani N Greece

yunior junior (at work or school)

Z

zaitun N olive

zakat, jakat N alms

zaman, jaman N age, era, time, period

zamrud, jamrud N emerald

zat, jat N element, substance

ziarah N pilgrimage, visit to a holy place or cemetery; **berziarah** V to make a pilgrimage, visit a holy place

A

English–Indonesian

A

a ART satu, suatu, se~; per, tiap;
~ *dog* seekor anjing → **ékor**;
~ *house* sebuah rumah → **buah**;
~ *man* seorang lelaki → **orang**

abacus N sempoa

abandon V mengabaikan, menelantarkan; **abandoned** V, ADJ terabaikan, telantar

abattoir N [abatuar] pejagalan

abbreviate V menyingkatkan, memendekkan; **abbreviation** N singkatan, kependekan

abdomen N perut

ability N [abiliti] kemampuan, kesanggupan, kepandaian ← **able**

able ADJ [ébel] bisa, mampu, sanggup

abnormal ADJ tidak normal, tidak biasa

aboard ADJ di atas kendaraan

abolish V menghapus, meniadakan

aborigine N [Aborijini] orang Aborijin, penduduk asli Australia; **aboriginal** ADJ, N orang Aborijin

abortion N pengguguran, aborsi

about PREP tentang, mengenai, seputar (sebuah topik); sekitar, keliling (sebuah tempat); kurang lebih, kira-kira (jumlah)

above PREP [abav] (di) atas; lebih daripada

abridged ADJ singkat

abroad ADV luar negeri, negeri orang

abrupt ADJ tiba-tiba; kasar, kurang sopan

absence N ketidakhadiran; **absent** ADJ tidak hadir

absolute ADJ mutlak, total; **absolutely** ADV secara mutlak, betul

absorb V menyerap; **absorption** N serapan, absorpsi; penyerapan

abstract ADJ abstrak; tidak konkret

absurd ADJ gila, tidak masuk akal

abundant ADJ berlimpah (ruah)

abuse N [abyus] penganiayaan, penyalahgunaan; kekerasan; V [abyuz] menganiaya, menyalahgunakan, memperlakukan dengan kasar

academic ADJ akademis; N akademisi; **academy** N akademi, sekolah tinggi

accelerator N (pedal) gas

accent [aksént] N logat, aksen, nuansa

accept V menerima; **acceptable** ADJ layak, dapat diterima

access N akses; V mendapat, memakai

accessory: accessories N, PL aksesoris, variasi (pada mobil), perlengkapan

accident N [aksident] kecelakaan; **accidental** ADJ kebetulan, tidak disengaja

accommodation N penginapan, akomodasi

accompany V menemani, mengantarkan, mengiringi

accomplice N [akamplis] kaki tangan, antek

accomplishment N prestasi

accord N persepakatan, persetujuan; **according** ~ *to* menurut

account N rekening (bank); pertanggungjawab; laporan, cerita; **accountant** N akuntan

accurate ADJ teliti, cermat, tepat

accusation N tuduhan; **accuse** V menuduh, menuding

accustomed ADJ terbiasa

ace N (kartu) as; ADJ, COLL mahir, hebat

ache N [ék] sakit, pegal; *tooth*~ gigi ngilu; V sakit

achieve V mencapai, meraih; **achievement** N prestasi

acid N asam; ADJ pahit

acknowledgment N pengakuan; ucapan terima kasih

acne N, PL [akni] jerawat

acquaintance N kenalan

acquire V memperoleh; **acquisition** N perolehan, barang yang diperoleh

A

acre N [éker] ukuran tanah (0.46 hektar)

acrobat N akrobat, pesenam

across PREP (di) seberang, melintang, lintas; mendatar

act N perbuatan; babak, lakon (dalam pertunjukan); undang-undang; V berbuat, bertindak; **action** N perbuatan, aksi; proses; **activate** V menghidupkan, menggerakkan; **active** ADJ giat, rajin, sibuk, aktif; hidup (telepon genggam); **activist** N aktivis; **activity** N kegiatan, kesibukan; **actor** N, M aktor, pemain (film); **actress** N, F aktris, pemain (film); **actual** ADJ **actually** ADV sebenarnya

acupuncture N tusuk jarum

adapt V menyesuaikan; **adaptable** ADJ mudah menyesuaikan diri, supel

add V bertambah, menambah, menambahkan

addict N pecandu

addition N tambahan, penambahan, jumlah; **additional** ADJ tambahan, ekstra ← add

address N alamat, adres; pidato; V mengalamatkan (surat); berpidato; menegur, menyapa

adequate ADJ cukup, memadai

adjoining ADJ berdampingan

adjust V menyetel, mencocokkan, mengatur, menyesuaikan

administration N; **administrative** ADJ pemerintahan; pemerintah; pelaksanaan; pemberian; **administrator** N pemerintah, pelaksana, pengurus

admirable ADJ mengagumkan, patut dikagumi ← admire

admiral N laksamana

admiration N kekaguman; **admire** V mengagumi

admission N penerimaan, izin masuk; pengakuan; **admit** V menerima, mengizinkan masuk; mengakui

adopt V mengangkat atau memungut anak; mengambil

adorable ADJ lucu, menggemaskan, manis, jelita; **adore** V memuja; sangat mencintai, gila akan

adult ADJ dewasa; N orang dewasa

adultery N zinah

advance N kemajuan; uang muka; V maju; memajukan, mempercepat

advantage N untung, keuntungan

adventure N petualangan

adverb N kata keterangan (pada kata kerja)

advertise V mengiklankan, memasangiklan; **advertisement** N iklan, pariwara, reklame

advice N [advais] nasihat, saran; **advise** V [advaiz] menasihati; **advisor** N penasihat

aerial N [érial] antena; ADJ angkasa, udara

aeronautical ADJ, N aeronautika, ilmu penerbangan

affair N perkara, hal, soal, urusan; perselingkuhan, cerita cinta

affect V mempengaruhi; **affection** N rasa kasih sayang; **affectionate** ADJ memperlihatkan kasih sayang

afford V mampu (membayar dll); **affordable** ADJ terjangkau (harganya)

afraid ADJ takut

Africa N Afrika; **African** ADJ, N orang Africa

Afro-American N orang Amerika berkulit hitam (keturunan Afrika); orang Negro

after PREP, CONJ, ADV kemudian; PREP setelah, sesudah; **afternoon** N sore, petang; sesudah jam 12 siang sampai dengan matahari terbenam; *good* ~ selamat siang (jam 12–15); selamat sore (jam 15–19); **afterwards** PREP sesudahnya, kemudian

again ADV (sekali) lagi; *then* ~ tapi

against PREP terhadap; berlawanan, bertentangan

agate N [aget] batu akik

age N umur, usia

agency N agen, perwakilan; *news* ~ kantor berita ← agent

agenda N agenda, acara; rencana

agent N agen, wakil

aggressive ADJ galak, bersifat menyerang, agresif

ago ADV lalu, lampau, silam

agony N kesakitan, penderitaan; sakratulmaut

agree V setuju, bersepakat; menyetujui, mengiyakan; **agreement** N persetujuan, kesepakatan, perjanjian

agricultural ADJ berkaitan dengan pertanian; **agriculture** N pertanian

A

ENGLISH–INDONESIAN

AH ABBREV *after hours* r, rmh (rumah)

ahead ADV [ahéd] di depan, di muka, terlebih dahulu ← head

aid N bantuan, pertolongan; *first ~* pertolongan pertama

AIDS (Acquired Immune Deficiency Syndrome) N AIDS

aim N sasaran, maksud, tujuan; V membidik, mengincar, menuju

air N udara; angin; *~ mail* pos udara; V menjemur, menganginkan; **aircraft** N pesawat terbang, kapal terbang; **air crew** N awak kabin; **air force** N angkatan udara; **airer** N jemuran; **airline** N perusahaan penerbangan, maskapai penerbangan; **airplane, aeroplane** N pesawat terbang; **airport** N bandara, bandar udara; **air raid** N serangan udara; **airtight** ADJ kedap udara

aisle N [ail] lorong

alarm N weker; tanda bahaya; rasa kaget

albatross N elang laut

alcohol N alkohol, minuman keras; **alcoholic** ADJ beralkohol

alert N tanda (bahaya); V memperingatkan; ADJ siaga, waspada

algebra N aljabar

Algeria N Aljazair

alien N [élien] makhluk asing, orang asing; ADJ asing

alike ADJ serupa, mirip ← like

alive ADJ (dalam keadaan) hidup ← live

all ADJ [ol] semua, seantero; sekalian, seluruh; *~ day* sepanjang hari, seharian; *~ over* habis; di mana-mana; *~ right* baiklah; *~ of us* kita semua; *not at ~* sama sekali tidak; **all-round** ADJ umum

allergic ADJ mempunyai alergi; **allergy** N alergi

alley N [ali] lorong, gang

alligator N [aligétor] buaya (bermoncong pendek)

allow V mengizinkan, memperbolehkan, memperkenankan; **allowance** N tunjangan, uang harian, uang saku

alloy N logam campuran

almighty ADJ [olmaiti] maha kuasa

almond N kacang almond, buah badam

almost ADV [olmost] hampir, nyaris

alone ADJ, ADV sendiri, seorang diri; hanya, saja

along PREP sepanjang; **alongside** ADJ di sisi, di tepi

aloud ADJ dengan suara keras, dengan suara nyaring

alphabet N abjad, aksara, alfabet

already ADV [olrédi] sudah, telah

also ADV [olso] juga, pula, pun

alter V mengubah; memperbaiki

alternate V berselang-seling, menyelang-nyeling; **alternative** N pilihan lain, alternatif

although CONJ [oltho] meskipun, walaupun

altitude N ketinggian, tinggi

altogether ADJ [oltogéther] semuanya, secara keseluruhan; neg sama sekali

aluminium, aluminum N aluminium

always ADV selalu, senantiasa

am ABBREV *ante meridiem* pagi, siang (jam 0.00–12.00)

amateur ADJ, N [amater] amatir; tidak profesional

amaze V mengherankan, menakjubkan, mengagumkan

ambassador N duta besar

ambition N ambisi, cita-cita; **ambitious** ADJ berambisi, mempunyai cita-cita tinggi

ambulance N ambulans

ambush N serangan mendadak, penyergapan; V menyerang secara mendadak, menyergap

amen EJAC amin

amendment N pembetulan; amandemen

amenities N, PL fasilitas, sarana

America N Amerika (Serikat); **American** N orang America

amethyst N batu kecubung

amiable ADJ [émiabel] ramah, baik hati

among [amang], **amongst** PREP di tengah, di antara

amount N jumlah, banyaknya; V berjumlah, menjadi

amuse V menghibur; **amused** ADJ terhibur, tertawa; **amusement** N hiburan, kesenangan; **amusing** ADJ lucu, menyenangkan

an ART (sebelum huruf vokal) satu,

suatu, se~; per, tiap; ~ *apple* sebuah apel → **buah**; ~ *owl* seekor burung hantu → **ekor**

anal ADJ ~ *sex* sodomi ← **anus**

analysis N analisa, analisis, uraian; **analyze** V menganalisa, meneliti

ancestor N leluhur, nenek moyang

anchor N [anker] sauh, jangkar; V membuang sauh, berlabuh

ancient ADJ [énsyent] kuno, zaman purbakala

and CONJ dan, serta, bersama; ~ *so on* dan lain sebagainya

anecdote N lelucon, cerita, anekdot

anesthetic N obat bius

angel N [énjel] malaikat

anger N [angger] kemarahan, murka; V membuat marah

angle N [anggel] sudut

angry ADJ marah, murka ← **anger**

animal N binatang, hewan, satwa

animation N semangat; kartun animasi, anime

ankle N [angkel] pergelangan kaki

annexe, annex N pavilyun

anniversary N (hari) ulang tahun, hari jadi; hari peringatan

announce V mengumumkan, memberitahukan; **announcer** N penyiar; **announcement** N pengumuman, maklumat

annoy V mengganggu, mengusik; **annoying** ADJ mengganggu, menjengkelkan

annual ADJ tahunan; **annually** ADV setiap tahun

anonymous ADJ tanpa nama, anonim; ~ *letter* surat kaleng

another N, ADJ satu lagi, yang lain

answer N [anser] jawaban, jalan keluar (dari masalah); V menjawab, membalas (surat)

ant N semut; *white* ~s rayap

Antarctic ADJ berasal dari Antartika; *the* ~, **Antarctica** N Antartika, Kutub Selatan

antenna N antena

anthem N lagu wajib; *national* ~ lagu kebangsaan

anthology N kumpulan, antologi, bunga rampai

anthropologist N antropolog; **anthropology** N ilmu antropologi

antics N, PL tingkah lucu, kelucuan

antidote N penawar ← **anti**

antique N barang kuno, barang antik; ADJ kuno, antik

anus N [énus] dubur

anxiety N [angzayeti] kecemasan, kegelisahan, kekuatiran; **anxious** ADJ [angsyes] gelisah, cemas

any ADJ [éni] sesuatu, beberapa, sembarang; NEG sedikit pun; **anybody**, **anyone** N siapa pun, siapa saja; **anyhow** ADV bagaimanapun; **anything** N apa saja, apa pun; **anywhere** N di mana saja; ADV ke mana saja

apart ADV terpisah; ~ *from* selain, kecuali

apartment N apartemen, rumah susun

ape N kera, siamang

apologize V minta maaf; **apology** N permintaan maaf

apparent ADJ nyata, jelas, kentara; **apparently** ADV tampaknya, ternyata ← **appear**

appeal N permohonan, permintaan, seruan; banding; V naik banding

appear V tampak, muncul, timbul, menghadap; **appearance** N tampang, penampilan

appendix N lampiran; usus buntu

appetite N selera, nafsu makan

apple N buah apel

appliance N peranti, pesawat, alat

applicant N pelamar, pemohon; **application** N (surat) lamaran; penerapan, pemakai; **apply** V berlaku; menerapkan, menggunakan

appreciate V [aprisyiét] berterima kasih; menghargai, menilai; mengerti

apprentice N [apréntis] murid

approach N pendekatan; V mendekati, menuju (tempat); menjelang (waktu)

appropriate ADJ patut, layak, pantas, sesuai

approval N [apruval] izin, persetujuan; **approve** V memperkenankan, mengizinkan, menyetujui

approximate ADJ kira-kira, kurang lebih; **approximately** ADV kira-kira, kurang lebih

April N [Épril] bulan April

aqua ADJ biru toska

aquarium N akuarium, kolam ikan

ENGLISH–INDONESIAN

A

aquatic ADJ [akuotik] berhubungan dengan air atau laut

aqueduct N jalan air (di atas tanah)

Arab N orang Arab; *Saudi* ~ Arab Saudi; **Arabic** N [Arabik] bahasa Arab

arch N garis lengkung; busur; **archer** N pemanah; **archery** N panahan

archeologist N ahli purbakala; **archeology** N ilmu purbakala

archipelago N [arkipélago] kepulauan, gugusan pulau

architect N [arkitekt] arsitek; **architecture** N arsitektur

archive, archives N [arkaiv] arsip

Arctic ADJ Arktik, Artik, berasal dari kawasan Kutub Utara

are V, PL → be

area N [éria] daerah, wilayah, kawasan

Argentina N [Arjentina] Argentina; **Argentinian** N orang Argentina

argue V [argyu] berdebat, bertengkar; memperdebatkan, membantah; **argument** N pertengkaran; alasan, dalih

arid ADJ gersang, kering

aristocracy N kaum ningrat; **aristocrat** N orang ningrat, bangsawan

arithmetic N ilmu berhitung

arm N lengan, tangan (baju)

arm N senjata; V mempersenjatai

armchair N kursi sofa, kursi tamu

armor N baju baja

armpit N ketiak

army N tentara, bala tentara; angkatan darat

aroma N bau harum, aroma; **aromatic** N berbau harum

around PREP sekeliling, sekitar, seputar; dekat; ADJ kira-kira

arrange V mengurus, menata, mengatur; mengaransemen (lagu); **arrangement** N penataan, pengaturan, perjanjian; aransemen

arrest N penahanan, penangkapan; V menahan, menangkap

arrival N kedatangan; **arrive** V datang, tiba

arrogant ADJ sombong, angkuh

arrow N (anak) panah

art N seni lukis; kesenian; **arts** N kesenian; sastra (jurusan)

artery N pembuluh nadi, arteri

arthritis N [arthraitis] encok, radang sendi

article N barang, benda; pasal, bab(hukum); kata sandang

artificial ADJ buatan, palsu

artist N seniman, seniwati; artis (seni peran); **artistic** ADJ artistik, indah ← **art**

as ADV, CONJ sama, se-; seperti; karena, sebab; ~ *big* ~ *a house* sebesar rumah; ~ *for me* kalau saya; ~ *if* seolah-olah

asbestos N asbes

ash N abu

ashamed ADJ malu

ashore ADV di darat; *to go* ~ naik ke darat ← **shore**

ashtray N asbak

Asia N Asia; *Southeast* ~ Asia Tenggara

aside ADV di sebelah; ~ *from* selain dari ← **side**

ask V bertanya, minta, memohon

asleep ADJ sedang tidur

assassinate V membunuh tokoh terkenal; **assassination** N pembunuhan tokoh terkenal

assemble V berkumpul, berhimpun, bersidang; mengumpulkan; merakit; **assembly** N perkumpulan, perhimpunan, sidang; perakitan; apel (di sekolah)

assess V menaksir, menilai; **assessment** N taksiran, penilaian

asset N aset, modal

assignment N tugas

assist V menolong, membantu; **assistance** N pertolongan, bantuan; **assistant** N pembantu, asisten

associate N kawan, mitra, rekan; V bergaul; mengaitkan, menghubungkan; **association** N gabungan, persatuan, asosiasi

assorted ADJ bermacam jenis

assume V menganggap; **assumption** N asumsi, prasangka

asterisk N tanda bintang

asthma N (penyakit) asma, sesak dada

astonish V mengherankan, menakjubkan; **astonished** ADJ heran

astound V **astounding** ADJ mengejutkan, mengherankan

B

ENGLISH–INDONESIAN

astrologer N [astrolojer] peramal; **astrology** N nasib menurut bintang, astrologi

astronomer N astronom, ahli bintang; **astronomy** N (ilmu) astronomi, ilmu bintang

asylum N [asailum] suaka, tempat perlindungan; ~-*seeker* pencari suaka

at PREP di; pada; ~ *all* sama sekali; ~ *home* di rumah; betah; ~ *last* akhirnya; ~ *least* paling tidak; ~ *once* sekarang juga

atheist N [éthiest] ateis

athlete N [athlit] atlet, olahragawan; pelari; **athletic** ADJ [athlétik] kuat, berotot, fit; **athletics** N cabang atletik, lari

atlas N atlas, buku peta

ATM ABBREV *automated teller machine* ATM (anjungan tunai mandiri)

atmosphere N suasana; hawa, udara; angkasa, atmosfer

atoll N pulau karang, atol

atom N atom; **atomic** ADJ berkaitan dengan atom, nuklir

attach V menambat, melekatkan, mengaitkan, melampirkan; **attached** ADJ terlampir; berpasangan; sayang; **attachment** N lampiran; rasa sayang

attack N serangan; V menyerang

attempt N usaha, percobaan; V mencoba, berusaha

attend V hadir; menghadiri; **attendance** N kehadiran; **attendant** N pelayan

attention N perhatian; **attentive** ADJ penuh perhatian

attic N loteng

attitude N sikap, pendirian; SL keberanian

attorney N [atérni] pengacara

attract V menarik atau memikat(hati); **attraction** N daya tarik, daya pikat; atraksi; **attractive** ADJ menawan

auction N lelang

audible ADJ kedengaran, terdengar

audience N para penonton, tamu, hadirin

August N bulan Agustus

aunt N [ant] **aunty, auntie** SL bibi, tante

Australia N [Ostrélia] Australia

authentic ADJ asli, otentik

author N pengarang, penulis

authority N otoritas, kekuasaan; yang berwajib, instansi; ahli, pakar; **authorization** N kewenangan; **authorize** V mengizinkan

autism N [otizem] autisme; **autistic** ADJ autis

autobiography N otobiografi

automatic ADJ otomatis, dengan sendirinya

autonomous ADJ otonom; **autonomy** N otonomi

autopsy N otopsi, bedah mayat

autumn N [otum] musim gugur

Av, Ave *Avenue* Jl (Jalan)

available ADJ tersedia

avenge V membalas dendam (terutama atas kematian)

avenue N [avenyu] jalan

average N, ADJ rata-rata

aviary N [éviari] kandang burung yang besar

avocado N alpukat

awake V awoke awoken bangun; ADJ dalam keadaan bangun; **awaken** V bangun ← **wake**

award N penghargaan; V memberi penghargaan

aware ADJ sadar akan, menyadari; **awareness** N kesadaran

away ADV tidak di sini, tidak ada; dari tempat itu; *go* ~! pergilah!

awe N [o] perasaan kagum; **awful** ADJ dahsyat, mengerikan

awkward ADJ kikuk, canggung

ax, axe N kapak

axis N poros, sumbu

axle N as roda

B

babble V berceloteh, mengoceh; bicara tanpa kendali

babe N, SL [béb] bayi; cewek; **baby** N bayi; ADJ anak; *a* ~ *elephant* anak gajah; ~-*sit* V menjaga anak; **babysitter** N penjaga anak

bachelor N bujangan, jejaka; ~'s *degree* S1 (Strata Satu)

back N belakang, punggung, balik; ADJ di belakang; ADV ke belakang,

B

mundur; ~ *seat* jok belakang; v mendukung, mendanai; **background** N latar belakang; **backing** N sokongan, dukungan; **backside** N, SL pantat; **backstroke** N gaya punggung; **backward, backwards** ADJ, ADV ke belakang, mundur

bacon N irisan daging babi asap

bacteria N, PL bakteri, kuman

bad ADJ jelek, buruk, kurang baik; ~ *dream* mimpi buruk

badge N lencana, pin

baffled ADJ bingung

bag N tas, karung

baggage N [bagej] bagasi, koper, tas

baggy ADJ kendor, kebesaran

bail N uang jaminan

bait N umpan

bake v membakar; **baker** N tukang memasak roti; **bakery** N toko roti

balance N keseimbangan; neraca, timbangan; FIN saldo; v menimbang; **balanced** ADJ berimbang

balcony N balkon, teras, beranda

bald ADJ botak, gundul, plontos

ball N bola; N pesta berdansa

ballerina N pebalet, penari balet; **ballet** N [balé] balet

balloon N balon

bamboo N bambu

ban N larangan; v melarang; **banned** ADJ dilarang

banana N pisang

band N gerombolan, geng, kawanan; grup (band); gelang

bandage N [bandej] perban; v memerban, membalut

bank N bank; tepi, sisi (sungai); **banker** N bankir

banner N spanduk

baptism N permandian; **Baptist** N pembaptis; **baptize** v mempermandikan, membaptis

bar N palang pintu, batang, halangan, rintangan; tempat minum, kafe

barb N duri

barbecue, barbeque, BBQ N acara memanggang daging di luar rumah

barber N tukang cukur

bare ADJ telanjang, polos; hanya; **barefoot** ADJ dengan kaki telanjang; **barely** ADJ hampir tidak

bargain N [bargen] pembelian yang murah; v tawar-menawar, menawar

bark N kulit kayu

barn N gudang (tempat menyimpan jerami, rumput kering dsb)

barricade N [barikéd] rintangan, barikade; v memblokir, merintangi

barrier N palang, penghalang, rintangan

barter N niaga tukar-menukar barang, barter; v tukar-menukar barang, barter, membarter

base N markas, dasar; v berdasar, mendasarkan

basic ADJ asasi, pokok

basin N baskom, wastafel

basket N keranjang, bakul, basket; ~*ball* bola basket

bat N alat pemukul (dalam olahraga); v memukul bola (dalam kriket, bisbol dsb)

bat N kelelawar, kampret, kalong

batch N sejumlah; seri (keluaran barang)

bath N (bak) mandi; ~*robe* kimono; ~*tub* badkip; **bathe** v [béth] mandi; **bathroom** N kamar mandi

battery N baterai

battle N pertempuran, peperangan; perjuangan; v bertempur, berjuang

bay N teluk; ~ *leaf* daun salam

bazaar N [bezar] pasar kaget

be v was been menjadi, adalah

beach N pantai, pesisir; v mendamparkan diri

bead N manik-manik; tetesan

beam N balok; sinar (cahaya); v bersinar, tersenyum lebar

bean N buncis, kacang

bear N beruang; *polar* ~ beruang putih

bear v bore, born memikul, menahan; bersalin; melahirkan

beard N [bird] jenggot

beast N binatang

beat N pukulan; irama, ritme; v beat, beaten memukul; mengalahkan

beautiful ADJ [byutifal] cantik (perempuan), asri (pemandangan), bagus, indah; **beauty** N kecantikan, keindahan; wanita cantik

became v, PF → become

because CONJ [bikoz] (oleh) karena, sebab

B

become v [bikam] became become menjadi

bed n tempat tidur, ranjang; **bedroom** n kamar (tidur); **bedspread, bedcover** n selimut

bee n lebah, tawon, kumbang

beef n daging sapi

beehive n sarang lebah ← bee

beer n bir

beetle n kumbang

before prep di muka, depan; sebelum; adv sebelum

beg v meminta-minta, mengemis; memohon; ~ *your pardon* maaf; **beggar** n pengemis

begin v **began begun** mulai, memulai; **beginning** n awal, permulaan

behave v berkelakuan (baik); **behavior** n perilaku

behind n [behaind] belakang; sl pantat; prep di belakang, ke belakang; adv tertinggal, ketinggalan

being n makhluk; keadaan → be

Belgium n [Béljum] Belgia

belief n **beliefs** pendapat, kepercayaan, iman, agama; **believe** v percaya, berpendapat

bell n bel, lonceng, genta

belly n (bagian bawah) perut

belong v milik, termasuk kepunyaan; **belongings** n, pl barang milik

beloved n [belovéd] adj yang dicintai, yang disayangi

below prep di bawah, ke bawah

belt n ikat pinggang, sabuk; *seat* ~ sabuk pengaman

bench n bangku, tempat duduk

bend n belokan; v **bent bent** membelok, melengkung

beneath prep di bawah

benefit n manfaat, untung; v menguntungkan

bent v, pf → bend; adj bengkok, tidak lurus

beside prep di sisi, di dekat; kecuali, di luar, selain dari; **besides** adv, prep lagipula, ditambah lagi

best adj paling bagus, paling baik, terbaik

bet n taruhan; v **bet bet** bertaruh

betray v mengkhianati; **betrayal** n pengkhianatan

better adj lebih baik; sembuh

between prep (di) antara, di tengah

beverage n minuman (terutama yang panas)

beware adj awas, berhati-hati

beyond prep (di) sebelah, lebih (jauh), melampaui, melebihi

BH abbrev *business hours* k, ktr (kantor)

bias n [bayas] kecenderungan; **biased** adj tidak berimbang

Bible n [baibel] Injil, Alkitab

bicycle n [baisikel] sepeda

big adj besar, gemuk; raksasa; ~ *toe* jempol kaki

bike n sepeda (motor); v naik sepeda; **biker** n penggemar sepeda motor

bilingual adj [bailingguel] dwibahasa

bill n bon, rekening, nota; wesel, daftar; paruh (pada burung); v menagih

billiards n, pl bilyar

billion n satu milyar (1 000 000 000); **billionaire** n milyarder

bin n tempat sampah, tong

bind v [baind] **bound bound** menjilid; mengikat; **binder** n map; **binding** n penjilidan

binoculars n, pl teropong, binokular

biography n biografi, riwayat hidup

biologist n [bayolojist] ahli biologi; **biology** n ilmu biologi

bird n burung

birth n kelahiran; ~*day* hari ulang tahun, hari jadi

biscuit n [bisket] biskuit, kue kering

bishop n uskup

bit n sedikit, sepotong; v, pf → bite

bite n gigitan; v **bit bitten** menggigit

bitter adj pahit

black adj hitam, gelap; **blackmail** n pemerasan; v memeras

bladder n kandung kemih

blade n mata pisau

blame n kesalahan; v menyalahkan, menyalahi (orang)

blank n tempat kosong; peluru kosong; adj kosong, hampa

blanket n selimut; v menyelimuti

blast n angin kencang, letupan, tiupan

B

blaze N kebakaran; v menyala; **blazing** ADJ menyala
blazer N jas (setengah resmi)
bleach N pemutih; v memutihkan (baju)
bleak ADJ suram, gelap
bleed *nose~* mimisan; v bled bled berdarah; **bleeding** ADJ berdarah
blend N campuran; v berbaur; mencampur
bless v memberkati; **blessing** N pemberkatan; doa restu
blew v, PF → blow
blind N [blaind] horden, penutup jendela, kerai; *~ed* silau; ADJ buta; **blindly** ADJ membabi buta, tanpa melihat atau berpikir
blink N kedipan mata, kejapan mata; v mengedip, mengejapkan mata
blister N lecet, lepuh; v menjadi lecet, melepuhkan
block N balok; blok; v merintangi, membatasi, menghambat; *~ed* tersumbat, mampet
blond ADJ, M blonde F (berambut) pirang
blood N darah; **bloodstain** N bekas darah; **bloody** ADJ berdarah
blossom N bunga; v berbunga
blouse N [blauz] blus
blow N pukulan, tamparan; tiupan; v blew blown bertiup; meniup; *~ your nose* membuang ingus, bersin; **blowpipe** N sumpitan
blue ADJ biru
blunder N [blander] kesalahan besar; v berbuat salah
blunt ADJ tumpul
blur N kabur; **blurred, blurry** ADJ kabur, kurang jelas
blush v memerah (muka); **blusher** N pemerah pipi, perona pipi
board N papan; karton, kertas tebal, kardus; dewan; v naik pesawat; mondok, kos; **boarder** N anak kos; **boarding** *~ house* rumah kos, asrama (sekolah); *~ pass* N pas naik pesawat
boast N bualan; v membual
boat N kapal, perahu
bob v membungkuk; turun naik
body N badan, tubuh; organisasi, himpunan; **bodyguard** N pengawal pribadi

bog N rawa, payau; v terhenti (kendaraan)
boil N bisul; v mendidih; merebus; **boiler** N ketel (kukus)
bold ADJ berani
bolt N baut, slot; v mengunci; kabur
bomb N [bom] bom; v mengebom; **bomber** N pesawat pengebom; **bombing** N pengeboman
bond N pengikat; ikatan; kewajiban
bone N tulang; gading
book N buku, kitab, novel; v memesan; *~case, ~ shelf* lemari buku; **booking** N pemesanan, buking; **booklet** buku kecil, buklet; **bookshop** N toko buku
boot N sepatu (bot), sepatu lars; v menghidupkan (komputer)
booth N loket, gerai
border N tepi, sisi; perbatasan, tapal batas; v berbatasan dengan; membatasi
bore v, PF → bear
boring ADJ membosankan, menjemukan
born v, PF dilahirkan, lahir, terlahir → bear
borrow v pinjam, meminjam
boss N pemimpin, bos; **bossy** ADJ suka menyuruh
both ADJ kedua, kedua(-kedua)nya; *both … and …* baik … maupun …
bother N repot, kesusahan; v merepotkan, menyusahkan; mengganggu
bottle N botol
bottom N bawah, pantat, alas; ADJ bawah
bought v, PF [bot] → buy
bounce N lambungan; semangat; v melambung, memantul
bound v melompat, berlari-lari; v, PF → bind
boundary N (tapal) batas
bow N [bau] tundukan; v membungkukkan badan, menunduk; menyerah
bow N [bo] busur
bowels N, PL [bauls] usus, pencernaan
bowl N [bol] mangkuk, pinggan
bowling N boling
box N kotak, dus, peti; tinju; v bertinju; meninju; **boxer** N petinju; **boxing** N tinju

ENGLISH–INDONESIAN

boy N anak lelaki
boycott N boikot; v memboikot
boyfriend N, M pacar
bracelet N [bréslét] gelang (berantai)
bracket N tanda kurung
brag v membual, menyombong
brain N otak, benak; **brainwash** v mencuci otak
brake N rem; *hand~* rem tangan; v mengerem
branch N cabang; bagian
brand N cap, merek
brandy N brendi
brass N kuningan
brave ADJ berani; **bravery** N keberanian
brawl N tawuran, pertikaian; v tinju, bergumul
Brazil N Brasil; **Brazilian** N orang Brasil
bread N [bréd] roti
break N [brék] istirahat, rehat, jeda; patah, putus; v broke broken memecahkan, mematahkan; **breakdown** N perincian; kegagalan, kerusakan; **breakfast** N, v [brékfast] sarapan, makan pagi
breast N [brést] dada, payudara; SL susu, tetek; ~ *milk* ASI (air susu ibu)
breath N [bréth] nafas, napas; **breathe** v [brith] bernafas, menarik nafas
breed N ras; v bred bred mengembangbiakkan; mendidik; **breeder** N peternak; **breeding** N trah, nenek moyang; sopan santun
breeze N angin sepoi-sepoi
bribe N uang sogok, uang suap; v menyogok, menyuap; **bribery** N suapan, sogokan
brick N batu bata
bridal ADJ berkaitan dengan acara pernikahan; **bride** N, F pengantin wanita, mempelai wanita; **bridegroom** N, M pengantin pria
bridge N jembatan; v menjembatani, mempertemukan
brief ADJ pendek, ringkas, singkat; **briefing** N rapat pendek, penyebaran informasi
brigade N [brigéd] regu, pasukan; *fire ~* pasukan pemadam kebakaran

bright N [brait] terang, gemilang; cerdik, cemerlang, pandai
brilliant ADJ gemilang, berseri
bring v brought brought [brot] membawa; ~ *up* membesarkan
Britain N [Briten] Britania COLL Inggris
broad ADJ lebar, luas
broadcast N siaran; v broadcast broadcast menyiarkan
broccoli N brokoli
broke, broken v, PF → break ADJ rusak
broker N makelar, calo, perantara
bronze N perunggu
brooch N [broc] bros
broom N sapu
brother N [brather] kakak atau adik lelaki; saudara; **brotherhood** N persaudaraan
brought v, PF → bring
brown ADJ (warna) coklat
bruise N [bruz] memar; **bruised** ADJ memar, bengkak
brush N sikat, kuas (alat seni); v menyikat
brutal ADJ brutal, bengis, kasar
bubble N gelembung
buck N rusa jantan; SL dolar
bucket N ember
Buddha N Budha; **Buddhist** N orang Budha
budget N [bajét] anggaran; v menganggarkan
buffalo N kerbau
buffet N [bafé] bufet, prasmanan
bug N serangga, kumbang, kutu
buggy N kereta atau kendaraan kecil
build v [bild] built built mendirikan, membangun, membina; **builder** N pemborong; **building** N gedung, bangunan
bulb N lampu pijar, bola lampu, bohlam
bull N sapi jantan
bullet N peluru
bulletin N selebaran, berita kilat
bully N orang yang menakut-nakuti atau mengejek orang lain; v menakut-nakuti orang lain
bump N pukulan, tonjokan; v menabrak; **bumpy** ADJ tidak rata, bergelombang

bun N roti berbentuk bola, biasanya manis

bunch N tandan, gugus, segenggam; segerombolan

bundle N [bandel] berkas, paket; v membungkus

bunk N ranjang yang sempit

bunny N, SL kelinci

buoy N [boi] pelampung

burden N beban; muatan, tanggungan; v membebani, memberatkan

bureau N [byuro] kantor, biro; meja tulis; **bureaucrat** N birokrat

burglar N maling; **burglary** N kemalingan

burial N [bérial] pemakaman ← **bury**

burn N luka terkena panas, luka bakar; v burned burnt menyala; membakar; **burner** N sumbu

burst v burst burst meletus; menyembur

bury v [béri] mengubur, menanam

bus N bis

bush N semak belukar

business N pekerjaan; perkara, urusan; perdagangan, perniagaan; perusahaan; N, M businessman; N, F businesswoman pengusaha, wiraswasta

busy ADJ [bizi] sibuk

but CONJ tetapi, tapi, namun; kecuali

butcher N [bucer] jagal, tukang potong, tukang daging; toko daging

butter N mentega

butterfly N kupu-kupu; gaya kupu-kupu

button N kancing

buy N [bai] pembelian; v bought bought [bot] membeli; **buyer** N pembeli

by PREP oleh, dengan

bye EJAC selamat jalan, selamat tinggal; ~~ CHILD selamat jalan, selamat tinggal

C

c *cent* sen

cab N bagian depan truk; ~ *driver* supir taksi

cabbage N [kabej] kol, engkol, kubis

cabin N bagian depan truk; ~ *crew* awak kabin

cabinet N kabinet; lemari

cable N [kébel] kabel

cactus N cacti kaktus

café, cafe N kafe, warung kopi

cage N sangkar, kurungan; v mengurung

cake N kue

calculate v menghitung-hitung, memperhitungkan, menaksir; **calculator** N kalkulator

calendar N kalender, almanak; penanggalan

calf N [kaf] anak sapi

call N [kol] panggilan, seruan; percakapan telepon; kunjungan; v memanggil; menelepon; **caller** N penelepon; tamu

calligrapher N [kaligrafer] orang yang bisa membuat tulisan tangan indah; **calligraphy** N tulisan tangan yang indah

calm N [kam] ketenangan, keteduhan; ADJ tenang, teduh

Cambodia N Kamboja

came v, PF → come

camel N [kamel] unta

camera N kamera

camp N perkemahan, kamp; v berkemah

can N kaleng

can AUX, v could/was able, been able dapat, bisa

Canada N Kanada

canal N terusan

cancel v membatalkan, mencoret, menghapus

cancer N kanker

candidate N calon, kandidat

candle N lilin

candy N permen, kembang gula

cane N tongkat

canoe N [kanu] kano

cantaloupe N [kantalop] melon, blewah

canteen N kantin

canyon N ngarai

cap N topi pet; tutup

capable ADJ bisa, mampu, dapat

capacity N daya tampung, kapasitas

cape N tanjung

capital N modal; huruf besar; ~ *(city)* ibukota

capitol N ibukota

C

captain N kapten, nahkoda; kapitan
capture N penangkapan; V menangkap
car N mobil; gerbong; ~ *park* tempat parkir
caramel N gula bakar, permen rasa karamel
caravan N kafilah; karavan
carbon N karbon, zat arang
card N kartu; kardus
cardboard N karton, kertas tebal
care N pemeliharaan, perawatan; V peduli, memedulikan; *child* ~ penitipan anak-anak; *to take* ~ berhati-hati, jaga diri; *to take* ~ *of* memelihara, mengurus
career N karir
careful ADJ hati-hati; **careless** ADJ teledor, lalai ← care
carer N perawat, penjaga anak ← care
caretaker N penjaga ← care
cargo N muatan kapal
carnival N pesta, pasar malam, karnafal
carpenter N tukang kayu
carpet N permadani, karpet
carport N garasi, atap untuk perlindungan mobil
carriage N [karij] kereta; gerbong ← carry
carrot N wortel; insentif
carry V mengangkut, membawa
cart N kereta, pedati, gerobak
cartoon N (film) kartun; komik
cartridge N [kartrij] pelor, peluru; isi pulpen, kartrid
carve V mengukir
case N peti, koper; kasus, perkara, hal, perihal
cash N uang kontan, uang tunai
cashew N kacang mede
cashier N [kasyir] kasir, kassa ← cash
cast N pemain-pemain sandiwara; V cast cast melempar, melontar; menuangkan; memilih untuk peran; ~ *iron* besi tuang
castle N [kasel] puri, benteng, istana
casual ADJ santai
casualty N korban kecelakaan
cat N kucing
catalog N katalog, daftar; V mendo-

kumentasi
catch N angkapan, hasil; jepitan, gesper; V caught caught [kort] menangkap; terkena, terjangkit (penyakit)
category N kategori, golongan
cater V melayani; menyediakan makanan; **caterer** N perusahaan jasa boga; **catering** N jasa boga
caterpillar N ulat
cathedral N [kathidral] katedral
Catholic (orang) Katolik
cattle N sapi, ternak
caught V, PF → catch
cauliflower N [koliflauer] kembang kol
cause N [coz] sebab; V menyebabkan, mengakibatkan
caution N sikap hati-hati, kewaspadaan; V mengingatkan
cave N gua
cavity N rongga, lubang (gigi)
ceiling N [siling] langit-langit, plafon
celebrate V [sélébrét] merayakan; **celebration** N perayaan
celebrity N selebriti
celery N seledri
cell N sel; bilik penjara; ~ *phone* telepon seluler (ponsel), telepon genggam
cement N semen, beton
cemetery N kuburan, tempat pemakaman umum (TPU)
censor N sensor; V menyensor
census N sensus
center N pusat; **central** ADJ pusat, tengah, pokok
centimeter N senti, sentimeter
centipede N [sentipid] kaki seribu, lipan
century N abad
cereal N [sirial] sereal
ceremony N upacara
certain ADJ [serten] tentu, pasti, yakin; **certainly** ADJ tentu saja
certificate N sertifikat, ijazah
chain N rantai; kalung; serangkaian; V merantai
chair N kursi; ketua; **chairman** N, M **chairperson** N ketua
chalk N kapur
challenge N tantangan; V menantang
chamber N [cémber] kamar

C

champagne N [syampéin] sampanye
champion N juara
chance N kesempatan, peluang
change N perubahan; uang kembali; v menukar, mengubah
channel N saluran, selat
chant v bernyanyi; menyanyikan (berulang-ulang)
chapter N bab, pasal
character N [karakter] sifat; peran; huruf; **characteristic** N ciri; ADJ khas
charcoal N arang
charge N muatan; ongkos, harga; serangan, serbuan; tuduhan; v menyerang; meminta bayaran, menagih; (me)ngecas
charity N amal
charm v memesonakan, menarik hati; menyihir
chart N grafik; peta
charter N piagam; v mencarter
chase N pengejaran; v mengejar
chat N percakapan; v mengobrol; **chatter** N celotehan, obrolan; v berceloteh, mengobrol; **chatting** N kegiatan berkomunikasi lewat internet
chauffeur N [syofer] supir, sopir
cheap ADJ murah
cheat N penipu; v menipu; curang; **cheating** N curang, kecurangan
check, cheque N cek
check N pemeriksaan, uji, cek; v memeriksa, menguji, mengecek
cheek N pipi; **cheeky** ADJ berani, nakal
cheer N kegembiraan; sorak; v memberi semangat, bersorak; mendukung; **cheerful** ADJ gembira, senang hati
cheese N keju
chef N [syéf] juru masak
chemical N [kémikel] bahan kimia; ADJ kimiawi; **chemist** N ahli kimia; apoteker; **chemistry** N ilmu kimia
cherry N buah ceri
chess N catur
chest N dada; peti, kopor
chew v mengunyah
chicken N (rasa) ayam; ~ pox cacar air
chief N chiefs kepala (suku), pemimpin; ADJ utama, pokok; **chiefly** ADV terutama, pertama-tama

child N [caild] **children** [cildren] anak, putra; **childish** ADJ kekanak-kanakan
Chile N [Cili] Cile
chill N udara dingin
chilli N cabe; ~ *sauce* (saus) sambal
chilly ADJ sejuk, dingin ← chill
chimney N **chimneys** cerobong asap
chimpanzee N simpanse
chin N dagu
China N [Caina] (negeri) Cina; **china** N, ADJ porselen; **Chinatown** N Pecinan; **Chinese** N orang Cina, orang Tionghoa; ADJ Cina, Tionghoa; ~ *New Year* (Tahun Baru) Imlek
chip N keping; keripik; *hot* ~*s* kentang goreng; v pecah
chocolate N, ADJ coklat
choice N pilihan, terpilih ← choose
choir N [kuaier] koor
choke v mencekik
cholera N kolera
cholesterol N kolesterol
choose v chose chosen memilih
chop N potong; steik yang bertulang; v memotong, mencincang
chopsticks N, PL sumpit
chose, chosen v, PF ← choose
Christ N [Kraist] (Yesus) Kristus; **christening** N permandian; **Christian** N orang Kristen atau Katolik; ADJ Kristiani, Nasrani, Masehi; **Christmas** N (hari) Natal
chubby ADJ gemuk, berlebihan berat badan
chunky ADJ berisi, berat
cigar N [sigar] cerutu; **cigarette** N [sigarét] rokok
cinema N [sinema] (gedung) bioskop
cinnamon N kayu manis
circle N [serkel] lingkaran, bulatan; kawasan, lingkungan; v melingkari; mengedari
circular ADJ [serkyuler] bulat, bundar; **circulate** v beredar; mengedarkan; **circulation** N peredaran, sirkulasi
circumcision N [sirkumsisyen] sunatan
circus N sirkus
citizen N [sitizen] warganegara
city N [siti] kota

C

ENGLISH—INDONESIAN

civil ADJ sipil; sopan; **civilian** N orang sipil; **civilization** N [sivilaizé-syen] peradaban

claim N tuntutan; tagihan; pengakuan; v menuntut; menagih; mengaku; meminta

clam N kerang

clan N suku bangsa, kaum, marga

clap N tepuk; v bertepuk tangan; **clapper** N anak lonceng

clarify v [klarifai] menjelaskan, menerangkan

clarinet N klarinet

clash N bentrokan; v bentrok

clasp N jepitan, gesper; pelukan

class N kelas; pelajaran; golongan; **classify** v menggolongkan; **classroom** N ruang kelas

class N mutu, kualitas (tinggi); **classic** ADJ klasik

clause N ayat, klausa; syarat; anak kalimat

claw N cakar, jepit

clay N tanah liat

clean ADJ bersih; v membersihkan; **cleaning** N pembersihan

clear ADJ terang, jernih, jelas; nyaring, nyata; v membereskan

clever ADJ [klever] pandai, cerdas, pintar

client N [klaient] nasabah, pelanggan, tamu, klien

cliff N tebing

climate N [klaimet] iklim

climax N [klaimaks] puncak, klimaks, orgasme

climb N [klaim] perjalanan naik; v memanjat; menaiki

clinic N klinik, pusat kesehatan masyarakat (puskesmas)

clip N jepitan; v menjepit, menggunting, memotong; **clippers** N gunting (kuku)

clock N jam; *alarm ~* weker; *three o'~* jam tiga; v mencatat waktu

close v [kloz] menutup

close ADJ [klos] dekat, akrab

closet N [klozet] lemari baju

cloth N kain, bahan; **clothes** N, PL pakaian, baju

cloud N awan; **cloudy** ADJ berawan

clove N cengkeh

clown N badut, pelawak; v melucu

club N perhimpunan, klub, kelab; **clubbing** N pergi ke diskotek

clue N tanda, petunjuk

clumsy ADJ canggung, kikuk

cluster N gugus, tandan; v berkerumun

clutch N genggam; kopling

cm *centimeter* cm (sentimeter)

coach N pelatih; bis pariwisata; v melatih

coal N batu bara

coarse ADJ [kors] kasar

coast N pantai, pesisir

coaster N alas gelas

coat N mantel, jas; lapisan; kulit atau bulu binatang; v melapisi

coax v membujuk

cobra N kobra, ular sendok

cobweb N sarang laba-laba

cock N ayam jantan; **cocky** ADJ arogan

cockatoo N [kokatu] burung kakatua

cockpit N kokpit

cockroach N kecoa

cocktail N sejenis minuman keras, koktil

cocoa N [koko] (biji) coklat

coconut N (buah) kelapa

code N sandi, kode

coffee N kopi; *white ~, milk ~* kopi susu

coffin N peti mati

coil N gulungan, gulung; v bergelung

coin N uang logam, koin

coincidence N [koinsidens] kebetulan

cold N masuk angin, pilek; rasa dingin; ADJ dingin

collaborator N orang yang bekerja sama

collapse N keruntuhan, kerobohan; v runtuh, ambruk, roboh

collar N kerah, leher baju

colleague N [kolig] rekan, kolega, teman kantor

collect v mengumpulkan, memungut; **collection** N kumpulan, koleksi; **collector** N kolektor

college N [kolej] sekolah, kolese; perguruan tinggi, universitas

collide v bertabrakan, menabrak; **collision** N [kolisyen] tabrakan

C

colon N titik dua

colonel N [kernel] kolonel

colonial ADJ kolonial, penjajah; **colonize** v menjajah, menduduki; **colony** N jajahan

color N [kaler] warna; v mewarnai; **colorful** ADJ berwarna-warni

coma N koma, mati suri

comb N [koom] sisir; v menyisir

combination N gabungan, kombinasi; **combine** v menggabungkan, memadukan

come v [kam] came come datang, tiba, sampai; ~ *from* berasal dari, datang dari; ~ *in* masuk; ~ *out* keluar; **comeback** N kembali

comet N bintang berekor

comfort N [kamfert] v menghibur; **comfortable** ADJ, **comfy** SL nyaman

comic N pelawak; ADJ lucu ← **comedy**

coming N [kaming] kedatangan; ADJ mendatang ← **come**

comma N koma

command N perintah; komando; v memimpin

commemorate v memperingati, merayakan; **commemoration** N peringatan, perayaan

commence v mulai, memulai

comment N komentar; v berkomentar, memberi komentar; mengomentari

commerce N perdagangan, perniagaan; **commercial** N, ADJ dagang, perniagaan; komersial

commission N pesan; komisi

commit v berjanji; melakukan

committee N [komiti] panitia, komite

common ADJ biasa, umum; bersama; rendah

communicate v berkomunikasi; memberitahu, menghubungi; **communication** N komunikasi, perhubungan

communism N komunisme

community N masyarakat, umat, komunitas ← **commune**

commuter N pelaju

compact ADJ kompak; padat

companion N kawan, teman; **company** N [kampeni] kawan-kawan; perusahaan, maskapai (penerbangan)

compare v membandingkan; **comparison** N perbandingan

compass N [kampas] pedoman, kompas; jangka

compete v [kompit] bersaing, bertanding

competent ADJ mampu, kompeten

competition N persaingan; pertandingan; **competitive** ADJ (suka) bersaing; **competitor** N pesaing, saingan ← **compete**

complain v mengadu, mengeluh

complete ADJ lengkap, komplit; v menyelesaikan; **completely** ADJ, NEG sama sekali

complex N kompleks; ADJ rumit, ruwet

complicate v mempersulit; **complication** N kesulitan; komplikasi (penyakit)

compliment N pujian; v memuji

component N unsur, komponen, suku cadang

compose v menyusun, membentuk, mengarang; **composer** N komponis

compound N kompleks (perumahan)

comprehend v mengerti, memahami; **comprehension** N pengertian, pemahaman

compromise N [kompromaiz] kompromi; v mencari jalan tengah, berkompromi

compulsory ADJ paksa, wajib

computer N komputer

comrade N [komrad] kawan, teman; kamerad

concave ADJ cekung

conceal v menyembunyikan

conceited ADJ sombong, angkuh

concentrate v memusatkan (perhatian), konsen; **concentration** N pemusatan, konsentrasi

concern N perkara, hal; perhatian; perusahaan

concert N konser

concession N izin, kelonggaran; konsesi ← **concede**

concise ADJ pendek, ringkas, singkat

conclude v menyimpulkan; memutuskan; **conclusion** N kesimpulan; akhir

concrete N [konkrit] semen, beton; ADJ nyata

condemn v [kondém] menghukum; menghakimi, mengutuk

condition N keadaan, kondisi; syarat; conditional ADJ dengan syarat

condolences our ~ kami ikut berduka cita, kami ucapkan belasungkawa

condom N kondom

conduct N kelakuan, cara; conductor N dirigen (musik); kondektur (angkutan umum); penghantar

cone N kerucut; marka jalan

confess v mengaku; confession N pengakuan

confetti N guntingan kertas yang dilempar saat berpesta, hujan kertas

confidence N kepercayaan; confident ADJ berani, percaya diri

confine v membatasi, mengurung; memingit

confirm v menegaskan, memastikan; confirmation N kepastian, penegasan, konfirmasi

conflict N perselisihan, pertikaian, percekcokan, konflik; perang; v bertentangan

confront v menghadapi; menentang, melawan; confrontation N konfrontasi

confuse v membingungkan

congratulations N, PL ucapan selamat; EJAC selamat

connect v menyambung, menghubungkan; connection N hubungan, sambungan; koneksi

conquer v [konker] mengalahkan, menaklukkan, merebut

conscience N [konsyens] hati nurani; conscientious ADJ rajin

conscious ADJ [konsyus] sadar

consecutive ADJ berturut-turut

consequence N akibat, dampak; consequently ADV oleh karena itu, maka

conservation N perlindungan, pemeliharaan; conservative ADJ kolot, konservatif

consider v menganggap, mengindahkan; mempertimbangkan; considerable ADJ cukup banyak; considering CONJ mengingat

consist v terdiri atas, terdiri dari

consistent ADJ konsekuen, tetap

console v menghibur

consonant N huruf mati, konsonan

conspiracy N [konspirasi] komplotan, persekongkolan

constant ADJ tetap, selalu

constellation N gugus bintang, konstelasi

constipated ADJ sembelit

constitution N undang-undang dasar (UUD), konstitusi

construct v membangun, membuat, membentuk; construction N bangunan, pembangunan (gedung), konstruksi; ~ site proyek

consul konsul, wakil; consulate N konsulat

consult v menanyakan, mencari pendapat, berkonsultasi; consultation N perundingan, konsultasi

consume v memakan, menghabiskan; memakai; consumer N pengguna, pemakai, konsumen; consumption N pemakaian

contact N hubungan, kontak; v menghubungi

contagious ADJ menular, menjangkit

contain v berisi, memuat, mengandung; container N tempat; ~ ship kapal barang

contamination N kontaminasi

contemporary ADJ modern, kini, kontemporer

contempt N penghinaan

content N [kentént] kepuasan

content N [kontént] isi, bahan; contents N, PL isi, muatan

contest N pertandingan, lomba; v bertanding; memperjuangkan; contestant N peserta

continent N benua

continuation N terusan, lanjutan, sambungan; continue v terus; melanjutkan, meneruskan; continuous ADJ terus-menerus

contraceptive N, ADJ kontrasepsi; ~ pill pil KB

contract N kontrak, surat perjanjian; contraction N kontraksi; contractor N kontraktor, pemborong

contradict v membantah, menyanggah

contrast N perbedaan, kontras; v berbeda; membandingkan

C

ENGLISH–INDONESIAN

C

contribute v menyumbang, memberikan; **contribution** N sumbangan, kontribusi

control N kendali, kontrol; v mengendalikan

controversial ADJ kontroversial

convenience N kesempatan; kemudahan; **convenient** ADJ enak; dekat

convention N seminar, rapat, konvensi; kebiasaan; **conventional** ADJ biasa ← convene

conversation N percakapan, pembicaraan

conversion N perubahan; **convert** v masuk agama baru; mengubah

convex ADJ cembung

convey v [konvé] membawa, mengangkut; menyampaikan

convict N narapidana; v menghukum

conviction N keyakinan, kepercayaan

convince v meyakinkan

convoy N iring-iringan, konvoi

cook N juru masak, koki; v memasak; **cookery** N cara memasak; **cookie** N kue kering yang keras

cool ADJ sejuk, dingin; v menyejukkan

coolie N kuli

co-operate, cooperate v bekerja sama; **co-operation** N kerja sama

cope v menghadapi, hidup dengan (kesulitan)

copper N tembaga

copy N salinan, kopi; v menyalin, meniru; memfotokopi; **copyright** N hak cipta

coral N karang

cord N tali

core N inti, hati

coriander N ketumbar

cork N gabus; sumbat

corn N jagung

corner N sudut, penjuru

corporal N kopral

corporate ADJ berkaitan dengan perusahaan; **corporation** N perusahaan, perkumpulan, persekutuan, grup

corpse N [korps] mayat (manusia)

correct ADJ benar, betul; v membetulkan, memperbaiki

correspond v surat-menyurat; sesuai dengan; **correspondent** N orang yang menulis surat atau artikel; wartawan

corridor N lorong

corrupt ADJ korup, dapat disuap; **corruption** N korupsi, suap

cosmetics N, PL alat-alat kecantikan (seperti lipstik, perona pipi dsb)

cost N harga (barang), ongkos (perjalanan), biaya (jasa); v cost cost berharga

costume N pakaian, busana, kostum

cosy, cozy ADJ enak, mungil

cottage N pondok, bungalo

cotton N, ADJ kapas, katun

cough N, v [kof] batuk

could v [kud] bisa, dapat, mampu; PF → can

council N dewan; pemerintah setempat (seperti kecamatan)

counsellor N konselor

count N penghitungan; v berhitung; menghitung

counter N loket

country N [kantri] negeri, negara; tanah air; **countryside** N pedesaan, pedalaman

couple N [kapel] pasang, pasangan

coupon N kupon

courage N [karej] keberanian; **courageous** ADJ [karéjus] berani

courier N kurir

course N [kors] kursus; jalan, arah

court N [kort] pengadilan

court N [kort] jalan buntu; taman; lapangan main

courtesy N [kertesi] kesopanan, sopan-santun

cousin N [kazen] (saudara) sepupu

cover N [kaver] tutup, penutup; sampul (buku); sarung (bantal); perlindungan; v menutup; meliputi

cow N sapi, lembu

coward N pengecut, penakut; **cowardly** ADJ penakut, pengecut

crab N kepiting, rajingan

crack N retak; bunyi; v retak, pecah dengan bunyi gemeretak; **cracker** N petasan; biskuit kering

craft N kerajinan tangan; ketrampilan; **craftsman** N perajin, tukang

cramp N kejang

crash N tabrakan, ambruknya; v bertabrakan, menubruk; jatuh (pesawat terbang)

ENGLISH–INDONESIAN

D

crate N peti kayu

crater N kawah

crawl V merangkak, merayap

crayon N krayon, kapur tulis lilin

crazy ADJ gila

cream N krim, kepala susu

create V [kriét] menciptakan, membuat; **creation** N ciptaan, kreasi; **creature** N makhluk

credit N penghargaan; kredit; ~ *card* kartu kredit

creep V merangkak, merayap, menjalar; **creepy** ADJ angker, mengerikan

cremation N kremasi, pembakaran mayat

crescent N jalan yang melingkar

crew N awak kapal; regu, kru

cricket N jangkrik, belalang; semacam olahraga seperti kasti

crime N kejahatan; **criminal** N penjahat; ADJ jahat

crisis N [kraisis] krisis

crisp ADJ garing; segar

criteria N, PL syarat; patokan, norma

critical ADJ kritis, genting; **criticism** N kritik; **criticize** V mengritik

crocodile N buaya

crooked ADJ bengkok

crop N panen; V memotong

cross N silang; salib; persimpangan, persilangan; V melintasi, menyeberangi; **crossing** N penyeberangan; **crossroads** N simpang, perempatan; **crossword** N teka-teki silang (TTS)

crouch V berjongkok

crow N [kro] burung gagak

crowd N orang banyak, gerombolan orang, kerumunan orang

crown N mahkota; ubun-ubun

crude ADJ kasar, mentah; primitif

cruel ADJ bengis, kejam

cruise N [kruz] pelayaran pesiar

crunchy ADJ garing

crusader N orang yang memperjuangkan sesuatu

crust N kerak, kulit

crutch N; **crutches** PL kruk

cry N [krai] teriak, pekik; tangis; V berteriak, memekik; menangis

crystal N, ADJ hablur, kristal

Cuba N Kuba

cube N kubus

cucumber N [kyukamber] timun, mentimun

cuddle N [kadel] pelukan; V memeluk, mengemong

cuisine N [kuisin] santapan, masakan

cultivate V memelihara, menanam; **cultivation** N pemeliharaan, penanaman

cultural ADJ **culture** N kebudayaan, budaya

cunning N, ADJ cerdik, licik

cup N cangkir, cawan; piala; **cupboard** N [kaberd] lemari; **cupcake** N kue kecil

cure N obat, pengobatan; V mengobati (sampai sembuh)

curfew N jam malam

curiosity N penasaran, keingintahuan; **curious** ADJ penasaran, ingin tahu; aneh

currant N kismis (kecil, berwarna hitam)

currency N mata uang

current N arus; ADJ kini; berlaku

curry N kari, gulai

curse N kutukan; umpatan, makian; V mengutuk; mengumpat, memaki

curtain N [kerten] horden, gorden, tirai

curve N lengkung; V melengkung

cushion N [kusyen] bantal

custard N sejenis puding

custom N adat, kebiasaan; **customer** N langganan, nasabah (bank)

customs N bea cukai, pabean

cut N potongan; V cut cut memotong, menggunting

cute ADJ lucu; mungil, manis

cyberspace N dunia maya

cycle N [saikel] daur, siklus; V bersepeda, naik sepeda; **cyclist** N pengendara sepeda; pembalap sepeda

cyclone N [saiklon] angin topan, siklon

cylinder N silinder

Czech ADJ Ceko

D

Dad N, SL Pak; **Daddy** N, SL, CHILD Papa

dagger N keris

D

daily N harian; ADV tiap hari

dairy N perusahaan susu

dam N bendungan; V membendung

damage N [damej] kerusakan; rugi, kerugian; V merugikan, merusak

damn V mengutuk; ADJ terkutuk; EJAC persetan

damp N kelembaban, iklim lembab; ADJ lembab

dance N tari, tari-tarian; dansa; V menari; berdansa; **dancer** N penari

dandruff N ketombe

danger N [dénjer] bahaya; **dangerous** ADJ berbahaya

dare N tantangan; V menantang; ADJ berani; daring N keberanian; ADJ berani

dark N gelap, kegelapan; ADJ gelap; ~ *green* hijau tua; **darkness** N kegelapan

darling N sayang, buah hati; ADJ tersayang

dash N garis datar; V berlari

dashboard N dasbor, panel peralatan

data N data; **database** N bank data

date N korma

date N tanggal; kencan; V mengencani, memacari

daughter N, F [doter] anak perempuan, putri

dawn N dini hari, fajar; permulaan

day N hari; siang; *all* ~ sepanjang hari; *one* ~ sekali waktu; *during the* ~ siang hari; **daybreak** N dini hari, fajar; **daydream** N lamunan, khayalan; **daylight** N siang; sinar matahari; **daytime** N, ADJ siang hari

daze N keadaan pusing

dazzle V menyilaukan, memesonakan

dead ADJ mati; sunyi senyap; ~ *end* jalan buntu; **deadline** N batas waktu; **deadly** ADJ mematikan; sungguh-sungguh → die

deaf ADJ [déf] tuli

deal N persetujuan; V dealt dealt [délt] membagi (kartu); ~ *in* jual-beli; ~ *with* memperlakukan, menghadapi; **dealer** N pedagang; **dealings** N, PL urusan, transaksi

dear N yang baik, yang terhormat (*in letters*); *my* ~ sayangku; ADJ mahal

death N [déth] kematian

debate N perdebatan; V berdebat; memperdebatkan

debt N [dét] hutang

decay N kerusakan, kebusukan; V melapuk, membusuk

deceased ADJ telah meninggal, mangkat, wafat

deceitful ADJ penuh tipu daya, bersifat menipu; **deceive** V menipu; ~*d* tertipu

December N bulan Desember

decent ADJ sopan, patut, layak

deception penipuan ← deceit

decide V memutuskan, menentukan, menetapkan

decision N [desisyen] keputusan ← decide

deck N geladak, dek

declaration N pernyataan, pengumuman, maklumat, deklarasi; **declare** V menyatakan, mengumumkan

decline N kemunduran, kemerosotan; V mundur, menjadi kurang; menolak

decorate V menghiasi; **decoration** N hiasan, perhiasan; tanda kehormatan

decrease N pengurangan, penurunan; V berkurang; mengurangi, menurunkan

dedicate V mempersembahkan, mengabdikan; **dedication** N pengabdian, persembahan

deduct V memotong, mengurangi; **deduction** N potongan, pengurangan

deduction N kesimpulan; pengurangan ← deduce

deep ADJ dalam; **deepen** V mendalam; memperdalam

deer N rusa, menjangan

default V gagal; lalai membayar

defeat N kekalahan; V mengalahkan, menggagalkan

defect N [difékt] cacat, cela, kerusakan; **defective** ADJ rusak, cacat ← defect

defend V membela, mempertahankan; **defendant** N tergugat; **defender** N pembela; bek; **defense** N pertahanan, pembelaan, perlawanan;

defensive ADJ bersikap bertahan, defensif

defiant ADJ bersifat menentang, bersifat melawan

define v menentukan, menetapkan, mengartikan; **definite** ADJ tertentu, pasti; **definition** N definisi

deflate v kempes; mengempeskan

deforestation N deforestasi, penebangan hutan

deformed ADJ cacat

degree N (suhu) derajat; gelar sarjana

dehydrated ADJ [dihaidréted] dehidrasi, kurang minum

delay N keterlambatan, penundaan; v menunda, memperlambat

delegate N wakil, utusan; v menyerahkan; mengutus; **delegation** N delegasi, perwakilan

delete v menghapus, mencoret

deliberate ADJ (dengan) sengaja

delicate ADJ halus; sering sakit

delicious ADJ [delisyus] enak, sedap, lezat

delight N [delait] kesenangan, kegembiraan; **delightful** ADJ menyenangkan, membahagiakan

deliver v mengirim, menghantarkan, memberi; membidani; melahirkan; **delivery** N penyerahan, pengiriman; ~ *boy* kurir

demand N tuntutan; persediaan; v menuntut, minta

democracy N demokrasi, kerakyatan; **democrat** N demokrat; **democratic** ADJ demokratis

demolish v membongkar, merobohkan

demonstration N pertunjukan; demonstrasi, demo, unjuk rasa

dengue [déngi] ~ *fever* demam berdarah

dense ADJ padat, rapat, lebat; SL bodoh; **density** N kepadatan

dentist N dokter gigi

deny v [denai] menyangkal, memungkiri, menolak

depart v berangkat, pergi; **departure** N keberangkatan

department N departemen; bagian; ~ *store* toko serba ada (toserba)

depend v bergantung, tergantung

deposit N deposito, simpanan; endapan

deputy N wakil

derail v anjlok, keluar dari rel

descend v turun; **descendant** N keturunan, anak cucu; **descent** N jalan turun; keturunan

describe v melukiskan, menggambarkan; **description** N penggambaran, deskripsi

desert N [désert] gurun, padang pasir

deserted ADJ sunyi (senyap)

deserve v berhak mendapat, patut (menerima)

design N rancangan, contoh, gambar, desain; v merancang, mendesain; **designer** N perancang, desainer ← **design**

desire N keinginan, nafsu, hasrat; v ingin, menginginkan, mendambakan

desk N meja (tulis); bangku (di sekolah)

desperate ADJ sudah putus asa

despite PREP meskipun, kendati

dessert N [desert] pencuci mulut, puding

destination N tujuan, jurusan

destiny N nasib, takdir

destroy v menghancurkan, memusnahkan, membinasakan; **destruction** N kerusakan, kehancuran, pemusnahan, pembinasaan; **destructive** ADJ merusak, membinasakan

detail N rinci, perincian, seluk-beluk; v merincikan

detective N reserse, detektif

detention N penahanan, penawanan ← **detain**

detergent N sabun, obat, deterjen

deteriorate v [detiriorét] memburuk, merosot

determination N tekad bulat; **determine** v menetapkan, menentukan, memutuskan

detest v membenci

devastate v menghancurkan; **devastation** N penghancuran

develop v mengembangkan, membangun, membina; mencuci (film); **developer** N pengembang, pembo-

D

rong; **development** N pembangunan, perkembangan; pengembangan, pembinaan

device N alat

devil N setan, iblis

devoted ADJ tekun

devout ADJ soleh, beriman ← devote

dew N embun

diabetes N [daiabitis] penyakit gula, kencing manis

diagnose V mendiagnosa, menentukan; **diagnosis** N diagnosa

diagonal ADJ sudut-menyudut, diagonal

diagram N denah, bagan

dial V memencet (nomor telepon)

dialect N dialek

diameter N garis tengah, diameter

diamond N berlian, intan

diaper N popok

diarrhoea, diarrhea N [daiaria] mencret, sakit perut, diare

diary N [daiari] buku harian

dice N, PL dadu

dictate V mendikte; **dictation** N dikte, imla

dictator N diktator

dictionary N kamus

did V, PF → do

die V [dai] died died mati, meninggal, wafat; gugur, wafar (dalam perang)

diesel N [disel] minyak solar; mesin disel

diet N [daiet] diet; makanan; V mengikuti diet, membatasi makan

differ V berbeda; **difference** N beda, perbedaan; **different** ADJ beda, lain, berbeda

difficult ADJ susah, sulit, sukar; **difficulty** N kesulitan, kesusahan

dig V dug dug menggali

digit N [dijit] angka; jari; **digital** ADJ digital

dignified ADJ [dignifaid] bermartabat, mulia; **dignity** N martabat

dike N pematang, bendung, tanggul

dilemma N pilihan sulit, dilema

diligent ADJ rajin, telaten

dim V meredup; meredupkan; ADJ redup, suram

dine V bersantap (malam)

dining N santapan ← dine

dinner N makan malam; makan siang

dinosaur N [dainosor] dinosaurus

diploma N ijazah, diploma

diplomat N pegawai kedutaan, diplomat; **diplomatic** ADJ diplomatik, berkaitan dengan kedutaan

direct ADJ langsung; serta merta; terus terang; V memimpin, mengarahkan, memerintahkan, menunjukkan; menyutradarai; **direction** N arah, petunjuk; **directly** ADV secara langsung, serta merta, segera; **director** N direktur, pemimpin; sutradara

directory N buku alamat, buku daftar

dirt N kotoran, debu; tanah; **dirty** ADJ kotor, dekil

disabled ADJ cacat; orang cacat

disadvantage N rugi, kerugian

disagree V tidak setuju; **disagreement** N percekcokan, perbedaan pendapat

disappear V hilang, lenyap

disappoint V mengecewakan; **disappointment** N kekecewaan, rasa kecewa

disapprove V tidak menyetujui, tidak suka, menolak

disaster N musibah, malapetaka, bencana; **disastrous** ADJ malang, celaka

disc, disk N cakram

discipline N disiplin, tata tertib, ketertiban

discount N potongan (harga), diskon, korting; V memotong harga, mendiskon

discourage V [diskarej] mengecilkan hati, tidak menganjurkan

discover V menemukan, mendapat; **discovery** N penemuan

discriminate V membedakan, mendiskriminasikan; **discrimination** N pembedaan, diskriminasi

discuss V [diskas] berembuk membicarakan; **discussion** N pembicaraan, diskusi

disease N penyakit

disgrace N aib, malu; V mencoreng muka, memalukan; **disgraceful** ADJ memalukan

disguise N [disgaiz] samaran

ENGLISH–INDONESIAN

disgust N rasa muak; V menjijikkan, memuakkan

dish N piring, pinggan; sajian, hidangan; ~*cloth* lap piring

dishwasher N mesin pencuci piring ← dish

dislike N ketidaksukaan; V tidak suka

dismay N kecemasan; V mencemaskan

dismiss V menolak; membubarkan, memecat; **dismissal** N pembubaran, pemecatan

disobedient ADJ tidak patuh, nakal; **disobey** V melawan, tidak mematuhi

dispensation N kelonggaran, dispensasi

dispenser N alat atau mesin dengan persediaan

displace V menggantikan

display N pameran, pertunjukan; V memperlihatkan, mempertunjukkan, memamerkan

disposal N persediaan; pembuangan

disprove V [dispruv] membantah, menyangkal; membuktikan salah

dispute N perselisihan, percekcokan; V membantah; mempermasalahkan

disqualified ADJ, V dinyatakan tidak berhak atau keluar, dibatalkan

dissatisfaction N ketidakpuasan, kekecewaan

dissolve V larut; melarutkan

distance N jarak, kejauhan; **distant** ADJ jauh

distinct ADJ jelas, kentara; **distinction** N perbedaan; nilai unggul

distorted ADJ berubah; diubah

distract V mengalihkan perhatian; menyesatkan; **distraction** N selingan; gangguan, kesesatan

distress N kesulitan, kesusahan; ~*ed* menderita

distribute V menyebarluaskan, membagikan, menyalurkan, mendistribusikan; **distribution** N penyebarluasan; pembagian; penyaluran, pendistribusian; **distributor** N penyalur, pengecer

district N, ADJ distrik, daerah

disturb V mengganggu; **disturbance** N kekacauan, kegaduhan, gangguan

ditch N selokan, parit

dive V menyelam, terjun; **diver** N penyelam; **diving** N selam; loncat indah

diverse ADJ berbagai (macam), aneka, pelbagai; **diversity** N keanekaragaman

divide N jurang, kesenjangan; V membagi

division N pembagian; bagian; divisi

divorce N perceraian; V bercerai

DIY ABBREV *do it yourself* barang yang dirakit atau dikerjakan sendiri

dizzy ADJ pusing (kepala), pening, bingung

do V [du] did done berbuat, bikin; membuat, melakukan, mengerjakan

dock N galangan, dok; **dockyard** N galangan

doctor N dokter; doktor (S3)

document N surat, dokumen; **documentary** N film dokumenter; **documentation** N catatan, dokumentasi

dodge V mengelakkan, menghindar

dog N anjing

doing N [duing] perbuatan

doll N **dolly** CHILD boneka

dollar N dolar; *US* ~ dolar AS

dolphin N [dolfin] lumba-lumba

dome N kubah

domestic ADJ dalam negeri, domestik

dominant ADJ berkuasa, berpengaruh, dominan; **dominate** V menguasai, mendominasi; **domination** N penguasaan, dominasi

donate V menyumbangkan; **donation** N sumbangan

done V, PF [dan] → do

donkey N keledai

donor N pemberi, donor; *blood* ~ donor darah ← donate

don't V jangan ← do

donut N donat

door N pintu

dorm, dormitory N asrama

dot N titik, noktah, percik

D

double ADJ [dabel] ganda; kembaran; v melipatgandakan; ~ *bed* tempat tidur untuk dua orang

doubt N [daut] ragu, keraguan; v menyangsikan, meragukan; **doubtful** ADJ sangsi, ragu-ragu

dough N [do] adonan; **doughnut** → donut

dove N [dav] burung merpati

down ADV di bawah, ke bawah; **downstairs** ADV di lantai bawah; **downtown** N (di) pusat kota; **downward, downwards** ADV ke bawah

doze N tidur sebentar, tidur ayam

dozen N [dazen] lusin; ~*s* berpuluh-puluh, puluhan

draft N rancangan; v merancang

drag N menyeret, menarik

dragon N naga

dragonfly N capung

drain N saluran, parit, got; kali; aliran; v menguras, mengalirkan, mengeringkan; **drainage** N pengaliran, drainase

drama N seni peran, drama, sandiwara

drank v, PF → drink

draw v drew drawn menggambar; menarik; **drawback** N kekurangan, sisi buruk; **drawer** N laci; **drawing** N lukisan, gambar

dreadful ADJ menakutkan, dahsyat

dream N mimpi, impian; v mimpi, bermimpi, mengimpikan

dress N rok; pakaian, baju, kostum; v berpakaian, mengenakan pakaian; menghiasi; **dressing** N perban; saus (untuk salada)

drew v, PF → draw

drift N arus, aliran, arah; v terbawa arus, terhanyut

drill N bor; v mengebor

drink N minuman; v **drank drunk** minum, meminum; **drinker** N peminum

drip N tetes, tetesan; v menetes

drive N semangat, dorongan; v **drove driven** [driven] membawa (mobil), mengemudikan, menyupir; **driver** N supir, sopir, pengemudi, pengendara (mobil); kusir, sais (kendaraan berkuda); **driveway** N jalanan masuk halaman

untuk mobil; **driving** ADJ mendorong

drizzle N, v hujan rintik-rintik

drop N titik, tetes; v jatuh, turun, terjun; menjatuhkan, menurunkan

drought N [draut] masa kering tanpa hujan

drove v, PF → drive

drown v tenggelam; menenggelamkan

drowsy ADJ mengantuk

drug N obat (bius), obat-obatan; v membius

drum N gendang, tambur; v mengetuk

drunk N mabuk; v, PF → drink

dry ADJ kering, haus; membosankan; v menjemur, mengeringkan; ~~-cleaning binatu, waserai; ~ *season* musim kemarau; **dryer** N alat atau mesin pengering

duck N itik, bebek; v berjongkok menghindari; **duckling** N anak itik

due ADJ jatuh tempo; perlu, wajib

dug v, PF → dig

dull ADJ bodoh, dungu

dumb ADJ bisu; bodoh

dummy N, ADJ tiruan

dump N *(rubbish)* ~ tempat pembuangan sampah, tempat pembuangan akhir (TPA); v membuang

dumpling N pangsit

dune N bukit pasir

duplicate N rangkap kedua, salinan, kopi, duplikat

duration N lamanya

during CONJ, PREP selama, sementara

dusk N senja

dust N abu, debu; v membersihkan, menghilangkan debu; **dustbin** N tempat sampah; **duster** N lap debu, penyapu; **dusty** ADJ berdebu

Dutch N bahasa Belanda

dutiful ADJ patuh, menurut; **duty** N kewajiban; pekerjaan, tugas; bea

dwarf N katai, cebol

dye N zat pewarna; v mencelupkan, mengecat (rambut)

dynamic ADJ dinamis, hidup

dynamite N dinamit, bahan peledak

E

each ADJ masing-masing; tiap-tiap; saban; ~ *other* saling, satu sama lain

ENGLISH–INDONESIAN

eager ADJ ingin sekali, pengen
eagle N burung rajawali
ear N telinga, kuping; **eardrum** N gendang telinga
early ADJ [érli] pagi-pagi, dini
earn V [érn] mendapat gaji, memperoleh
earnings N, PL pendapatan, gaji, upah ← earn
earring N anting ← ear
earth N [érth] bumi, dunia; tanah, debu; on ~ di dunia; **earthquake** N gempa bumi
east ADJ timur; ~ Timor Timor Loro Sae
Easter N Paskah
eastern ADJ (daerah) timur ← east
easy ADJ mudah, gampang
eat V ate eaten makan
echo N [éko] gema, gaung, kumandang; V bergema, bergaung, berkumandang
eclipse N gerhana
ecological ADJ berkaitan dengan ekologi; **ecology** N ekologi
economic ADJ berkaitan dengan ekonomi; **economical** ADJ hemat, ekonomis; **economist** N ekonom; **economy** N ekonomi, dunia usaha; kehematan
ecstasy N kegembiraan, kebahagiaan; ekstasi; **ecstatic** ADJ sangat gembira atau bahagia
edge N [éj] pinggir, sisi, tepi; mata (pisau); on ~ tegang
edible ADJ dapat dimakan
edit V menyunting, mengedit; **edition** N terbitan, keluaran, edisi, cetakan; **editor** N redaktur, penyunting, editor; **editorial** N tajuk rencana
educate V mendidik; **education** N pendidikan
eel N [iel] belut
effect N pengaruh, efek; akibat, hasil; **effective** ADJ berhasil, efektif
efficient ADJ berdaya guna, tepat guna, efisien
effort N usaha, upaya
egg N telur; **eggplant** N terong
Egypt N [Ijipt] Mesir
eight ADJ, N [éit] delapan; **eighteen** ADJ, N delapan belas; **eighteenth** ADJ kedelapan belas; **eighth** ADJ

kedelapan; **eighty** ADJ, N delapan puluh
either ADJ [ither, aither] salah satu; ~ ... or ... ... atau...
elaborate ADJ rumit, panjang lebar, teliti
elastic N karet; ADJ karet, kenyal, elastis
elbow N siku; V menyikut
elder N yang lebih tua; sesepuh; ADJ kakak; ~ brother kakak (laki-laki); **elderly** ADJ sepuh, sudah tua; **eldest** ADJ anak paling tua, sulung
elect V memilih; **election** N pemilihan
electric ADJ listrik; **electrician** N tukang listrik; **electricity** N listrik
electronic ADJ elektronik; **electronics** N, PL barang elektronik, elektronika
element N unsur, bagian, bahan, elemen; **elementary** ADJ dasar
elephant N [élefant] gajah
elevator N lift
eleven ADJ, N sebelas; **eleventh** ADJ kesebelas
elf N elves peri
eligible ADJ memenuhi syarat, dapat dipilih
eliminate V menyisihkan, menyingkirkan
elite ADJ elit
else ADV lain; **elsewhere** ADV di lain tempat
embarrass V memalukan, mempermalukan
embassy N kedutaan
embrace V memeluk
embroidery N sulaman, bordiran
emerald N zamrud; ADJ hijau
emerge V [emérj] timbul, muncul
emergency N [emérjénsi] keadaaan darurat
emigrant N emigran; **emigrate** V pindah, beremigrasi; **emigration** N emigrasi
emission N pancaran, buangan, emisi
emotion N perasaan, emosi; **emotional** ADJ emosi
emperor N kaisar ← empire
emphasis N [émfasis] tekanan; **emphasize** V menekankan, menitikberatkan

empire N kekaisaran, kerajaan

employee N pegawai, buruh, pekerja, karyawan, karyawati; **employer** N majikan; **employment** N pekerjaan

empty ADJ kosong, hampa; V mengosongkan

enable V memungkinkan

enchant V memesonakan, memikat, menyihir

enclose V memagari; melampirkan, menyertakan

encounter N pertemuan; V bertemu, berjumpa

encourage V [énkarej] mendorong, mendukung, memberi semangat; **encouragement** N dorongan, desakan

end N akhir, ujung; V berakhir; menyudahi; mengakhiri; **endless** ADJ tanpa ujung, tiada hentinya, tidak ada akhirnya, tak terhingga, tidak berkeputusan ← **end**

endurance N daya tahan; **endure** V bertahan; menahan, menderita, menempuh

enemy N musuh, seteru

energetic ADJ [énerjétik] energik, bersemangat; **energy** N tenaga, usaha

engage V memasang; **engagement** N janji; pertunangan

engine N [énjin] mesin; **engineer** N insinyur; masinis; V merekayasa; **engineering** N ilmu teknik

England N [Ingland] Inggris; **English** N bahasa Inggris

enhance V meningkatkan

enjoy V menikmati; **enjoyable** ADJ menyenangkan; **enjoyment** N kenikmatan, kesenangan

enlarge V membesarkan, memperbesar, memperluas

enormous ADJ sangat besar

enough ADJ [enaf] cukup, sudah

enrich V memperkaya

enroll V mendaftarkan; **enrolled** ADJ terdaftar

ensure V memastikan, menjamin

enter V masuk; memasuki, memasukkan

entertain V menghibur; **entertainment** N hiburan

enthusiasm N semangat, gairah, antusiasme, gelora; kegemaran, hobi; **enthusiastic** ADJ antusias, bersemangat

entire ADJ seluruh, seantero; **entirely** ADV benar-benar

entitled ADJ berhak

entrance N pintu masuk ← **enter**

entrepreneur N [ontreprenur] pengusaha, wiraswasta

entry N jalan masuk, pintu masuk ← **enter**

envelope N amplop

envious ADJ iri

environment N lingkungan; ~*ly friendly* ramah lingkungan

epidemic N wabah

epilepsy N penyakit ayan, epilepsi, sawan

equal N [ikuel] bandingan; V menyamai, menyamakan; ADJ sama, setara; **equality** N kesamaan

equator N katulistiwa

equestrian ADJ berkaitan dengan penunggangan kuda

equipment N perlengkapan

equivalent N yang sama atau setara

eraser N penghapus

erect V mendirikan, membangun; ADJ tegak, tegang

erotic ADJ erotis, merangsang

errand N urusan, pesan

erratic ADJ tidak menentu, tidak teratur

error N salah, kesalahan

erupt V meletus; **eruption** N letusan, erupsi

escalator N tangga berjalan, eskalator

escape N pelarian; V melarikan diri, kabur, menghindari

escort N pendamping, rombongan

especially ADV khususnya, terutama ← **special**

essay N karangan

essential ADJ mutlak

establish V mendirikan, mengadakan; menentukan, menetapkan; **establishment** N pendirian, penentuan, penetapan; pembangunan

estate N tanah milik; kebun, perkebunan

estimate N taksiran, anggaran,

perkiraan; pendapat; v menaksir, memperkirakan

estuary N muara, kuala

eternal ADJ abadi, kekal

ethical ADJ etis; **ethics** N, PL etika

ethnic ADJ etnis, kesukuan; tradisional; ~ *group* suku (bangsa), kelompok etnis

etiquette N tata cara, sopan santun, etiket

Europe N [Yurop] Eropa

evacuate v mengungsi; mengungsikan; **evacuation** N pengungsian, evakuasi

evaluate v menilai; **evaluation** N evaluasi, penilaian

evaporate v menguap; **evaporation** N penguapan

eve N [iv] malam (sebelumnya); *New Year's* ~ Malam Tahun Baru

even ADJ rata; genap; pun; PREP bahkan; ~ *if* kalaupun; ~ *though* meskipun

evening N sore, petang; malam; *good* ~ selamat malam; *this* ~ nanti malam

event N peristiwa, kejadian, acara; **eventually** ADV akhirnya

ever ADJ [éver] pernah; ~ *since* (mulai) sejak; *have you* ~? pernahkah?; **everlasting** ADJ kekal, abadi

every ADJ [évri] setiap, tiap; **everybody, everyone** PRON semua orang, setiap orang; **everyday** ADJ seharihari; **everything** N semua; **everywhere** ADV di mana-mana

evidence N bukti; **evident** ADJ jelas, nyata, terang

evil N [ivel] kejahatan; ADJ jahat

evolution N evolusi

exact ADJ tepat, persis; betul; **exactly** ADV persis

exaggerate v [egzajerét] membesarbesarkan; **exaggeration** N pernyataan yang berlebihan

exam, examination N ujian; **examine** v menguji, memeriksa

example N contoh, teladan; *for* ~ (seperti) misalnya, seumpamanya

excellent ADJ bagus sekali, hebat

except PREP kecuali; v mengecualikan; **exception** N kekecualian,

pengecualian; **exceptional** ADJ luar biasa, istimewa

excess N kelebihan

exchange N pertukaran, penukaran; kurs; v menukar

excite v merangsang, membangkitkan

exclaim v berseru

exclude v mengecualikan; **excluding** v tidak termasuk; **exclusive** ADJ eksklusif, elit

excursion N kunjungan

excuse N [ékskyus] alasan, dalih; v [ékskyuz] memaafkan; ~ *me* permisi

execute v melakukan, melaksanakan; menjalankan keputusan; melakukan hukuman mati; **execution** N pelaksanaan (hukuman mati); **executive** N pemimpin (harian), eksekutif; ADJ eksekutif

exercise N olahraga; latihan, pelajaran; v berlatih; melakukan

exhaustion N kecapekan yang luar biasa

exhibition N pameran

exile N buangan; pembuangan

exist v ada eksis; **existence** N keberadaan

exit N pintu atau jalan keluar; kepergian

exotic ADJ eksotik, dari negeri asing

expand v memperluas, mengembangkan; memuai; **expansion** N perluasan, pengembangan

expat, expatriate N orang asing, orang yang tinggal di luar negeri, ekspatriat

expect v berharap; mengharapkan, menantikan; **expectation** N harapan

expense N belanja, biaya, ongkos; **expensive** ADJ mahal

experience N pengalaman; v mengalami

experiment N percobaan, uji coba; v mengadakan percobaan, menguji coba

expert N ahli, pakar; ADJ ahli

expire v kedaluwarsa, jatuh tempo; mati

explain v menjelaskan, menerangkan, menyatakan; **explanation** N penjelasan

explode v meletus, meledak

exploit v memanfaatkan, mengeksploitasi

explore v menjelajah; mengadakan penelitian; **explorer** N penjelajah

explosion N letusan, ledakan; **explosive** ADJ dapat meledak ← explode

export N, ADJ ekspor; v mengekspor; **exporter** N pengekspor, eksportir

expose v menyingkapkan, mempertunjukkan, memamerkan, membuka

express N yang cepat, kilat, ekspres; ADJ cepat, kilat; v mengucapkan, mengungkapkan, menyatakan, mengutarakan; **expression** N ucapan, peribahasa; raut muka; **expressive** ADJ ekspresif, menyatakan perasaan

extend v merentangkan, membentangkan; memperluas; memperpanjang; **extension** N perpanjangan; **extensive** ADJ luas, panjang lebar

exterior N luar, luarnya

extinct ADJ punah; **extinction** N pemadaman; kepunahan

extra ADJ ekstra

extract v mencabut (gigi); mengambil

extraordinary ADJ [ékstrodinari] luar biasa, istimewa

extravagant ADJ boros, berfoya-foya

extreme ADJ terlampau, ekstrem

eye N [ai] mata; **eyebrow** N alis; **eyelash** N bulu mata; **eyelid** N kelopak mata; **eyesight** N penglihatan; **eyewitness** N saksi mata

F

fable N dongeng, cerita rakyat

fabric N kain, bahan

fabulous ADJ hebat, menakjubkan

face N muka, paras, wajah; v menghadapi; **facial** N perawatan wajah

facility N sarana, fasilitas; kemudahan

facsimile N salinan, kopi → fax

fact N kenyataan, fakta; in ~ sebenarnya

factory N pabrik

fade v luntur, pudar; mengecil (suara)

fail v gagal; tidak jadi; jatuh; tidak lulus; **failure** N kegagalan, gagalnya

faint N pingsan; v (jatuh) pingsan; ADJ lemah, kecil

fair N pameran, pekan raya, pasar malam; ADJ adil, berimbang

fairy N peri; ~ tale dongeng

faith N iman, kepercayaan; **faithful** ADJ beriman, setia

fake N tipuan; ADJ palsu

fall N kejatuhan, keruntuhan, keguguran; musim gugur, musim rontok; v fell, **fallen** jatuh, runtuh, gugur

fallen v, PF → fall

false ADJ palsu

fame N ketenaran

familiar ADJ dikenal; akrab; **family** N keluarga; rumah tangga

famous ADJ terkenal, ternama ← fame

fan N kipas; penggemar, fans

fanatic ADJ fanatic

fancy ADJ rumit, megah

fantastic ADJ ajaib, fantastis, tidak masuk akal; **fantasy** N fantasi, khayalan

far ADJ jauh

fare N ongkos perjalanan

farewell EJAC selamat tinggal, selamat jalan

farm N pertanian, peternakan; **farmer** N petani

farther, further ADJ, ADV lebih jauh

fascinate v memesonakan, menarik hati

fashion N mode; cara; v membentuk; **fashionable** ADJ bergaya, gaya

fast N puasa; v berpuasa

fast ADJ cepat, laju; kokoh

fat N lemak; ADJ gemuk, tambun

fatal ADJ mematikan

fate N nasib

father N ayah, bapak; **father-in-law** N mertua (lelaki)

fatigue N [fatig] kelelahan, kecapekan; kerusakan

faucet N keran

fault N kesalahan, salah; cacat; **faulty** ADJ cacat, rusak, kurang sempurna

favor N pertolongan; karunia, anugerah; ampun; v lebih suka

favorite N kesukaan, anak emas; ADJ kesukaan, yang paling disukai, favorit

fax N ~ *(machine)* mesin faks; V (me)ngefaks, mengirim lewat faks ← **facsimile**

fear N ketakutan, rasa takut; V takut akan; **fearless** ADJ tidak takut, berani

feast N pesta, perjamuan, perayaan

feather N bulu

feature V mempertunjukkan, memperlihatkan

February N bulan Februari

fed V, PF → **feed**

federal ADJ federal, berserikat

fee N upah, gaji, biaya

feed N pakan, makanan hewan; ~ *on* makan (dari) V **fed fed** memberi makan; **feedback** N tanggapan

feel N rasa; V **felt felt** berasa, merasa; meraba; **feeling** N perasaan

feet N, PL → **foot**

fell V, PF → **fall**

fellow N lelaki; ADJ sesama

felt V, PF → **feel**

female N, ADJ perempuan, wanita; betina (binatang)

feminine ADJ feminin; yang berkaitan dengan kewanitaan

fence N pagar

ferocious ADJ ganas, buas

ferry N feri; V membawa penumpang bolak-balik, menyeberangkan

fertile ADJ subur; **fertilizer** N pupuk; **fertility** N kesuburan

festival N pesta, perayaan, hari raya, festival

fetch V menjemput (orang), mengambilkan

fever N demam; **feverish** ADJ demam, panas

few ADJ (hanya) sedikit; *a* ~ beberapa

fiancé N [fiansé] tunangan (laki-laki); **fiancée** N tunangan (perempuan)

fiber N [faiber] serabut, serat

field N bidang, daerah; padang, medan, ladang

fierce ADJ buas, galak, ganas

fifteen ADJ, N lima belas; **fifteenth** ADJ kelima belas ← **five**

fifth ADJ kelima ← **five**

fifty ADJ, N lima puluh

fight N [fait] pertengkaran; perkelahian; pertempuran, perjuangan; V **fought fought** bertengkar; berkelahi; bertempur, berperang, berjuang

figure N rupa, bentuk; bagan, gambar; angka; harga

file N berkas, arsip, dokumentasi; V menyimpan; mengikir

fill N jatah; V mengisi, menempati, memenuhi

film N film

filter N saringan, filter; V menyaring, menyeleksi

filthy ADJ kotor sekali

fin N sirip

final N (pertandingan) final; ADJ final, penghabisan, terakhir; **finally** ADV akhirnya

finance N keuangan; V membiayai, mendanai; **financial** ADJ keuangan

find N [faind] (hasil) temuan; V **found found** menemukan; menyimpulkan

fine N denda, tilang

fine ADJ bagus, baik; halus

finger N jari; **fingerprint** N sidik jari

finish N (garis) akhir; penghabisan, penyelesaian; V berhenti; mengakhiri, menghentikan; menyelesaikan; menghabiskan

Finland N Finlandia

fire N api; kebakaran; V melepaskan tembakan, menembak; **fireworks** N, PL kembang api, petasan, mercon

firm ADJ tetap, pasti, tegas

first ADJ pertama; ~ *name* nama depan; *at* ~ pada awalnya, semula; **firstly** ADV pertama-tama

fish N ikan; V memancing; **fisherman** N nelayan; **fisheries** N perikanan; **fishing** N memancing; ~ *rod* joran

fist N tinju, kepalan tangan

fit ADJ pas, tepat, layak, patut; fit, sehat; V menyesuaikan; **fitness** N kebugaran, kesehatan

five ADJ lima

fix N masalah; V memperbaiki; menetapkan, memasang; **fixed** ADJ tetap

flag N bendera

flame N (kobaran) api

flannel N kain panas, flanel; handuk kecil untuk menyabuni

flap N tutup, penutup; V mengepak

flash N kilau; blits; V berkilat-kilat; **flashlight** N (lampu) senter

flask N botol minuman

flat N apartemen; ADJ rata, datar; **flatten** V meratakan

flavor N rasa; V membumbui

flea N kutu (binatang); ~ *market* pasar loak

fled V, PF → flee

flee V fled fled melarikan diri, kabur, minggat

fleet N armada (angkatan laut)

flesh N daging

flight N [flait] penerbangan; terbangnya

fling V flung flung melemparkan

flip N salto; V membalik, memutar-balikkan

flirt V bermain mata

float V mengapung, terapung

flood N banjir, air bah; V banjir; membanjiri; **flooded** ADJ banjir

floor N lantai, tingkat

flop V gagal; jatuh, tidak berdiri; **floppy** ADJ tidak tegak, lembut

florist N (pemilik) toko bunga

flour N tepung (terigu)

flow N aliran; V mengalir

flower N bunga, kembang

flown V, PF → fly

flu N flu, selesma ← influenza

fluent ADJ lancar, fasih

fluid N cairan

flung V, PF → fling

flush V memerah (muka); ~ *the toilet* menyiram WC

flute N suling

fly N lalat

fly V flew flown [flon] terbang; berkibar-kibar; mengibarkan

flyer, flier N selebaran, brosur

foam N buih, busa

focus N titik perhatian, pusat perhatian, fokus; V memfokuskan, memusatkan perhatian; **focused** ADJ terarah

fog N kabut

foil N kertas perak

fold N lipatan; V melipat

folk N orang; ~ *tale* cerita rakyat

follow V mengikuti, menuruti; **following** yang berikut

fond ADJ suka, gemar

font N jenis huruf (cetakan)

food N makanan, pangan, pakan (hewan)

fool N orang bodoh; **foolish** ADJ bodoh

foot N feet kaki; **football** N sepak bola; **footpath** N jalan setapak, trotoar; **footprint** N tapak kaki; **footwear** N sepatu

for PREP bagi, untuk; selama; CONJ karena

forbid V forbade forbidden melarang; **forbidden** ADJ terlarang, dilarang

force N kekuatan, tenaga, daya; V memaksa

forecast N ramalan

forehead N dahi, kening

foreign ADJ [foren] asing, luar negeri; **foreigner** N orang asing

forest N hutan; **forestry** N perhutanan

forever, forevermore ADV untuk selamanya

forgave V, PF → forgive

forget V forgot forgotten lupa, melupakan, terlupa; **forgetful** ADJ pelupa

forgive V forgave forgiven memaafkan, mengampuni

forgot, forgotten V, PF → forget

fork N garpu; belokan, pertigaan

form N bentuk, rupa; formulir, blangko; V merupakan, membentuk

formal ADJ formal, resmi

former ADJ dahulu, bekas, mantan (orang), lama

formula N rumus, formula

fort N benteng ← fortress

fortnight N dua minggu

fortunate ADJ beruntung; **fortunately** ADV secara beruntung; **fortune** N rezeki; harta karun

forty ADJ, N empat puluh ← four

forward ADJ, ADV ke depan, maju; V mengirimkan

fossil N fosil

foul ADJ jorok, kotor, najis, jijik; V melanggar peraturan (olahraga); mengotori

found V mendirikan; V, PF → find; **foundation** N yayasan; fondasi, alas; bedak dasar

G

fountain N air mancur, pancuran air
four ADJ, N empat; **fourteen** ADJ, N empat belas
fox N rubah; v menipu
fraction N pecahan
fracture N keretakan, patah
fragile ADJ mudah pecah atau patah
fragrance N fragrant ADJ [frégrant] harum, wangi
frame N rangka, kerangka; bingkai, lis (gambar); kusen (pintu); tubuh, badan; v membingkai
France N Perancis
frangipani N bunga kamboja
fraud N penipuan, penipu
freak N orang dengan cacat yang luar biasa; ADJ luar biasa, kebetulan
freckle N bintik-bintik
free v membebaskan, melepaskan; ADJ bebas, merdeka; cuma-cuma, gratis; **freedom** N kemerdekaan, kebebasan
freeze v froze frozen membeku; **freezer** N lemari es
freight N [frét] muatan, kargo; v mengirim
French N bahasa Perancis
frequent ADJ berulang kali, sering; v sering mengunjungi
fresh ADJ segar; baru; sejuk
Friday N hari Jumat
fried ADJ goreng → fry
friend N [frénd] kawan, sahabat, teman; **friendly** ADJ ramah, bersahabat; **friendship** N persahabatan
fright N [frait] rasa takut; **frighten** v menakut-nakuti, menakutkan
fringe N pinggir; poni
frog N kodok, katak
from PREP dari
front N bagian muka; hadapan; ADJ muka; **frontier** N tapal batas, perbatasan
frost N embun beku; **frosty** ADJ dingin, tidak ramah
frown N [fraun] muka cemberut; v mengernyit dahi
froze, frozen v, PF → freeze
fruit N buah, buah-buahan
frustrate v menghambat; **frustration** N frustasi
fry v menggoreng; menjadi panas

fuel N bahan bakar
fulfill v memenuhi
full ADJ penuh; kenyang; lengkap
fun N keasyikan; ADJ asyik
function N fungsi; v berfungsi, berjalan, bekerja
fund N dana
funeral N (upacara) pemakaman
funnel N corong
funny ADJ lucu, jenaka; aneh
fur N bulu (binatang); **furry** ADJ berbulu
furious ADJ marah sekali, geram, naik pitam ← fury
furniture N mebel, perabot rumah
further ADJ lebih jauh, lebih lanjut; **furthermore** ADV lagipula
fury N kemarahan, berang
fuse N sumbu, sekering; v melebur, menyatu
fuss N repot; kekacauan; v cerewet; **fussy** ADJ teliti, cerewet
future N masa depan; ADJ yang akan datang, mendatang, bakal, calon (orang)

G

gadget N alat, perkakas
gain N untung, keuntungan, laba; v memperoleh, mendapat, mencapai
gale N angin besar, badai
gallery N serambi, ruang pameran, galeri
gamble v berjudi, bertaruh; **gambling** N judi, perjudian
game N permainan, pertandingan; ADJ berani
gang N kawanan, gerombolan, geng; **gangster** N preman, penjahat, perampok, garong
gap N lubang, celah, jurang pemisah
garage N [garaj] garasi; bengkel
garden N kebun, taman; **gardener** N tukang kebun; **gardening** N berkebun
gargle v berkumur
garlic N bawang putih
gas N gas; bensin
gasoline N [gasolin] bensin ← gas
gasp N embusan napas; v menarik nafas dengan cepat
gate N pintu (masuk), gerbang

G

gather v berkumpul; mengumpul-kan, memetik; **gathering** n per-kumpulan

gauge n [géj] ukuran, kadar; v men-gukur, menaksir

gay n orang homoseksual; ADJ se-nang hati, meriah

gaze v menatap, memandangi

gazelle n semacam rusa

gear n peralatan, perkakas, perabot; persneling, gigi; gir

gecko n cicak

gee EJAC, SL wah, aduh

geese n, PL → goose

gem, gemstone n permata

gender n jenis kelamin; jender

gene n gen

general n jenderal; ADJ umum; *in* ~ pada umumnya

generation n angkatan, generasi

generator n pembangkit listrik ← generate

generous ADJ murah hati, der-mawan

genital n kemaluan

genius n [jinius] kecerdasan; jenius, orang berotak cemerlang

genre n [jonre] gaya, aliran

gentle ADJ (lemah) lembut, halus, jinak; **gentleman** n gentlemen tuan; orang pria; orang sopan; **gently** ADV perlahan-lahan, lemah lembut

genuine ADJ [jényuin] asli, sejati, tulen

geography n [jiografi] ilmu bumi, geografi

geologist n [jiolojist] geolog, ahli geologi; **geology** n geologi

geothermal ADJ [jiotérmal] ber-hubungan dengan panas bumi

germ n kuman

German n bahasa Jerman; **Germany** n Jerman

get v got gotten mendapat, menerima; mengerti; menjadi; ~ *better* sembuh; menjadi lebih baik; ~ *off* turun; ~ *up* bangun; ~ *well soon* semoga lekas sembuh

ghost n hantu

giant n, ADJ [jaiant] raksasa

gift [gift] kado, hadiah, pemberian; bakat

gigantic ADJ [jaigantik] besar sekali, raksasa

giggle v cekikik; tertawa terkikik-kikik

gin n [jin] jenewer, minuman keras

ginger n [jinjer] jahe; ADJ merah (rambut); kuning (bulu kucing)

gipsy → gypsy

giraffe n [jiraf] jerapah

girl n [gerl] anak perempuan, putri, gadis

give v gave given memberi; ~ *birth* bersalin, melahirkan; ~ *in* mengalah; ~ *up* menyerah, menye-rahkan; **given** ADJ tertentu

glacier n gletser

glad ADJ gembira, senang

glamorous ADJ memesona, menarik, menawan, glamor

glass n kaca; gelas; **glasses** n kaca-mata; **glasshouse** n rumah kaca

glide v meluncur; **glider** n pesawat peluncur, pesawat layang; *hang-~* gantole

glitter n kegemilapan, kemegahan; v gemilap

global ADJ seluruh dunia; ~ *warming* pemanasan bumi; **globalization** n globalisasi; **globe** n bola dunia; bola lampu, bohlam

glorious ADJ megah, mulia, agung; **glory** n kemuliaan; kemenangan

gloss n kilau, kilap

glossary n daftar istilah

glossy ADJ licin, mengkilap ← gloss

glove n [glav] sarung tangan

glow n sinar, cahaya; v bersinar, berseri; menyala

glue n [glu] lem, perekat; v mengelem

gnome n [nom] orang kerdil, katai

go v went gone [gon] pergi, berja-lan; hilang; ~ *on* meneruskan; ~ *out* keluar; ~ *under* bangkrut; *to have a* ~ berusaha

goal n gawang, gol; tujuan; v *(to score a)* ~ mencetak gol; **goal-keeper** n penjaga gawang, kiper

goat n kambing

god n dewa; **God** ISL, CHR Allah, Tuhan; CHR Bapa; **goddess** n, F dewi

going ~ *to* mau, akan; naik ← go

ENGLISH–INDONESIAN

G

ENGLISH–INDONESIAN

gold N emas; **golden** ADJ terbuat dari emas; **goldfish** N ikan emas

golf N golf; **golfer** N pegolf, pemain golf

gone V, PF ← go

good ADJ baik, bagus; ~ *evening* selamat malam; ~ *night* selamat tidur; **goodbye** EJAC selamat tinggal, selamat jalan; **goodness** ~ *me* ampun; **goods** N, PL barang-barang

goose N **geese** [gis] angsa

gorge N jurang, ngarai

gorgeous ADJ [gorjes] sangat menawan atau menarik, indah

gorilla N gorila

gosh EJAC wah!

gossip N gosip, isu, gunjingan, buah bibir, kabar burung

got, gotten V, PF ← get

govern V [gavern] memerintah; **government** N [gaverment] pemerintah, pemerintahan; **governor** N gubernur

gown N gaun; jubah

grab V merampas, menjambret, menyerobot, menangkap

grace N keanggunan; rahmat, anugerah, karunia; **graceful** ADJ anggun

grade ADJ tingkat, pangkat, derajat; nilai (rapot); kelas; **gradual** ADJ lama-kelamaan, berangsurangsur

graduate N [gradyuet] lulusan, tamatan; sarjana; V [gradyuét] lulus, tamat; wisuda; **graduation** N tamat sekolah, acara lulus-lulusan; wisuda

grain N butir; sereal, biji-bijian

gram N gram

grand N besar, agung; bagus, mewah

grandchild N cucu; **grand-daughter** N cucu (perempuan); **grandfather** N kakek; nek; **grandma** N, SL nenek; nek; **grandmother** N nenek; **grandpa** N, SL kakek; kek; **grandson** N cucu (lelaki); **granny** N nenek, perempuan tua ← **grandmother**

grant N (dana) pemberian, sumbangan, subsidi, beasiswa

grape N buah anggur; ADJ (rasa) anggur; **grapefruit** N semacam jeruk kuning yang besar

graphic ADJ grafik, bergambar, jelas

grasp V memegang, menggenggam, menangkap, mengerti

grass N rumput; **grasshopper** N belalang

grate V memarut; mengganggu; **grate, grating** N riol, kisi; ADJ kasar, mengganggu

grateful N berterima kasih

grave ADJ berat, genting, gawat, serius

grave N kuburan, makam; **graveyard** N kuburan, tempat pemakaman

gravity N daya tarik bumi, gaya berat

gravy N [grévi] saus atau kuah daging

gray ADJ (warna) abu-abu, kelabu; suram

graze N goresan pada kulit; V mendapat goresan pada kulit

grease N [gris] gemuk, minyak; V [griz] memberi gemuk, meminyaki; **greasy** ADJ berlemak, berminyak

great ADJ [grét] besar, agung, mulia, raya

great-grandchild N cicit; **great-grandfather** N kakek buyut

Greece N Yunani

greedy ADJ rakus, tamak, loba

Greek N bahasa Yunani; orang Yunani ← **Greece**

green ADJ hijau; mentah; baru, muda; ramah lingkungan; **greenhouse** N rumah kaca; **greens** N, PL sayuran, sayur-mayur; partai hijau, partai peduli lingkungan

greet V memberi salam, menegur, menyambut; **greeting** N salam, ucapan selamat

grenade N granat

grew V, PF → grow

grey → gray

grid N jaringan

grief N kesedihan, duka cita

grill N pemanggangan, barbekiu; V memanggang

grin senyum, seringai

grind V **ground ground** menggerinda, menggiling, mengasah; **grinder** N gerinda

grip N pegangan, genggaman; V memegang, menggenggam

grit N kerikil, pasir; kenekatan

groan N keluh, erang; V berkeluh, mengeluh, mengerang

G

grocery N toko bahan makanan; **groceries** N, PL bahan makanan

groom N *(bride)*~ mempelai pria, pengantin pria, calon suami

gross N gros, 12 lusin, 144; ADJ sangat gemuk

ground V, PF → grind

ground N [graund] tanah, bumi; V mendasarkan; **grounds** N, PL pekarangan, taman; alasan

group N kelompok, grup; V mengelompokkan

grow V [gro] grew grown tumbuh; bertambah; menjadi; menanam

growl N [graul] geram; V menggeram

growth N pertumbuhan, pertambahan; benjolan ← grow

grudge N dendam

grumble N bersungut-sungut, menggerutu; keluhan

grumpy ADJ mengomel, marah-marah

grunt N dengkur; V mengeluarkan bunyi dengkur

guarantee N [garanti] jaminan; V menjamin, menanggung

guard N [gard] jaga, pengawal; kondektur; V menjaga, pengawal; **guardian** N wali, orang tua asuh; penjaga

guava N jambu

guess N [gés] tebakan, terkaan, sangkaan; V menebak, menerka

guest N [gést] tamu

guide N pemandu, pembimbing; V membimbing, memandu; **guidebook** N buku petunjuk, buku panduan; **guidelines** N, PL pedoman

guilt N [gilt] kesalahan, rasa bersalah; **guilty** ADJ bersalah

guitar N gitar

gulf N teluk besar; jurang

gum N getah

gum N gusi

gun N bedil, senapan, revolver, pistol; V menembak

gush N pancaran, semburan; V memancar, mengalir dengan deras

gut N usus; **guts** N, PL nyali, keberanian

gutter N parit, selokan

guy N, SL [gai] orang, lelaki, cowok

gym N [jim] aula, tempat senam; pusat kebugaran; **gymnasium** N aula, tempat senam, gimnasium; **gymnast** N pesenam

gymnastics N senam

gynecologist N [gainekolojist] ginekolog

gypsy, gipsy N nomaden, orang jipsi

H

habit N kebiasaan

hack V memotong-motong, mencincang; memasuki jaringan komputer; **hacker** N orang yang memasuki jaringan komputer

had V, PF → have

hadn't (had not) ← have

hail, hailstone N hujan es

hair N rambut, bulu; **hairbrush** N sikat rambut; **hairdresser** N penata rambut, potong rambut; **hairspray** N semprot rambut; **hairy** ADJ berbulu

half N [haf] halves ADJ setengah, separuh; ~ *past three* (jam) setengah empat; **halfway** ADJ setengah jalan

hall N [hol] aula, balai, ruang; lorong, koridor; **hallway** N lorong, koridor

halt N [holt] pemberhentian

ham N irisan daging babi

hamburger N burger

hammer N palu

hamper N bakul, keranjang (makanan)

hamster N marmot

hand N tangan; jarum (jam); jangan disentuh; **handbag** N tas tangan; **handbook** N buku panduan, pedoman

handicap N rintangan, cacat

handicraft N kerajinan tangan ← hand

handkerchief N sapu tangan

handle N pegangan; V menangani, memegang

handmade ADJ buatan tangan ← hand

handsome ADJ [handsam] ganteng, tampan

handwriting N [handraiting] tulisan tangan ← hand

ENGLISH–INDONESIAN

handy ADJ berguna, praktis; **handyman** N tukang ← **hand**

hang V bergantung; menggantung; ~~*gliding* gantolé

happen V terjadi; **happening** N kejadian, peristiwa

happiness N kebahagiaan; **happy** ADJ bahagia, berbahagia, senang

harbor N [harber] pelabuhan

hard ADJ keras; susah, sulit; dengan rajin

hardly ADV nyaris tidak, hampir tidak

hardware N alat-alat pertukangan; barang-barang dari logam dan besi; peranti keras ← **hard**

harm N bahaya, kerugian, kerusakan, kejahatan; V merusak, mengganggu; **harmful** ADJ membahayakan, merusak, merugikan; **harmless** ADJ tidak jahat

harmonica N harmonika

harness N tali pengaman, tali keselamatan; pakaian kuda

harsh ADJ kasar, keras hati; tidak ramah

harvest N (hasil) panen

hash N pagar (#)

hate N kebencian, rasa benci; V membenci; **hatred** N [hétred] kebencian, rasa benci

haul V menarik, menghela

haunt V menghantui

have V [hav] **had had** mempunyai, memiliki; ada; mendapat; menyuruh

hawk N burung elang

hawker N penjaja, pedagang kaki lima

hay N rumput kering, jerami; ~ *fever* alergi rumput

hazard N bahaya, risiko

he PRON, M [hi] dia, ia (subyek); **He** PRON Dia, Tuhan

head N [héd] kepala; pemimpin, direktur; V mengepalai; menyundul (bola); V mengepalai, memimpin; **headache** N sakit kepala, pusing; **heading** N judul (karangan); **headlights** N, PL lampu depan (mobil); **headline** N kepala berita; **headquarters** N markas besar

heal V menyembuhkan, menyehatkan; **health** N [hélth] kesehatan; **healthy** ADJ sehat

heap N timbunan, tumpukan, susunan

hear V **heard heard** [hérd] mendengar; **hearing** N (indera) pendengaran, sidang

heart N [hart] jantung; hati, inti; **heartbeat** N denyut jantung; **heartbreak** N patah hati

heat N panas, kepanasan, hangat; V memanaskan, menghangatkan; **heater** N alat pemanas

heaven N [héven] surga

heavy ADJ [hévi] berat, berbobot

hedge N pagar hidup

hedgehog N landak

heel N tumit; hak

height N [hait] ketinggian; tinggi badan; puncak

heir N [ér] **heiress** F ahli waris

helicopter N helikopter, heli

hell N neraka

hello, hallo EJAC halo; apa kabar?

helmet N helm

help N pertolongan, bantuan; V menolong, membantu; **helpful** ADJ suka menolong; berguna; **helpless** ADJ tidak berdaya

hemorrhoid N [hémeroid] wasir, ambeien

hen N, F ayam betina

hepatitis N [hépataitis] hepatitis, radang hati

her PRON, F -nya (kepunyaan); dia, ia (obyek)

herb N jamu, bumbu

herd N kawanan; V menggembala

here ADV di sini

heritage N [héritej] warisan, harta pusaka

hero N [hiro] pahlawan

heroin N [héroin] heroin, putau

heroine N, F [héroin] pahlawan (wanita) ← **hero**

herring N ikan haring

hers PRON, F miliknya; **herself** PRON dirinya, sendiri ← **her**

hesitant ADJ hesitate V ragu-ragu, bimbang

hey EJAC he, oi

hiccup V cegukan, bersedu

hid, hidden V, PF → hide

hide V **hid hidden** bersembunyi,

berlindung, mengumpet; menyembunyikan
hiding N persembunyian; *in ~* bersembunyi ← hide
high ADJ [hai] tinggi, mulia; *~ chair*
kursi bayi; *~ school* sekolah
menengah (atas); **highlands** N
tanah tinggi, pegunungan; **highway**
N jalan raya, jalan besar
hijack V membajak; **hijacker** N
membajak; **hijacking** N pemba-
jakan
hike N perjalanan kaki; V berjalan
kaki, mendaki gunung
hill N bukit; **hillside** N lereng bukit
him PRON, M dia, ia (obyek); **himself**
PRON dirinya, sendiri
Hindu N orang Hindu; ADJ Hindu;
Hinduism N agama Hindu
hinge N [hinj] engsel; sendi
hint N tanda, isyarat, sindiran
hip N pangkal paha, pinggul
hire N sewa; V menyewa; mem-
pekerjakan
his PRON, M -nya (kepunyaan)
historic ADJ bersejarah; **history** N
sejarah, hikayat
hit N pukulan; V hit hit memukul,
kena, mengenai
hitchhike V menumpang mobil
orang yang lewat
hobby N hobi, kegemaran, kesukaan
hockey N hoki; *ice ~* hoki es
hoe N [ho] pacul, cangkul
hold N pegangan, genggaman;
palka; V held held memegang,
menggenggam; bermuatan
hole N lubang, liang
holiday N hari libur; *religious ~* hari
raya; V berlibur
Holland N, SL Belanda
hollow N rongga, ruang; ADJ hampa,
kosong
holy ADJ suci, kudus
home N rumah; panti (jompo); ADJ
di rumah, di kandang sendiri;
hometown N kampung (halaman);
homemade ADJ buatan sendiri;
homesick ADJ rindu pada rumah,
kampung halaman atau negeri
sendiri; **homework** N pekerjaan
rumah (PR)
homo SL orang homo; homoseksual

honest ADJ [onest] jujur; **honesty** N
kejujuran
honey N [hani] madu; sayang, sayangku; **honeymoon** N bulan madu
honorable ADJ terhormat; **honorary**
ADJ kehormatan; **honor** N hormat,
kehormatan; V menghormati
hoof N **hooves** kuku (binatang)
hook N kait, kali; V mengait; **hooked**
ADJ keranjingan
hooligan N penggemar sepak bola
yang brutal
hop N lompat (pada satu kaki); V
melompat-lompat, melonjak-lonjak
hope N harapan; V berharap; mengharapkan; **hopeful** ADJ penuh
harapan; **hopeless** ADJ putus asa
horizon N [horaizon] cakrawala,
kaki langit, ufuk, horison; **horizontal** ADJ [horizontel] melintang, horisontal
horn N tanduk; terompet, klakson
hornbill N burung enggang
horrible, horrific ADJ mengerikan,
dahsyat; **horror** N kengerian, ketakutan, horor
horse N kuda; **horsepower** N daya
kuda, PK (paardekracht); **horseshoe** N ladam, sepatu kuda
hose N selang
hospital N rumah sakit
hospitality N keramahtamahan
host N, M [hoost] tuan rumah
hostage N sandera, tawanan
hostel N asrama
hostess N, F [hoostés] nyonya
rumah ← host
hot ADJ panas, hangat; pedas
hotel N hotel
hound N anjing pemburu
hour N [auer] jam; *half-~, half an ~*
setengah jam; *quarter of an ~* seperempat jam
house N rumah; dewan; **household**
N rumah tangga; **housekeeper** N
kepala pembantu; **housemaid** N, F
pembantu, pramuwisma; **housewife** N, F ibu rumah tangga; **house-
work** N pekerjaan rumah; **housing**
N perumahan
how ADV bagaimana; betapa; *~
much?, ~ many?* Berapa banyak?;
~ much is it? Berapa harganya?;

however ADV biarpun, akan tetapi, namun; bagaimanapun

howl N gonggong; teriak, tangis; V melolong; menangis (dengan keras)

hub N pusat (kota)

hug N pelukan; V berpelukan; memeluk

huge ADJ besar sekali

hum V bersenandung; mendengung

human N, ADJ manusia, orang; **humane** ADJ manusiawi, berperikemanusiaan

humble ADJ rendah hati; V merendahkan

humid ADJ lembab; **humidity** N kelembaban

humiliate V menghina, merendahkan; **humiliation** N penghinaan

humorous ADJ lucu, kocak, menggelikan; **humor** N kelucuan; sifat

hump N ponok (unta), bongkol

hunch N perasaan, firasat, dugaan

hunchback N, ADJ bungkuk

hundred N ratusan; ADJ seratus; ADJ keseratus

Hungary N Hongaria

hunger N [hangger] rasa lapar; **hungry** ADJ lapar

hunt N perburuan, buruan; V berburu; memburu; **hunter** N pemburu; **hunting** N pemburuan, perburuan

hurdle N gawang; rintangan; V melompati; mengatasi; **hurdles** N, PL lari gawang

hurrah, hurray EJAC hore

hurricane N angin topan

hurry N ketergopoh-gopohan; V bergegas; menggegaskan

hurt N sakit hati, luka; V melukai, menyakiti, mencederai, merusak

husband N suami

hush V diam

hut N pondok, gubuk

hydraulic ADJ [haidrolik] hidrolik, hidrolis

hygiene N [haijin] kebersihan; higiene; **hygienic** ADJ bersih; higienis

hypertension N hipertensi, darah tinggi

hypocrite N [hipokrit] orang munafik; **hypocritical** ADJ munafik

hysterical ADJ histeris

I PRON saya, aku

ice N es; **ice cream** N es krim; **iceberg** N gunung es; **icing** N lapisan gula di atas kue

icy ADJ [aisi] dingin sekali, sedingin es ← **ice**

idea N [aidia] ide, gagasan; **ideal** ADJ [aidil] yang diinginkan atau diidamkan, ideal, yang terbaik

identical ADJ sama, serupa, identik

identification N pengenalan, identifikasi; **identify** V mengenal, mengidentifikasi; **identity** N identitas, jati diri

idiom N ungkapan, idiom

idiot N orang dungu

idol N idola; berhala; **idolize** V mendewakan, memuji

if CONJ kalau, jika; apabila, bila

ignorant ADJ tidak tahu; **ignore** V tidak menghiraukan, tidak mengindahkan

iguana N iguana, sejenis biawak

ill N penyakit; ADJ sakit; jahat, salah; **illness** N penyakit

illegal ADJ melanggar hukum, tidak sah, ilegal

illegitimate ADJ lahir di luar nikah

illiterate ADJ buta huruf

illusion N ilusi, khayal

illustrate V menggambarkan, melukiskan; **illustration** N gambar, lukisan, ilustrasi

image N gambar; **imaginary** ADJ khayal; **imagination** N daya cipta, khayal, fantasi; **imagine** V membayang; membayangkan

imitate V meniru; **imitation** N tiruan, imitasi

immediate ADJ langsung; **immediately** ADV serta merta

immigrant N pendatang, imigran; **immigration** N imigrasi

immoral ADJ tuna susila, cabul

immortal ADJ kekal, abadi

immunization N imunisasi, pengebalan

impartial ADJ tidak memihak, adil, obyektif

impatient ADJ tidak sabar

imperial ADJ [impirial] kaisar;

imperialism N imperialisme; **imperialist** N orang penjajah, imperialis; ADJ imperialis, penjajahan ← empire

impersonal ADJ bersikap dingin; tidak mengenai orang tertentu

implement N perkakas, perabot, alat; v menerapkan, melaksanakan; **implementation** N penerapan, implementasi

implicate v melibatkan

import N barang impor, pemasukan; v mengimpor, mendatangkan

important ADJ penting

impossible ADJ mustahil, tidak mungkin

impractical ADJ tidak praktis

impress v memberi kesan, mengesankan; **impression** N kesan; cetakan; **impressive** ADJ mengesankan, hebat, dahsyat

imprisonment N hukuman penjara

improve v [impruv] memperbaiki; meningkatkan; menjadi sembuh, membaik; **improvement** N perbaikan, peningkatan, kemajuan

impulse N kata hati, dorongan hati; **impulsive** ADJ menurut kata hati

in PREP di (dalam), dalam, pada; ~ Indonesian dalam Bahasa Indonesia

inability N ketidak mampuan

inaccurate ADJ tidak teliti, tidak tepat

inadequate ADJ kurang, tidak cukup

inappropriate ADJ tidak pantas

inaugural ADJ [inogyural] perdana

incense N dupa, kemenyan

inch N inci

incident N peristiwa, kejadian, insiden

include v mengandung, meliputi; **inclusive** ADJ inklusif; sampai dengan

income N [incam] pendapatan, penghasilan, gaji; **incoming** ADJ yang masuk

incompatible ADJ tidak cocok

incompetent ADJ tidak mampu

incomplete ADJ kurang lengkap, tidak komplet

inconsiderate ADJ tidak memperhatikan (perasaan orang lain)

inconsistent ADJ tidak konsisten

inconvenient ADJ merepotkan, mengganggu

incorrect ADJ tidak benar, salah

increase N pertambahan, kenaikan; v tambah, bertambah; menambah, menaikkan, meningkatkan

incredible ADJ luar biasa, tidak dapat dipercaya, hebat

indecent ADJ tak senonoh, tidak sopan

indeed ADJ, ADV betul, sebetulnya; CONJ memang; bahkan

independence N kemerdekaan; kebebasan; **independent** ADJ mandiri, merdeka, bebas, tidak tergantung

index N daftar, indeks

India N India; **Indian** N orang India; orang Indian

indicate v menunjukkan; **indication** N tanda, petunjuk, alamat; **indicator** N penunjuk; indikator; lampu sein

Indies the East ~ Hindia Belanda

indigenous ADJ asli

indigestion N salah cerna

indignant ADJ marah, jengkel

indigo N nila; ADJ biru tua

indirect ADJ tidak langsung

individual N pribadi, orang, oknum; ADJ per seorangan

Indonesia N Indonesia; **Indonesian** N Bahasa Indonesia; orang Indonesia

indoor ADJ indoors ADV di dalam rumah atau gedung

industry N industri, perindustrian; kegiatan

inefficient ADJ tidak efisien, tidak jalan dengan baik

infant N, ADJ bayi, balita, anak kecil

infect v menulari, menjangkiti; **infection** N penyakit, infeksi, penularan; **infectious** ADJ menular

inferior ADJ [infirior] kurang bagus atau baik, bermutu rendah

infertile ADJ mandul, tidak subur

infinite ADJ [infinit] tak terhitung; **infinity** N jumlah tak berakhir

inflate v membesar

inflexible ADJ kaku

influence N [influens] pengaruh, efek; v memengaruhi

influenza N flu, selesma

inform v memberitahu, mengabarkan, menginformasikan

ENGLISH–INDONESIAN

informal ADJ santai, tidak resmi
information N informasi, keterangan, penerangan ← **inform**
ingredient N [ingridient] bahan (mentah)
inhabit V mendiami, menghuni; **inhabitant** N penduduk, penghuni
inhale V menarik nafas, mengisap; **inhaler** N isapan, sedotan
inherit V mewarisi; **inheritance** N warisan
initial N huruf pertama, paraf; V teken, memaraf; ADJ pertama, perdana, permulaan; **initiation** N (upacara) pengenalan; **initiative** N prakarsa, inisiatif
inject V menyuntik, menyuntikkan; **injection** N suntik, suntikan; injeksi
injure V merugikan, melukai; **injury** N luka; kerugian; hinaan
injustice N ketidakadilan
ink N tinta
inland N pedalaman
inn N penginapan
inner ADJ (di) dalam; batin
innocent ADJ tidak bersalah, tanpa dosa
innovation N ciptaan baru; **innovative** ADJ mampu menciptakan yang baru
input N masuknya; V memasukkan
inquiry, enquiry N pertanyaan; penyelidikan, pemeriksaan
insane ADJ gila, sakit jiwa
inscription N tulisan, suratan, prasasti
insect N serangga
insert N sisipan; V menyisipkan, menyelipkan, memasukkan
inside PREP, ADJ (di) dalam; **insider** N orang dalam
insight N [insait] wawasan, pemahaman
insist V mengotot, bersikeras, bersikukuh; mendesak
inspect V memeriksa; **inspection** N pemeriksaan, inspeksi; **inspector** N pemeriksa
inspiration N ilham, inspirasi; **inspire** V mengilhami, memberi inspirasi
install, instal V melantik; memasang; **installation** N pelantikan;

pemasangan; **instalment, installment** N angsuran
instance for ~ misalnya, seumpamanya
instant N saat; **instantly** ADV saat itu juga, serta-merta
instead CONJ [instéd] alih-alih, melainkan, malah
institute N lembaga, institut
instruct V mengajar; memerintahkan, menginstruksikan; **instruction** N pengajaran; perintah, instruksi
instrument N alat, perkakas, pesawat
insult N cemoohan, hinaan; V menghina, mencemoohkan
insurance N asuransi, pertanggungan; **insure** V mengasuransikan
intake N masukan, asupan
integral ADJ perlu; pokok
intellect N akal budi, intelek; **intellectual** N cendekiawan; ADJ pandai
intelligence N kecerdasan; intelijen; **intelligent** ADJ cerdas, pandai
intend V berniat, bermaksud
intense ADJ hebat, mendalam, kuat, intens; **intensify** V meningkatkan; **intensive** ADJ intensif
intent, intention N maksud, niat, kehendak, tujuan; **intentional** ADJ sengaja ← **intend**
interaction N pergaulan, interaksi
interchange N simpang, belokan
interest N kepentingan; perhatian, minat; daya tarik; bunga (uang); **interested** ADJ tertarik, berminat; **interesting** ADJ menarik (perhatian)
interfere V [interfir] campur tangan; mencampuri, mengganggu
interior N [intirior] pedalaman, dalamnya
intermediate ADJ sedang
internal ADJ dalam (negeri); **international** ADJ internasional, antar bangsa
interpret V menafsirkan; menerjemahkan (secara lisan); **interpreter** N penerjemah, juru bahasa; **interpreting** N penerjemahan
interrogate V [intérogét] memeriksa, menginterogasi, menanyai; **interrogation** N pemeriksaan, interogasi

ENGLISH–INDONESIAN

interrupt v menyela, menyeletuk, memotong pembicaraan

intersection N perempatan, simpang; persilangan

interval N antara, selang, jeda, waktu istirahat

intervention N halangan, campur tangan, intervensi

interview N wawancara, tanya jawab, interpiu; v mewawancarai

intestine N [intéstin] usus, isi perut

intimate ADJ [intimet] mesra, intim, karib

intimidate v menakuti-nakuti, mengintimidasi

into PREP ke (dalam); menjadi; menuju

introduce v memperkenalkan; **introduction** N perkenalan; (kata) pengantar

intrude v mengganggu; **intruder** N orang yang memasuki tempat tanpa izin; maling

invade v menyerang, menyerbu

invaluable ADJ tak ternilai

invasion N serangan, serbuan ← invade

invent v menciptakan, menemukan; membuat-buat; **invention** N ciptaan

invest v menanamkan (modal), menginvestasikan

investigate v menyelidiki; **investigation** N penyelidikan; **investigator** N penyelidik

investment N penanaman modal, investasi ← invest

invisible ADJ tak terlihat, gaib

invitation N undangan, ajakan; **invite** v mengundang, mengajak; mempersilakan

involve v melibatkan

Iran N Iran

Iraq N Irak; **Iraqi** N orang Irak

Ireland N Irlandia

iron N besi; setrika; v menyetrika; **ironing** N setrikaan; kegiatan menyetrika

ironic ADJ ironis; **irony** N ironi

irregular ADJ tidak teratur, luar biasa

irrelevant ADJ tidak relevan

irresponsible ADJ tidak bertanggung jawab

irrigate v mengairi; **irrigation** N pengairan, irigasi

irritable ADJ cepat marah, marah-marah; **irritate** v mengganggu, membuat jengkel

Islam N agama Islam; **Islamic** ADJ berkaitan dengan agama Islam

island N [ailand] pulau

Israel N [Isrél] Israel

issue N [isyu] masalah, isu; terbitan

it PRON dia, ia (barang); -nya; itu

italics N, PL [italiks] tulisan miring

Italy N Italia

itch N, v **itchy** ADJ gatal

item N [aitem] barang; pasal, ayat; nomor

its PRON -nya (barang)

itself PRON sendiri

ivory N [aivori] gading

J

jack N dongkrak, tuas, kuda-kuda

jacket N jaket; sampul buku

jade N batu giok

jaguar N semacam macan di Amerika

jail, gaol N penjara

jam N selai; v macet; menyumbat, menjepit

janitor N petugas pembersihan, penjaga

January N bulan Januari

Japan N Jepang

jar N kendi, stoples, botol

jasmine N [jasmin] bunga melati

Java N pulau Jawa; **Javanese** N bahasa Jawa

jaw N rahang

jealous ADJ [jélus] cemburu

jeep N mobil jip

jelly N agar-agar; **jellyfish** N ubur-ubur

jerk N sentakan, renggutan; v menyentak, merenggut

jersey N [jérsi] switer

Jesus N [Jisus] CHR Yesus; ISL Isa; ~ Christ Yesus Kristus

jet N semburan air; pancar gas; jet; v, SL terbang

jetty N jeti, dermaga

jewel N [jul] (batu) permata; **jeweler** N tukang emas; **jewelry** N perhiasan

Jewish ADJ Yahudi ← Jew
jigsaw N gergaji ukir; ~ *puzzle* teka-teki menyusun potongan kayu
job N pekerjaan, tugas; *part-time* ~ pekerjaan paruh waktu; **jobless** ADJ menganggur
jockey N joki
jog N, V lari pagi, lari sore
join V bergabung, ikut serta; menghubungkan, menggabungkan
joint N sendi, ruas; ADJ bersama
joke N senda gurau, lelucon, guyonan; **joker** N pelawak; joker (kartu)
jolly ADJ riang, gembira
Jordan N Yordania
journal N (buku) harian, majalah; **journalist** N wartawan, jurnalis
journey N [jurni] perjalanan
joy N kebahagiaan, kegembiraan
judge N hakim; V menghakimi, menilai; **judgment** N keputusan
judo N judo, yudo
jug N tempat untuk saus atau minuman; teko
juggle V bermain sunglap; bermain sulap; **juggling** N sunglapan
juice N air (buah), sari buah, jus; **juicy** ADJ berair banyak
jukebox N kotak musik, mesin pemutar lagu
July N bulan Juli
jumbo ADJ (berukuran) besar
jump N lompatan, loncatan; V melompat, meloncat; melompati
jumper N switer, baju hangat
junction N simpang (jalan), perempatan
June N bulan Juni
jungle N [janggel] hutan, rimba (raya)
junior N yunior; ADJ yunior, lebih muda, lebih rendah pangkatnya
junk N barang bekas, barang loak, sampah
jury N juri
just ADJ, ADV hanya, saja; tepat, persis; ~ *now* baru saja
just N adil; **justice** N keadilan; **justify** V membenarkan

K

kangaroo N kanguru, kangguru
kayak N dayung; kayak, kano; sampan
keen ADJ antusias; tajam
keep V kept kept menyimpan, memegang, menaruh, memelihara, menjaga; **keeper** N pemegang, penjaga, kurator
kennel N kandang anjing
kept V, PF → keep
kerosene N [kerosin] minyak tanah; ~ *lamp* lentera, lampu petromaks
kettle N teko; **kettledrum** N genderang kecil
key N [ki] (anak) kunci; tuts; nada; ADJ pokok; **keyboard** N kibor; papan tuts; **keyhole** N lubang kunci
kick N tendangan; V menendang, menyepak
kid N anak kambing; SL anak
kidnap V menculik; **kidnapper** N penculik
kidney N [kidni] ginjal
kill V membunuh; **killer** N pembunuh; **killing** N pembunuhan
kilogram, kilo N kilo, kilogram
kilometer, kilo N kilo, kilometer
kind N [kaind] macam, jenis, ragam; ADJ baik hati, simpatis; ~ *of* agak
kindness N [kaindness] kebaikan hati ← kind
king N raja; **kingdom** N kerajaan
kiosk N kios, loket, warung
kiss N ciuman, sun, kecupan; V mencium, (memberi) sun
kit N peralatan, perlengkapan
kitchen N dapur
kite N layang-layang
kitten N anak kucing; **kitty** N, COLL kucing (kecil)
kiwi N burung kiwi; **kiwifruit** N (buah) kiwi
knee N [ni] lutut, dengkul
kneel V [nil] knelt knelt berlutut
knew V, PF → know
knife N [naif] knives pisau; V menikam
knight N [nait] kesatria
knit V [nit] merajut; **knitting** N rajutan
knob N [nob] tombol, pegangan

K

knock N [nok] pukulan, ketok; v mengetuk; memukul; **knockout** N (pukulan) yang sangat hebat

knot N [not] simpul; buku, mata kayu; mil laut; v menyimpulkan

know v [no] knew known tahu, mengetahui; mengenal; mengerti; **knowledge** N [nolej] pengetahuan; **knowledgeable** ADJ banyak tahu; **known** ADJ dikenal

knuckle N [nakel] buku jari

koala N koala

Koran the ~ al-Quran

Korea N [Koria] Korea (Selatan)

L

label N merek; nama; v memberi nama, menulis nama pada barang

laboratory, lab N laboratorium

labor N pekerjaan (kasar); **laborer** N buruh, tukang, pekerja

lace N renda

lack N kekurangan; v kurang, tidak memiliki, tidak mempunyai

lacquer N [laker] lak, pernis; v memberi pernis

ladder N tangga, jenjang

lady N, F [lédi] nyonya, wanita; gelar bangsawan; **ladybird, ladybug** N kepik

lagoon N laguna

laid v, PF → lay

lain v, PF → lie

lake N danau, telaga

lamb N [lam] anak domba, anak biri-biri

laminate v melaminasi, melapis dengan lembaran plastik, laminating

lamp N lampu, pelita

land N tanah, bumi, darat; negeri, negara; v mendarat; **landing** N pendaratan; tempat beristirahat di tangga; **landmark** N patokan, petunjuk; peristiwa penting; **landscape** N pemandangan, lanskap; **landslide** N tanah longsor

lane N gang, lorong; jalur; lajur

language N [languej] bahasa

lantern N lentera

Lao N bahasa Laos, orang Laos; ADJ berasal dari Laos

lap N haribaan, pangkuan

lapse N jatuh; kehilangan; selang; v kambuh, menjadi; habis

laptop N komputer laptop

large ADJ besar, luas; ~ size ukuran besar

laser N (sinar) laser

last v tahan, bertahan, berlangsung; awet; ADJ terakhir, penghabisan; ~ night tadi malam, semalam

late ADJ lambat, terlambat; mendiang; ISL almarhum; F almarhumah; **lately** ADV belum lama, belakangan ini, baru-baru ini

later ADJ, ADV nanti; kemudian ← late

latest ADJ, ADV terakhir, paling akhir

Latin N bahasa Latin, bahasa Romawi

latitude N lintang

latter N, ADJ yang kemudian, yang tersebut

laugh N, v [laf] tertawa, ketawa; **laughter** N ketawa, tawa

launch N peluncuran; kapal berkas; v meluncurkan

laundry N cucian, baju kotor; binatu

lava N lahar, lava

lavatory N [lavetori] kamar kecil, WC

lavender ADJ ungu muda; N semacam bunga harum berwarna ungu

law N hukum, undang-undang; peraturan

lawn N lapangan rumput

lawsuit N perkara, dakwaan ← law

lawyer N pengacara, advokat, praktisi hukum ← law

laxative N obat peluntur, pencahar

lay v laid laid meletakkan

layer N lapis, lapisan

layout N tata letak; rancangan, rencana ← lay

lazy ADJ malas

lead N [léd] timbal, timah hitam, plumbum

lead v [lid] led led memimpin; **leader** N pemimpin; **leadership** N kepemimpinan; **leading** ADJ penting, utama, terkemuka

leaf N leaves daun

leaflet N selebaran

leafy ADJ rimbun, rindang ← leaf

league N [lig] liga, persatuan, perserikatan

L

ENGLISH—INDONESIAN

leak N, V bocor, merembes; **leaky** ADJ bocor, rembes

lean N kurus; sedikit

lean V tidak lurus, condong, bersandar; **leaning** N kecenderungan

leap N lompatan; V melompat

leapt V, PF [lépt] → leap

learn V belajar; mendengar berita; **learner** N pelajar; **learning** N pembelajaran

lease N sewa; V mempersewakan

leash N pengikat binatang

least ADJ terkecil, paling sedikit; *at* ~ setidak-tidaknya, sekurang-kurangnya

leave N cuti; V left left berangkat, pergi, bertolak; membiarkan; meninggalkan

Lebanon N Libanon

lecture N kuliah, ceramah, pidato; V memberi kuliah; memberi teguran; **lecturer** N dosen, lektor

led V, PF → lead

leech N lintah

left ADJ (sebelah) kiri

left ADJ, V, PF tertinggal → leave; **leftover** N, ADJ sisa

leg N kaki

legal ADJ sah, legal, menurut undang-undang

legend N legenda; kunci peta; **legendary** ADJ terkenal

leggings N, PL [légings] stoking tebal ← leg

legible ADJ [léjibel] dapat dibaca

legislation N perundang-undangan; **legislative** ADJ legislatif

legitimate ADJ sah

leisure N [lésyer] waktu luang, waktu senggang

lemon N jeruk nipis, limun; **lemonade** N air jeruk nipis; Sprite

lend V meminjamkan; **lender** N pemberi pinjaman

length N panjang; jarak, lama; **lengthen** V memperpanjang; **lengthy** ADJ panjang lebar; panjang, lama

lens N lensa; *contact* ~ lensa kontak

leopard N [lépard] macan kumbang

lesbian N lesbi

less ADJ kurang, lebih kecil; **lessen** V mengurangi, mengecilkan

lesson N pelajaran; les

let V let let membiarkan; menyewakan (rumah); ~ *us*, *let's* marilah

lethal ADJ [lithal] mematikan

letter N surat; huruf, aksara

lettuce N [létes] selada

leukaemia, leukemia N [lukimia] kanker darah

level ADJ [lével] datar, rata; N tingkat; permukaan

lever N pengungkit, tuas, tuil

liar N [laier] pembohong ← lie

liberal ADJ murah hati; liberal; **liberate** V membebaskan; **liberation** N pembebasan; **liberty** N kemerdekaan, kebebasan

librarian N [laibrérian] pustakawan, kepala perpustakaan; **library** N perpustakaan

license, licence N [laisens] izin, ijazah

lick N jilatan; V menjilat

lie V bohong; V berbohong, membohong

lie V lay lain terletak, berada; berbaring

lieutenant N letnan

life N hidup, kehidupan; **lifeboat** N sekoci (penyelamat); **lifebuoy** N pelampung; **lifeguard** N penjaga pantai, penjaga kolam renang; **lifejacket** N baju pelampung; **lifelong** ADJ seumur hidup, sepanjang hidup; **lifesaver** N penjaga pantai; **lifestyle** N gaya hidup; **lifetime** N seumur hidup ← live

lift N lift, pengangkat barang; V mengangkat

light N [lait] cahaya, sinar; lampu; SL korek api; ADJ terang; ringan, enteng; V lit lit menyalakan, memasang (lampu); **lighten** V meringankan, menerangkan; **lighter** N korek api, geretan; **lighthouse** N mercu suar; **lightning** N kilat, halilintar, geledek

like ADJ sama, serupa, sepadan, setara; CONJ seperti, sama dengan; V suka, menyukai, gemar; **likeable** ADJ ramah, menyenangkan; **likely** ADJ agaknya, kemungkinan

lily N [lili] teratai

lime N limau; kapur

limit N batas, limit; V membatasi; **limited** ADJ terbatas

L

limousine N [limosin], **limo** N, SL limosin, limo

limp V berjalan pincang; ADJ lemah

line N garis, gores; tali; baris, deret; V melapisi

linen N kain linan

liner N kapal penumpang yang besar

lingerie N [lonjeri] pakaian dalam wanita

linguistics N ilmu bahasa, ilmu linguistik

lining N lapisan, furing ← line

link N mata rantai, hubungan

lion N [laion] singa

lip N bibir; **lipstick** N lipstik

liquid ADJ cair; N cairan, zat cair

list N daftar; V mendaftar, menyebutkan

listen V [lisen] mendengarkan, menyimak; **listener** N pendengar; **listening** N (pelajaran) menyimak

lit V, PF → light

liter N liter

literally ADV secara harfiah; benar-benar; **literate** ADJ melek huruf; terpelajar; **literary** ADJ sastra; **literature** N kesusastraan

litre → liter

litter N sampah (di jalan); V membuang sampah sembarangan

little ADJ kecil; sedikit; ~ finger kelingking; N sedikit

live V [liv] hidup, tinggal, berdiam; **live** ADJ [laiv] langsung; hidup

liver N [liver] hati, lever

livestock N hewan ternak

living N [living] mata pencarian ← live

lizard N [lizerd] kadal, biawak, cicak

load N muatan, beban; V memuat, diisi

loaf N loaves roti; sejenis sepatu santai

loan N pinjaman; V meminjamkan, meminjami → lend

lobby N lobi (hotel); gerakan; V berusaha memengaruhi, memperjuangkan

lobster N udang karang, udang laut

local ADJ setempat, lokal; N orang setempat; **locate** V mencari; **location** N lokasi, tempat; penempatan

lock N kunci, gembok; pintu air; ~-up sel tahanan; V mengunci; **locker** N loker

locket N liontin

locksmith N tukang kunci ← lock

locomotive N lokomotif, lok

lodge N pondok, pemondokan; V mondok, menginap; **lodging** N pemondokan; akomodasi

loft N loteng; **lofty** ADJ tinggi, mulia

log N catatan, buku harian; V mencatat; ~ in memasukkan nama atau kata kunci

log N batang kayu, kayu gelondongan; V menebang (pohon); **logging** N penebangan

logic N [lojik] logika, akal; **logical** ADJ logis, masuk akal

lone ADJ tunggal, sendiri; **loneliness** N (rasa) kesepian; **lonely** ADJ sepi, kesepian, sunyi, sendirian

long ADJ panjang; lama; as ~ as selama

long ~ for rindu akan, merindukan, mengidamkan

look N penampilan, gaya; V melihat; ~ after merawat, menjaga; ~ for mencari; ~ on menonton; ~ out! awas!; **lookout** N tempat meninjau; pengintai

loop N lingkaran, ikal, putaran; V menyimpulkan

loose ADJ longgar, kendur, terurai; lepas; **loosen** V melonggarkan, mengendurkan

looting N penjarahan

lord PRON tuan; **Lord** N, CHR Tuhan

lorry N truk

lose V [luz] hilang, kehilangan; rugi, kalah; **loser** N yang kalah; **loss** N rugi, kerugian, kehilangan; **lost** ADJ hilang; tersesat; tewas

lotion N salep

lottery N lotere, undian ← lot

lotus N bunga seroja, bunga teratai

loud ADJ berisik, riuh, gempar, bising; **loudspeaker** N pengeras suara

louse N lice kutu; **lousy** ADJ, SL [lauzi] jelek

love N [lav] cinta, asmara; kasih (sayang); PRON kekasih, sayang; V mencintai, menyayangi; **lovely** ADJ manis, cantik, asri; **lover** N kekasih, penggemar

ENGLISH–INDONESIAN

M

low ADJ rendah, hina; murah; N titik rendah, nadir; **lower** ADJ lebih rendah; v menurunkan

loyal ADJ setia, setiakawan

lubricant N [lubrikant] pelumas

luck N untung; *good* ~ untung; semoga; **lucky** ADJ beruntung

luggage N bagasi, barang-barang

lukewarm ADJ [lukworm] suam-suam kuku

lullaby N [lalabai] (kidung) ninabobo

lumber N kayu; **lumberjack** N penebang kayu

lump N gumpal, bongkah; benjolan

lunar ADJ berkaitan dengan bulan

lunatic ADJ gila; N orang gila

lunch N, v makan siang

lungs N, PL paru-paru

luxurious ADJ [laksyurius] mewah, lux; **luxury** N kemewahan

lychee N buah leci

lyric N lirik, kata-kata yang dinyanyikan

M

m *meter* m (meter)

ma'am PRON Nyonya, Nona ← madam

macaroni N makaroni

machine N [masyin] mesin, alat

mad ADJ gila, tergila-gila; marah

madam PRON Nyonya

madness N kegilaan, penyakit gila ← mad

magazine N majalah

magic N [majik] ilmu sihir, ilmu sulap; **magical** ADJ berkaitan dengan sihir; ajaib; **magician** N penyihir, penyulap

magnet N magnet, maknit; **magnetic** ADJ magnetik

magnificent ADJ sangat bagus, mewah

magpie N burung murai

mahogany N pohon mahoni, kayu mahoni

maid N pembantu; gadis

mail N pos; surat email; v mengepos, mengirim lewat pos; **mailbox** N kotak surat

main ADJ utama; **mainly** ADV terutama

maintain v memelihara, mempertahankan; **maintenance** N pemeliharaan

maize N jagung

majesty N keagungan; *Your* ~ Baginda, Sri Paduka

major ADJ utama, terbesar; N mayor; **majority** N kebanyakan, mayoritas

make N jenis, macam; v membuat, membikin, mengadakan; **make-up** N rias wajah; ~ *artist* perias; **maker** N pembuat, pencipta

Malay ADJ Melayu; N bahasa Melayu, bahasa Malaysia; orang Melayu; **Malaysia** N Malaysia; **Malaysian** N orang Malaysia

Maldives [Maldivs] *the* ~ (Kepulauan) Maladewa

male ADJ lelaki, pria; jantan

malfunction N kerusakan, kegagalan; v gagal

mama, mamma N, PRON ibu

man N **men** orang laki-laki, pria; suami, pasangan, pacar; v bertugas di

manage v mengelola, memimpin; mengurus, menangani; **management** N pimpinan, direksi; pengelolaan, pemerintahan, pengurusan, manajemen; **manager** N manajer, pemimpin, pengurus

mango N mangga

mangosteen N manggis

mangrove N bakau

mania N [ménia] kegilaan, demam

manicure N perawatan tangan, manikur

manipulative ADJ suka memanipulasi

mankind N [mankaind] umat manusia ← man

manner N cara, jalan; macam

mansion N [mansyen] rumah besar

mantelpiece N rak di atas perapian

manual ADJ dengan tangan, tidak otomatis; N pedoman, buku panduan

manufacture N pembuatan; v membuat; **manufacturer** N pabrik

manure N pupuk (kotoran)

manuscript N naskah

many ADJ [méni] banyak

map N peta; v memetakan

marble N marmer, pualam; kelereng

M

ENGLISH–INDONESIAN

March N bulan Maret

march N perjalanan (militer); mars; v jalan kaki

margarine N [marjarin] mentega

marijuana N [marihuana] ganja

marina N dermaga; **marine** ADJ berhubungan dengan laut

mark N tanda, alamat; cap; sasaran; bekas; nilai; v menandai, mengecap; mencatat, memperhatikan; mengoreksi; **marker** N penanda; spidol besar; penilai

market N pasar, pasaran; **marketing** N pemasaran

marmalade N selai jeruk

marriage N [marij] perkawinan, pernikahan; **married** ADJ kawin, nikah; M beristri; F bersuami ← marry

marry v menikah, kawin; menikahi

marsh N rawa

marshmallow N penganan manis yang putih dan empuk

marvelous ADJ ajaib, hebat, mengagumkan

masculine ADJ [maskulin] laki-laki, lelaki, jantan

mask N topeng; masker; v menyamarkan

mass N massa; banyak sekali; misa

massage N pijatan; v memijat, mengurut

massive ADJ raksasa, besar sekali ← mass

mast N tiang (kapal)

master N tuan (rumah); ahli, guru; v menguasai; ~'s (degree) S2, magister

mat N tikar; matras

match N korek api; tara, jodoh; pertandingan; v menyesuaikan; menyamai, menandingi; **matchmaker** N mak jomblang

mate N kawan, sahabat; pasangan; v kawin (binatang)

material N bahan, perkakas, alat; materi

maternal ADJ keibuan; dari pihak ibu

mathematics N, PL math, maths SL matematika

matron N [métron] kepala perawat, suster

matter N perkara, hal, perihal; bahan; v berarti

mattress N kasur

mature ADJ dewasa, tua, matang

maximal ADJ maksimal, sebanyak-banyaknya; **maximum** ADJ, N maksimum, sebanyak-banyaknya

May N bulan Mei

may v, AUX boleh, dapat; **maybe** ADV [mébi] mungkin, barangkali, boleh jadi

mayor N [mér] walikota

maze N labirin

me PRON, OBJ saya, aku

meadow N [médo] padang rumput

meal N makanan, santapan

mean ADJ jahat, membuat sakit hati

mean v meant meant [mént] berarti, bermaksud; memaksudkan, menghendaki; **meaning** N arti, maksud

meanwhile ADV sementara itu

measles N, PL [mizels] penyakit campak

measure N [mésyer] ukuran, takaran; besarnya; tindakan; v mengukur

meat N daging

mechanic N [mekanik] montir, ahli mesin; **mechanical** ADJ teknik

medal N medali

media N, PL [midia] pers; perantara, bahan ← medium

medical ADJ kedokteran, medis; **medicine** N [médisin] obat; jurusan kedokteran, ilmu kedokteran

medieval ADJ [médiivel] dari Abad Pertengahan

meditate v bermeditasi, bersemadi

medium ADJ sedang; **media** N cenayang, dukun, perantara; bahan

meet N perlombaan atletik atau renang; v met met bertemu, berjumpa; menemui; berkumpul; **meeting** N rapat, pertemuan

melody N lagu

melon N semangka

melt v meleleh, mencair, melebur; melelehkan, meleburkan

member N anggota

memo N memorandum, surat peringatan; **memorial** ADJ peringatan; N tanda atau tugu peringatan; **memo-**

rize v menghafalkan; **memory** N ingatan, memori

mend v memperbaiki, membetulkan; menambal

menstruation N datang bulan, mens

mental ADJ jiwa

mention N [ménsyen] sebutan; v menyebutkan

menu N daftar makanan, menu

merchant N pedagang, saudagar

mercy N belas kasih, kemurahan hati

merge v menyatu; menggabungkan

mermaid N putri duyung

merry ADJ ria

mess N kekacauan, keadaan berantakan; v mengacaukan; mengacaukan

message N pesan; **messenger** N pesuruh, kurir

messy ADJ berantakan, tidak rapi ← mess

metal N logam

meteor N [mitior] bintang jatuh

meter N meter

method N metode, cara, jalan

metre → meter

Mexico N Meksiko

mice N, PL ← mouse

microphone N [maikrofon] mikrofon, corong radio

microscope N [maikroskop] mikroskop

midday N tengah hari, jam 12 siang

middle ADJ tengah, menengah; N pertengahan, titik tengah

midnight N [midnait] tengah malam, jam 12 malam

midwife N bidan

might v, AUX [mait] mungkin, boleh jadi

mighty ADJ berkuasa; besar

migraine N [maigrén] migren, sakit kepala sebelah

migrant N [maigrant] pendatang; **migrate** v pindah, bermigrasi

mild ADJ [maild] lembut, ringan, enteng

mile N mil

military ADJ, N militer, ketentaraan

milk N susu; v memerah susu

millimeter N mili, milimeter

million N juta; **millionaire** N jutawan, milyuner

mimic v mimicked mimicked meniru

minaret N [minarét] menara (mesjid)

mince N (daging) cincang; v mencincang, mengiris

mind N [maind] akal (budi), pikiran, jiwa; v ingat akan, memperhatikan, mengindahkan; merasa keberatan

mine PRON, POSS milikku, saya punya

mine N ranjau; **minefield** N daerah ranjau

mine N tambang; **miner** N buruh tambang; **mineral** N [mineral] barang tambang, barang galian

mini ADJ, SL kecil, mungil, mini; **miniature** ADJ kecil

minimum ADJ, N minimum, sedikit-sedikitnya, terendah

mining N [maining] pertambangan

minister N menteri; pendeta; **ministry** N kementerian, departemen

minor ADJ [mainor] kecil; **minority** N golongan kecil, minoritas

mint N percetakan mata uang

mint N sejenis kemangi; permen penyegar mulut

minus v [mainus] kurang; tanpa

minute N [minet] menit

miracle N [mirakel] keajaiban, mukjizat

mirror N cermin; v mencerminkan

miscarriage N [miskarej] keguguran

mischievous ADJ nakal, jahil

miserable ADJ [mizerabel] sedih, murung

mislead v misled misled menipu, menyesatkan

misprint N salah cetak

miss N, PRON Nona (before a surname)

miss v meleset; rindu akan, merindukan

missionary N misionaris

mist N kabut, halimun

mistake N kesalahan; v mistook mistaken keliru, salah mengerti

mister PRON Tuan (before a surname); **mistress** N kekasih, gundik

misty ADJ berkabut ← mist

misunderstand v misunderstood misunderstood salah mengerti, salah paham, salah tangkap

M

mitten N sarung tangan, kaus tangan

mix N campuran; V mencampur(kan); **mixture** N campuran, adonan

moan N erangan; keluhan; V mengerang, mengeluh

mobile ADJ dapat bergerak, dapat dipindahkan; ~ *phone* telepon genggam, ponsel

mock ADJ palsu, pura-pura, tiruan; V mengejek

model ADJ contoh; N contoh, macam, model; peragawati, peragawan; V memperagakan

modern ADJ modern, baru, kini

moist ADJ basah, lembab; **moisture** N embun, kelembaban; **moisturizer** N pelembab

moldy, mouldy ADJ berjamur, jamuran, apak

mole N sejenis tikus; tahi lalat

Moluccas *the* ~ Maluku

Mom, Mum PRON Bu, Mak

moment N saat; *in a* ~, *just a* ~ sebentar

mommy, mummy PRON Ibu, Mama, Mami ← mom

Monday N [Mandé] hari Senin

monetary ADJ [manetéri] keuangan, moneter; **money** N uang; **money-box** N celengan

Mongolia N Mongolia

mongrel N [manggrel]; anjing kampung

monitor N pengawas; layar (komputer); V mengawasi

monkey N [mangki] monyet

monorail N monorel

monsoon N musim hujan, muson

monster ADJ raksasa; N makhluk besar yang mengerikan

month N [manth] bulan; **monthly** ADJ, ADV bulanan

monument N monumen, tanda peringatan, tugu peringatan

mood N suasana hati

moon N bulan, rembulan; **moonlight** N [munlait] sinar bulan

moral N [morel] kesusilaan, etika; moral, moril

more ADV lebih, lagi; **moreover** ADV lagipula

morning N pagi (hari); *good* ~ sela- mat pagi (diucapkan sampai jam 12 siang)

Morocco N Maroko

Moslem → Muslim

mosque N [mosk] mesjid

mosquito N [moskito] nyamuk; ~ *net* kelambu

most ADV paling, maha; **mostly** ADV kebanyakan

motel N hotel transit

moth N ngengat

mother N [mather] ibu; induk; PRON Ibu; ~*in-law* (ibu) mertua; ~ *tongue* bahasa ibu

motion N gerak; mosi, usul

motivation N dorongan, dukungan, motivasi; **motive** N [motiv] alasan, dalil, motif

motor N motor, mesin; **motorboat** N perahu bermotor; **motorcycle** N motorbike SL sepeda motor; **motorist** N pengendara mobil; **motorway** N jalan bebas hambatan

mould → mold

mount N (nama) gunung; ~ *Bromo* Gunung Bromo; **mountain** N [maunten] gunung

mouse N mice tikus; **mousetrap** N perangkap tikus

mouth N mulut; muara; **mouthful** N sesuap; **mouthwash** N obat kumur

move N perpindahan, gerakan; V bergerak; berpindah (rumah); menggerakkan, memindahkan; **movement** N gerak, gerakan, pergerakan

movie N, SL [muvi] film

mower N mesin pemotong rumput

Mt *Mount* Gg., (gunung)

much ADV, N banyak; *so* ~ sekian; *as* ~ *as* sebanyak

mud N lumpur

muddle N kekacauan, kekusutan; V mengacaukan

muddy ADJ berlumpur ← mud

mudguard N [madgard] sepakbor ← mud

muffler N kenalpot; selendang

mug N cangkir besar; V menodong, merampok; **mugger** N penodong

muggy ADJ lembab (cuaca)

multi- PREF lebih dari satu, aneka; **multi-colored** ADJ warna-warni, beraneka warna

ENGLISH–INDONESIAN

multiple ADJ [maltipel] berlipat ganda; **multiplication** N perkalian; **multiply** V berkembang biak; mengalikan

mumble V bergumam, berkomat-kamit

mummy N mumi → **mommy**

mumps N penyakit gondok

munch V mengunyah

municipality N [munisipaliti] kota (praja), kotamadya

mural N lukisan pada tembok atau dinding

murder N pembunuhan; V membunuh; **murderer** N pembunuh

murmur N bisikan; V berbisik

muscle N [masel] urat, otot; kekuatan

museum N musium

mushroom N cendawan, jamur

music N musik, lagu; **musical** ADJ (berbakat) musik; **musician** N musikus, pemain musik

Muslim, Moslem ADJ Islam, Muslim; N orang Islam

must N keharusan; V, AUX harus, wajib, terpaksa

mustache, moustache [mustasy] kumis, misai

mute ADJ bisu

mutilate V memotong

mutter V bergumam, berkomat-kamit

mutual ADJ [myutyual] saling, dari kedua pihak, timbal balik

my PRON, POSS saya, -ku

myself PRON saya sendiri; sendirian

mysterious ADJ gaib, misterius; **mystery** N kegaiban, misteri

myth N [mith] isapan jempol, dongeng, mitos

N

nail N paku; kuku; V memaku; **nailbrush** N sikat kuku

naked ADJ [néked] telanjang

name N nama; V menamai, menamakan, memberi nama; **named** ADJ bernama; **namely** CONJ yakni, yaitu

nanny N penjaga anak, pengasuh anak

nap N tidur siang

napkin N serbet; popok; **nappy** N popok; *disposable* ~ pampers, popok plastik

narrator N orang yang bercerita

narrow ADJ sempit

nasty ADJ buruk, jahat

nation N [nésyen] negara, bangsa; **national** N, ADJ [nasyonal] nasional, kebangsaan; **nationality** N kebangsaan, kewarganegaraan

native ADJ [nétif] asli; N orang asli, pribumi

natural ADJ [natyurel] alami, alamiah; **naturally** ADJ tentu, memang; **nature** N alam (semesta); tabiat, kepribadian, sifat

naughty ADJ [noti] nakal, jahil

nausea N [nozia] (rasa) mual, mabuk

navel N pusar

navigate V [navigét] melayari, mengemudikan kapal; **navigator** N mualim, navigator; **navy** N [névi] angkatan laut

near ADJ dekat; **nearby** ADV [nirbai] dekat; **nearly** ADV hampir

neat ADJ apik, rapi, bersih; SL hebat, bagus

necessary ADJ [néseséri] perlu; **necessity** N kebutuhan, keperluan

neck N leher; **necklace** N kalung; **necktie** N dasi

need N kebutuhan, keperluan; V membutuhkan, memerlukan

needle N jarum; **needlepoint, needlework** N semacam sulaman

negative ADJ negatif, buruk; N klise

neglect N keadaan telantar; V mengabaikan

negotiate V bermusyawarah, berunding; merundingkan; **negotiation** N negosiasi, perundingan

neigh V [néi] meringkik

neighbor N [nébor] tetangga; **neighborhood** N lingkungan (dekat rumah)

neither CONJ [nither, naither] keduaduanya (tidak); ~ ... *nor* bukan ... maupun

nephew N, M [néfyu] keponakan (lelaki)

nerve N saraf; nyali, keberanian; **nervous** ADJ gelisah, gugup

nest N sarang; V bersarang

net ADJ bersih, netto; N jala, jaring

Netherlands *the* ~ (negeri) Belanda

network N jaringan; v menjalin hubungan

neutral ADJ [nutral] netral, tidak memihak

never ADV [néver] tidak pernah

nevertheless CONJ [néverthelés] walaupun demikian, namun

new ADJ baru; ~ *Year* tahun baru; ~ *Zealand* Selandia Baru; *Papua* ~ *Guinea* Papua Nugini; **newborn** ADJ baru saja lahir; **newcomer** N pendatang baru; **newly** ADV baru saja, belum lama; **news** N, s berita, warta, warta berita; kabar; **newsletter** N selebaran; **newspaper** N surat kabar, koran

next PREP berikut, sebelah, samping

nibble N [nibel] gigit; v menggigit, mengunggis

nice ADJ enak, sedap; manis, cantik, apik

nick N torehan; v, SL mengutil

nickname N nama kecil, nama panggilan

niece N, F [nis] keponakan (perempuan)

night N [nait] malam; *at* ~ pada waktu malam, malam hari; *good* ~ selamat tidur; *last* ~ tadi malam, semalam; **nightie** SL daster; **nightfall** N senja, magrib; **nightingale** N bulbul; **nightlife** N kehidupan malam; **nightly** ADV tiap malam; **nightmare** N mimpi buruk

nine N, ADJ sembilan; **nineteen** N, ADJ sembilan belas; **ninety** ADJ, N sembilan puluh; **ninth** ADJ [nainth] kesembilan

nip N gigitan kecil; v mencubit, menggigit

nipple N [nipel] puting, pentil, dot

no tidak; bukan

noble ADJ bangsawan, ningrat

nobody N [nobodi] bukan siapa-siapa; PRON tidak seorang pun

nod N anggukan, tanda setuju

noise N bunyi, kegaduhan, keributan, suara bising; **noisy** ADJ gaduh, ribut, berisik, bising

nominate v mencalonkan; **nomination** N pencalonan, nominasi

non- PREF tidak, non-

none N [nan] seorang pun tidak, sesuatu pun tidak; tidak sama sekali

nonsense N omong kosong

noon *(at)* ~ jam duabelas siang

nor → neither

normal ADJ biasa, lazim, lumrah, umum; normal; **normally** ADV biasanya, pada umumnya

north ADJ, ADV utara; N (sebelah) utara; ~ *Korea* Korea Utara (Korut); **northeast** ADJ, N timur laut; **northern** ADJ utara; **northwest** ADJ, N barat laut

Norway N Norwegia; **Norwegian** ADJ [Norwijen] berasal dari Norwegia

nose N hidung; **nostril** N lubang hidung; **nosy** ADJ ingin tahu

not ADV tidak, tak; belum; bukan; ~ *yet* belum

note N catatan, peringatan; nada, not; nota; v mencatat, menulis; memperhatikan; **notebook** N buku catatan, buku tulis, notes; **noted** ADJ masyhur, tersohor, kenamaan; **notepaper** N kertas tulis

nothing N [nathing] tidak sesuatu pun

notice N [notis] perhatian; pemberitahuan, maklumat; v melihat; memerhatikan; **noticeable** ADJ [notisabel] nyata, tampak, kelihatan

notification N [notifikésyen] pemberitahuan, surat panggilan; **notify** v memberitahu, memberitahukan

nought, naught N, ARCH [not] nol, kosong; tanpa hasil

noun N [naun] kata benda

nourishing ADJ bergizi

novel ADJ baru; N buku roman, novel

November N bulan November

now PREP [nau] sekarang, kini; *just* ~ baru saja, tadi; *from* ~ *(on)* mulai sekarang; CONJ nah; **nowadays** PREP sekarang (ini)

nowhere ADV, PRON [nowér] tidak di mana-mana

nuclear ADJ nuklir

nude ADJ telanjang, bugil

nudge N [naj] sentuhan; v menyentuh, menyinggung

nuisance N [nusens] gangguan; orang pengganggu

O

numb ADJ [nam] mati rasa, kesemutan

number N nomor; bilangan, angka; banyaknya; **numeral** N angka; *Roman* ~s angka Romawi

nun N biarawati, suster

nurse N juru rawat, perawat; V merawat; menyusui; **nursery** N kamar anak; toko tanaman; **nursing** ADJ menyusui; ~ *home* panti asuhan

nut N kacang; SL penggemar berat, penggila; **nutmeg** N pala

nutrient N [nutrient] gizi; **nutrition** N [nutrisyen] ilmu gizi; **nutritious** ADJ bergizi

O

oar N dayung

oatmeal N havermut

oath N sumpah; umpatan

oats N, PL sejenis gandum

obese ADJ [obis] gemuk sekali

obey V [obé] taat, patuh

object N benda, obyek; V berkeberatan; **objection** N keberatan; **objective** ADJ obyektif, tidak memihak; N tujuan

oboe N obo

obscene ADJ [obsin] cabul, jorok

observe V mengamati, meninjau; menghormati; **observer** N pengamat, peninjau

obsession N obsesi

obstacle N [obstakel] rintangan, hambatan

obtain V memperoleh, mendapatkan, menerima

obvious ADJ [obvius] jelas, terang, nyata

occasion N [okésyen] kesempatan; peristiwa, acara

occupant N penghuni; **occupation** N pekerjaan; pendudukan; **occupy** V [okupai] mengisi; menduduki

occur V terjadi; **occurrence** N kejadian, peristiwa

ocean N [osyan] samudera, lautan

o'clock jam, pukul; *it's six* ~ sekarang jam enam

octagon N segi delapan

October N bulan Oktober

octopus N ikan gurita

odd ADJ aneh, ganjil

odor N bau

of PREP [ov] milik; dari, daripada

off PREP jauh; ADJ mati, tidak hidup; basi (makanan); tidak jadi; *day* ~ hari libur

offend V menghina, membuat tersinggung; melanggar hukum; **offensive** ADJ menghina, tidak sopan; serangan

offer N tawaran, penawaran; V menawarkan, menawari; mempersembahkan; **offering** N persembahan, sesajen

office N [ofis] kantor, ruangan, tempat kerja; jabatan; **officer** N pegawai, petugas; perwira; **official** ADJ resmi; N pegawai, pejabat

often ADV sering

ogre N [oger] raksasa

oil N minyak; V meminyaki; ~ *colors*, ~ *paint* cat minyak; ~ *palm* kelapa sawit; **oilfield** N ladang minyak; **oily** ADJ berminyak

ointment N salep, balsem

OK, okay [oké] baik, oke, jadi; V menyetujui

old ADJ tua; sepuh, lanjut usia; *olden* ~ *days* masa lalu, tempo dulu, zaman baheula

olive N [oliv] (buah) zaitun

Olympic ADJ Olimpiade; ~ *Games* Pertandingan Olimpiade; **Olympics** *the* ~ Olimpiade

omelet, omelette N telur dadar

omen N tanda, pertanda, alamat

omit V melupakan, menghilangkan

on ADJ hidup; PREP di (atas), pada; ~ *the way* sedang dalam perjalanan; sedang berjalan, sedang berlangsung

once ADV [wans] sekali (waktu); dahulu kala; *all at* ~ serentak; tiba-tiba; *at* ~ pada saat itu juga, segera ← one

one N, ADJ [wan] satu, suatu; seorang; PRON orang; ~ *another* satu sama lain; ~-*way street* jalan satu arah; ~ *by* ~ satu per satu

ongoing ADJ terus-menerus ← on

onion N [anien] bawang

only ADJ tunggal; ~ *child* anak tunggal; *one and* ~ satu-satunya; ADV

O

saja, hanya; *not* ~ ... *but also* tidak hanya ... tetapi juga

onyx N [oniks] batu akik

opal N opal, baiduri

opaque ADJ [opék] tidak tembus pandang, buram

open ADJ buka, terbuka; terang-terangan; V membuka; **opener** N pembuka; **opening** ADJ pembuka; N pembukaan; lubang, celah, lowongan

opera N opera

operate V [operét] membedah, mengoperasi; beroperasi; menjalankan (mesin), mengoperasikan; **operation** N pembedahan, operasi; cara menjalankan; **operator** N penjaga mesin, penjaga telepon

opinion N [opinion] pendapat; *in my* ~ menurut pendapat saya

opium N candu

opossum, possum N semacam tupai

opponent N lawan

opportunity N kesempatan, peluang

opposite N, ADJ [opozet] berlawa-nan, bertentangan, lawan (kata); **opposition** N perlawanan, oposisi

optical ADJ optik; **optician** N ahli kaca mata

optimist N optimistic ADJ optimis

option N [opsyen] opsi, pilihan; **optional** ADJ bebas (memilih)

optometrist N dokter mata; ahli kacamata

or CONJ atau; *either* ... ~ salah satu

oral ADJ lisan, berkaitan dengan mulut

orange ADJ [orenj] oranye, jingga; N jeruk

orangutan N orang hutan

orchard N [orced] kebun buah

orchestra N [orkestra] orkes

orchid N [orkid] (bunga) anggrek

order N urutan; peraturan; perintah; pemesanan; V memerintahkan, menyuruh, mengatur, memesan

ordinary ADJ [ordineri] biasa, lazim

organ N orgel, organ

organ N bagian badan; **organic** ADJ organik

organization N organisasi, persa-tuan; penyusunan, pengaturan;

organize V menyusun, mengatur, mengurus

oriental ADJ timur, ketimuran

origin N asal, asal-usul; **original** ADJ orisinil, asli

ornament N hiasan

orphan N [orfan] anak yatim (piatu); **orphanage** N rumah yatim piatu

ostrich N burung unta

other PRON, ADJ [ather] lain, ber-lainan; *the* ~ *day* kemarin, belum lama ini; **otherwise** CONJ kalau tidak, bila tidak

otter N berang-berang

ouch EXCL [auc] aduh, sakit

ought AUX, V [out] seharusnya, semestinya, sebaiknya

ounce N [auns] ons

our PRON kita, kami; **ours** PRON milik kita, milik kami; **ourselves** PRON kita sendiri, kami sendiri

out PREP (di) luar; ADJ di luar, tidak ada; tidak berlaku lagi; **outburst** N letusan, ledakan; **outdated** ADJ ketinggalan zaman, kuno; **outdoor** ADJ outdoors PREP (di) luar (rumah); **outer** ADJ bagian luar; **outfit** N busana; **outgoing** ADJ ramah; **outlet** N jalan keluar, salu-ran pembuangan; toko, cabang; **outline** N garis besar; **outlook** N wawasan; **output** N hasil, produksi; keluaran; **outside** N, PREP (di) luar, ke luar, bagian luar; **outsider** N orang luar; **outspoken** ADJ blak-blakan, terang-terangan; **outstand-ing** ADJ luar biasa

oval ADJ lonjong; N (lapangan) bulat panjang

oven N [aven] oven, kompor, tungku

over ADJ selesai, rampung; PREP di atas; melalui; tentang, mengenai; lebih daripada; **overact** V bertindak secara berlebihan; **overall** ADJ secara keseluruhan; **overcharge** V meminta bayaran terlalu tinggi; **overcome** ADJ overcame over-come kewalahan; V mengalahkan, mengatasi; **overdose** N overdosis, OD; V OD; **overdue** ADJ kedalu-warsa, terlambat; **overhead** ADJ di atas (kepala); **overhear** V over-heard overheard menguping; terdengar; **overnight** ADJ, PREP semalaman; **overpass** N jembatan penyeberangan; **overpower** V menguasai; **overseas** ADV, ADJ (di) luar negeri; **overtake** V overtook overtaken menyalip; **overthrow** V overthrew overthrown menjatuhkan, meruntuhkan; **overweight** ADJ kelebihan berat (badan)

owe V [o] berhutang

owl N [aul] burung hantu

own ADJ [oun] sendiri; V memiliki, mempunyai; **owner** N pemilik; **ownership** N kepemilikan, hak milik

ox N oxen sapi, lembu

oxygen N [oksijen] oksigen

oyster N tiram

ozone N, PL ozon

P

p *page*, **pp** (*pages*) halaman

Pa PRON, SL Pak, Yah

pace N langkah; kecepatan

Pacific ~ *Ocean* Lautan Teduh, Samudera Pasifik

pack N bungkusan, pak; V membungkus, mengepak, menyusun; **package** N bungkus; bingkisan, paket; **packet** N paket, pak, bungkus

pact N pakta, perjanjian

pad N bantalan

paddle N [padel] kayuh; V mengayuh

paddy N ~ *(field)* sawah

padlock N gembok; V mengunci, menggembok

page N halaman, lembar

pagoda N kuil

paid V, PF → pay

pain N rasa sakit, rasa nyeri; *in* ~ kesakitan; **painful** ADJ sakit, pedih

paint N cat; V mengecat; **painter** N tukang cat; pelukis; **painting** N lukisan; seni lukis

pair N pasang, rangkap; pasangan

pajamas → pyjamas

Pakistan N Pakistan; **Pakistani** N orang Pakistan

palace N [pales] istana, puri

palate N [palet] langit-langit

pale ADJ pucat, lemah

Palestine N [Palestain] Palestina; **Palestinian** N orang Palestina

palm N [pam] palem; telapak tangan

pamphlet N brosur, selebaran, pamflet

pan N panci, wajan, kuali; **pancake** N panekuk

panel N panel; sehelai papan

panic N panik, ketakutan; V panik

panther N macan kumbang

pantry N [pantri] gudang (dapur), lemari untuk menyimpan makanan kering

pants N, PL celana

panty ~ *liner* pembalut (tipis); **panties** N, PL celana dalam wanita

papa PRON pak, ayah

papaya N pepaya

paper N kertas; koran, surat kabar; makalah; **paperboy** N tukang koran, loper koran; **paperwork** N pekerjaan tulis-menulis

Papua N Irian (Jaya); ~ *New Guinea (PNG)* Papua Nugini

parachute N payung, parasut; V terjun payung

parade N [paréid] pawai, arakarakan; jalan

paradise N surga

paragraph N paragraf, alinea

parakeet N burung bayan, burung parkit

parallel ADJ sejajar, paralel

paralyzed ADJ lumpuh

parasite N [parasait] parasit, benalu

parcel N bingkisan, paket; parsel

pardon N ampun, maaf; grasi; V mengampuni, memaafkan

parent N [pérent] orang tua, ibu bapak, ayah bunda

park N taman; V parkir; memarkirkan mobil

parliament N Dewan Perwakilan Rakyat (DPR), parlemen

parrot N burung nuri

parsley N [parsli] peterseli

part N bagian, potong; peranan; belahan; V membagi, memisahkan; ~ *with* melepaskan

participant N peserta; **participate** V ikut serta, mengambil bagian

particular ADJ istimewa, spesial, khusus

parting N perpisahan; belahan (rambut) ← part

partly ADV sebagian ← part
partner N pasangan, mitra
party N pesta, perayaan; partai, kelompok, pihak; rombongan; v berpesta
pass N surat izin masuk, pas jalan; jalan kecil; v lulus ujian; lewat; melalui, melewati; mengesahkan; ~ *away* meninggal dunia, berpulang; **passage** N [pasej] jalan lintas, jalan tembus, lorong, terusan; bagian dari tulisan; pelayaran; **passenger** N [pasenjer] penumpang
passion N [pasyen] hawa nafsu, gairah; **passionate** ADJ [pasyenet] bernafsu, bergairah, bersemangat
passive ADJ pasif, terdiam
passport N paspor
password N kata sandi
past ADJ lalu, lewat, lampau, silam; N masa lalu
paste N [pést] adonan, pasta; v tempel
pastel N warna pastel; kapur berwarna
pastor N pastor, pendeta
pastry N [péstri] kue
pat N tepukan; v menepuk, mengelus
patch N tambal, tempelan
paternal ADJ [patérnal] dari pihak bapak
path N jalan (tapak), lorong
patience N [pésyens] kesabaran; soliter; **patient** ADJ sabar; N pasien
patriotic ADJ cinta tanah air
patrol N patroli, ronda; v berpatroli, meronda
pattern N pola, corak; patron, contoh
patty N perkedel
pause N [pouz] jeda, waktu istirahat; v berhenti sebentar; menghentikan sementara
pavement N trotoar
pavilion N [pavilion] anjungan; tenda besar; bangunan dekat taman atau lapangan
paw N kaki binatang
pay N pembayaran; gaji, upah; v paid paid membayar; **payment** N pembayaran; **payphone** N telepon umum
pea N kacang polong

peace N perdamaian; **peaceful** ADJ damai, tenteram, tenang
peach N buah persik
peacock N, M burung merak
peak N, ADJ puncak; v memuncak
peanut N kacang tanah
pear N [pér] buah pir
pearl N mutiara
peculiar ADJ [pekyulier] aneh, ganjil
pedal N [pédel] injakan kaki, pedal; v mengayuh (sepeda)
pedestrian N [pedéstrien] pejalan kaki
pedicab N [pedikab] becak
pedicure N pedikur, perawatan kaki
pee v, SL kencing, pipis
peek v mengintip, menengok sejenak
peel N kulit (buah); v mengelupas; menguliti, mengupas; **peeler** N alat pengupas
peep v mengintip, mengintai; menengok
peer v melihat dengan susah
peg N pasak; sangkutan; patokan; v mematok, memasak
pelican N [pélikan] burung pelikan
pen N pena, kalam; bolpoin, pulpen
penalize v menghukum; **penalty** N denda, hukuman, penalti
pencil N pensil
penguin N pinguin
peninsula N [peninsula] semenanjung
penknife N [pén naif] pisau lipat ← pen
pension N [pénsyen] pensiun
penthouse N [pént haus] apartemen (mewah)
people N, PL [pipel] orang, bangsa, rakyat, kaum
pepper N merica, lada; **peppermint** ADJ mint, mentol; N permen
per PREP setiap, tiap, per
percent ADJ persen; **percentage** N persentase
perfect ADJ [pérfekt] sempurna
perform v melakukan, menyelenggarakan, memainkan (peran); **performance** N pertunjukan; **performer** N pemain, pemeran
perfume N wewangian, minyak wangi, parfum; wangi
perhaps N mungkin, barangkali

P

ENGLISH–INDONESIAN

period N [piried] zaman, masa, kala, waktu; titik; COLL datang bulan, haid

permanent ADJ tetap, permanen

permission N izin; **permit** N surat izin; V mengizinkan, memperboleh

persist V tetap (melakukan), bertekun, bertahan

person N people [pipel] orang, pribadi; **personal** ADJ pribadi; perorangan; **personality** N kepribadian; tokoh; **personnel** N [pérsonél] personalia, para karyawan

persuade V [pérsuéd] meyakinkan

pessimistic ADJ pesimis, bersangka buruk

pest N hama; gangguan

pesticide N [péstisaid] pestisida, obat pembasmi serangga

pestle N alu

pet ADJ kesayangan; N hewan peliharaan; V mengelus

petal N [pétel] daun bunga

petition N [petisyen] permohonan, petisi; V memohon

petrol N bensin

petticoat N rok dalam

phantom N [fantom] hantu, momok

pharmacy N apotik

Philippines [filipins] the ~ Filipina

philosophy N (ilmu) filsafat

phone N, SL telepon; V menelepon ← telephone

photo N, SL foto; **photocopy** N fotokopi; V memfotokopi; **photograph** N foto, potret, gambar; V memotret; **photographer** N tukang foto, tukang potret, fotografer; **photography** N potret-memotret, fotografi

phrase N [fréz] frasa, kelampok kata

physical ADJ (secara) fisik; jasmani

physics N, PL ilmu fisika

physiotherapy N fisioterapi

piano N piano

pick V memilih; mencungkil; memetik; ~ up mengambil; menjemput

pickpocket N copet, pencopet

pickup N pikap

picnic N piknik

picture N gambar, lukisan

piece N [pis] potong, keping, bagian

pier N [pir] jeti, dermaga, pelabuhan

pierce V [pirs] menembus, menindik, menusuk

pig N babi

pigeon N [pijen] burung merpati, burung dara

pile N timbunan; V menimbun

pilgrim N haji; peziarah

pill N pil, obat

pillar N [piler] tiang, soko guru

pillow N [pilo] bantal

pilot ADJ percontohan; N pilot, penerbang, pandu; contoh

pimple N [pimpel] jerawat

pin N peniti; V menyematkan

pinch V mencubit

pine N ~ (tree) pohon pinus

pineapple N nanas

pingpong N tenis meja, pingpong

pink ADJ merah muda, merah jambu, pink

pioneer N [payonir] perintis, pelopor

pipe N pipa; V menyalurkan; **pipeline** N saluran pipa

pirate N [pairat] bajak laut, pembajak; **pirated** ADJ bajakan

pit N lubang, terowongan dalam tambang

pitch N pola titinada; V melemparkan; **pitcher** N kendi, tempat air

pitiful ADJ [pitiful] memelas, menyedihkan; **pity** N belas kasihan; V mengasihani; what a ~ sayang (sekali)

place N tempat; kedudukan

plague N [plég] penyakit sampar, wabah

plain ADJ polos; sederhana, bersahaja; nyata; N medan, dataran; **plainly** ADV terus terang

plan N rencana, rancangan, bagan, denah; V merancang, merencanakan; **planning** N perencanaan

plane N, SL pesawat terbang ← airplane

planet N planet; ~ Earth Bumi

plank N papan

planner N perencana ← plan

plant N tetumbuhan, tanaman; pabrik; V menanam, menanamkan; **plantation** N perkebunan

plaster N kapur, gips, plester

P

plastic ADJ, N plastik; ~ *bag* keresek, kantong plastik

plate N piring; pelat

platform N peron; panggung

platinum N [platinum] platina, emas putih

play N pertunjukan, sandiwara; permainan; V main, bermain; memainkan; **playboy** N lelaki yang suka mempermainkan perempuan; seorang Arjuna; **player** N pemain; **playground** N tempat bermain, tempat ayunan; **playpen** N boks (bayi)

plaza N alun-alun

pleasant ADJ [plézant] menyenangkan, enak, nyaman, nikmat; sopan; **please** tolong; silahkan; coba; ~ *help me* tolong bantu saya; ~ *sit down* silahkan duduk; ~ *try* cobalah; V menyenangkan; **pleasure** N [plézyur] kesukaan, kenikmatan

plenty ADJ banyak, cukup

plot V merencanakan; berkomplot, bersekongkol

plow, plough N [plau] bajak; V membajak

plug N sumbat; steker, stopkontak; V menyumbat

plumber N [plamer] tukang ledeng

plump ADJ tambun, subur

plural ADJ jamak

plus [plas] plus, ditambah

pneumonia N [nyumonia] radang paru-paru

pocket N saku, kantong, kocek; **pocketknife** N [poketnaif] pisau lipat

poem N [poem] syair, pantun; **poet** N penyair; **poetry** N puisi

point N titik, noktah; tanjung; V menunjuk, menunjukkan; **pointed** ADJ runcing, tajam; **pointless** ADJ tiada gunanya

poison N racun; bisa; V meracuni; **poisonous** ADJ beracun, berbisa

poke V menyodok, menusuk

Poland N Polandia

polar ADJ berhubungan dengan kutub; ~ *bear* beruang kutub; **pole** N kutub

pole N tiang

police N [polis] polisi; ~ *station* kantor polisi, pos polisi; **policeman** N, M polisi; **policewoman** N, F polisi wanita (polwan)

policy N kebijaksanaan

polio N penyakit lumpuh layuh, penyakit polio

polish N pelitur, semir; V menggosok, menyemir

polite ADJ sopan (santun)

political ADJ politik; **politician** N [politisyen] politikus, politisi

pollute V mencemarkan; **pollution** N pencemaran, kecemaran, polusi

polygamy N poligami

pond N kolam

pony N kuda kerdil, kuda poni

poo, pooh N, SL tahi; V berak

pool N kolam (renang); bilyar

poor ADJ miskin, papa; hina, malang

pop V meletup; ~ *up* muncul

Pope *the* ~ Sri Paus

popular ADJ populer, laku; **population** N (jumlah) penduduk, populasi

pork N daging babi

pornography N pornografi

porpoise N [porpus] lumba-lumba

porridge N [porij] bubur

port ADJ kiri (di kapal); N pelabuhan; lubang, colokan

portable ADJ dapat dibawa ke mana-mana, jinjing

porter N kuli

portion N porsi, bagian

portrait N potret, lukisan, gambar

pose N [poz] gaya, lagak; V bergaya

position N [posisyen] letak, kedudukan, pangkat, jabatan; keadaan

positive ADJ, N positif, pasti, tentu

possess V memiliki, mempunyai

possibility N kemungkinan; **possible** ADJ [posibel] mungkin; **possibly** ADV barangkali, mungkin

post ADJ sesudah, pasca

post N pos; jabatan; tiang; layanan pos; ~ *office* kantor pos; V mengeposkan; menempelkan; **postcard** N kartu pos; **poster** N plakat, gambar

postman N tukang pos

postpone V menunda, mengundurkan

pot N pot, periuk, tempat bunga, tempat tanaman

potato N [potéto] kentang; ~ *chips* kentang goreng

P

potential ADJ mungkin, berpeluang, calon

pothole N [pot hol] lubang di jalan

pottery N tembikar, pecah belah, keramik

poultry N [poltri] unggas

pour V mengalir; menuangkan, mencurahkan; menyiram

poverty N [poverti] kemiskinan

powder N [pauder] bubuk, serbuk, puyer; bedak; V membedaki

power N kekuasaan, kekuatan, daya, tenaga; **powerful** ADJ berkuasa, kuat

practical N praktis, berguna; **practically** ADV hampir-hampir, benar-benar; **practice** N praktek, kebiasaan, adat; latihan; mempraktekkan, melatih

praise N [préiz] pujian; V memuji

pram N kereta bayi, kereta anak-anak

prank N gurauan, permainan

pre- PREF [pri] pra-, sebelum

preacher N pemuka agama; ISL khatib, dai

precious ADJ [présyus] berharga, mahal; mulia

precise ADJ tepat, saksama

predict V meramalkan; **prediction** N ramalan

prefer V lebih suka, memilih; **preference** N kecenderungan, pilihan

prefix N awalan

pregnancy N (masa) kehamilan; **pregnant** ADJ hamil, mengandung

prehistoric ADJ prasejarah

prejudice N [préjudis] prasangka

premature ADJ prematur, sebelum waktunya, pradini

premier ADJ utama, terbaik

premiere N [prémiér] pemutaran perdana, pertunjukan perdana

prepaid ADJ prabayar

preparation N [préparésyen] persiapan; **prepare** V menyiapkan, mempersiapkan

preposition N [préposisyen] kata depan

prescription N resep

presence N [prézens] hadirat, hadapan; kehadiran; **present** ADJ [prézent] sekarang, kini; hadir; N hadiah, kado, pemberian; V [prezént] menyajikan, mempersem-

bahkan; **presentation** N penyajian, presentasi; **presently** ADV segera

preservation N [préservésyen] perlindungan; preservasi; **preserve** N [presérv] cagar; selai; V mengawetkan, melindungi, memelihara

president N presiden; ketua

press N percetakan; pers; alat penekan; V menekan, menindih, mendesak; **pressure** N [présyur] tekanan

presume V menganggap; mengira

pretend V berpura-pura, berdalih

pretty ADJ [priti] manis, cantik, molek; ADV cukup

prevent V [prevént] mencegah, menghalangi, menangkis; **prevention** N pencegahan

previous ADJ yang dahulu, yang sebelumnya

price N harga; **priceless** ADJ tidak ternilai

prick N tusukan; V menusuk; **prickly** ADJ tajam, berduri, menusuk

pride N kesombongan, kebanggaan, harga diri

priest N, CATH [prist] pastor; HIND pedanda

primary ADJ pertama, terpenting, dasar; **prime** ADJ perdana, utama; ~ *minister (PM)* Perdana Menteri (PM)

primitive ADJ sederhana, primitif

prince N, M pangeran; **princess** N, F putri, permaisuri

principal ADJ utama; N kepala sekolah; uang pokok

principle N [prinsipel] asas, prinsip

print N tapak (kaki); gambar, reproduksi; tulisan, ketikan; V mencetak; **printer** N printer, pencetak; **printout** N hasil cetak

prior ADJ [praior] terlebih dahulu; **priority** N prioritas

prison N [prizon] penjara; **prisoner** N orang yang dipenjara, terpidana

private ADJ [praivet] pribadi; swasta; milik sendiri

privilege N [privilej] hak istimewa

prize N hadiah

probably ADV kemungkinan besar, mungkin

problem N masalah, soal

procedure N prosedur, tata cara; **process** N cara, proses; V mem-

P

proses, mengolah; **procession** N arak-arakan, prosesi

proclamation N proklamasi, pengumuman

produce N hasil; V menghasilkan; **producer** N produsen; **product** N hasil, produk; **production** N produksi, pertunjukan

profession N profesi, pekerjaan; pernyataan; **professional** ADJ profesional

professor N guru besar

profile N profil

profit N untung, keuntungan, laba; V beruntung, memperoleh keuntungan; **profitable** ADJ menguntungkan

program, programme N acara, program; V memprogram

progress N kemajuan; V maju

project N proyek; V memproyeksikan; **projector** N proyektor

promise N [promis] janji; V berjanji; menjanjikan

promote V memajukan, menaikkan pangkat, mempromosikan; **promotion** N kenaikan pangkat; promosi

pronunciation N lafal

proof N bukti

propeller N baling-baling

proper ADJ benar, betul, patut, layak; **properly** ADV benar-benar, dengan betul

property N kepunyaan, (harta) milik; sifat

proposal N usul; lamaran; **propose** V mengusulkan; meminang

protect V melindungi; **protection** N perlindungan; **protective** ADJ [protéktif] bersifat melindungi; pencegah

protest N protes, pembangkangan, unjuk rasa; V memprotes, melawan, membangkang, berunjuk rasa

proud ADJ bangga; angkuh, sombong

prove V [pruv] membuktikan

proverb N peribahasa

provide V menyediakan, membekali, melengkapi; **provided, providing ~ (that)** asal, asalkan

province N propinsi; **provincial** ADJ berhubungan dengan provinsi; picik, kampungan

prune N buah prem kering

pseudonym N [siudonim] nama samaran

psychiatrist N [saikayetrist] psikiater, ahli jiwa

psychic ADJ, N [saikik] mempunyai indera keenam, cenayang

psychologist N psikolog, ahli ilmu jiwa; **psychology** N ilmu jiwa, psikologi

PTO ABBREV *please turn over* di halaman berikut

public N orang banyak, umum; **publication** N terbitan, keluaran; pengumuman

publish V menerbitkan, mengeluarkan, mengumumkan; **publisher** N penerbit

pudding N puding, pencuci mulut, podeng

puddle N [padel] genangan

pull N tarikan, daya tarik; V [pul] menarik; **pullover** N switer, baju hangat

pulse N nadi

pump N pompa; V memompa

pumpkin N labu

punch V menghantam, meninju, menonjok

punctual ADJ tepat waktu

punctuation N [pangktyuésyen] pemberian tanda-tanda baca

punish V [panisy] menghukum; **punishment** N hukuman

pupil N murid; anak mata

puppet N boneka; wayang

puppy N [papi] anak anjing

purchase V membeli

pure ADJ murni, bersih

purple ADJ ungu, lembayung

purpose N maksud, niat, tujuan; **on ~** dengan sengaja

purr N dengkur (kucing); V mendengkur

purse N dompet

push N [pusy] dorongan; V mendorong; **pusher** N kereta anak

puss, pussycat N, SL [pus, pusikat] kucing

put V put put [put] meletakkan, menaruh, menyimpan; menempatkan

puzzle N [pazel] mainan, teka-teki

pyjamas, pajamas N, PL piyama, baju tidur

ENGLISH–INDONESIAN

python N [paithon] ular sanca, piton

Q

quake N gempa; V gemetar
qualification N kualifikasi, ijazah; **qualified** ADJ berkualifikasi, berhak, berijazah
quality N mutu, kualitas; sifat
quantity N [kuontiti] banyaknya, kuantitas
quarantine N [kuorantin] karantina
quarrel N [kuorel] pertengkaran, percekcokan
quarter N [kuorter] perempat; kampung, daerah, lingkungan
quay N [ki] dermaga
queen N ratu
queer ADJ aneh
query N [kuiri] pertanyaan; V menanyakan, meragukan
quest N pencarian
question N pertanyaan; masalah, soal; V bertanya; memeriksa; **questionnaire** N [kuéstionér] angket
queue N [kyu] antre, antrean; V antri, berantri
quick ADJ cepat
quiet ADJ [kuayet] teduh, tenang
quilt N selimut tebal
quit V quit quit putus asa, berhenti, meninggalkan
quite ADV cukup sama, rada, lumayan
quiz N kuis, ulangan singkat, tanya jawab; V menanyai
quotation N kutipan; penawaran; **quote** V mengutip, menyebut, mencatat

R

rabbit N kelinci
race N lomba, balap, pacuan; V berlomba, membalap; **racehorse** N kuda pacu, kuda balap; **racetrack** N sirkuit; pacuan kuda
race N (suku) bangsa, ras; **racism** N [résizem] rasisme, pembedaan rasial; **racist** ADJ rasis
rack N rak
racket, racquet N raket
radio N [rédio] radio
radish N [radisy] lobak

raffle N [rafel] undian
raft N rakit
rag N lap, kain jelek
rage N kemarahan, geram
raid N razia, serangan, penggerebekan; V merazia, menyerang, menyerbu
rail N rel; **railing** N susuran; **railroad**, **railway** N jalan kereta api
rain N, V hujan; **rainbow** N pelangi, bianglala; **raincoat** N jas hujan; **rainy** ADJ banyak hujan
raise V mengangkat, menaikkan, meninggikan; membesarkan (anakanak); menimbulkan
raisin N kismis
rally N reli; pertemuan
ramp N jalur mendaki, jalur yang melandai
ranch N peternakan, pertanian
range N [rénj] jajaran, barisan; kisaran, jangkauan; lapangan, tempat; **ranger** N penjaga hutan
rank N pangkat, derajat; V menduduki; mengatur, menyusun; menggolongkan; **ranking** N urutan
ransom N (uang) tebusan, penebusan
rap N musik rap; ketukan; V mengetuk
rape N perkosaan, pemerkosaan; V memerkosa
rapid ADJ [rapid] cepat, lekas; **rapids** N, PL jeram
rare ADJ mentah; jarang; **rarely** ADV jarang
raspberry N frambozen
rat N tikus (besar)
rate N tarif, perbandingan, angka; kecepatan
rather ADV agak, rada, cukup; melainkan; ~ **than** daripada
rating N penilaian
ration N rangsum, jatah
rattan N rotan
raven N burung gagak
raw ADJ mentah; kasar
ray N sinar
razor N pisau cukur
reach V sampai, tiba, mencapai; menghubungi
react V [riakt] bereaksi; menanggapi; **reaction** N tanggapan, reaksi
read V read read [réd] membaca; **reader** N pembaca; buku bacaan;

R

reading N membaca; bacaan ← read

ready ADJ [rédi] siap, sedia; selesai, sudah

real ADJ nyata, betul, sejati; ADV sangat, benar-benar; **reality** N kenyataan, realitas; **realize** V sadar; mewujudkan, melaksanakan

rear ADJ, N (bagian) belakang; pantat

reason N sebab, alasan; akal (budi); **reasonable** ADJ masuk akal

rebel N [rébel] pemberontak; **rebellion** N pemberontakan

recall V ingat; memanggil kembali, menarik kembali

receipt N [risit] kuitansi, tanda terima, struk; penerimaan; **receive** V menerima, mendapat, memperoleh; menyambut

recent ADJ baru; **recently** ADV baru-baru ini

reception N resepsi ← receive

recharge V mengecas, mengisi ulang

recipe N [résipi] resep

recognize V mengenal, mengenali; mengakui, menghargai

recommend V menganjurkan; memuji; **recommendation** N rekomendasi, saran

record N [rékord] catatan; daftar; rekor; piringan hitam; dokumen; V [rekord] mencatat, mendaftar, merekam

recover V [rikaver] sembuh, pulih; menemukan kembali, menyelamatkan

recreation N [rékriésyen] hiburan, rekreasi

recruit N rekrut; V merekrut

rectangle N [rektanggel] empat persegi panjang

recycle V [risaikel] didaur ulang; **recycling** N daur ulang

red ADJ merah

reduce V mengurangi, memperkecil

reef N (batu) karang

refer V mengacu; menunjukkan; mengenai; **referee** N wasit; **reference** N surat keterangan, referensi

refill N isi ulang; pengisian kembali

refine V menghaluskan, menyaring; **refinery** N kilang

reflect V membayang; mencerminkan, memantulkan; merenung, merenungkan; **reflection** N bayangan; renungan

reforestation N reboisasi

reform N perubahan, reformasi; V berubah; mengubah; menyusun kembali

refresh V menyegarkan

refrigerator N lemari es, kulkas

refugee N pengungsi

refund N pembayaran kembali; V mengembalikan uang

refusal N penolakan; **refuse** V [refyuz] menolak

regard N hormat; V menganggap

regency N kabupaten; daerah; **regent** N bupati

region N daerah, wilayah; **regional** ADJ daerah

register N [réjister] daftar; V daftar; mendaftarkan; mencatat; **registration** N pendaftaran, pencatatan; **registry** N (kantor) pendaftaran

regret N rasa sesal; V menyesal

regular ADJ biasa; teratur; tetap

rehearsal N [rihérsal] latihan

reign N [réin] pemerintahan, masa bertakhta

reindeer N [reindir] reindeer rusa kutub

reject V [rejékt] menolak; **rejection** N penolakan

relate V menceritakan; mengaitkan, menghubungkan; **relation** N saudara, keluarga; hubungan; **relationship** N hubungan; **relative** ADJ relatif; N saudara, keluarga

relax V bersantai-santai; mengendurkan; **relaxation** N relaksasi; **relaxing** ADJ santai

release N pembebasan; rilis, keluaran; V melepaskan, membebaskan, memerdekakan

relevant ADJ bersangkut paut, relevan

reliable ADJ andal, terpercaya ← rely

relief N [rilif] bantuan, pertolongan, sumbangan; rasa lega; **relieve** V membantu, menolong

religion N [rilijen] agama

reluctant ADJ enggan

rely V [relai] mengandalkan

remain v tinggal, tetap; ~s N sisa; **remainder** N sisa

remark N komentar; catatan; v berkomentar, mengomentari; berkata; **remarkable** ADJ pantas diperhatikan, luar biasa

remember v ingat

remind v [remaind] mengingatkan; **reminder** N surat peringatan

remote ADJ, N terpencil; ~ *control* remot

removal N [remuvel] pemindahan; **remove** v memindahkan; menjauhkan

renew v memperbarui, memperpanjang

renovate v merenovasi, memperbaiki

rent N (uang) sewa; v menyewa; ~ *out* menyewakan

repair N perbaikan, reparasi; v memperbaiki

repay v repaid repaid membayar kembali, mengganti

repeat N tayangan ulang; v mengulangi

replace v mengganti, menggantikan

reply N [replai] jawaban, sahutan, balasan; v menjawab, menyahut, membalas

report N laporan, pemberitaan; v melapor; melaporkan, memberitakan; **reporter** N wartawan

represent v mewakili; menggambarkan, melambangkan; **representative** N wakil, utusan

reprint N cetak ulang; v mencetak ulang

reproduce v mempunyai keturunan, berkembang biak; meniru; **reproduction** N reproduksi

reptile N binatang melata

republic N republik; **republican** ADJ berkaitan dengan republik, republikan

reputation N nama baik, reputasi

request N permohonan, permintaan; v memohon, minta

require v memerlukan

rescue N penyelamatan; v menolong, menyelamatkan

research N penelitian, riset; v meneliti, meriset

resemble v menyerupai, mirip

reservation N reservasi, pesanan, buking; **reserve** N cadangan, persediaan; v memesan, menyediakan

reshuffle N perombakan; v merombak

residence N kediaman; **resident** N penduduk, penghuni; ARCH residen

resign v [rizain] mundur, mengundurkan diri, berhenti bekerja

resist v [rezist] melawan, menahan; **resistance** N perlawanan, pertahanan

resort N tempat beristirahat, resor

resource N sumber daya

respect N hormat; hal; **respectable** ADJ baik-baik, terhormat; **respectful** ADJ (penuh) hormat

respective ADJ masing-masing

respond v membalas, menjawab, menanggapi; **response** N tanggapan, jawaban, respons

responsibility N [responsibiliti] tanggung jawab; **responsible** ADJ bertanggung jawab

rest N (waktu) istirahat; sisa; v berhenti, beristirahat, mengaso; tinggal; **restroom** N toilet, WC

restaurant N restoran, rumah makan

restrict v membatasi; **restriction** N pembatasan

result N akibat, hasil

resumé, resume N [rézumé] riwayat hidup

resume v mulai lagi, meneruskan

resurrect v menghidupkan kembali

retail ADJ [ritél] eceran, ritel; N perdagangan eceran; **retailer** N pengecer, pedagang eceran

retain v menyimpan, menahan, tetap

retarded ADJ tunagrahita, terkebelakang

retire v pensiun; **retirement** N masa pensiun

retreat N [retrit] retret; v mundur, menarik diri

retrieve v [retriv] mengambil, mendapat kembali

return N kembali, pemulangan, perjalanan pulang; v pulang, kembali; mengembalikan, membalas

reveal v [revil] membuka, menyingkapkan; menyatakan

R

revenge N (rasa) dendam, pembalasan

reverse ADJ terbalik; N sisi balik; V mundur, memundurkan kendaraan; membalikkan

review N [revyu] tinjauan; resensi; majalah; V meninjau kembali; menilai; **reviewer** N penulis resensi

revolution N revolusi; peredaran

reward N [reword] hadiah, imbalan, ganjaran; V mengganjar; menghadiahi; **rewarding** ADJ menguntungkan, berguna

rheumatism N [rumatizem] encok, rematik, sengal

rhinoceros N [rainoseres] **rhino** SL badak

rhyme N [raim] sajak; V bersajak; **rhythm** N [rithem] irama, ritme

rib N tulang rusuk, iga

ribbon N pita

rice N padi; beras; nasi

rich ADJ kaya, subur

rickshaw N becak

rid V membersihkan, membebaskan

riddle N teka-teki

ride N perjalanan; V rode ridden mengendarai, naik; **rider** N penunggang; pengendara

ridiculous ADJ menggelikan

rifle N [raifel] senapan, bedil

right ADJ [rait] (sebelah) kanan; betul, benar; patut, layak

ring N cincin; lingkaran; jaringan; gelanggang; dering; V rang rung berdering; COLL telepon, menelepon

rink ice (skating) ~ gelanggang es

rinse N bilasan; V membilas

riot N [raiot] kerusuhan; kegaduhan

rip N robekan, sobekan; V menyobek, merobek

ripe ADJ masak, matang

rise N kenaikan; V rose risen [rizen] bangkit, terbit, berdiri

risk N risiko; V mengambil risiko

ritual N upacara (agama)

rival N saingan, lawan; V menyaingi

river N [river] sungai, kali

road N jalan (raya); **roadwork** N perbaikan jalan

roast ADJ panggang; N daging panggang; V memanggang, membakar

rob V merampok, merampas;

robber N perampok; **robbery** N perampokan

rock N batu, cadas; V mengayunkan; menggoncang

rocket N roket; V meroket

role N peran, peranan

roll N gulung, gulungan; roti bulat; daftar; V berguling, berputar; menggulung, menggulingkan, menggelindingkan; **roller** ~ blades, ~ skates sepatu roda

Roman ADJ Romawi

romance N cerita cinta

roof N atap

room N ruang, ruangan; kamar; V kos

rooster N ayam jago

root N akar

rope N tali

rose N bunga mawar, bunga ros; V, PF → rise

rot V membusuk

rotate V berputar, berkisar

rotten ADJ busuk ← rot

rough ADJ [raf] kasar; mentah; **roughly** ADV kurang lebih, kira-kira; secara kasar

round ADJ bulat, bundar; di sekitar; N giliran, putaran, ronde; V mengelilingi; **roundabout** N bundaran; komidi putar

route N [rut] trayek, jalur, rute

row N [ro] baris, jajar, deretan

row V [ro] berkayuh; mendayung, mengayuh

rub V menggosok, menggosok-gosok; ~ out menghapus; **rubber** N karet; penghapus

rubbish N sampah; omong kosong

ruby N batu mirah

rucksack N ransel

rude ADJ kasar, tidak sopan

ruin N reruntuhan, puing-puing; V meruntuhkan, merobohkan, merusak

rule N aturan, peraturan; pemerintahan; V memerintah; **ruler** N kepala pemerintah; penggaris

rum N room

rumor N kabar angin, kabar burung, desas-desus

run N perjalanan, latihan berlari, perlombaan; V ran run lari; berlangsung; mengalir; memimpin; menjalankan; **runaway** N pelarian

ENGLISH–INDONESIAN

S

runner N pelari; pesuruh, pengantar ← run

runway N landasan terbang

rural ADJ pedesaan, pedalaman

rush N ketergesa-gesaan; ~ *hour* jam padat; v terburu-buru; menyerbu

Russia N Rusia; **Russian** N bahasa Rusia; orang Rusia

rust N karat; v berkarat; **rusty** ADJ berkarat, karatan

ruthless ADJ [ruthles] keji, kejam, tanpa belas kasihan

S

sabotage N [sabotaj] sabotase; v menyabotase

sachet N [sasyé] sase, saset, kemasan (kecil) (berisi saus, sampo dll)

sack N karung, goni

sacred ADJ [sékred] suci, kudus

sacrifice N [sakrifais] korban, pengorbanan; ISL kurban, qurban; v berkurban; mengorbankan

sad ADJ susah, sedih

saddle N pelana, sadel, tempat duduk

safe ADJ selamat; aman, dapat dipercaya; **safety** N keselamatan; keamanan

sail N layar; v berlayar; **sailing** N berlayar; **sailor** N pelaut, anak buah kapal (ABK)

salad N selada

salary N [salari] gaji

sale N obral; *for* ~ dijual; **sales** N penjualan; **salesperson** N agen; pelayan toko

salmon N [samen] ikan salmon

salt N garam; **salty** ADJ asin

salute N pemberian hormat; v memberi hormat

same ADJ sama; serupa

sample N [sampel] contoh; v coba

sand N pasir

sandal N [sandel] sepatu sandal

sandpaper N kertas gosok, ampelas ← sand

sandwich N [sandwij] roti lapis

sapphire N [safair] batu nilam, batu safir

sarong N sarung

satellite N [satelait] satelit; bulan; ~ *dish* parabola

satisfaction N kepuasan; **satisfactory** ADJ memuaskan, cukup; **satisfy** v [satisfai] memuaskan; memenuhi

Saturday ADJ, N [saterdé] hari Sabtu

sauce N kuah, saus

saucer N piring cawan

Saudi Arabia N Arab Saudi

savage ADJ [savej] buas, liar, ganas

save N penyelamatan, tangkapan; PREP kecuali; v menyelamatkan; **savings** N, PL (uang) tabungan, simpanan

saw N gergaji; v, PF → see; **sawdust** N serbuk kayu

sax, saxophone N saksofon

say v said said [séd] kata, berkata; mengatakan; **saying** N pepatah, peribahasa

scale N skala, ukuran; sisik, kulit; **scales** N, PL timbangan, neraca

scan N peninjauan; v meninjau; pindai, memindai

scandal N skandal, keonaran

scanner N pemindai, scanner ← scan

scar N bekas (luka); v membekas, menggoresi

scare N [skér] peristiwa yang menakutkan; v menakut-nakuti, menakutkan; **scared** ADJ takut

scarf N syal

scary ADJ [skéri] menakutkan ← scare

scavenger N pemulung

scene N [sin] pemandangan; adegan; **scenery** N pemandangan alam

scent N [sént] (minyak) wangi, harum, bau

schedule N [skédyul] jadwal, program, daftar acara; v merencanakan, mengatur

scheme N [skim] rencana; bagan, skema, rancangan; v merekayasa

scholar N [skolar] pelajar; orang terpelajar; **scholarship** N beasiswa; **school** N sekolah

science N ilmu (pengetahuan alam, IPA); sains; **scientist** N ilmuwan

scooter N otopet, skuter

scorch v membakar (tidak sengaja)

score N skor, angka, nilai; v mencetak gol, angka atau poin; memperoleh nilai; **scoreboard** N papan angka

scorpion N kalajengking
Scotland N Skotlandia
scout N pandu, pramuka; pengintai
scramble N perebutan; v berebut; mengocok
scrap ADJ bekas; ~ *metal* besi tua; ~ *paper* kertas bekas; N sisa, carik
scrape v bergeseran; menggores, menggesekkan
scratch N goresan; v menggores, menggaruk, mencoret
scrawl N tulisan cakar ayam
scream N jeritan; v berteriak, menjerit
screen N tabir; layar putih; **screening** N pemutaran film
screw N sekrup; v menyekrup; **screwdriver** N obeng
scribble v mencoret-coret
script N tulisan; naskah
scroll v menggulung, naik
scrub N semak, belukar
scrub v menggosok
scuba ~ *diving* selam dengan tangki udara
sculptor N perupa, pematung, pemahat patung
sea N laut; ~ *level* permukaan laut; ~ *urchin* bulu babi; **seafood** N makanan laut; **seagull** N burung camar; **seahorse** N kuda laut
seal N anjing laut
seal N meterai, cap; v menutup
sealion N [silayon] singa laut ← **sea**
search N [sérc] pencarian, penggeledahan; v mencari, memeriksa, menggeledah
seashell N kerang (laut) ← **sea**
seashore N pantai laut ← **sea**
seasick ADJ mabuk laut ← **sea**
seaside N tepi laut ← **sea**
season N [sizen] musim; *the dry* ~ musim kemarau
seasoning N bumbu
seat N tempat duduk, bangku, kursi
seaweed N ganggang laut, rumput laut
second N [sékond] detik
second ADJ [sékond] kedua; ~-*hand* bekas; **secondary** ADJ sekunder
secretary N sekretaris, panitera
section N seksi, bagian, belahan; **sector** N sektor, bidang

security N keamanan
see v saw seen melihat; berkunjung
seed N biji, benih
seek v sought sought [sot] mencari
seem v nampak; ternyata, kelihatannya; rupanya, rasanya
seize v [siz] menangkap; menyita
seldom ADV jarang
select v [sélékt] memilih, menyaring; **selection** N pilihan, pemilihan, seleksi
self PRON sendiri, pribadi; **selfish** ADJ egois, suka mementingkan diri sendiri
sell v sold sold menjual, berjualan; **seller** N penjual
semi- PREF tengah, separuh; ~-*colon* titik koma
send v sent sent mengirim, mengirimkan, mengirimi
senior ADJ [sinior] lebih tua, tertua, senior; N orang yang lebih tua; ~ *high school* sekolah menengah atas (SMA)
sensation N kegemparan, sensasi
sense N indera; perasaan; arti, pengertian; **sensible** ADJ waras, berpikiran sehat, berakal sehat; **sensitive** ADJ peka, sensitif
sentimental ADJ sentimentil
separate ADJ [séperet] terpisah; v [séperét] berpisah; pisah ranjang; memisahkan
September N bulan September
sequel N [sikuel] lanjutan, sambungan
sergeant N [sarjen] sersan
serial N [siriel] seri; film seri; cerita bersambung (cerber); **series** N seri, rangkaian
serious ADJ sungguh-sungguh, serius
servant N pembantu, pelayan, pramuwisma, babu; **serve** v melayani, mengabdi; menghidangkan; **service** N pelayanan; pemeliharaan; kebaktian; masa bakti; jasa; v memperbaiki (mobil)
serviette N [sérviét] serbet
sesame N [sésami] wijen
set ADJ sudah ditentukan; siap; N sepasang, seperangkat, perlengkapan; pesawat (radio/televisi);

kelompok; **v set set** menaruh; memasang, menyetel; menetapkan; terbenam (matahari)

settle v [sétel] berdiam; menempati; menyelesaikan, menenangkan; mengatur, mengurus; **settlement N** perkampungan; penyelesaian; **settler N** pendatang, pemukim awal

seven ADJ, N [séven] tujuh; **seventeen ADJ, N** tujuh belas; **seventh ADJ** ketujuh; **seventy ADJ, N** tujuh puluh

several ADJ [séveral] beberapa

sew v [so] sewed sewn menjahit

sewn v, PF [son] → **sew**

sex N jenis kelamin; (hubungan) seks, persetubuhan, sanggama; **sexy ADJ** seksi

shade N naungan, tempat teduh; krei; warna

shadow N [syado] bayangan; **v** membayangi; membuntuti

shake N minuman bercampur (coklat, dsb) ← **milkshake**; goncangan, gelengan (kepala); jabat tangan; **v shook shaken** mengguncang, mengocok

shall v, AUX akan

shallow ADJ dangkal

shame N malu

shampoo N [syampu] sampo; **v** berkeramas

shan't v takkan, tidak akan ← **shall**

shape N bentuk; **v** membentuk

share N bagian, andil, saham; **v** berbagi; membagi; **shareholder N** pemegang saham

shark N ikan hiu

sharp ADJ tajam, runcing; cerdik; **sharpen v** meruncingkan, mengasah, meraut; **sharpener N** raut pensil

shave v bercukur; mencukur; mengiris; **shaver N** alat cukur (listrik)

shawl N syal, selendang

she PRON, F [syi] dia

shed N gudang

sheep N sheep domba, biri-biri; **sheepdog N** anjing gembala

sheet N helai, lembar; seprai

shelf N papan, rak

shell N kulit, kerang; **v** mengupas; **shellfish N** kerang-kerangan

shelter N tempat berlindung, tempat teduh; **v** berlindung, bernaung; melindungi

shepherd N [shéperd] gembala

shield N [syild] perisai, tameng; **v** melindungi

shift N perubahan, pergeseran; jam kerja; **v** berpindah tempat, beralih; mengubah, menggeser

shine N cahaya, sinar; **v shone shone** [syon] bercahaya, bersinar; memancarkan

shiny ADJ berkilap, mengkilap ← **shine**

ship N kapal, perahu; **shipping N** perkapalan, pengiriman dengan kapal; **shipwreck N** [syiprék] peristiwa kapal karam; **shipyard N** galangan kapal

shirt N baju, kemeja

shiver v menggigil, gemetar

shock N guncangan; kejutan; *electric* ~ kena setrum; **shocking ADJ** mengejutkan

shoe N [syu] sepatu; **shoelace N** tali sepatu

shoot v shot shot menembak; merekam; **shooting N** penembakan; menembak (olahraga); syuting, pengambilan gambar

shop N toko; **v** berbelanja; **shopkeeper N** pemilik toko; **shoplift v** mengutil atau mencuri dari toko; **shopper N** orang yang berbelanja, pembeli; **shopping N** hasil belanja, belanjaan; ~ *center*, ~ *mall* (pusat) pertokoan, mal

shore N pantai, tepi

short ADJ pendek, ringkas, singkat; kurang; kekurangan; **N** film pendek; **shortage N** [shortej] kekurangan; **shortly ADV** tidak lama lagi; **shorts N, PL** celana pendek, kolor

shot N tembakan; suntikan; **v, PF** → **shoot**

should v, AUX [syud] seharusnya, sebaiknya, semestinya

shoulder N [syolder] bahu, pundak; *hard* ~ bahu jalan

shout N [syaut] teriakan; **v** berteriak

shove N [shav] dorongan; **v** mendorong dengan kasar

shovel N [shavel] sekop; **v** menyekop

show N [sho] pertunjukan, tontonan; acara di televisi; pameran; v memperlihatkan, mempertunjuk-kan; menunjukkan, menampakkan; membuktikan; **showdown** N [shodaun] bentrokan

shower N [syauer] pancuran (mandi); hujan sebentar; v mandi (di pancuran); menghujani, menaburi

shred N carik, sobekan; v mencarik, memarut

shriek N [syrik] jeritan, pekikan; v menjerit

shrimp N udang

shrine N kuil, tempat keramat

shrink v shrank shrunk susut; menyusutkan

shrunk v, PF → shrink; **shrunken** ADJ berkerut, menyusut

shuffle v mengocok; menyeret kaki

shut v shut shut tutup; menutup; **shutter** N daun penutup jendela

shuttle ADJ [syatel] ulang-alik; N kendaraan ulang-alik

shy ADJ [syai] malu, pemalu

sick ADJ sakit

sickly ADJ sering sakit, sakit-sakitan ← sick

side N sisi, segi; samping; **sidewalk** N trotoar; **sideways** ADV miring, ke samping

sieve N [siv] ayakan, saringan

sift v mengayak; menyaring

sigh N [sai] keluh, nafas panjang; v menarik nafas panjang; mendesah

sight N [sait] pemandangan; pengli-hatan; **sightseeing** N wisata, tamasya

sign N [sain] tanda, pertanda, isyarat; rambu; plang; v menandatangani; teken, memberi paraf; **signal** N [signal] tanda, isyarat; v memberi tanda; mengisyaratkan; **signature** N [signatyur] tanda tangan

significant ADJ berarti, penting

signpost N [sainpost] rambu

silence N keheningan; v mendiam-kan; **silent** ADJ diam

silk ADJ, N sutera

silly ADJ bodoh, tolol; lucu

silver ADJ, N perak

similar ADJ [similer] serupa, mirip

simple ADJ [simpel] sederhana, ber-sahaja; **simply** ADV dengan seder-hana; hanya; benar-benar, sungguh-sungguh

sin N dosa; v berdosa

since CONJ sejak, sedari; sebab, karena

sincere ADJ [sinsir] tulus (hati), ikhlas; bersungguh-sungguh

sing v sang sung bernyanyi, men-yanyi; menyanyikan; **singer** N penyanyi

Singapore N Singapura

singer N penyanyi

single ADJ [singgel] tunggal, sendiri; lajang; M bujangan; lagu

singlet N singlet

sink N tempat cuci (piring); v sank sunk tenggelam, mengendap; menenggelamkan

sip N isapan; v mengisap, meminum sedikit

sir PRON tuan

siren N sirene

sister N saudara perempuan, adik atau kakak perempuan; kepala perawat, suster

sit v sat sat duduk

site N lokasi, situs

situated ADJ [sityuéted] terletak; **situation** N keadaan, situasi

six ADJ, N enam; **sixteen** ADJ, N enam belas; **sixth** ADJ keenam; **sixty** ADJ, N enam puluh

size N ukuran, nomor; besarnya

skate N sepatu luncur, sepatu es; ice-~ sepatu es; v bermain sepatu luncur atau sepatu roda; **skating** N bermain sepatu luncur

skeleton N [skéleton] kerangka

sketch N sketsa; gambar

ski N (sepatu) ski; v main ski; **skiing** N main ski

skill N keterampilan, keahlian; **skill-ful, skilful** ADJ terampil

skin N kulit

skinny ADJ [skini] kurus, ceking

skip v melompat-lompat; melewati; meloncati

skirt N rok

skull N tengkorak, batok kepala

sky N langit, angkasa, udara; **sky-diving** N terjun payung; **skyscraper** N pencakar langit

slang N bahasa percakapan, bahasa gaul

slap N tampar, tamparan; V menampar

slaughter N [sloter] pembantaian; penyembelihan; V membantai; memotong, menyembelih

slave N budak; **slavery** N perbudakan

sled, sledge N kereta luncur

sleep V slept slept tidur; **sleepy** ADJ mengantuk

sleeve N lengan baju; sisipan kertas di CD; **sleeveless** ADJ tanpa lengan

slender ADJ ramping, langsing

slice N irisan, sayatan; V mengiris, menyayat

slide N perosotan; V slid slid meluncur; tergelincir

slightly ADV sedikit

slim ADJ ramping, langsing, lampai

slip N kesalahan; longsor; rok dalam; V tergelincir; terlupa

slipper N selop; sandal

slippery ADJ licin ← slip

slogan N semboyan, slogan

slope N lereng; V melandai

sloppy ADJ tidak rapi; cengeng

slow ADJ perlahan-lahan, pelan-pelan; lambat, lamban; lama; **slowly** ADV pelan-pelan

slug N semacam siput

slum N daerah kumuh

slump N kemerosotan; V merosot; terjatuh

smack N tampar, tamparan, tempeleng; SL heroin; V menampar, menempeleng

small ADJ kecil

smart ADJ cerdas, pintar; cantik, tampan; cepat; V pedih, sakit

smash N tabrakan, kecelakaan (mobil); V memecahkan, menghancurkan

smell N bau; V bau; **smelly** ADJ berbau (tidak sedap)

smile N senyum, senyuman; V tersenyum

smith N pandai besi

smog N asbut (asap kabut)

smoke N asap; SL rokok; V berasap; merokok; **smoking** no ~ dilarang merokok; **smoky** ADJ berasap

smooth ADJ licin; lancar

smuggle V [smagel] menyelundupkan

snack N makanan kecil, camilan

snail N keong, siput

snake N ular

snapshot N potret, foto

snatch V menjambret, merampas

sneak N orang yang melaporkan kawan; V menyelinap; **sneakers** N sepatu kets, sepatu olahraga; **sneaky** ADJ tidak suka terus terang

sneer N mimik wajah yang menyeringai; V menyeringai

sneeze N, V bersin

sniff N hirupan; V mencium, mencium-cium

sniffle N [snifel] pilek; V tersedu-sedu

sniper N penembak jitu

snob N, SL orang sombong

snooze N, SL tidur sebentar

snore V mendengkur; SL mengorok

snow N salju; V hujan salju; **snowball** N bola salju; **snowman** N boneka salju; **snowy** ADJ bersalju

snug ADJ hangat, nyaman; pas

so ADV begitu; sangat; demikian; CONJ jadi, maka, oleh sebab itu

soak V merendam

soap N sabun

sob N sedu; V tersedu-sedu

soccer N sepak bola

social ADJ [sosyal] sosial, kemasyarakatan; ramah; **socialism** N [sosyalizem] sosialisme; **society** N [sosayeti] masyarakat; perkumpulan, perhimpunan; **sociology** N sosiologi, ilmu masyarakat

sock N kaus kaki

socket N lubang, stopkontak

soda ~ water air soda

sofa N dipan, sofa, kursi empuk

soft ADJ lunak, lembek, lembut; ~ toy boneka; **softball** N sofbal

soil N tanah; V mengotori

solar ADJ [soler] berhubungan dengan matahari

soldier N [soljer] tentara, laskar, serdadu

sole N telapak kaki, alas sepatu

solicitor N [solisiter] pengacara, ahli hukum

solid ADJ padat; kuat, kokoh

solo ADJ, ADV sendiri, solo

solution N cara pemecahan, cara penyelesaian, solusi; **solve** V memecahkan; menyelesaikan

some ADJ [sam] beberapa; kurang lebih; salah satu; sedikit; **somebody** PRON seseorang, ada orang; **somehow** ADV bagaimanapun juga; **someone** PRON [samwan] seseorang, ada orang; **something** PRON [samthing] sesuatu; **sometimes** ADV [samtaimz] kadang-kadang; **somewhere** ADV [samwér] entah di mana

son N [san] anak (lelaki), putera; ~*-in-law* menantu

song N nyanyian, lagu

soon ADV segera, lekas

sophisticated ADJ [sofistikéted] canggih, pintar, berpengalaman

sore ADJ sakit, pedih

sorry ADJ menyesal; maaf

sort N macam, jenis; V menyortir, memilih, memilah-milah

soul N sukma, nyawa, jiwa, semangat

sound ADJ sehat, kuat; N bunyi, suara

soup N [sup] sop, sup

source N [sors] sumber, mata air; narasumber

south ADJ, N [sauth] selatan; **southeast** ADJ, N [sauth ist] tenggara

souvenir N [suvenir] oleh-oleh, kenang-kenangan, cenderamata

sow V [so] menaburkan

soy ~ *milk* susu kedelai; **soya** ~ *bean* kacang kedelai

space N ruang, tempat; spasi, jarak; angkasa

spaghetti N spageti

Spain N Spanyol

spare ADJ cadangan

spark N (percikan) api; **sparkle** N kilau; V berkilau-kilauan, bergemerlapan

sparrow N [sparo] burung gereja

speak V spoke spoken berbicara, berkata; **speaker** N pembicara; Ketua Dewan

spear N tombak, lembing

special ADJ [spésyal] istimewa, khusus, spesial; **specialist** N spesialis, ahli

specific ADJ khusus, tertentu, spesifik

spectacular ADJ hebat, spektakuler; **spectator** N penonton

speech N pidato; cara bicara ← speak

speed N laju, kecepatan; **speedboat** N perahu motor cepat; **speedy** ADJ lekas, cepat

spend V spent spent membelanjakan, memakai

sperm N sperma, air mani

spice N bumbu, rempah-rempah; **spicy** ADJ pedas

spider N laba-laba

spill V tumpah; menumpahkan

spin V spun spun berputar-putar; memintal

spinach N [spinec] bayam

spine N tulang punggung

spiral ADJ [spairal] spiral; V bergerak naik/turun

spirit N [spirit] semangat; roh, hantu; **spiritual** ADJ batin, rohani; keagamaan

splash N bunyi ceburan atau cemplungan; V bepercikan; memercikkan

splendid ADJ bagus sekali

split ADJ retak, sobek; N belahan, retakan; V split split retak, membelah; membagi

spoil V memanjakan; merusak; **spoilt** ADJ manja

spokesperson N juru bicara

sponge N [spanj] spons, bunga karang

sponsor N sponsor

spoon N sendok

sport N olahraga; **sporting** ADJ sportif; **sportsperson** N olahragawan

spot N titik, noda; SL jerawat; V melihat; **spotlight** N lampu sorot; **spotty** ADJ berjerawat, jerawatan

spout N bibir, corot

sprain N, V salah urat, keseleo

spray N percikan, semprotan; V menyemprot, memerciki

spread N [spréd] penyebaran; sajian; mentega, selai; V spread spread mengolesi; menyiarkan, menyebarkan, membentangkan

spring N musim semi, musim

bunga; sumber (air); per, pegas; v
sprang sprung melompat, meloncat
sprinkler N alat penyiram
spy N mata-mata, spion; v memata-
matai
square ADJ [skuér] persegi; N
persegi empat; alun-alun, medan
squash N [skuosy] semacam labu; v
memasukkan dengan paksa
squat v [skuot] jongkok, berjongkok
squeak N [skuik] ciutan; cicit; v
menciut-ciut; mencicit
squeeze v memeras; memeluk
squirrel N bajing
stab v menikam
stable ADJ [stébel] mantap, stabil;
kandang kuda, istal
stadium N stadion, gelanggang,
arena
staff N staf, para karyawan, para
pegawai; para guru atau pengajar
stage N panggung, pentas; tahap
stain N noda
stair N anak tangga; **stairs** PL tangga;
staircase, stairway N tangga
stale ADJ keras (roti); basi, pengap,
apak
stall N [stol] warung, kedai, kios;
kandang
stamina N daya tahan
stamp N perangko; meterai, segel,
tera, cap; v membubuhi prangko,
memberi meterai, mengecap
stand N tribune; pendirian, sikap;
kios; v **stood stood** berdiri; tahan
standard ADJ baku, standar, tolok; N
patokan, ukuran, norma, standar
staple v [stépel] menjepret (kertas);
stapler N jepretan
star N bintang
stare v memelototkan mata;
memandang, menatap
starfish N bintang laut ← star
start v mulai, berangkat; memulai;
menghidupkan mesin
starve v (mati) kelapar
state ADJ kenegaraan; N negara
(bagian); keadaan, suasana; v
menyatakan, menyebutkan, mema-
parkan; **statement** N pernyataan,
pengumuman
station N stasiun, pos; pangkalan

stationery N alat tulis
statistics N, PL statistik, angka
statue N [statyu] patung
status N keadaan, kedudukan, status; pangkat, derajat
stay N (masa) tinggal; v tinggal,
menginap; bertahan
steady ADJ [stédi] tetap, terus-
menerus, teguh, mantap
steak N [sték] stek, bistek
steal v **stole stolen** mencuri
steam N uap; v beruap; mengukus
steel N baja
steep ADJ curam, terjal; SL mahal
steer v mengemudikan
stem N batang
step N langkah, jejak; anak tangga;
tahap; v melangkah; **stepfather** N
bapak tiri, ayah tiri; **stepmother** N
ibu tiri
sterile ADJ [stérail] steril, sucihama;
mandul; **sterilize** v menyucihama-
kan, mensterilkan
stick N tongkat, batang; v **stuck
stuck** bertekun, bertahan; melekatkan; **sticker** N stiker, tempelan
stiff ADJ keras, kaku; pegal
still ADJ tenang, teduh, sepi; ADV
masih; CONJ bahkan, tetapi
sting N sengat; v **stung stung**
menyengat
stir N [ster] keributan, kekacauan; v
bergerak; mengaduk; mengacaukan
stitch N jahitan; v menjahit
stock N persediaan; hewan ternak
stocking N stoking
stomach N [stamek] perut, lambung
stone N batu; biji (buah)
stool N bangku, dingklik
stop v berhenti, menahan
store N toko; persediaan, perbeka-
lan, gudang; v menyimpan
stork N (burung) bangau
storm N angin badai; **stormy** ADJ
(berangin) ribut
story, storey N lantai, tingkat
story N cerita, riwayat, kisah, dongeng
stove N kompor
straight ADJ [strét] lurus, terus; ADV
langsung; jujur, terus terang;
straighten v meluruskan
strain N ketegangan; v bersusah

S

ENGLISH–INDONESIAN

payah; mengejan; menyaring; memaksakan; **strainer** N saringan

strait N selat

strange ADJ [strénj] aneh, ganjil, asing; **stranger** N orang asing, orang luar

strangle V [stranggel] mencekik

strap N tali; cambuk

straw N sedotan; jerami, merang

strawberry N stroberi, arbei

stream N sungai, kali; aliran; V mengalir

street N jalan; **streetcar** N trem

strength N kekuatan, tenaga, kekuasaan; **strengthen** V memperkuat, memperkokoh ← strong

stress N tekanan; ketegangan, stres; V menekan, mementingkan, menitikberatkan

stretch V menegangkan; merentangkan

stretcher N usungan

strict ADJ keras; streng (guru)

strike N pukulan; pemogokan, mogok kerja; serangan; V **struck struck** memukul; menyerang; mogok

string N tali; senar (raket, alat musik); untaian

strip N garis, jalur; V menghilangkan, membersihkan

stripe N garis, belang

stroke N pukulan; gaya (renang); serangan otak

strong ADJ kuat, kokoh; keras (minuman)

struggle N [stragel] perjuangan; V berjuang

stubborn ADJ keras kepala

stuck ADJ terjebak, terjepit; V, PF → stick

student N pelajar, murid, mahasiswa

studio N studio; sanggar

study N [stadi] pelajaran, studi; penelitian, riset; ruang belajar; V belajar, mempelajari, mengkaji

stuff N bahan; barang-barang; V mengisi

stunt N perbuatan yang luar biasa; pertunjukan, akrobatik

stupid ADJ bodoh, dungu

sturdy ADJ kokoh

style N [stail] gaya, cara; **stylish** ADJ bergaya

sub- PREF (di) bawah

subject N soal, topik, subyek; mata pelajaran

submarine N [sabmarin] kapal selam

submit V menyerahkan, menyampaikan

subscribe V berlangganan; menganut

subsequent ADJ berikut

subsidize V mensubsidi, memberi subsidi; **subsidy** N tunjangan, subsidi

substitute ADJ, N ganti, pengganti; wakil; V mengganti

subtitles N, PL teks

subtract V mengurangi

suburb N [sabérb] daerah perumahan, daerah perkotaan

subway N kereta api bawah tanah; terowongan penyeberangan

succeed V [saksid] berhasil, menjadi sukses; mengganti; **success** N keberhasilan, sukses; **successful** ADJ berhasil, sukses

such ADJ seperti itu, sedemikian; sungguh; ADV demikian, begini, begitu; PRON demikian, begitu

suck V mengisap, mengemut

sudden ADJ tiba-tiba, mendadak; **suddenly** ADV tiba-tiba, secara mendadak

suffer V menderita

sufficient ADJ [safisyent] cukup

sugar N [syuger] gula

suggest V [sejést] menyarankan, mengusulkan, menganjurkan; **suggestion** N saran, usul, anjuran

suicide N [suisaid] bunuh diri

suit N [sut] setelan (pakaian); rupa (kartu); V cocok; berpadanan; **suitable** ADJ patut, layak, cocok; **suitcase** N koper

Sumatra N (pulau) Sumatera

summary N ringkasan, ikhtisar

summer N musim panas

sun N matahari; **sunburn** N, V terbakar sinar matahari; **sunny** ADJ cerah; riang

sundae N [sandé] es krim dengan sirop

Sundanese N bahasa Sunda; orang Sunda

Sunday N hari Minggu ← sun

sundown N matahari terbenam, matahari tenggelam, magrib ← sun

sunglasses N, PL kacamata hitam ← sun

sunk ADJ tenggelam; V, PF → sink

sunlight N [sanlait] cahaya matahari ← sun

sunrise N matahari terbit ← sun

sunset N matahari terbenam, matahari tenggelam, magrib ← sun

sunshine N sinar matahari, cahaya matahari ← sun

super ADJ luar biasa, hebat

superior ADJ [supirior] ulung, unggul, tinggi; sombong; N atasan

supermarket N (toko) swalayan

superstitious ADJ [superstisyes] sering percaya takhayul

supervise V mengawasi; **supervisor** N [supervaizer] pengawas

supper N makan malam

supply N pasokan, persediaan, suplai; V memasok, menyediakan

support N dukungan, bantuan; V mendukung, membantu; **supporter** N pendukung

suppose V mengandaikan, menganggap, mengira

supreme ADJ unggul, teratas

sure ADJ [syur] tentu, pasti; yakin

surf N buih ombak; V berselancar

surface N [sérfes] muka, permukaan

surgeon N [serjen] ahli bedah; **surgery** N pembedahan, operasi; tempat praktek dokter

surname N nama keluarga, nama marga

surprise N kejutan; V membuat kejutan, mengejutkan

surround V mengelilingi, mengepung

survey N angket; penelitian; peninjauan

survival N kelangsungan hidup; **survive** V bertahan (hidup), tetap hidup, selamat

suspect N [saspekt] tersangka; V [saspékt] menyangka; **suspicious** ADJ curiga, mencurigakan

swallow V [swolo] menelan

swamp [swomp] paya, rawa

swap, swop N pertukaran; V bertukar; menukar

swear V [suér] swore sworn bersumpah; mengumpat

sweat N [swét] keringat, peluh; V berkeringat

Sweden N Swedia

sweep V swept swept menyapu

sweet ADJ manis; N permen

swim V swam swum berenang, mandi; **swimming** N renang; **swimsuit, swimwear** N baju renang

swing N swung swung ayunan; pergeseran; V bergoyang, berayun

swipe V menggesek; memukul; mencuri

switch N sakelar, penghubung; pertukaran

Switzerland N (negeri) Swis

swollen ADJ bengkak, kembung ← swell

sword N [sord] pedang

symbol N lambang, simbol

symptom N gejala

syringe N [sirinj] alat suntik, suntikan

syrup N sirop

system N sistem, susunan, jaringan

T

T ~-shirt kaus (oblong)

tab N label

table N [tébel] meja; daftar; **tablecloth** N taplak meja; **tablespoon** N sendok besar

tablet N pil, tablet

tag N label, merek, nama, kartu

tail N ekor, buntut; bagian belakang

tailor N tukang jahit, modist

Taiwan N Taiwan

take V took taken mengambil, membawa (pergi); menganggap; menangkap, menerima; makan (waktu), memerlukan; **takeaway** ADJ, N dibungkus, bawa pulang

talcum ~ powder bedak

tale N cerita, dongeng

talent N [talent] bakat; **talented** ADJ berbakat

talk N [tok] percakapan, pembicaraan, ceramah; V berbicara, berun-

T

ding, bertutur; **talkshow** N acara diskusi

tall ADJ [tol] tinggi, jangkung

tambourine N [tamburin] rebana

tame ADJ jinak; v menjinakkan

Tamil ADJ berasal dari kebudayaan Tamil atau Keling; N bahasa Tamil

tan ADJ coklat muda; N kulit berwarna coklat

tangerine N [tanjerin] jeruk garut, jeruk keprok

tangle N [tanggel] kekusutan, kekacauan

tank N tangki; panser; **tanker** N kapal tangki

tap N keran; ketukan; v mengetuk; menyadap

tape N pita; plester; kaset; v membalut; merekam

target N sasaran, tujuan, target; v mengincar

tariff N tarif, ongkos

taro N talas

tart N kue kecil yang bulat

task N tugas, pekerjaan

taste N [tést] (cita) rasa; nuansa; selera; v mengecap, merasai; **tasty** ADJ enak, sedap

tattoo N tato, rajah

tax N pajak, bea; v mengenakan pajak atau bea; **taxation** N pajak, perpajakan

taxi, taxicab N taksi

taxpayer N pembayar pajak ← tax

tea N [ti] teh

teach v taught taught [tot] mengajar; **teacher** N guru, pengajar

teacup N cangkir teh, cawan teh ← tea

teak N (kayu) jati

team N regu, tim; **teamwork** N kerjasama sekelompok

tear N [tér] sobekan, robekan; v tore torn menyobek, merobek, mengoyak

tear N [tir] air mata

tease v mengganggu, meledek, mengusik

teaspoon N sendok teh ← tea

technical ADJ [téknikel] teknis; **technician** N teknisi

technology N teknologi

teenage ADJ remaja, umur belasan

tahun; **teenager** N (anak) remaja

telephone N (pesawat) telepon, telefon; v menelepon

telescope N teropong (bintang), teleskop

television (TV) N televisi (teve, tivi)

tell v told told bercerita; menceritakan, memberitahukan; menyuruh, memerintahkan

temper N sifat, watak

temperature N suhu

temple N candi, kuil; HIND pura, kuil

temporary ADJ untuk sementara

ten ADJ, N sepuluh

tend v cenderung; merawat, memelihara

tennis N tenis

tense N masa; *past* ~ bentuk lampau

tense ADJ tegang; **tension** N ketegangan, tegangan

tent N kemah, tenda

tenth ADJ kesepuluh ← ten

term N istilah; jangka waktu; **semester** triwulan, caturwulan (cawu); **terms** N, PL syarat-syarat; hubungan

terminal N terminal, pangkalan

termite N rayap, anai-anai

terrace N teras

terrible ADJ [téribel] mengerikan, menakutkan, buruk sekali

terrific ADJ [terifik] hebat

territory N ndaerah, wilayah

terror N rasa takut, teror; **terrorism** N [térorizem] terorisme; **terrorist** N teroris; terrorize v meneror

tertiary ADJ [térsyeri] ketiga; ~ *education* pendidikan di perguruan tinggi

test N ujian, pemeriksaan, tes; percobaan, uji coba; v memeriksa, menguji; mengujicoba

text N naskah, teks; v mengirim pesan singkat; **textbook** N buku pelajaran

textiles N, PL tekstil, barang tenunan

Thailand N Thailand

than CONJ daripada, dari; *bigger* ~ lebih besar daripada

thank v mengucapkan terima kasih; ~ *God* ISL alhamdulillah; CHR puji Tuhan; **thanks** COLL terima kasih, makasih; ~ *very much* terima kasih banyak

ENGLISH–INDONESIAN

that CONJ bahwa; yang; supaya; ~ *way* begitu; ke arah sana; PRON those itu

the ART itu, -nya

theater N (gedung) teater

theft N pencurian ← thief

their PRON, POSS, PL [thér] theirs mereka (punya), milik mereka; **them** PRON, OBJ, PL mereka; **themselves** PRON, PL mereka sendiri

then ADV pada waktu itu; CONJ sesudah itu, kemudian, lalu; maka; N waktu itu

there ADV [thér] (di) situ; (di) sana; EJAC nah; N sana; itu; ~ *is*, ~ *are* ada; **therefore** CONJ maka, oleh sebab itu

thermometer N termometer

these PRON, PL ini ← this

they PRON, PL [thé] mereka

thick ADJ gemuk; tebal; kental

thief N [thif] thieves pencuri, maling

thigh N [thai] paha

thin ADJ kurus; tipis; encer

thing N barang, benda, alat

think V thought thought [thot] pikir, berpikir; berpendapat

third ADJ, N ketiga; pertiga

thirsty ADJ haus

thirteen ADJ, N tiga belas

thirty ADJ, N tiga puluh

this PRON these ini; ~ *evening* nanti malam; malam ini; ~ *morning* tadi pagi; pagi ini

thorn N duri

those PRON, PL itu ← this

though ADV [tho] bagaimanapun; CONJ sungguhpun, meskipun, biarpun; *even* ~ walaupun

thought N [thot] pikiran, ide; V, PF → think

thousand ADJ, N ribu; *one* ~, *a* ~ seribu

thread N [thréd] benang; urutan

threat N [thrét] ancaman; **threaten** V mengancam

three ADJ, N tiga

thriller N film atau buku yang menyeramkan; **thrilling** ADJ menggetarkan

throat N tenggorokan, kerongkongan

through ADJ [thru] selesai; ADV terus; PREP melalui, melewati, oleh, karena, terus

throw N lemparan; V threw thrown membuang, melemparkan

thumb N [tham] jempol, ibu jari; V membaca sepintas lalu (buku)

thunder N gemuruh, geluduk; **thunderbolt**, **thunderclap** N petir; **thunderstorm** N gemuruh dan petir

Thursday ADJ, N (hari) Kamis

thus CONJ, ARCH maka

tick N tanda ✓; detik; kutu (binatang); V berdetik

ticket N karcis, tiket

tickle V [tikel] menggelitik

tide *high* ~, ~*'s in* air pasang; *low* ~, ~*'s out* air surut

tidy ADJ apik, rapi; N tempat menyimpan barang

tie N tali, ikat; dasi; pertalian; seri

tiger N harimau, macan

tight ADJ [tait] erat, tegang, ketat; COLL sukar, sulit

tile N ubin, tegel, keramik; genteng

till CONJ, COLL sampai, sehingga

timber N kayu (bahan bangunan)

time N waktu, masa; kali; *in* ~ sebelum waktunya; *on* ~ tepat waktu; *all the* ~ selalu, senantiasa; sejak semula; V mencatat waktu; **times** kali; **timer** N jam (pasir), pencatat waktu; **timetable** N jadwal

tin N timah; kaleng; **tinfoil** N kertas perak

tiny ADJ [taini] kecil sekali, mungil

tip N ujung; uang rokok, tip; saran, tips; tempat pembuangan akhir (TPA); V memberi tip; menumpahkan

tiptoe V jalan berjinjit

tire, tyre N ban

tired ADJ lelah, capek, letih

tissue N tisu; jaringan

title N [taitel] gelar; judul

T-junction N pertigaan, simpang tiga

to PREP [tu] ke, kepada; untuk; lawan; *five (minutes)* ~ *three* jam tiga kurang lima (menit)

toad N katak, kodok; **toadstool** N cendawan, jamur payung

toast N sulangan; V bersulang

toast N roti panggang; **toaster** N alat pemanggang roti

tobacco N tembakau

T

today ADV, N [tudé] hari ini; (masa) kini

toddler N (anak) batita (bawah tiga tahun)

toe N [to] jari kaki; ujung (kaus kaki)

together ADV [tugéther] bersama, bersama-sama

toilet N kamar kecil, WC; kloset; **toiletries** N, PL perlengkapan mandi, alat-alat kecantikan

token N tanda (penghargaan), tanda masuk

toll N tol, bea; jumlah korban; ~ *road* jalan tol

tomato N tomatoes tomat

tomorrow ADV, N [tumoro] besok, esok (hari); masa depan; *the day after* ~ lusa

tone N bunyi, nada; warna, rona

tongs N, PL jepitan

tongue N [tang] lidah; bahasa

tonight ADV, N [tunait] malam ini, nanti malam

tonsils N, PL amandel

too ADV terlalu, terlampau; sekali; juga

tool N alat, perkakas; **tools** N, PL peralatan; **toolbox** N tempat peralatan

tooth N teeth gigi; **toothbrush** N sikat gigi; **toothpaste** N pasta gigi; **toothpick** N tusuk gigi

top ADJ atas; teratas, terbaik, tertinggi; N puncak, (bagian) atas, ujung; tutup; gasing

topic N topik, isu

torch N obor, suluh; senter

tortoise N [tortes] kura-kura

torture N siksaan; V menyiksa

toss N lemparan; V melemparkan, melontarkan, melambungkan; mengundi

total ADJ sama sekali, seluruh; N jumlah, total

touch N [tac] sentuhan, nuansa; V menyentuh, menyinggung, mengenai; **touching** ADJ bersentuhan; mengharukan

tough ADJ [taf] kasar; liat, alot, awet; ~ *luck* sayang sekali

tour N tamasya, tur, perjalanan, pelayaran; **tourism** N wisata, pariwisata, turisme; **tourist** N wisatawan, turis

tournament N kejuaraan, pertandingan, turnamen

tow V [to] menarik, menderek

toward [tuwod] **towards** PREP ke (arah); kepada, akan, untuk, terhadap; menjelang, menuju

towel N [taul] handuk

tower N [tauer] menara

town N kota; **township** N kota

toy N mainan

trace N bekas, jejak; V merunut, mengikuti jejak, memetakan

track N jejak, tapak jalan

tractor N traktor

trade N niaga, perniagaan, perdagangan; V berdagang, berbisnis; bertukar; tukar-menukar; **trader** N pedagang; **tradesman** N tukang

tradition N [tradisyen] adat (istiadat), tradisi; **traditional** ADJ menurut adat, tradisional

traffic N lalu lintas; peredaran, perdagangan

tragedy N [trajedi] cerita sedih; kecelakaan

trail N tapak jalan, bekas, jejak

train N kereta api

train V melatih; **trainee** ADJ calon; orang yang ikut latihan, orang yang magang; **trainer** N pelatih; **training** N latihan, pelatihan, pendidikan

tram N trem

transfer N pemindahan, mutasi; V memindahkan

translate V menerjemahkan; **translation** N terjemahan, penerjemahan; **translator** N penerjemah

transmigration N transmigrasi

transparent ADJ bening, tembus cahaya

transport N angkutan, pengangkutan, transportasi; V mengangkut, membawa; **transportation** N transportasi

trap N perangkap, jerat, jebakan; V memerangkap, menjerat, menjebak; **trapdoor** N pintu di lantai atau plafon

trash N sampah

trauma N [troma] pengalaman buruk, trauma

travel V jalan, berjalan; bepergian; **traveler** N orang yang sedang dalam perjalanan, musafir

ENGLISH—INDONESIAN

tray N dulang; baki

tread V [tréd] **trod trodden** menginjak, memijak

treasure N [trésyur] barang berharga tinggi

treasurer N [trésyurer] bendahara; Menteri Keuangan

treat N [trit] sesuatu yang menyenangkan; V mengobati; memperlakukan; **treatment** N pengobatan, perawatan; perlakuan

tree N pohon

tremendous ADJ [treméndus] hebat, dahsyat

tremor N gemetaran; gempa bumi

trend N mode, gaya, tren; kecenderungan; **trendy** ADJ gaya, bergaya, modis

triangle N [trayanggel] segi tiga; kerincing

tribe N suku (bangsa)

trick N tipu daya; permainan; V menipu; **tricky** ADJ sulit, rumit

tricycle N [traisikel] sepeda roda tiga

trim ADJ langsing, rapi; V menggunting; menghiasi

trip N perjalanan; V tersandung; menjebloskan

triple ADJ [tripel] lipat tiga; N rangkap tiga

tripod N [traipod] (tumpuan) kaki tiga, tripod

triumph N [trayemf] kemenangan, keberhasilan; V menang, berhasil

trolley N kereta dorong, troli

troop N pasukan; V jalan ramai-ramai; **trooper** N polisi

trophy N [trofi] piala

tropical ADJ tropis

trouble N [trabel] kesusahan, kesulitan; gangguan; kerusakan; repot

trousers N, PL [trauzerz] celana panjang

truck N truk

true ADJ [tru] benar, betul, sungguh; setia; **truly** ADV sesungguhnya, sungguh-sungguh

trumpet N trompet

trust N kepercayaan; V memercayakan, mempercayai

truth N [truth] kebenaran; **truthful** ADJ jujur

try N usaha, percobaan; V mencoba, berusaha; **tryout** N seleksi, percobaan

T-shirt N kaus (oblong) ← T

tub N bak mandi

tube N tabung; pipa, pembuluh

tuberculosis N radang paru-paru, tebese, TBC

Tuesday ADJ, N [Tyusdé] (hari) Selasa

tug N sentakan, tarikan; V menarik, menyentak; **tugboat** N kapal penarik

tuition N [tuwisyen] pengajaran; uang belajar

tulip N bunga tulip, tulpen

tumor N benjolan, tumbuhan, tumor

tuna N ikan tongkol

tune N bunyi, lagu; melodi; V menyetel; menala

tunnel N terowongan; V menggali terowongan atau lubang

Turkey N Turki

turkey N kalkun

turn N putaran; giliran; belok; V berputar, membelok, menoleh; memutar, membalikkan

turnip N lobak cina

turnoff N pintu keluar (jalan tol) ← turn

turquoise ADJ [térkoiz] biru toska; N (batu) pirus

turtle N kura-kura, penyu

tutor N guru pribadi; wali kelas; V memberi les privat kepada; **tutorial** N kelas diskusi

TV ABBREV *television* teve, tivi, TV (televisi)

tweezers N, PL pinset, penyepit

twelfth ADJ kedua belas; **twelve** ADJ, N dua belas

twenty ADJ, N dua puluh

twice ADV dua kali

twilight ADJ, N [twailait] senjakala

twin N kembar

twist N tikungan; pelintir; putaran; V memutar, memintal, menganyam

two ADJ, N [tu] dua

tycoon N [taikun] hartawan, taipan

type N macam, jenis, bentuk, tipe; golongan; huruf cetak; V mengetik

typhoid N [taifoid] ~ *(fever)* tifus, tipus

typhoon N [taifun] (angin) topan

U

U

UFO ABBREV *unidentified flying object* piring terbang

ugly ADJ buruk (rupa), jelek

UK ABBREV *United Kingdom* Kerajaan Inggris

Ukraine N [Yukrén] Ukraina

ulcer N bisul, borok

um INTERJ anu, er

umbrella N payung

umpire N wasit

UN ABBREV *United Nations* PBB (Persatuan Bangsa-Bangsa)

unable ADJ [anébel] tidak mampu, tidak dapat, tidak bisa ← **able**

unauthorized ADJ [anothoraizd] tanpa wewenang, tidak sah ← **authorize**

unbearable ADJ [anbérabel] tak tertahankan ← **bear**

unbelievable ADJ [anbelivabel] tidak dapat dipercaya, bukan main ← **believe**

unbolt V membuka (kunci selot) ← **bolt**

unborn ADJ belum lahir; ~ *baby*, ~ *child* janin ← **born**

unbreakable ADJ [anbrékabel] tahan banting, anti pecah ← **break**

uncle N [angkel] paman, om

unclear ADJ kurang jelas ← **clear**

uncomfortable ADJ [ankamftabel] tidak enak, kurang nyaman ← **comfortable**

unconscious ADJ [ankonsyus] pingsan, tidak sadar ← **conscious**

uncover ADJ [ankaver] membuka ← **cover**

under CONJ menurut; PREP (di) bawah; **underage** ADJ di bawah umur; **underclothes**, **underwear** N, PL pakaian dalam; **undergo** V **underwent undergone** menempuh, mengalami; **undergraduate** ADJ, N sarjana muda; **underground** ADJ (di) bawah tanah; **underline** V menggarisbawahi; **underneath** ADV, PREP (di) bawah; **underpass** N terowongan (di bawah jalan); **underscore** N tanda

understand V **understood understood** mengerti, paham; memahami;

understanding ADJ pengertian; N pengertian, pemahaman

undertake V **undertook undertaken** menjalankan, melakukan

underwater ADJ [anderwoter] (di) dalam air ← **under**

underwear N pakaian dalam ← **under**

undo V [andu] **undid undone** membuka ← **do**

undress V membuka pakaian, melepas pakaian ← **dress**

unemployed ADJ, N [anemploid] pengangguran ← **employ**

uneven ADJ [aniven] tidak rata, bergelombang; tidak konsisten, tidak seimbang ← **even**

unexpected ADJ [anékspékted] tidak terduga; **unexpectedly** ADV tiba-tiba ← **expect**

unfair ADJ tidak adil, tidak jujur ← **fair**

unfaithful ADJ tidak setia, durhaka; menyeleweng ← **faithful**

unforgettable ADJ [anforgétabel] tak terlupakan ← **forget**

unfortunate ADJ [anfortyunet] malang, sial; **unfortunately** ADV sayang ← **fortunate**

unhappy ADJ tidak bahagia; sedih; malang ← **happy**

uniform ADJ, N [yuniform] (pakaian) seragam

union N [yunien] persatuan, serikat, uni

unique ADJ tunggal, unik, tiada duanya

unit N [yunit] unit, satuan

unite V [yunait] bersatu, menyatu; menyatukan, mempersatukan; **united** ADJ bersatu, serikat

universal ADJ [yunivérsel] umum, universal; **universe** N alam semesta

university N [yunivérsiti] universitas

unkind ADJ [ankaind] kejam, bengis ← **kind**

unknown ADJ tidak ketahuan, tidak dikenal ← **known**

unless CONJ (kecuali) kalau

unlike ADJ tidak seperti, tidak sama ← **like**

unlikely ADJ kemungkinan kecil; tidak dapat dipercaya ← **likely**

V

unlucky ADJ celaka, sial, malang ← lucky

unmarried ADJ [anmarid] belum kawin, tidak kawin, lajang ← married

unpaid ADJ tidak dibayar, belum dibayar ← pay, paid

unrealistic ADJ tidak realistis ← real

unreasonable ADJ [anriznabel] tidak masuk akal ← reasonable

unreliable ADJ [anrelayabel] tidak dapat dipercayai, tidak dapat diandalkan ← reliable

unsafe ADJ tidak aman, berbahaya ← safe

unstable ADJ [anstébel] goyah, tidak stabil; mudah tergoncang ← stable

unsuccessful ADJ [ansaksésful] tidak berhasil, tidak lulus, gagal ← successful

unsuitable ADJ [ansutabel] tidak cocok ← suitable

unsure ADJ [ansyur] tidak yakin, tidak pasti ← sure

untidy ADJ [antaidi] tidak rapi, tidak teratur, jorok ← tidy

untie V [antai] membuka (tali), menguraikan ← tie

until CONJ sampai; PREP hingga, sampai (dengan)

unusual ADJ [anyusuyel] tidak biasa, tidak lazim ← usual

unwell ADJ tidak enak badan ← well

unwrap V [anrap] membuka (bungkus)

unzip V membuka ritsleting ← zip

up ADJ habis; bangun; naik; *what's ~?* apa kabar? ada apa?; ADV ke atas; naik; PREP (di) atas; ke atas; **upcoming** ADJ [apkaming] yang mendatang; **update** N laporan terbaru; V memperbarui; **upfront** ADJ [apfrant] terus terang, jujur; **upgrade** N penataran; V menaikkan kelas

upon PREP [apon] (di) atas → on

upper ADJ (tingkat) atas; tinggi ← up

uprising N pemberontakan ← up

upset ADJ tersinggung; tidak tenang; terganggu; V membuat tersinggung, mengganggu, merusak

upside *~ down* terbalik ← up

upstairs ADJ di (lantai) atas; ADV ke (lantai) atas; N lantai atas ← up

urban ADJ [érben] perkotaan

urgent ADJ mendesak, penting, genting

urinate V [yurinét] kencing, buang air kecil; **urine** N air kencing, air seni

US ABBREV *United States* AS (Amerika Serikat)

us PRON, OBJ kita (termasuk lawan bicara); kami

use N [yus] pemakaian, penggunaan; V [yuz] memakai, menggunakan; *~ up* menghabiskan; **used** ADJ bekas (pakai); *~ to* terbiasa; dulu; **useful** ADJ [yusfel] berguna, bermanfaat; **useless** ADJ tidak berguna, sia-sia; tidak dapat dipakai; **user** N [yuzer] pemakai

usual ADJ [yusyual] biasa, lazim, lumrah; *as ~* seperti biasa; **usually** ADV biasanya ← use

utensil N [yuténsil] alat (masak)

V

vacancy N lowongan; ada kamar; **vacant** ADJ kosong

vacation N [vakésyen] liburan

vacuum N [vakyum] menyedot debu

vague ADJ [vég] tidak jelas, samar-samar

valet N, M [valé] pelayan pria

valid ADJ [valid] berlaku, sah

valley N [vali] lembah

valuable ADJ [valyuabel] berharga; mahal; **valuables** N, PL barang-barang berharga; **value** N nilai; PL norma, nilai; V menghargai, menilai

valve N [valv] klep, katup, pentil

van N mobil bagasi; gerbong

vanilla N panili, vanili

vanish V [vanisy] hilang, menghilang, lenyap

variable ADJ [vériabel] berubah-ubah, tidak tetap ← vary

variety N [varayeti] macam; keanekaragaman; **various** ADJ [vérius] berjenis-jenis, bermacam-macam ← vary

V

varnish N pernis
vary V [véri] berubah-ubah, ber-beda-beda; mengubah
vase N vas, jambangan
vast ADJ luas, besar sekali
vat N tong
vault N kuda-kuda loncat; V meloncat (dengan galah)
veal N daging anak sapi
vegan N orang yang tidak makan atau memakai produk dari hewan
vegetable ADJ [véjtebel] nabati; N sayur, PL sayur-sayuran, sayur-mayur; **vegetarian** N [véjetérien] orang yang hanya makan sayur, orang vegetarian
vehicle N [viekel] kendaraan, wahana
veil N [vél] kerudung, kudungan; jilbab; tudung
vendor N penjaja, penjual
vent N lubang angin; **ventilation** N ventilasi, peredaran udara, sirkulasi udara
venue N [vényu] tempat acara berlangsung
veranda(h) N beranda
verb N kata kerja
verse N [vérs] ayat; sajak, syair; pantun; bagian (dari sajak)
version N [vérsyen] versi
versus (vs) CONJ lawan, melawan
vertical ADJ tegak lurus, vertikal
very ADV [véri] amat, sangat, sekali; benar, betul
vest N rompi; singlet
vet N, COLL dokter hewan (drh) ← veterinarian
veteran ADJ [vétran] kawakan; N veteran
veterinarian, vet N [véterinérian] dokter hewan
via PREP [vaya] lewat, via; melalui
vibrate V bergetar; **vibration** N getaran, vibrasi
vice N sifat buruk atau jahat
vice- PREF wakil, muda
vicious ADJ [visyes] kejam, jahat
victim N korban
video [vidio] alat perekam kaset video; **videotape** N kaset video; V merekam pada kaset video
Vietnam N Vietnam

view N [vyu] pemandangan; pandangan, pendapat; V melihat, meninjau; **viewer** N pemirsa
villa N vila
village N [vilej] desa, kampung, dusun; **villager** N orang desa
vine N tanaman anggur; tanaman merambat
vinegar N [vineger] cuka
vineyard N [vinyerd] kebun anggur
violence N [vayolens] kekerasan; **violent** ADJ kasar; suka memukul; keras, hebat
violet ADJ [vayolet] ungu muda
violin N [vayolin] biola
virgin N [vérjin] perawan, gadis
virtual ADJ [vértyuel] nyaris; maya
virus N [vairus] virus
visa N [viza] visa
visit N [vizit] kunjungan; V berkunjung; mengunjungi; **visitor** N tamu, pengunjung
visual ADJ [visyuel] berkaitan dengan mata atau penglihatan; ~ *arts* seni rupa
vital ADJ penting sekali
vitamin N vitamin
vivid ADJ [vivid] hidup, jelas, terang
vocabulary N **vocab** COLL [vokabuleri] kosa kata
vocal ADJ bersuara; berkaitan dengan suara; N pembawaan lagu; **vocalist** N penyanyi, vokalis
voice N [vois] suara; V menyuarakan, mengatakan
volcano N [volkéno] gunung api, gunung berapi
volleyball N bola voli
volume N [volyum] isi, muatan, volume; jilid
volunteer ADJ sukarelawan
vomit N muntah; V muntah
vote N (pemungutan) suara; hak memilih; V memberikan suara; memutuskan; memilih; **voter** N pemilih; **voting** N pemungutan suara
voucher N [vaucer] vocer, bon
vow N janji; V bersumpah
voyage N [voyej] pelayaran, perjalanan lewat laut

W

wade v berjalan dalam air; mengarungi

wafer N biskuit tipis

waffle N [wofel] wafel

wag v mengibas, mengibasibas; mengibaskan

wage N upah

wagon N [wagon] gerbong, kereta

wail N ratapan; v meratap

waist N pinggang; **waistcoat** N rompi

wait N masa menunggu; penantian; v menunggu, menanti; **waiter** N, M pelayan; **waitress** N, F pelayan

wake N selamatan sesudah upacara pemakaman; v **woke woken** membangunkan; **waken** v bangun; membangkitkan

walk N [wok] jalan-jalan, jarak yang dijalani; v jalan (kaki), berjalan (kaki); **walking** ADJ berjalan; **walkout** N aksi mogok

wall [wol] N tembok, dinding

wallet N [wolet] dompet

wallpaper N [wolpéper] kertas dinding

walnut N [wolnat] sejenis kenari

walrus N [wolras] singa laut

wander N jalan-jalan; v mengembara, berkelana, berputar-putar

want N [wont] keinginan; v ingin; menginginkan, menghendaki; membutuhkan, memerlukan; **wanted** ADJ dicari

war N [wor] perang

ward N [word] bangsal, ruang; wilayah

wardrobe N [wordrob] lemari baju, lemari pakaian

warehouse N [wérhaus] gudang

warm ADJ [worm] hangat, panas; v memanaskan, menghangatkan; **warmth** N panas, kehangatan

warn v [worn] memperingatkan; **warning** N peringatan

warranty N [woranti] jaminan, garansi

warrior N [worier] pejuang, prajurit, kesatria

wart N [wort] kutil

was v, PF [woz] → be

wash N [wosy] cucian; mandi; v mencuci, membasuh; memandikan (orang); **washbasin** N tempat cuci muka, wastafel; **washcloth** N lap; **washing** N cucian; **washroom** N kamar kecil, WC

wasp N [wosp] tawon

waste N [wést] sampah; pemborosan; v memboroskan; membuang; **wasteful** ADJ boros

watch N [woc] jam tangan; jaga

watch v [woc] menonton; menjaga; **watchdog** N (anjing) penjaga

water N [woter] air; v berliur; menyirami, mengairi; **watercolors** N, PL cat air; **waterfall** N air terjun; **watermelon** N semangka; **waterproof** ADJ kedap air; **waterski** N [woterski] ski air

wave N ombak, gelombang; v berkibar; melambaikan; **wavy** ADJ bergelombang, berombak

wax N lilin; malam (untuk batik)

way N jalan; arah; cara

we PRON, PL kami; kita

weak ADJ [wik] lemah

wealth ADJ [wélth] kekayaan; **wealthy** ADJ kaya

weapon N [wépen] senjata

wear N [wér] pakaian; perlengkapan; v **wore worn** memakai

weather N [wéther] cuaca

weave v [wiv] **wove woven** bertenun; menenun; **weaver** N penenun, tukang tenun

web N jaringan; rumah laba-laba

wedding N (acara) perkawinan, pernikahan

Wednesday ADJ, N [Wénsdé] (hari) Rabu

week N minggu; **weekday** N hari kerja; **weekend** N akhir minggu, akhir pekan

weep v **wept wept** menangis

weigh v [wé] menimbang; **weight** N berat, bobot; **weightlifting** N angkat besi

weird ADJ [wird] aneh, ganjil

welcome N [wélkem] sambutan; v (mengucapkan) selamat datang

well ADV baik; sehat; *as ~* (begitu) juga, demikian juga

well N (sumber) mata air, sumur

ENGLISH–INDONESIAN

W

Welsh ADJ berasal dari Wales
west ADJ, N barat; **western** ADJ barat; **westerner** N orang Barat
wet ADJ basah, berair; V wet wet membasahi
whale N [wél] ikan paus
wharf N [worf] **wharves** dermaga
what ADJ [wot] apa; alangkah; INTER-ROG [wot] apa; ~'s your name? siapa namanya?; **whatever** ADJ apa saja, apa pun
wheat N [wit] gandum
wheel N [wil] roda; **wheelbarrow** N [wilbaro] kereta dorong, gerobak; **wheelchair** N kursi roda
when CONJ [wén] ketika; bila, kalau; INTERROG kapan; **whenever** ADV, CONJ [wénéver] kapan saja
where ADV, CONJ, PRON [wér] di mana; INTERROG di mana
whereas CONJ [wéraz] sedangkan, padahal
wherever ADV, CONJ [wéréver] di mana saja, di mana pun
whether CONJ [wéther] apakah
which CONJ, PRON [wic] mana; **whichever** PRON [wicéver] mana saja
while, whilst CONJ [wail] selama; saat, ketika; sedangkan; N waktu
whip N [wip] cambuk, cemeti; V mencambuk, mencemeti
whisper V [wisper] berbisik; membisikkan
whistle N [wisel] peluit; V bersiul
white ADJ [wait] (berkulit) putih
who CONJ [hu] yang; INTERROG, PRON siapa; **whoever** PRON [huéver] barang siapa
whole ADJ [hol] seantero, seluruh, semua; lengkap, utuh; N semua, keseluruhan; **wholemeal** ADJ tepung terigu yang masih mengandung biji-biji; gandum
whom PRON, OBJ [hum] siapa
whose CONJ yang; PRON, POSS [huz] milik siapa
why CONJ, interrog [wai] mengapa; EJAC nah
wicked ADJ [wiked] jahat
wide ADJ [waid] lebar, longgar, luas; ADV jauh, lebar
widespread ADJ [waidspréd] tersebar luas

widow N, F [wido] janda (mati)
width N lebar(nya) ← wide
wife N wives isteri
wig N rambut palsu, wig
wild ADJ [waild] liar, ganas, buas; gila; **wildlife** N [waildlaif] margasatwa, fauna
will N kehendak, kemauan; wasiat; V **would** [wud] akan, mau, hendak; **willing** ADJ rela, bersedia, sudi
win V won won [wan] menang; memenangkan; memperoleh, mendapat
wind N (mata) angin
wind N [waind] belok, belokan, belitan; V **wound wound** memutar, menggulung; membelit, membalutkan
windmill N kincir angin ← wind
window N [windo] jendela
windscreen, windshield N [windsyild] kaca depan mobil ← wind
windy ADJ banyak angin, berangin ← wind
wine N (minuman) anggur
wing N sayap; sisi (panggung)
wink N kedip, kedipan; V kedip, berkedip; mengedipkan mata
winner N pemenang; **winnings** N hasil kemenangan ← win
winter ADJ, N musim dingin; in ~ pada musim dingin
wipe V menyapu, menyeka, menghapus
wire N [wair] kawat
wisdom N kearifan, kebijaksanaan; **wise** ADJ arif, bijaksana
wish N keinginan; V ingin; menginginkan; mengharapkan
witch N, F penyihir, tukang sihir
with PREP dengan, bersama, serta; pakai; **withdraw** V withdrew **withdrawn** mundur, mengundurkan diri; menarik, mencabut; **withdrawal** N pengunduran; penarikan (uang); **withdrawn** ADJ pendiam, suka menyendiri
within ADV, PREP (di) dalam ← with
without PREP tanpa, dengan tidak ← with
witness N saksi; V menyaksikan
wives N, PL → wife

ENGLISH–INDONESIAN

wizard N, M [wizerd] penyihir, tukang sihir

wobbly ADJ goyang

woke, woken V, PF → wake

wolf N [wulf] **wolves** serigala

woman N [wumen] **women** [wimen] perempuan, wanita

wonder N [wander] keajaiban; V berpikir, berpikir-pikir; **wonderful** ADJ ajaib, mengherankan

won't V, AUX takkan → will

wood N kayu; hutan; **wooden** ADJ terbuat dari kayu; **woods** N, PL hutan; **woodwork** N prakarya, pelajaran memotong dan mengolah kayu

wool N wol, bulu domba; **woolen** ADJ terbuat dari wol

word N [wérd] kata

wore V, PF → wear

work N [wérk] pekerjaan, karya, kerja; kantor, tempat kerja; *at* ~ sedang bekerja; di kantor; *hard* ~ kerja keras; V bekerja, berjalan, jalan; **workbook** N buku tulis; **worker** N pekerja, buruh; **workforce** N tenaga kerja; **working** ADJ ~ *class* kaum buruh, rakyat jelata; **workman** N pekerja, tukang; **workout** N latihan; **works** N, PL pabrik; mesin; **worksheet** N kertas tugas belajar; **workshop** N bengkel

world N [wérld] dunia, alam; planet; **worldwide** ADJ yang meliputi seluruh dunia

worm N [wérm] cacing, ulat

worn V, PF → wear

worry N [wari] kekhawatiran, beban pikiran, urusan, kesusahan; V khawatir, merasa cemas; ~ *about* mencemaskan; *don't* ~ jangan khawatir; *no worries* tidak masalah

worse ADJ, ADV [wérs] lebih buruk, lebih jelek ← bad

worship V memuja, menyembah

worst ADJ, ADV [wérst] paling buruk, paling jelek, terburuk ← bad

worth ADJ bernilai, bermanfaat, berharga; N [wérth] nilai, harga, guna; **worthwhile** ADJ berguna, bermanfaat

would V, AUX, PF [wud] akan → will; **wouldn't** V AUX, NEG [wudent] tidak

akan, takkan

wound N [wund] luka; V melukai

wow EJAC [wau] wah

wrap N [rap] semacam roti isi yang digulung; V membungkus; **wrapper** N bungkus, pembungkus

wreck V merusak, menghancurkan

wrench N [rénc] *(monkey)* ~ kunci Inggris; renggutan; V merenggut

wrestle N [résel] pergumulan, pergulatan; V bergumul, bergulat; **wrestler** N [résler] pegulat; **wrestling** N [résling] gulat

wrinkle N [ringkel] (garis) keriput, kerut

wrist N [rist] pergelangan tangan; **wristwatch** N jam tangan

write V [rait] **wrote written** menulis, mengarang; **writer** N penulis, pengarang; **writing** N tulisan, karangan; **written** ADJ tertulis

wrong ADJ [rong] salah, keliru; N kesalahan

X

X-ray N [éksré] rontgen, sinar X; V merontgen, menyinar

xylophone N [zailofon] xilofon

Y

yacht N [yot] kapal layar, kapal pesiar

yard N pekarangan, halaman; ukuran panjang sebesar 0.9144 m

yarn N benang (rajutan)

yawn V menguap

yeah SL [yéa] ya, iya ← yes

year N [yir] tahun

yell N pekik, pekikan; V memekik

yellow ADJ [yélo] kuning; SL takut

yes ya

yesterday ADV, N kemarin; *the day before* ~ kemarin dulu

yet ADV masih (belum); *as* ~ sampai sekarang, sehingga kini; CONJ namun

yolk N [yok] kuning telur

you PRON [yu] kamu, engkau; FORM Anda; PL kalian; ~ *all* kalian, anda sekalian; **you'll** anda akan ← you will

young ADJ [yang] muda; N anak (binatang)

your PRON -mu, kamu punya, milik anda, kepunyaan anda; **you're** kamu adalah ← you are; **yours** PRON, POSS milikmu, milik anda; **yourself** PRON **yourselves** engkau sendiri, kamu sendiri, Anda sendiri ← you

youth N [yuth] masa muda; kaum muda; ~ *hostel* losmen

you've [yuv] kamu sudah ← you have

yum EJAC sedap, enak; **yummy** ADJ enak, sedap; EJAC enak, nyam-nyam

Z

zebra N kuda zebra, kuda belang

zero ADJ, N [ziro] nol, kosong

zigzag ADJ, V berkelok-kelok, ber-liku-liku

zinc N seng

zipper, zip N ritsleting, kancing tarik

zone N zona, daerah

zoo N kebun binatang

zoom ~ *in* memfokuskan lebih dekat pada

ENGLISH–INDONESIAN